Course   MSP 1011
          Introduction to Media Theory
          2014-2015

Professor   John Edward Campbell
             School of Media and Communication
             Temple University

             **Department of Media Studies
             and Production**

http://create.mheducation.com

ISBN-10: 1308280475   ISBN-13: 9781308280479

Contents

Credits

Introduction

CHAPTER

1   Conceptual Foundations:

What Is Communication?

In the classic movie *Cool Hand Luke*, Paul Newman was the recipient of a now famous line: "What we have here," he was told, as he stood with insouciant charm, "is a failure to communicate." Though this comment was delivered well over 30 years ago, the sentiment is a timeless one and still has traction in the early years of the 21st century. In today's society, such a failure would seem a serious—or perhaps fatal—problem because the central concerns in our lives are predictably connected to the ubiquitous concept of communication. We are told that open communication is the key to a good relationship. We are told that the Internet and World Wide Web are part of a global communication revolution. We are told that the communication industry is instilling negative values in our children. We are told that productive organizations are those that communicate effectively with both employees and customers. With all these messages ringing in our ears, it is little wonder that anyone accused of failing to communicate would be highly concerned.

Communication, then, is seen as central to our everyday ideas about what makes life worth living. Thus, it is not surprising that academics have attempted to unravel the secrets of the communication process. This desire to study and understand communication is not new. Indeed, Pearce and Foss (1990) trace the systematic study of communication back to the Sophists in the 5th century B.C.; through the times of Plato and Aristotle; through the Middle Ages, the humanistic revival of the Renaissance, and the scientific study of the Enlightenment; and through to the establishment of communication as an academic discipline in the 20th century. In other words, scholars have sought a systematic understanding of the communication process—communication theory, that is—for several thousand years.

Our concern in this book rests primarily with contemporary views of communication theory that have emerged in the communication discipline since the 1950s. Even this limitation is far from straightforward, however. What we now think of as the discipline of communication has incredibly diverse roots. For example, scholars in rhetoric and public communication might trace their forebears to English departments in the early 20th century and the subsequent creation of speech departments. Other scholars might trace their lineage through early studies in mass communication in departments of sociology and political science. Still

> *"Scholars have sought a systematic understanding of the communication process—communication theory, that is—for several thousand years."*

others might see their roots in the work of social and industrial psychologists. In spite of these diverse histories, we can now identify a discipline of communication. We examine in this book the theorizing and theories of this community of scholars—this discipline of communication.

This textbook considers several important ways to approach communication theory, and it analyzes a wide range of theoretical statements that have sprung from such approaches. Before moving into these important discussions, however, we must draw a map of the terrain. That is, before we start discussing the wide variety of ideas that make up the body of communication theory, it is important to establish an understanding of what communication theory is.

Drawing this map of communication theory requires two distinct but interrelated tasks: understanding the nature of communication and understanding the nature of theory. We undertake the task of understanding the nature of theory in Chapter 2. In this chapter, we consider the first term in the phrase "communication theory" by exploring definitional controversies regarding what communication is, by considering the implications of these debates for the disciplinary study of communication theory, and by previewing the contents of subsequent chapters in our consideration of communication theory.

▥ DEFINING COMMUNICATION

In 1998, political pundits reacted with derision to President Bill Clinton's comment in a deposition that "it all depends on what your definition of the term 'is' is." Though this comment was seen as ludicrous by some, it hits on a central truth of both academia and everyday life: People define terms in different ways, and those differences in definition can have a profound impact on the extent to which we understand each other and can move forward with both academic and everyday pursuits. Given the variety of ways in which words are used and understood, we are often ill-served to search for the single, so-called correct definition of a term. Rather, it is typically more practical to consider the appropriateness

and usefulness of particular definitions for the specific context in which those definitions will be employed and to consider the extent to which interactants converge on definitions of relevant terms. In other words, it is better to evaluate definitions in terms of their utility than in terms of their correctness. This is not to suggest that "anything goes" with regard to definitions. However, we should not assume that there is always a single right way to define a concept.

Nowhere is this cautionary note more appropriate than in considering the nature of communication. Conceptualizations of communication have been abundant and have changed substantially over the years. In the middle of the 20th century, defining communication was a popular sport among communication scholars. Consider the following titles of articles published in the mid-1960s: "On Defining Communication: Another Stab" (G. R. Miller, 1966) and "On Defining Communication: Still Another View" (Gerbner, 1966). So widespread was the sport of defining communication that Dance and Larson (1976) reported over 126 definitions proposed in the literature. To illustrate the variety of definitions proposed during this definitional heyday, a sampling is included in Table 1.1.

As Table 1.1 illustrates, however, a great deal of variation existed among these definitions. Some take a very abstract view of communication, whereas others are extremely specific. Some include myriad situations and contexts in which communication might occur, whereas others are very narrow in their specification. For example, consider two of the early conceptualizations put forth in the middle of the 20th century that offer vastly different views of what communication is:

> [Communication is] the process by which an individual (the communicator) transmits stimuli (usually verbal) to modify the behavior of other individuals (the audience). (Hovland, Janis, & Kelley, 1953, p. 12)

> [Communication is] all of the procedures by which one mind can affect another. (W. Weaver, 1949, p. 95)

Table 1.1	Some Sample Definitions of Communication
Definition	**Source**
[Communication is] all of the procedures by which one mind can affect another.	Weaver (1949)
Communication means that information is passed from one place to another.	Miller (1951)
From a communication point of view, the event may be observed in the employment of symbols (act), under specific circumstances (scene), by an individual or individuals (agent), using selected media (agency), for defined ends (purposes).	Babcock (1952)
[Communication is] the process by which an individual (the communicator) transmits stimuli (usually verbal) to modify the behavior of other individuals (the audience).	Hovland, Janis, and Kelley (1953)
Communication is the process by which we understand others and in turn endeavor to be understood by them. It is dynamic, constantly changing and shifting in response to the total situation.	Andersen (1959)
[Communication] is a process that makes common to two or several what was the monopoly of one or some.	Gode (1959)
Communication does not refer to verbal, explicit, and intentional transmission of messages alone. . . . The concept of communication would include all those processes by which people influence one another.	Ruesch and Bateson (1961)
Communication means, fundamentally, the stimulation in the minds of others of essentially your awareness, understanding, and sense of importance of the event, feeling, fact, opinion, or situation you are attempting to depict.	Oliver, Zelko, and Holtzman (1962)
Communication among human beings is the art of transmitting information, ideas, and attitudes from one person to another.	Emery, Ault, and Agee (1963)
Communication is a process by which a person reduces the uncertainty about some state of affairs by the detection of cues which seem to him to be relevant to that state of affairs.	Lewis (1963)
Communication: The transmission of information, ideas, emotions, skills, etc., by the use of symbols—words, pictures figures, graphs, etc. It is the act or process of transmission that is usually called communication.	Berelson and Steiner (1964)
Communication is social interaction through symbols and message systems.	Gerbner (1966)
In the main, communication has as its central interest those behavioral situations in which a source transmits a message to receiver(s) with conscious intent to affect the latter's behavior.	Miller (1966)
Human communication is the eliciting of a response through verbal symbols.	Dance (1967)
Communication cannot be understood except as a dynamic process in which listener and speaker, reader and writer act reciprocally, the speaker acting to provide direct and indirect sensory stimulation of the listener; the listener acting on the stimulation by taking it in, investing it with meaning by calling up images in the mind, testing those images against present information and feelings and sooner or later acting upon those images.	Martin and Anderson (1968)

Table 1.1	Some Sample Definitions of Communication (continued)	
Definition	**Source**
Communication [is] the sharing of experience, observable as the extent to which the responses of a generator and perceiver (both of which are necessarily living organisms) are systematically correlated to a referent stimulus.	Goyer (1970)
Communication [is] patterned space-time behavior with a symbolic referent.	Hawes (1973)

Source: All definitions drawn from Appendix A of Dance, F. E. X., & Larson, C. E. (1976). *The functions of human communication*. New York: Holt, Rinehart and Winston.

Hovland, Janis, and Kelley provide a relatively narrow view of communication, defining it as a one-way activity encompassing primarily verbal signals used to modify another's behavior. In contrast, Weaver's definition is incredibly broad, including all the procedures by which one "mind" could have an effect on another. For example, if one person decided to plant a flower and another person noticed it, this would count as communication. For most contemporary scholars investigating communication processes, neither of these definitions would pass muster in terms of utility. The definition by Hovland and others excludes too many activities that we normally think of as communication (e.g., just chatting to pass the time of day), whereas the Weaver definition includes practically everything and thus doesn't help us distinguish communication from other forms of human activity.

Through all this definitional turmoil, however, a number of conceptual features have emerged as important points of discussion throughout the years. Some of these features are widely accepted as appropriate to definitions of communication, and we consider these as points of convergence. These concepts—communication as a process, as symbolic, and as transactional—are not considered in detail because they have really become truisms about communication rather than issues of theoretical contention. Other conceptual dimensions, in contrast, have met with a great deal of discussion and debate in the literature. These features are considered in more detail as points of divergence in the conceptualization of communi-

cation. Because this textbook serves as an introduction to a wide range of theoretical positions regarding communication, we do not settle on any singular, specific definition to guide our investigations here. However, it is important to lay out the issues of contention in order to draw a map of the conceptual terrain.

Conceptualizing Communication: Points of Convergence

Communication Is a Process   Perhaps the most widespread point of convergence in defining communication is the notion that communication is a process. A process-oriented conceptualization of communication suggests that it is continuous and complex and cannot be arbitrarily isolated. That is, communication unfolds over time. David Berlo (1960) popularized this idea over 40 years ago, stating:

> If we accept the concept of process, we view events and relationships as dynamic, on-going, ever-changing, continuous. When we label something as a process we also mean that it does not have a beginning, an end, a fixed sequence of events. It is not static, at rest. It is moving. The ingredients within a process interact; each affects all others. (p. 24)

Think, for instance, of a relatively simple interaction between a child and a parent in which the child is reprimanded for not cleaning up after play. When we see communication as a process, we realize that this interaction is really not all that simple. Rather, the interaction is influenced by the past behavior of these two individuals (e.g., Does the child habitually fail to clean up? Is the parent under other kinds of stress?), by relationships each has had with others (e.g., perhaps an older child was excessively neat, setting up parental expectations for this child), and by the situation surrounding the interaction (e.g., perhaps grandparents are arriving for a visit and neatness is seen as an important priority). Further, this so-called simple interaction will affect subsequent interactions between the child and the parent. In short, when we look at communication as a process, we see that even simple interactions are influenced in complex ways by the past and will also have important implications for the future.

In early conceptualizations of communication, this process was seen as a primarily linear one, in which communication moved from a source to a receiver. For example, a source-message-channel-receiver (SMCR) model of communication characterizes the communication process as a straightforward activity of transmission through a singular conduit. Similarly, Lasswell's (1964) classic model of communication asks a series of linear questions: Who? Says what? To whom? Through what channel? With what effect? Though this conceptualization can be seen as a process (i.e., a sequence of steps), most communication scholars today do not accept this simple linear model, or even one that incorporates a feedback loop from receiver to source. Rather, most communication researchers now take a transactional approach to communication. This point of convergence is considered next.

Communication Is Transactional   A second point of widespread convergence in conceptualizations of communication is the notion that communication is **transactional** and hence highly complex. In unpacking the concept of *transaction*, it is useful to contrast it with the related ideas of *action* and *interaction* (see Dewey & Bentley [1949] for an early explication of this distinction).

If we consider communication to be strictly action, we would look at a source presenting a message to a receiver or an audience. We would not consider the reaction of the audience or feedback from it. This linear and one-way approach to communication (like the simple models discussed above) has been labeled the hypodermic needle model, or magic bullet model of communication (see Forsdale, 1981). This action model (which we revisit in our discussion of historical models of media effects in Chapter 14) suggests that communication is a simple process of injecting (with a needle) or shooting (with a bullet) our messages into receivers.

In contrast, if we view communication from an interaction perspective, we move beyond the hypodermic needle and magic bullet to consider the importance of feedback from the receiver. That is, in an interaction model, we look at not only the message of the source but also the reaction of the receiver. An interactional view is clearly a move forward because it acknowledges that communication is not strictly a one-way process with direct and linear effects. However, this model is still relatively simplistic in its isolation of a source and receiver and its consideration of limited influence between them.

Most communication scholars today, however, conceptualize communication in a transactional sense. A transactional view of communication, like an interactional view, includes the important role of feedback. However, a transactional view goes further in seeing communication as a process in which there is constant mutual influence of communication participants. As Burgoon and Ruffner (1978) note:

> People are simultaneously acting as source and receiver in many communication situations. A person is giving feedback, talking, responding, acting, and reacting continually through a communication event. Each person is constantly participating in the communication activity. All of these things can alter the other elements in the process and create a completely different communication event. This is what we mean by transaction. (p. 9)

Consider, again, our exchange between a parent and a child regarding picking up after play. If we view communication as an interaction, we look first at what the parent says, then consider what the child says, and so on. When looking at the exchange as a transaction, we need to look simultaneously at both parties involved. The parent, for instance, might vary the content or tone of the reprimand based on ongoing nonverbal feedback from the child. At the same time, the child might respond to the parent's cues by adjusting messages and behavior.

A view of communication as transactional also emphasizes the importance of context in the communication process. That is, not only do participants constantly influence each other, they are also influenced by the context in which they interact. For example, a comment made in an organization can take on very different meaning depending on whether it is heard in a formal performance appraisal meeting or in casual conversation in the cafeteria. A television show depicting violent acts might be viewed very differently by children alone as compared with children in the company of parents discussing the program's content. In short, a transactional perspective on communication recognizes the inherent complexity of the communication process and will enhance our understanding of a variety of communication exchanges.

Communication Is Symbolic   A third area of convergence in conceptualizations of communication is the belief that communication is symbolic. To explore this concept, it is useful to talk briefly about the more general concept of **sign,** investigated by the field of *semiotics* (for treatments in the field of communication, see A. A. Berger, 1989; Leeds-Hurwitz, 1993). Semioticians see a sign as consisting of two inextricably linked parts—the *signifier* and the *signified*. Consider the word *book* and the object made of paper and glue that you hold in your hand right now. In this case, the signifier is the word *book* and the signified is the physical object. In semiotics, a sign is the relationship between the signifier and the signified. This relationship is obviously not a perfect one-to-one correspondence and is often an arbitrary relationship in that there is no natural correspondence, for instance, be-

tween the letters *b-o-o-k* and the object to which they refer.

Once this basic semiotic notion is understood, a number of further elaborations can be made. First, many theorists follow I. A. Richards (1936), an early scholar in the field of semantics, in distinguishing between a sign and a symbol. This distinction deals with the arbitrariness of the connection between the signifier and the signified. For example, Langer, in her book *Philosophy in a New Key,* conceptualizes a sign as something that signals the presence of something else. In this sense, smoke is a sign of fire and tears are a sign of sadness. Of course, even with these signs there is not a perfect match because tears can be shed in joy as well as in sadness. However, a natural match exists between the signifier and the signified in this case. **Symbols,** in contrast, "are not proxy of their objects, but are vehicles for the conception of objects" (Langer, 1942, p. 61). Thus, symbols hold an arbitrary, rather than natural, relationship to what is symbolized, and a symbol has no inherent meaning.

What then is the relationship between the symbol and the referent? Ogden and Richards (1946) explained this relationship in terms of a semantic triangle in which the three points of the triangle are the *symbol* (e.g., the word *book*), the *referent* (e.g., the physical object), and the *reference* (e.g., what you mean by book when you use the symbol). In this triangle, the link between the symbol and the referent is typically represented with a dotted line because this relationship is arbitrary. That is, you might be quite clear about what you mean when you use the term *book*, but that symbol might have different meanings for different people. Not only are there a wide range of physical objects that could be described as books, but individuals also have a wide range of other concepts and emotions associated with the symbol. For some, books are sacred objects that are cherished and saved throughout a lifetime. For others, books are objects that weigh down the backpack and should be sold back as soon as the end of the semester arrives.

However, with most symbols, some degree of shared meaning exists between interactants.

This is true because the symbols are developed through shared social experience and exist within a system of other symbols. However, this imperfect relationship between symbol and referent suggests that there will always be gaps in understanding. These gaps will be smallest for individuals who have shared experiences (e.g., growing up in the same culture, being of the same generation, having professional similarities). They will be largest for those who have had radically divergent social experiences.

So, when theorists say that communication is symbolic, they mean that it requires signs and symbols that have relationships to referents that are to some extent arbitrary. These symbols can be verbal (e.g., the use of language) or nonverbal. Nonverbal symbols can be seen in a wide range of communicative activities and in many contexts. Some nonverbal behavior actually serves more as a sign than a symbol. For example, Ekman and Freisen (1975) have found that facial expressions are widely seen as unarbitrary indicators of emotion that are recognized across cultural bounds. Other nonverbal communication clearly takes on the arbitrary form of a symbol. Consider, for example, some communication examples in the organizational context. When you dress in a suit for a job interview, that suit could symbolize many things—your respect for the company, your willingness to conform, or your sense of organization and decorum. When a manager chooses to send a message by means of a paper memorandum rather than by phone, e-mail, or interpersonal channels, that choice could symbolize many things—the formality of the message or perhaps the need to file the message for future reference. In short, the nonverbal messages we send and receive are characterized by their symbolic nature, and because of the possible gaps between symbol and referent, "perfect" communication is unlikely.

The ways in which symbols function in communication have come under some scrutiny in recent years. This debate has considered not only the issue of whether communication is symbolic (but see Andersen, 1991, for a contrary definitional view), but also the ways in which

symbols are attached to referents in the real world—in essence the extent to which we can say that symbols hold any stable meaning. A number of theorists have argued that symbols do not have any stable connection to the world and that meaning is, instead, a function of power relationships, ideology, situational context, or history (e.g., Bochner, 1985; Deetz, 1973; Lannaman, 1991; Stewart, 1986). In contrast, others (see, especially, Ellis, 1995) have argued that though symbols do not have single, correct meanings, those symbols can be seen as having purposeful and significant attachments to referents. As we see in later chapters, this debate is one strand of the ontological discussions that mark important differences among postpositivist (Chapter 3), interpretive (Chapter 4), and critical (Chapter 5) perspectives on communication theory. This debate over the stability of meaning, however, does not detract from agreeing that communication is a symbolic process.

Conceptualizing Communication: Points of Divergence

As noted earlier, most contemporary communication scholars agree that communication can be conceptualized as a process that is symbolic and transactional, though different aspects of these conceptualizations will be emphasized depending on the theoretical needs of the researcher. However, communication scholars have agreed less often in several other areas. One of these areas involves the social nature of communication processes, and another involves whether communication should be conceptualized as a purely intentional behavior. These points of divergence are taken up in this section.

Communication as a Social Activity   The first point of some divergence is whether communication necessarily involves two or more people (e.g., is a social or interpersonal activity) or whether communication can occur within one individual (i.e., **intrapersonal communication**). That is, can you communicate with yourself?

Though the colloquialism of "talking to your-self" is frequently used in modern society, many communication scholars would prefer to label this phenomenon as cognition or thinking and leave the term *communication* for situations in which two or more people are involved. Other scholars see intrapersonal communication as distinct from thinking, and divisions within professional associations and numerous publications (see, e.g., C. V. Roberts & Watson, 1989; Vocate, 1994) now acknowledge the importance of intrapersonal communication.

In some ways, though, this issue may be a red herring in the conceptualization of communication. Even scholars who see communication as a clearly social process (e.g., involving two or more people) also acknowledge the importance of internal states such as cognition and emotion on communicative interaction. Indeed, we will see that many theories of message production (Chapter 7), message processing (Chapter 8), and discourse and interaction (Chapter 9) highlight the role of planning and other cognitive processes in the creation of messages in social situations and the regulation of behavior during conversation. Further, theories that look specifically at those intrapersonal and perceptual ways of understanding the symbolic world (Chapter 6) are central to our understanding of communication processes.

The more important point in conceptualizing communication as a social process is in the function that communication serves as a social vehicle. That is, when we see communication as something that occurs between people, the question arises of what communication is doing in that relationship. We deal more thoroughly with this issue in our discussion of speech act theory in Chapter 9. However, it is worth making some initial distinctions here among the various ways we can look at language:

- The *semantic* level of language study considers the links between signs and referents. Our brief discussion of semiotics in the preceding section dealt primarily with this level of analysis.

- The *syntactic* level of language study considers the rules that govern language use by considering various grammars.
- The *pragmatic* level of language study looks at language in use. That is, a pragmatic view looks at the ways in which we "do things with words" (Austin, 1962).

When we conceptualize communication as a social activity, we are then looking primarily at the pragmatic level. That is, communication, in this social sense, is a vehicle through which we are trying to do something. What we are trying to do with communication could vary greatly— we might be trying to get others to understand or appreciate our internal thoughts or emotions, or we might be trying to understand those internal states in others. We might be trying to coordinate behaviors with others or to have others behave in a specific desired way. In other words, we don't just seek to communicate. Instead, from the pragmatic viewpoint, we seek to do specific things in communicating.

In summary, then, in conceptualizing communication as a social activity, we are not discounting the importance of cognitive and internal psychological states in the communication process. Rather, we are emphasizing the point that communication is a critical part of social commerce and that through communication we seek to have an impact on the people around us.

Communication and Intention   Perhaps the most active debate in the area of defining communication revolves around the issue of **intentionality.** Many years ago, Watzlawick, Beavin, and Jackson (1967) wrote a highly influential book, *The Pragmatics of Human Communication.* We deal extensively with their ideas in our discussion of communication in ongoing relationships (Chapter 11). However, this book has probably been cited more for one phrase than for all the rest of the book combined. This is Watzlawick et al.'s dictum that "you cannot not communicate," suggesting that meaning is inherent in all human behavior. For example, an individual who pulls on an old pair of blue jeans and wears them to class may do so simply because everything else in the closet is dirty. Following Watzlawick et al., however, this behavior is communication because others might derive a variety of meanings from it (perhaps disrespect for authority or conformity to peer pressure). As Motley (1990, p. 1, emphasis in original) summarizes, Watzlawick et al.'s dictum "favors a broad approach to communication phenomena, making *communication* synonymous, or nearly synonymous, with behavior."

In early conceptualizations of communication, some theorists disagreed with the idea that you "cannot not communicate," arguing that only intentional behaviors should count as communication (e.g., Burgoon & Ruffner, 1978; G. R. Miller, 1966). In this view, communication occurs only when there is clear intent on the part of the source to communicate. G. R. Miller's (1966, p. 92) definition is a case in point: Communication occurs in "those situations in which a source transmits a message to a receiver with conscious intent to affect the latter's behavior." It should be noted that definitions such as Miller's did not suggest that the intent needed to be successfully realized in order for communication to occur (that is, the attempt doesn't have to be competent or effective in order to be communication), but rather that intent on the part of the source is a defining feature that moves us from the concept of behavior to the concept of communication.

In the early 1990s, this debate flourished once again, with Peter Andersen (1991), Janet Beavin Bavelas (1990), Wayne Beach (1990), Theodore Clevenger (1991), and Michael Motley (1990, 1991) all weighing in with varying positions on the issue. One of the most important underlying threads in the revival of this debate was the distinction between a **source perspective** on defining communication and a **receiver perspective.** Motley (1990, 1991) represents the source position, arguing that a source must have a "receiver-based intention" (either conscious or unconscious) in order for communication to occur. In contrast, Andersen (1991) represents the receiver perspective in arguing that any behavior

that is received (either through active attention or incidentally) counts as communication.

Consider, again, our example of wearing old blue jeans to class. From a source-based perspective (Motley, 1990, 1991), this behavior is not communication because there is no receiver-directed intent to communicate, either conscious or unconscious, on the part of the person putting on the blue jeans. From a receiver-based perspective, this behavior might be communication, depending on whether the professor (or perhaps other students) receive, either incidentally or through purposeful attention, a message from that wardrobe choice. If a message is received, the wearing of blue jeans is communication. Otherwise, communication has not occurred.

Recently, Burgoon and Hoobler (2002) have proposed a resolution of this debate with regard to nonverbal communication by proposing that theorists take a **message perspective** rather than a receiver or source perspective. In a message perspective, communication is defined as "those behaviors that could reasonably function as messages within a given speech community" (Burgoon & Hoobler, p. 244). They further elaborate on this position, noting that "[i]f a behavior is commonly encoded deliberately and interpreted as meaningful by receivers or observers, it does not matter if, on a given occasion, it is performed unconsciously or unintentionally" (p. 244). This move to a message orientation is interesting because it no longer relies on the intent or beliefs about intent of specific interactants. However, questions can still be raised within this approach as to the beliefs of "typical" interactants within speech communities.

A second critical issue highlighted in this debate about intentionality is the distinction among *verbal messages, analogic messages,* and *symptomatic behavior* (Andersen, 1987, 1991; Motley, 1990, 1991). Motley (1990, pp. 14–15) describes the distinctions among these three categories:

> Symptomatic behaviors (e.g., stomach growls, observable autonomic responses, scratching, etc.), at least in their pure form, exemplify behaviors

whose source is something other than an effort to influence a receiver. Verbal behaviors, on the other hand, are typically intended for receivers, as are analogic behaviors; i.e., intentional imitations of symptomatic behaviors—or "ritual" behaviors in the terms of Cronkhite (1986)—and other nonverbal "behaviors purposively displayed to receivers." (Andersen, 1987)

To illustrate this distinction, imagine that you are talking to a friend on the phone and you are exhausted. Because of your fatigue, you might let out an uncontrollable yawn. This is **symptomatic behavior.** Or you might tell your friend that you are very tired and need to get off the phone. This is **verbal behavior.** Or you might emit a fake yawn to communicate your exhaustion to your friend. This is **analogic behavior.** These distinctions are important for several reasons. First, by highlighting the role of analogic communication in much interaction, these distinctions emphasize the importance of nonverbal messages in our conceptualization of communication. Second, they emphasize that a wide range of consciousness is possible in communication, even when considering receiver-directed and intentional behavior. This issue has been further emphasized in discussions of the "mindlessness" of much communication (see, e.g., Langer, 1989). For example, Kellermann believes that communication is both "inherently strategic" and "primarily automatic" (Kellermann, 1992, p. 288). That is, she argues that though our communication is receiver directed and intentional, it is also often unconscious and guided by cultural scripts and ingrained habits.

In summary, early questions of "Is communication intentional?" have evolved in recent years to include sophisticated debates about receiver perception, strategic intent, automatic communication, and the nature of meaning. It is unlikely that these debates will be resolved to the satisfaction of all involved (see, e.g., the positions expressed by Ellis, 1991, p. 221; Mumby, 1997, p. 21). But perhaps these debates should not be resolved because, as noted earlier, definitions are not right or wrong but are more or less useful for the purposes at hand. It is important,

however, to be familiar with these issues as we embark on the study of a variety of communication theories. As Andersen (1991) emphasizes, "These perspectives launch scholars down different theoretical trajectories, predispose them to ask distinct questions, and set them up to conduct different kinds of communication studies" (p. 309). Thus, definitional choices about communication influence—and are influenced by—the theoretical and research commitments of communication scholars.

◼ MOVING BEYOND DEFINITIONS

It appears, then, that we do not have—and probably never will have—an undisputed definition of communication. As noted earlier, this is not necessarily a bad state of affairs because varying definitions can usefully serve different theoretical and practical purposes. Utility depends on the scholar, the research context, and a host of other factors. However, this lack of a singular definition of "what we study" makes it even more important to understand the varying ways that communication is approached by scholars. In the remainder of this chapter, we consider two procedures for "dividing up" communication studies. One of these procedures is the consideration of varying conceptual approaches to the study of communication. The other procedure involves the subdisciplinary domains that typically define our academic departments and professional associations. Following our discussion of these two frameworks, we consider the domains of communication that are included in this textbook.

Conceptual Domains of Communication Studies

An often-cited essay by Robert Craig (1999) makes a compelling case for the importance of considering distinctions among varying conceptual domains in communication theory. Craig argues that typical discussions of the concept of communication distinguish between a

---

☼ REAL LIFE INSIGHT

This chapter considers a variety of ways that scholars in the communication discipline have looked at the "meaning" of "communication." In her recent book, *Reconstructing Communicating: Looking to a Future*, Robyn Penman (2000) talks about these various views as different ways of "imagining" communication. She notes that most people in the "everyday world" hold a "transmission" imagining of communication, in which concern is centered on the need to improve communication and solve problems of communication. Penman acknowledges the prevalence of this imagining, but also invites both scholars and practitioners into an alternative imagining, one that "requires us to inquire into communicating and not communication; to treat communicating as the essential problematic of concern; and to recognize that we construct our reality in our communicating" (pp. 6–7). Penman provides substantial historical and theoretical argument regarding her "reconstruction" of communicating. She then closes her book with a fascinating look at several case studies in which she and her colleagues use a constitutive frame to look at the

ways in which context and lived experience influence the very nature of communicating.

One of the cases she considers is the information needs of HIV/AIDS patients as they were undertaking a new and complicated triple-combination drug regimen in the late 1990s. By actually listening to the way these patients talked about their lives, she realized how important it was to talk not about patient "compliance" (a physician's term) but about "commitment" to the treatment and "control" over their own lives. Further, her work highlighted that the medical profession's typical focus on "best practice" (e.g., take the medicine on a totally empty stomach three times a day) just didn't work, and that patients needed to know that there were "good" practices that didn't quite hit the ideal.

In short, Penman's work shows that by rethinking our models of communication and by giving credence to both the context and process of interaction, it is possible to address pressing problems of daily living. We won't necessarily find all the answers, but at least we'll be asking the right questions.

---

transmission model of communication and a constitutive model of communication. According to Craig, within the transmission model, "communication is a process of sending and receiving messages or transferring information from one mind to another" (p. 125), whereas the alternative is "a model that conceptualizes communication as a constitutive process that produces and reproduces shared meaning" (p. 125). In a constitutive model, communication "is not a secondary phenomenon that can be explained by antecedent psychological, sociological, cultural, or economic factors; rather, communication itself is the primary, constitutive social process that explains all these other factors" (p. 126).

Craig believes that seeing communication theory as a choice between a transmission and a constitutive model is problematic. First, he argues that a fair fight is rarely provided because

"the transmission model, as usually presented, is scarcely more than a straw figure set up to represent a simplistic view" (p. 127). Second, Craig argues that the transmission view of communication does resonate in many practical settings. That is, in everyday life we often think about communication as the sending and receiving of information rather than as the creation and recreation of social realities. For example, we talk about "sending that guy a message" or "picking up my e-mail" in ways that are clearly oriented toward transmission. Indeed, Penman (2000) argues that in the everyday world of organizations, communication is seen as "a relatively straightforward activity that we use to achieve effects—sending messages or controlling others" (p. 3). Hence, if we want to deal with communication in the way that "real life" actors see it, the transmission view should not be totally rejected. Finally, Craig argues that the simple contrasting of

Table 1.2	Conceptual Domains of Communication Theory	
	Communication Theorized as:	**Problems of Communication Theorized as:**
Rhetorical	The practical art of discourse	Social exigency requiring collective deliberation and judgment
Semiotic	Intersubjective mediation by signs	Misunderstanding or gap between subjective viewpoints
Phenomenological	Experience of otherness; dialogue	Absence of, or failure to sustain, authentic human relationship
Cybernetic	Information processing	Noise; overload; underload; a malfunction or "bug" in a system
Sociopsychological	Expression, interaction, and influence	Situation requiring manipulation of causes of behavior to achieve specified outcomes
Sociocultural	(Re)production of social order	Conflict; alienation; misalignment; failure of coordination
Critical	Discursive reflection	Hegemonic ideology; systematically distorted speech situation

Source: Adapted from Craig, R. T. (1999). Communication theory as a field. *Communication Theory, 9,* 119–61.

the transmission model and the constitutive model fails to account for the rich variety of ways in which scholars have often thought about the communication process.

To deal with these conceptual issues, Craig proposes that we recast the constitutive view of communication as a "metamodel," or an over-arching way of thinking about communication theory, rather than as a definition of communication. As Craig argues:

> That is, the constitutive model does not tell us what communication really is, but rather implies that communication can be constituted symbolically (in and through communication, of course) in many different ways, including (why not, if it is useful to do so for some purpose?) as a transmission process. (p. 127)

Craig then goes on to define seven different conceptual traditions in communication theory. These seven traditions are presented in Table 1.2, along with the ways in which each tradition theorizes communication and problems of communication. It should be emphasized that these

traditions all stand within the larger metamodel of communication as a constitutive process. That is, the traditions are not radically different—and incommensurate—paradigms of theory and research. Rather, these traditions are different ways of constituting and talking about communication. For example, a scholar working within the semiotic tradition might consider the ways in which specific linguistic choices are constituted within interaction. In contrast, a proponent of the critical tradition would take a broader view in looking at the means through which the cultural icons communicated in television advertising control the perceptions and actions of the viewing public.

Craig hopes that by establishing this constitutive metamodel, space will be opened up for more dialogue among the various ways of thinking about communication theory and research. As Craig summarizes:

> The scheme I am proposing divides the field according to underlying conceptions of communicative practice. An effect of this shift in perspective is that communication theories no

longer bypass each other in their different paradigms or on their different levels. Communication theories suddenly now have something to agree and disagree about—and that "something" is communication. (p. 135)

Craig's use of this conceptual matrix—and particularly his adoption of the constitutive view of communication as a "metamodel" has recently generated some interesting academic debate (see, e.g., Craig, 2001; Myers, 2001). For example, Myers critiques Craig for providing few criteria for adjudicating among various communication models and sees the constitutive metamodel as problematic as it doesn't allow for fundamental differences among those supporting various first-order models. Craig responds that the constitutive metamodel does not impose a grand unified theory but instead "seeks, by turning to the practical life world that all of us share, common ground on which to discuss some of those differences" (Craig, 2001, p. 235). The debate regarding this article suggests that it has already generated productive discussion about the nature of communication, and thus we will rely on some of Craig's points in our presentation of communication theory. For example, many of the arguments made by theorists in the socio-psychological and cybernetic approaches to communication theory resonate with the postpositivist perspectives on theory we consider in Chapter 3. Similarly, the ideas of phenomenological and sociocultural theorists are largely represented in the interpretive ideals of Chapter 4, and critical theory is considered in Chapter 5.

Useful as these conceptual distinctions are, however, they do not reflect the way the field is typically segmented in academic departments or in presentations of communication theory. Craig admits this ("the structure of the matrix differs radically from conventional ways of dividing up the field," p. 132) and argues that this reconceptualization is critical to the development of communication theory. However, it is also important to look at the ways in which the field of communication is typically divided within academic departments and within pedagogical treatments of communication theory and research. These divisions within the field are considered in the next section.

Disciplinary Domains of Communication Studies

There is little doubt that communication is a fragmented discipline. This fragmentation can, not surprisingly, be seen in the way we label ourselves and talk about ourselves. For example, Kellner (1995) notes the wide array of labels used by departments that study communication issues and even notes that there are idiosyncratic preferences for the terms *communication* or *communications* when referring to the discipline. Within the major professional associations of the field (the National Communication Association and the International Communication Association), a wide array of subdisciplines are represented in the divisions and commissions (see Table 1.3). These subdisciplines vary across the different associations (e.g., the National Communication Association has a larger and more diverse structure than the International Communication Association, with more emphasis on pedagogical issues), and their definitional criteria vary within associations. That is, some divisions are defined in terms of levels (e.g., interpersonal communication, group communication, mass communication), some in terms of a process (e.g., language and social interaction, communication technology, communication apprehension and avoidance), and others in terms of contexts (e.g., instructional, political, health). Even these distinctions are overly simplistic given that a term such as *organizational communication* could imply both a level and a context in which interaction occurs.

The debate regarding disciplinary divisions can be seen within a broader context as well. For instance, when considering the history of the field, we see that wide differences exist between those who look at the development of speech communication (e.g., H. Cohen, 1994) and those who consider the communication discipline as it

Table 1.3	Subdisciplinary Domains in Communication
Divisions and Interest Groups in the International Communication Association (ICA)	**Divisions and Commissions in the National Communication Association (NCA)**
Information systems	African American communication and culture
Interpersonal communication	American studies
Mass communication	Applied communication
Organizational communication	Argumentation and forensics
Intercultural and development communication	Asian Pacific American communication
Political communication	Basic course
Instructional and developmental communication	Communication and aging
Health communication	Communication and law
Philosophy of communication	Communication in the future
Communication and technology	Communication apprehension and avoidance
Popular communication	Communication assessment
Public relations	Communication ethics
Feminist scholarship	Communication needs of students at risk
Communication law and policy	Critical and cultural studies
Language and social interaction	Ethnography
Visual communication	Environmental communication
Gay, lesbian, bisexual, & transgender studies	Experiential learning in communication
Intergroup communication	Feminist and women studies
	Family communication
	Freedom of expression
	Gay, lesbian, bisexual, transgender studies
	Group communication
	Health communication
	Human communication and technology
	Instructional development
	International and intercultural communication
	Interpersonal communication
	Intrapersonal and social cognition
	Language and social interaction
	Latina/Latino communication studies
	Mass communication
	Organizational communication
	Peace and conflict
	Performance studies
	Political communication
	Public address
	Public relations
	Rhetorical and communication theory
	Semiotics and communication
	Spiritual communication
	Theatre
	Training and development
	Vietnamese communication
	Visual communication

developed from sociology and social psychology (e.g., E. M. Rogers, 1994). Craig (1995) argues that this fragmentation is evidence of the tenuousness of the communication discipline:

> The rationale for our field's existence, at core amounts to scarcely more than a single, culturally very potent symbol, "communication," a word still trendy enough to attract students, legitimate enough to keep skeptical colleagues at bay for awhile, and ambiguous enough to serve as a lowest common denominator for our otherwise largely unrelated scholarly and professional pursuits. Any further theoretical analysis of "communication," any attempt to define the field that goes much beyond the magic word itself, threatens to elevate some traditions over others and so upset our delicately balanced system of alliances. (p. 178)

"Definitional choices about communication influence—and are influenced by—the theoretical and research commitments of communication scholars."

Communication is not just fragmented within the discipline, it is also characterized by a high level of interdisciplinary pursuits. Clearly, the history of communication is an interdisciplinary one (see H. Cohen, 1994; Craig, 1995; E. M. Rogers, 1994) given that its development was shaped by fields such as journalism, sociology, psychology, theater, rhetoric, and English. Further, communication remains highly interdisciplinary, as many academics creating scholarship on communication do not reside in communication departments. For example, the study of concepts that we might see as communication is often a mainstay of departments of psychology, sociology, journalism, management, or anthropology.

Is all of this fragmentation a good thing or a bad thing? Commentators differ on this issue, and several representative views can be found in the 1993 "Future of the Field" issue of *Journal of Communication*. In this issue, Rosengren (1993) laments fragmentation, arguing that "it is as if the field of communication research were punctuated by a number of isolated frog ponds—with no friendly croaking between the ponds, very lit-

tle productive intercourse at all, few cases of successful cross-fertilization" (p. 9). In contrast, B. J. O'Keefe (1993, p. 75) notes that she is "struck by increasing interconnections between previously separate disciplines and by projects that deliberately attempt to forge connections," and she argues (following Bochner & Eisenberg, 1985) that we should not have a coherent discipline in which all agree on theoretical and methodological choices but should instead strive for cohesion in which there is room for subdisciplinary dialogue and in which proponents of those subdisciplines respect and protect each other. For some, the issue comes down to whether we should maintain our allegiance to the *concept* of communication or to the *discipline* of communication. Beninger (1993, p. 18), for instance, argues that we should "embrace the subject, not the field" by looking at communication in a broad conceptual sense rather than in what he sees as a narrow disciplinary way.

The Domain of This Textbook

This chapter so far has discussed a wide range of issues regarding the definition of communication, the conceptual domains of communication, and the somewhat fragmented and interdisciplinary nature of communication as a field of study. It is little wonder, then, that students of communication theory may learn very different things, depending on the predilections of their professors and the authors of their textbooks. Indeed, when J. A. Anderson (1996) analyzed the contents of communication theory textbooks, he found 249 distinct theories. Of these, only 22 percent appeared in more than one book and only 7 percent appeared in more than three books.

It appears, then, that writers of communication theory textbooks face a number of choices in order to delimit the topics under consideration and give some sense of coherence (or at least cohesion) to the subject matter of communication. Some of these choices are necessary for purposes of clarity and expediency—not everything can be covered in one book. All choices on domain must be made with a clear conceptual justification. Given the necessity of defining a domain, the following choices have been made regarding this textbook.

First, this book strives to give comprehensive and up-to-date coverage of the major theories considered rather than just considering thumbnail sketches. In order to evaluate theories and examine their usefulness for both scholarship and everyday life, it is critical that the theories be discussed in detail and not glossed over. This initial choice, then, means that it is impossible to consider all theoretical statements that might be included under the huge and multifaceted umbrella of communication. Thus, three major criteria were used to delimit the domain of *this* book.

Criterion One   I first decided to include only work that can be clearly distinguished as a specific theory of communication, given the descriptions of theory that are presented in Chapters 2 through 5 of this book. It should be emphasized that this criterion does not preclude the inclusion of a variety of perspectives on theory or types of theory: critical theories, interpretive theories, postpositivist theories—all are included in this book. However, this book does not cover individual research efforts on particular topics within the communication discipline that have not been codified into coherent theoretical statements. These research efforts will sometimes be briefly considered in order to provide context or support for theories under consideration, but the major emphasis of the book will be on the description and analysis of ideas that have been codified into coherent theoretical statements.

Criterion Two   I next decided to include only theories that have been either *developed by* scholars working within the communication discipline or *widely used and extended by* scholars in the communication discipline. To some extent,

then, I chose to embrace the field rather than the broader subject of communication (contrary to the recommendation of Beninger, 1993). I made this choice in order to concentrate on the work done by communication scholars that is largely (though certainly not always) published in communication journals. In other words, I have decided to define *communication theory* as "theory done by communication scholars."

Criterion Three   Finally, I limited the scope of this book to theories that would be largely considered social science theories within communication or that have had a major impact on work in the social science portions of the discipline. In other words, theories of a purely rhetorical nature are not included in this text. This is not to say that all theories of rhetoric are ignored. Indeed, Chapter 6 highlights two very influential rhetorical theories (narrative and dramatism). And other theories such as symbolic convergence theory (see Chapter 13) and concertive control theory (see Chapter 12) have clear roots in the rhetorical tradition of the communication field.

In grouping these chapters, I have followed the trend of professional associations in communication (the National Communication Association and the International Communication Association) of considering both communication processes and communication contexts as organizing factors. Theories are grouped into chapters that take on a relatively coherent topic area of explanation. However, it is clear that many theories could fit well into multiple chapters. For example, communication accommodation theory could find a home either in theories of interaction or in theories of intercultural contexts. Indeed, structuration theory was so difficult to place that it wound up as a central feature of three chapters (Chapters 5, 12, and 13). In spite of these classification difficulties, a (more or less) coherent structure for organizing the chapters emerged.

- The remainder of Part 1 (*Perspectives on Communication Theory*) considers the philosophical background that is essential for understanding the theory development process (Chapter 2) as well as the three dominant perspectives on theory development in communication and other social research disciplines: the post-positivist perspective (Chapter 3), the interpretive perspective (Chapter 4), and the critical perspective (Chapter 5). We talk more about the selection and structure of these perspectives at the end of Chapter 2.

- Part 2 (*Theories of Communication Processes*) reviews representative and influential theories that have considered major aspects of communicative behavior. This section includes theories of symbolic organization (Chapter 6), theories of message production (Chapter 7), theories of message processing (Chapter 8), theories of discourse and interaction (Chapter 9), theories of communication in developing relationships (Chapter 10), and theories of communication in ongoing relationships (Chapter 11).

- Part 3 (*Theories of Communication Contexts*) reviews influential theories that have been important for developing an understanding of communication in more specific situations and contexts. This section includes theories of organizational communication (Chapter 12), theories of small group communication (Chapter 13), theories of media processing and effects (Chapter 14), theories of media and society (Chapter 15), and theories of culture and communication (Chapter 16).

Each of the chapters in Parts 2 and 3 opens with a brief discussion of the communication process or context under consideration. Then, two to four specific theories are considered that have attempted to enhance our understanding of the communication process or context. Each theory is described in detail, including consideration of metatheoretical roots, assumptions and structure, underlying theoretical mechanisms, empirical support, critiques of the theory, and

basic and applied extensions. However, because the theories differ in terms of domain, level, context, application, and philosophical foundation, application of a cookie-cutter format for description and evaluation would not be productive. Instead, the description of each theory has been designed to provide the most insight into key issues for understanding that theory. Each chapter closes with a brief comparison of the theories in the chapter and commentary about theoretical strengths, weaknesses, and future directions.

▓ SUMMARY

In this chapter, we have explored the terrain surrounding the concept of communication. Some might say the terrain is rather treacherous, given the widespread definitional squabbles, conceptual quagmires, and disciplinary feuds that have sprung from the study of communication. It is hoped, though, that you will see this terrain not as treacherous but as ripe for challenging exploration. In the next chapter we explore the concept of theory and then, in Chapters 3, 4, and 5, analyze three different perspectives on the development and analysis of communication theory. We will then be ready to consider the wide and varied range of theories that have been used to describe, explain, understand, and even change communication processes.

Key Terms

communication process
transactional
sign
symbol
intrapersonal communication
intentionality
source perspective
receiver perspective
message perspective
symptomatic behavior
verbal behavior
analogic behavior

INTO YOUR WORLD

Though many of the issues considered in this chapter seem highly abstract, you can use concepts from these debates about the nature of communication to examine your own relationships—and perhaps even improve them. For example, when in the midst of a disagreement with parents, partners, or friends, you might use the notion of a "receiver perspective" on communication to consider the message that has been internalized by the other individual—even if it wasn't the message you meant to send. Indeed, a receiver perspective suggests that a friend could "get" a message when you weren't trying to communicate at all! Or, in a more general sense, you can use the idea of how communication "constitutes" various social situations to look at the very different perspectives that might be brought into interaction by individuals of different genders, ages, or cultural or socioeconomic backgrounds.

transmission model of communication
constitutive model of communication

Discussion Questions

1. How does viewing communication as a transaction make it more complex than when taking an action or interaction view?
2. Besides the examples of fire and tears offered in this chapter, what other signs can you think of? What makes these signs different from symbols?

3. Defend or attack Watzlawick, Beavin, and Jackson's statement that "you cannot not communicate." Does this idea make sense when you consider your interactions with friends and family?
4. In our everyday lives, do we typically view communication using a transmission model or a constitutive model? What are the implications of this distinction for our interactions?

CHAPTER

2 Philosophical Foundations:
What Is Theory?

Sir Karl Popper, a philosopher instrumental in shaping 20th-century views of knowledge, said that "theories are nets cast to catch what we call 'the world'" (Popper, 1959). Popper was primarily interested in investigating the ways in which we come to understandings of the natural and physical world, but his views are also highly appropriate in a consideration of how we come to know about the human and social world in which we live and communicate. We are faced every day with puzzles about communication and social life. Why does one friendship flourish and another flounder? Why do disciplinary tactics have different effects on different children? How can we manage workplace conflict in constructive ways? What effect will increasing use of the Internet and the World Wide Web have on our daily lives? In addressing these puzzles, we attempt to make sense of our social worlds, and that sense making often involves casting out the net of what we might think of as commonsense theory.

Consider, for example, the first puzzle mentioned in the preceding paragraph: Why does one friendship flourish and another flounder? We may have very practical reasons for gaining an understanding of this issue (e.g., we want to enhance the chances of a successful friendship with a particular individual), or we may simply be curious about the vagaries of social life. In either case, making sense of friendship development will involve creating and testing a variety of informal theories. Perhaps the success of friendship is based purely on the similarity of the two individuals involved in the relationship. Perhaps friendship development depends more on the specific communicative choices made by individuals as they get to know each other. Or perhaps events both inside and outside the relationship mark turning points that are influential in the process of relational development. All of these possibilities represent commonsense theories in that they enhance our understanding of how relationships develop and they are all somewhat abstract representations of relational development. In other words, these understandings move beyond the specific and concrete observation that "Bob and I are good friends because we both like country and western music" to the abstract statement that "friendship development is enhanced by the similarity of relational partners."

Everyone tries to make sense of their lives by developing and testing these commonsense theories. Indeed, we talk further about this concept of humans as "naive scientists" when we discuss attribution theory in Chapter 6. However, people who make sense of communication as part of an academic career are communication researchers and theorists. And though the explanations and understandings of communication developed by these scholars have a great deal in common with our everyday theories about communication (e.g., scholarly theory development also involves the consideration of both observations of the social world and abstract understandings of those observations), they are also different in a number of important respects.

This chapter explores the nature of theory by looking at what we mean by *theory* in the scholarly world and by looking at the foundations we bring to the development and use of theory. We first examine the basic questions of what theory is and how theory functions in fields of social research. We then consider metatheoretical assumptions that we bring to the theory development process, particularly assumptions about ontology (the nature of the world and reality), epistemology (the nature of knowledge), and axiology (the nature and role of values). Finally, we look at these ideas within the context of the communication discipline, building an argument for communication theory development as a pluralistic process.

▓ THE NATURE OF THEORY

Understanding the nature of theory in the scholarly world involves a consideration of two issues. First, it is important to develop a shared understanding of what a theory is. A variety of approaches to this issue have been proposed over the years, and although we will not reach any sense of closure about the "right" way to define *theory*, we will consider issues regarding the conceptualization of theory that guide our investigations throughout this book. Second, it is critical to look at how theory functions as a vehicle toward enhancing our understanding of the social world. Thus, we then consider the general question of what a communication theory should do.

Conceptualizing Theory: What Is Theory?

In discussing the problem of defining *theory* in social scholarship, D. C. Phillips (1992) argues,

"There is no divinely ordained correct usage, but we can strive to use the word consistently and to mark distinctions that we feel are important" (p. 121). This point is certainly well-taken, as in all problems of definition. Indeed, we talked about this issue extensively in Chapter 1, as we considered the various ways in which scholars have defined *communication*. As was pointed out in that discussion, we are seeking not the right definition of a particular term, but one that is most useful for our purposes (see G. R. Miller & Nicholson, 1976). That is, definitions should be judged in terms of their utility rather than in terms of their correctness.

Unfortunately, the search for a definition of *theory* that has high and broadly based utility is a difficult one. Phillips (1992) notes that we can define terms (like *theory*) either in a *stipulative* way by setting forth a group of characteristics that must be present or in a *reportive* way by looking at entities that have been called by a particular name in the past and analyzing the nature of those entities. For example, we could define *war* by either delineating an abstract list of the characteristics of war (a stipulative definition) or by describing characteristics of events that have been called *war* in the past. Neither of these approaches is entirely satisfying with regard to the definition of theory. The first approach seems overly restrictive in that only entities meeting our stipulations will count as theory, and the second approach seems overly inclusive in that anything that has been called a theory in the past will count as a theory now. Thus, combining these two approaches seems a reasonable compromise. A search for a workable conceptualization of *theory* necessarily involves a consideration of both what we think *theory* should look like (stipulative approach) and what it has looked like during the history of social research (reportive approach).

One final point about defining *theory* must be emphasized and will become increasingly apparent as we consider approaches to theory development in communication throughout this book. Specifically, different schools of thought will define *theory* in different ways depending on the needs of the theorist and on beliefs about the social world and the nature of knowledge. That is, the post-positivist perspective on theory presented in Chapter 3 defines theory in a way very different than either the interpretive perspective (Chapter 4) or the critical perspective (Chapter 5). To the extent possible, though, this chapter presents points of convergence among these various perspectives on theory development.

So, what is a theory in this most general sense of the term? As we noted at the beginning of this chapter, theories help us understand or explain phenomena we observe in the social world. They are the "nets with which we catch the world" or the ways in which we make sense of social life. Thus, a theory is necessarily an **abstraction** of the social world. A theory is not the communicative behavior itself but an abstract set of ideas that help us make sense of that behavior. Abstractions might take on a variety of forms and may be put together in a variety of ways, but it must be stressed that theories are at an abstract or higher level than actual observations, and theories have the goal of "explaining and systematizing lower-level findings" (Rosenberg, 1986, p. 342). In providing this abstract understanding of observations, a theory must go beyond or "look behind" phenomena in the social world (Hempel, 1966). In doing this, most theories include

"Theories help us understand or explain phenomena we observe in the social world. They are the 'nets with which we catch the world' or the ways in which we make sense of social life."

- Descriptions of phenomena in the social world
- Relationships among these phenomena (sometimes in the form of rules or laws)
- An underlying and abstract storyline that describes the mechanisms at work in these relationships
- Links between the storyline and the observed phenomena and relationships (sometimes called correspondence rules or

bridge principles; see Phillips, 1992, p. 130)

Several points about the parts of a theory should be emphasized. First, in moving beyond a mere description of the social world, we are distinguishing between a taxonomy (or typology) and a theory. That is, a theory is more than a cataloging of the social world: It is an attempt to provide an abstract understanding or explanation of that social world. For example, a list of relational "break-up strategies" would not count as a theory. Instead, a theory must move on to enhance our understanding of how, when, or why such strategies might be used. Second, theories could be formulated at a variety of levels of generality. For example, we will encounter some theories (e.g., structuration theory in Chapter 12 or coordinated management of meaning in Chapter 9) that are of broad scope and can apply to a wide range of communication situations. Other theories we will encounter are much narrower (e.g., uncertainty reduction theory in Chapter 10 or spiral of silence theory in Chapter 15) but still are important theoretical statements that help us explain or understand a portion of social life. Indeed, some grounded theories in the interpretive tradition of theorizing (see Chapter 4) do not attempt any kind of generalization, but they still serve as abstract understandings of events and processes observed in the social world.

To highlight the various parts of a theory, we briefly preview a theory we consider in much more detail in Chapter 10—social penetration theory. Earlier in this chapter, we discussed enhancing our understanding of relational development and friendship formation through the development of an informal theory. Social penetration theory is a formal and widely used theory that tackles this topic area. Social penetration provides a description of the relationship formation process (i.e., social penetration is a process through which we enhance the depth and breadth of our relationships over time through communication), an explication of the concepts and relationships that are part of the social penetration process (i.e., a consideration of the stages of relational development and self-disclosure processes), an explanation of the mechanisms that motivate the process of social penetration (i.e., we develop relationships because of our desire to enhance outcomes with reference to future alternatives and past comparisons), and a consideration of the links between observed interaction and the social penetration process (i.e., the theory specifies ways to define relational stages and instances of self-disclosure).

Of course, this is only one example of how these various parts can be seen in an actual theory, and we find very different ways of developing understanding in other theories. Various perspectives on theorizing tend to use these concepts in different ways, and in Chapters 3, 4, and 5 of this book, we consider some of the specific forms that theories can take when considered within the post-positive, interpretive, and critical schools of social theory. However, it makes sense to follow the lead of Richard Miller (1987, p. 135), who is "prepared to accept as a theory an explanatory . . . story even though it might not be as precise as we would often like" and to appreciate the variety of ways in which these theoretical understandings can be constructed.

Regardless of the precise form that theory takes, this consideration of what theory is emphasizes the clear distinction that should be made between the abstract world of theory and the empirical world of observation. We use an abstract theory to understand empirical observations. In the area of relational development, we understand our empirical observations and experiences with friends (and others) in the social world by invoking an abstract explanation involving the importance of similarity in the friendship formation process. This distinction, then, between abstract theory and empirical observation leads to the classic "chicken-or-the-egg" question of social theory: Which comes first, the theory or the observation? A **deductive**

approach to theory building (e.g., Dubin, 1978; Hage, 1972) tends to give primacy to theory. Poole, McPhee, and Canary (2002) exemplify this approach when they state that "theory should guide method; it should indicate what data are appropriate and suggest the types of evidence best suited to test ideas" (pp. 23–24). For example, in considering our theory of relational development and friendship formation, a deductive theorist might first formulate specific propositions about attitude similarity and relational development and then test those propositions with empirical data. The movement is from the general proposition to the specific instances seen in the research.

In contrast, an **inductive approach** to theory building (e.g., Glaser & Strauss, 1967) gives primacy to observation. In this approach, theoretical abstractions are based on—or grounded in—empirical observation. For example, an inductive approach to the study of relational development would advocate a great deal of observation of (and often participation in) developing relationships before any propositions or hypotheses are formed. Only after the scholar has been immersed in the process of developing relationships could he or she come to any conclusions about the abstract processes involved in the relational development process.

Not surprisingly, neither of these pure types is reflective of how theory development is most typically practiced in social research. Rather than working in a purely deductive or inductive mode, social theorists most often "tack" between observations and abstractions, using observations to hone previously developed theoretical statements and theory to guide subsequent empirical observation. The distinction then becomes whether *theory* is given primacy—as in the deductive theorizing of post-positivist perspectives (see Chapter 3)—or whether *observation* is given primacy—as in the inductive theorizing of interpretive perspectives (see Chapter 4).

In summary, then, the question of what a theory is can be answered by considering some ways in which we form abstract understandings and explanations about the way the observed social world works. These understandings can be formed at a variety of levels and through a variety of inductive and deductive processes, but they share the common feature of attempting to answer questions regarding how and why communicative processes work in the ways they do.

Conceptualizing Theory: What Should Theory Do?

A second issue in conceptualizing theory involves considering the function of theories. That is, what should theories do? Confronting the functions we want theory to play will help us consider the appropriate forms that theories can take and the standards by which we can evaluate the quality of a particular theory of social and communicative life.

Bernard Cohen (1994) draws on the work of Larry Laudan (1977, 1982) in proposing that the central function of theory is to solve problems. Laudan (1977) notes that "the first and essential acid test for any theory is whether it provides acceptable answers to interesting questions; whether, in other words, it provides satisfactory solutions to important problems" (p. 14). This approach suggests that theories can be evaluated both in terms of the importance or significance of the problems being addressed and in terms of the quality of the solution the theory provides. Cohen (1994) argues that questions of importance and significance are specific to particular disciplines and are often determined by values— and sometimes only in hindsight. However, determining the success of theoretical solutions to problems is an issue that is directly germane to the determination of what theories should do and how we should evaluate the quality of various social theories.

Theories can be used to address a number of types of problems. Laudan (1977) begins with two types: empirical problems and conceptual problems. An **empirical problem** is "anything about the . . . world which strikes us as odd, or otherwise in need of explanation" (Laudan,

1977, p. 15). For example, a communication researcher might notice that people from Eastern cultures (e.g., Japan, Korea, or China) behave differently in business meetings than people from Western cultures (e.g., North America or Western Europe). A theoretical explanation similar to the theories of face and culture that we will consider in Chapter 16 could then be forged to enhance our understanding of this phenomenon.

Laudan's second problem type, the **conceptual problem,** can be internal or external. An internal conceptual problem exists when a particular theory exhibits inconsistencies that need to be clarified. For example, a theory of group decision making may include statements that would lead to different predictions depending on whether a group was described as a decision- making group or an information-gathering group. If a group was involved in both of these activities, a conceptual problem within the theory (e.g., how to deal with dual-function groups) would need to be resolved. Conceptual problems can also be external, in which case a particular theory conflicts with an explanation provided by another theory. For example, in Chapter 10 we consider related theories of communication during initial interaction (uncertainty reduction theory and predicted outcome value theory) in which the underlying mechanisms proposed lead to conflicting predictions and explanations of relational development.

To empirical and conceptual problems, Cohen (1994) adds the category of the **practical problem,** arguing that "utility in solving practical problems has historically played a major role in both assessing and promoting theory construction" (pp. 70–71). Indeed, Kurt Lewin's (1951) oft-stated comment that "there is nothing so practical as a good theory" (p. 169) highlights the role of theory in solving practical problems. Within the field of communication, the role of theory in dealing with practical or applied problems is particularly important. Communication scholars often confront applied issues such as how to improve the provision of health care, how to enhance the effectiveness of problem solving within organizational groups, or

> ## ☼ REAL LIFE INSIGHT
>
> Theory can be seen as a problem-solving enterprise, addressing empirical, conceptual, and practical problems. However, recent work taking a *practical theory* perspective shows that these problem-solving functions are not independent goals of theory, but work together in addressing communication problems in families, workplaces, and communities. Recent work by Karen Tracy and Heidi Muller (2001) provides a case in point. These communication scholars examined 33 months of a school district's board meetings. Tracy and Muller argue that school board meetings "are quintessential sites of democracy in action: loosely knit groups of people, with partially shared and partially competing interests, making decisions about how to educate their community's children" (p. 85).
>
> These scholars used several theories as lenses for the analysis of interaction during school board meetings, and these theories helped to shed light on the *practical problems* facing the board. For example,
>
> Tracy and Muller conclude that the theories they used provided paths for improving communication such as changing structures for participation, developing "thicker skins" among school board members, and understanding the conversational work that is necessary for productive deliberation of contentious issues.
>
> Perhaps what is most interesting about this research, though, is that these scholars did not just use theory to address practical problems: They also used their research to address the *conceptual problems* of the theories they worked with. In other words, Tracy and Muller turned the lens the other way—from data to theory—in critiquing and suggesting changes for the specific theories that guided their work. This research, then, points both to the way theorizing addresses different kinds of problems (practical and conceptual) and to the way that productive theories often have to move fluidly between the concrete world of observation and the abstract world of theory in addressing these problems.

how to develop persuasive campaigns to promote desirable behavior. Practical problems exist at a much more abstract level as well, and communication theorists struggle with the challenge of creating and maintaining democratic workplaces and communities or enhancing the process of development on a global basis.

Within the discipline of communication, there are a variety of positions advocated with regard to this connection between theory and practice (see, e.g., Cissna, 1995; Petronio, 1999). For example, some scholars (e.g., Seibold, 1995; Miller, 1995) tend to regard theory development and the application of that theory to applied problems as relatively distinct processes. Others (e.g., Goodall, 1995) contend that applied problems can best be addressed through an intimate connection between a researcher or theorist and the "real-world" issues under consideration. Indeed, a recent movement advocating **practical theory** in the communication discipline (see, e.g., Barge, 2001; Craig, 1989, 1995; Cronen,

2001) highlights the role of communication theory in addressing the ongoing practical problems faced by individuals and community. Practical theory is a process in which theorists become engaged with individuals and groups and theorize with those community members in creating new understandings of communication processes and opening up possibilities for action.

Summary

In this section, we have considered formative ideas about what a theory is and what a theory should do. A theory is an abstract statement that provides an understanding or explanation of something observed in the social world. Further, a theory functions to answer empirical, conceptual, and practical questions. In the next section we take a step back from these questions of theory to examine some of the larger assumptions that guide any theorist during the theory development process.

■ METATHEORETICAL CONSIDERATIONS

Throughout the preceding discussion of theory form and function, frequent mention was made of the fact that different schools of social thought have very different ideas about what theory is and what theory does. In other words, the theory development process does not exist within a vacuum. Rather, a philosophical framework exists in which theory development and testing occurs. That framework strongly influences beliefs about what counts as theory and how theory should function within the academic community and within larger society. Indeed, Chapters 3, 4, and 5 are devoted to detailed discussions of three of these theoretical frameworks: post-positivist, interpretive, and critical approaches to theory development.

Some of the important distinctions among the philosophical frameworks that influence these schools of thought on theory development can be traced to their metatheoretical foundations. **Metatheory,** as the term implies, is theory about theory. That is, metatheoretical considerations involve philosophical commitments on issues such as what aspects of the social world we can and should theorize about, how theorizing should proceed, what should count as knowledge about the social world, and how theory should be used to guide social action. These metatheoretical themes have traditionally been the province of philosophers of science, but in recent years social theorists and social researchers have paid increasing attention to metatheoretical issues (see, e.g., edited volumes in the social sciences such as Fiske & Shweder, 1986; Guba, 1990b; M. Martin & McIntyre, 1994; and volumes specific to the communication discipline such as Dervin, Grossberg, O'Keefe, & Wartella, 1989).

These discussions of metatheoretical issues may have had their genesis in Thomas Kuhn's (1962) landmark publication, *The Structure of Scientific Revolutions*. Though Kuhn was writing primarily about the development of theory and knowledge within the "hard" sciences such as physics, his book has probably been even more widely read and cited within social research disciplines. We discuss some of Kuhn's more specific ideas about theory development and the cumulation of knowledge in Chapter 3, but one clear impact of his writing was to spur discussions about metatheory—and the theoretical approaches defined by metatheory—within social and behavioral scholarship. In the next few sections, we consider three specific areas of metatheory—ontology, epistemology (and related issues of methodology), and axiology—that help map the terrain for different schools of thought in social research. In these sections we attempt to merely draw and define the boundaries and contours of the map. The specific placement of approaches to theory on this map will be left for our discussions in Chapters 3, 4, and 5.

Ontological Considerations

The study of **ontology** within philosophy involves investigations into the nature of being. In metatheoretical discussions within social research, questions of ontology involve issues such as "What is the nature of reality?" and "What is the nature of the knowable?" (Guba, 1990a, p. 18). In other words, questions of ontology address the nature of the phenomena that we address in our scholarship—the "what" of our theorizing. For researchers in social fields such as communication, this involves considering the nature of the social world and the people, groups, and processes that populate that world.

Many typologies have been proposed to describe various ontological positions, and these typologies are the subject of much debate in social research (see, e.g., Phillips's [1992] chapter entitled "Objectivity and Subjectivity"). Space does not permit a full discussion of these debates here. However, it is important to distinguish among several important ontological positions that can be adopted in social scholarship. Few theorists take the pure or extreme versions of these positions but instead use these positions as landmarks in describing their own individual ontological positions.

Burrell and Morgan (1979) label one position on the ontological map as a **realist position.** Many scholars take a realist position with regard to the physical world (i.e., they believe in the hard reality of rocks, trees, planets, and so on), but views of the social world are more important for communication theorists. According to a social realist, "The social world external to human cognition is a real world made up of hard, tangible and relatively immutable structures" (Burrell & Morgan, 1979, p. 4). A social realist sees both the physical and the social world as consisting of structures that exist "out there" and that are independent of an individual's perception. That is, for a realist, an individual can have varying levels of a concept called communication competence just as one could possess a car or a house or have hair of a certain color. In this view, communication competence is a real entity that can be recognized and possessed.

At the other end of the ontological spectrum is the **nominalist position.** "The nominalist position revolves around the assumption that the social world external to individual cognition is made up of nothing more than names, concepts and labels which are used to structure reality" (Burrell & Morgan, 1979, p. 4). Thus, for a nominalist, there is no world "out there"—only the names and labels of entities that are created by individuals. In the nominalist view, then, communication competence is merely a label that an individual might apply to a specific experience of self or other in social life; it is not a real and objective thing.

A third—some would say intermediary—point on the ontological map is a stance that has been highly influential in social research since the late 1960s. This stance is often called a **social constructionist position** (e.g., Berger & Luckmann, 1967). According to this position, social reality cannot be construed as either totally objective (the realist position) or totally subjective (the nominalist position). Rather, social reality is seen as an intersubjective construction that is created through communicative interaction. As Leeds-Hurwitz (1992) states, "In this view, social reality is not a fact or set of facts

existing prior to human activity. . . . [W]e create our social world through our words and other symbols, and through our behaviors" (p. 133). However, most social constructionists would argue that these intersubjective realities are then reified or objectified because individuals treat the social constructions and are affected by the social constructions as if they were objective features of the social world. For example, the competence of communicators can be seen as socially constructed when different groups of individuals come to see different kinds of communication as competent during the course of one or more interactions. Further, the social construction of communication competence will vary depending on the social situation and the social actors in that situation. For example, what is seen as competent communication at a college fraternity party is likely to be very different from what is competent in a court of law or in the surgical suite of a hospital.

To further illustrate the differences among realists, nominalists, and social constructionists, these three ontological positions can be contrasted with regard to an additional concept. Consider, for example, the notion of *hierarchy* that is central to communication in organizational settings. A realist would contend that the existence of hierarchical levels in organizations is a very real thing that affects individuals every day. This hierarchy is demonstrated in a number of ways: the printed organizational chart that is distributed in organizational publications, the chain of command that governs organizational activities and communication, and the like. For a realist, hierarchy is a social fact of organizational life. In contrast, a nominalist would contend that the attribute of hierarchy is simply a social label created by individuals as they make their way through the social world. This label might be a convenient one to assist in interaction—especially for those wielding power in organizations—but it has no inherent reality or meaning outside the name. Finally, a social constructionist would argue that the concept of hierarchy is one that has been imbued with meaning through many communicative interactions, both historically (e.g., looking at how organizations have worked over time) and in current experience (e.g., the way things work in the organization at which you are employed). As the hierarchy concept becomes part of our social fabric, it influences subsequent communicative interaction (e.g., we try to follow the chain of command in organizational communication), and it also has the potential to be transformed by those interactions (e.g., we can try to buck the system by going over the boss's head). This illustrates the ways in which a concept is created through social interaction, enables and constrains communication, but may become so naturalized that we don't even notice its influence on us.

In summary, a central metatheoretical issue is the ontological stance one takes with regard to the social world. A social theorist's ontology might be realist by positing a hard and solid reality of both physical and social objects. Or a theorist's stance might be nominalist in proposing that the reality of social entities exists only in the names and labels we provide for them. Or a theorist's stance might be social constructionist in emphasizing the ways in which social meanings are created through historical and contemporary interaction and the manner in which these social constructions enable and constrain our subsequent behavior.

Epistemological Considerations

The study of **epistemology** within philosophy involves questions about the creation and growth of knowledge. Typical questions of epistemology might be "What counts as knowledge of the social world?" "What can we know?" "What is the relationship between the knower and the known?" and "How is knowledge about the social world accumulated?" Like questions of ontology, epistemological debates have recently come to the fore in social research. Indeed, many debates about epistemology have their roots in debates about ontology because our beliefs about the nature of the social world necessarily influence our beliefs about how we can come to know about that social world. For example, if you see

communication competence as a hard fact of social life, you could come to know about an individual's competence through standardized instruments and procedures. In contrast, if you believe that communication competence is created through social interaction, knowledge of competence would have to be based on an understanding of specific settings and conversations. As in our discussion of ontology, in this section we merely map out a few crucial epistemological positions and the distinctions among them as a way of setting the stage for discussions of approaches to theory development in communication in the next three chapters.

The epistemological position that has dominated thought in both the physical and social sciences throughout much of the 20th century is an **objectivist position.** Though this stance has many variants, several aspects of an objectivist epistemology are particularly important. First, objectivists believe that it is possible to understand and explain the social world and that these explanations about the social world accumulate through the work of a community of scholars. Second, objectivists believe that knowledge about the social world can best be gained through a search for regularities and causal relationships among components of the social world. Third, objectivists believe that regularities and causal relationships can best be discovered if a separation exists between the investigator and the subject of the investigation (i.e., between the knower and the known). Finally, objectivists argue that this separation can be guaranteed—or at least enhanced—through the use of the scientific method. We talk more about the scientific method in Chapter 3. In short, the methods of science emphasize observable evidence, clear definitions, distinctions between the observer and the observed, and, as much as possible, control over the phenomenon being studied. In the objectivist epistemological stance, the scientific method is necessary because "scientists, like all men and women, are opinionated, dogmatic, ideological. . . . That is the very reason for insisting on procedural objectivity; to get the whole business outside of ourselves" (Kerlinger, 1979,

Table 2.1	Objectivist and Subjectivist Positions in Epistemology	
	Objectivist Stance	**Subjectivist Stance**
Kind of Knowledge Gained through Theory	*Explanation* of social phenomena based on causal relationships	*Understanding* of social phenomena based on situated knowledge
Methodological Commitments in Search for Knowledge	Separation between knower and known through use of the scientific method	Inquiry from the "inside" through ethnography and reports of social actors
Knowledge Goals for Theory Development	Cumulation of general knowledge through testing of the community of scholars	Emergent and local understandings of cases of situated social life

p. 264). Methodological choices like this are tightly linked with issues of epistemology in social research.

In contrast, a **subjectivist position** rejects many of these foundational principles. For the subjectivist, "the social world is essentially relativistic and can only be understood from the point of view of the individuals who are directly involved in the activities which are to be studied" (Burrell & Morgan, 1979, p. 5). Thus, subjectivists reject the notion of a separation between the knower and the known and with it the scientific method that tries to enhance that separation. Instead, subjectivists support "inquiry from the inside" through the use of ethnographic methods in which understandings of motives and contexts are favored over causal and lawlike explanations. Because knowledge is situated and relativistic, a subjective epistemology also largely rejects the concepts of knowledge generalization and of knowledge cumulation, preferring instead local understandings that emerge through situated research. Table 2.1 summarizes some of the key issues that distinguish objectivist and subjectivist epistemological positions in social research.

To contrast these two positions, consider an objectivist and a subjectivist scholar, each interested in studying children's responses to televised violence. The objectivist scholar might choose to use either experimental or survey research methods in which a premium is placed on standardized instruments, random sampling, and control over procedures. Because this scholar hopes to add to the accumulation of knowledge on this topic, the objectivist would probably design the research project to test current media theories and would look for evidence that could either confirm or falsify those theories. The type of explanation sought by the objectivist scholar would probably be a causal one: for instance, investigating the extent to which viewing violent cartoons will cause children to be verbally or physically aggressive during interaction with others.

In contrast, a subjectivist scholar would argue that an understanding of children's responses to televised violence could be understood only from the inside—that is, by finding out more about the experiences of children while watching (and after watching) violent television programming. Thus, this researcher might choose to observe children watching cartoons over a number of Saturday morning sessions and might even become an active part of the viewing experience. This participant observation might be supplemented with in-depth interviews (with the children and perhaps their parents) designed to elicit each child's experience in television viewing. These observations could then be used to ground theoretical ideas about television violence and children within a particular context for a particular group of children.

In summary, epistemological foundations involve a theorist's ideas about what knowledge is and how knowledge is created and represented in the social world. To the objectivist, knowledge should consist of causal statements about the social world and should be generated through the efforts of a community of scholars using established scientific methods. In contrast, a subjectivist's epistemological stance posits that knowledge resides with social participants in specific situations and thus must be garnered through experience or through extended interaction with insiders.

Axiological Considerations

A final set of metatheoretical issues that should be considered involves **axiology,** or the study of values. The classical scientific view of this topic is that values should have no role in the practice of researchers. As Phillips (1992) argues, scholars holding this view believe that "social science must expunge any trace of values" because "if we allow any chink through which values can enter, then objectivity will escape through the very same crack" (p. 139). Most philosophers of science—and most social researchers—have rejected this hard-line position, however. Indeed, it is probably safe to say that no social researcher today believes that values can be totally expunged from the processes of research and theory development. As G. S. Howard (1985) states, "The controversy is no longer about whether values influence scientific practice, but rather about how values are embedded in and shape scientific practice" (p. 255). In this section, we briefly consider three positions that represent important and influential points of view on this issue.

One school of thought contends that theorists and researchers need to differentiate between the context of discovery in which research problems are chosen and formulated and the context of verification in which research hypotheses are checked, tested, and critically evaluated. Karl Popper (1976) argues that we cannot (and should not) eliminate values from the context of discovery, but that within the context of verification we must have mechanisms that will "achieve the elimination of extra-scientific values from scientific activity" (p. 97). For example, values might influence a social researcher's choice to study the ways in which physicians interact differently with representatives of different cultural groups. Indeed, this choice of research area might be spurred on by a scholar's encounters with the medical community. However, once the study begins, the scientific method should exclude the influence of values in the testing of theoretical propositions. Further, according to this view, even if some values "sneak in" during the actual conduct of research, other scholars should serve as a check on problematic findings through the review of research for publication and through the critical reading of that research once the research is disseminated.

A second position on the relationship between values and theory argues that it is impossible to eliminate the influence of values from any part of the research endeavor. This position argues that "some value orientations are so embedded in our modes of thought as to be unconsciously held by virtually all scientists" (Phillips, 1992, p. 142). For example, Sandra Harding (1987) argues from a feminist perspective that there is a male bias in fundamental aspects of scientific thought, and Stephanie Shields (1975) found that a great deal of research on sex differences in the 20th century was influenced by historical biases (e.g., ideas about natural and social differences between men and women). These values may enter the research and theory development process in either overt or very subtle ways.

More generally, N. R. Hanson's classic work, *Patterns of Discovery* (1965), argues that observation is always influenced by the observer's theoretical perspective and background knowledge. For example, Gould (1981) examines the ways in which intelligence has been studied over time and finds that values and theoretical perspectives have influenced the scientific process in a variety of ways. For example, intelligence has been measured using techniques that will lead white men to come out on top, or with statistical techniques that will favor a particular value about how intelligence is structured in individuals. Thus, according to this second axiological position, values and theoretical perspectives constitute lenses through which we view the world, and these lenses cannot be eliminated in any portion of the scholarly process.

A third position on the role of values in scholarship goes beyond the argument that we cannot expunge values from the research process to contend that we should not separate values from scholarship. This position, which we discuss extensively in our consideration of critical perspectives on theory in Chapter 5, argues not only that values guide choices of research topics and influence the practice of research, but also that scholarship involves active participation in social change movements. Thus, a scholar in this tradition interested in workplace participation would be influenced by values in the choice of research problem; in the formulation of theoretical positions; in the conduct of research; and in recommendations for social, structural, and communicative change that could improve the quality of life for organizational members. This axiological position goes beyond the acknowledgment of the role of values in research to a pointed consideration of *whose* values are given precedence. As Guba (1990a) summarizes, "If the findings of studies can vary depending on the values chosen, then the choice of a particular value system tends to empower and enfranchise certain persons while disempowering and disenfranchising others. Inquiry thereby becomes a *political act*" (p. 24).

Metatheoretical positions on axiology, then, consider the role of values in the process of theoretical development and testing. Though few social researchers would now suggest that theory development and testing can be a value-free process, many still advocate a very limited role of values. Other scholars, however, believe that values are so entrenched in our worldviews that we cannot avoid having them seep (or flow!) into our research. Finally, many scholars believe

that values should play a very active role in our research, directing our scholarship in the paths of social change.

Summary

Theory arises within a context bounded by and influenced by the assumptions of social researchers. We have considered several areas of important metatheoretical assumptions that guide the theory development process, including issues of ontology (the nature of reality), epistemology (the nature of knowledge), and axiology (the role of values). As we will see in subsequent chapters, these metatheoretical foundations have a strong influence on how theory is developed and assessed. We will also see that there are links—though not necessary ones—among these metatheoretical areas.

▀ THEORY IN THE COMMUNICATION DISCIPLINE

In the first two chapters of this book, we have developed two conceptual maps. The first map, presented in Chapter 1, charted the landscape of conceptualizations of communication by identifying key points of definitional convergence and divergence among communication scholars and by discussing the domain of communication in both conceptual and disciplinary terms. The second map, presented in this chapter, introduced the terrain of the theory-building enterprise by defining theory and how it functions and by considering important metatheoretical entailments regarding ontology, epistemology, and axiology. It should be clear from these discussions that any consideration of communication theory will be a complex and multifaceted endeavor. In the final few pages of this chapter, then, we briefly consider communication theory as a pluralistic activity and highlight some of the approaches to developing and working with communication and theories that we discuss throughout the remainder of this book.

Communication Theory as a Pluralistic Enterprise

In the early to middle part of the 20th century, there was widespread agreement among social researchers—including communication scholars—about the proper road for the development and testing of theory. This position held that social research disciplines would flourish if they followed the lead of the physical sciences with their realist ontology, objective epistemology, and value-free methodology. Though some communication scholars have retained aspects of this vision as an ideal (see discussion of post-positivists in Chapter 3), others have turned to alternative frameworks that emphasize the socially constructed nature of reality and an accompanying subjective epistemology (see discussion of interpretivists in Chapter 4) or that emphasize the role of values in social theory and active contributions to relevant societal change (see discussion of critical theorists in Chapter 5). Do we need to decide among these options for theorizing? Are they mutually exclusive and competing options for social theory and research? Or can a variety of approaches to communication theory coexist?

This book takes the position that a variety of perspectives on communication theory can and should coexist. Of course, there are clear points of tension—and even conflict—among these perspectives. As we will see in subsequent chapters, a post-positivist theorist and an interpretive theorist construct and evaluate their theories in very different ways. And critical theorists differ on both of these perspectives in their view of the role of theories and theorists in the social world. However, all these perspectives share a commitment to an increased understanding of social and communicative life and a value for high-quality scholarship. As Goodall (1995) states, "our joint interest is in . . . scholarly pluralism, not . . . scholarly unity. That we find fault with each other's research values should be expected; that we read each other's research carefully and with an open mind should be our goal" (p. 68).

This does not suggest that communication scholars typically endorse the "anything goes" view of epistemology often attributed to Paul Feyeraband (1970), an influential—and some say anarchist—philosopher of science. Indeed, within each guiding approach to communication theory, clear metatheoretical principles lead to judgments regarding the quality in theory and research. However, the view of communication theory adopted in this book suggests that the development of theory within the communication discipline can best be viewed as a pluralistic process in which a variety of viewpoints make valued contributions. This pluralistic enterprise requires an ability to communicate across these approaches, for as Jacobson (1991) argues, "As inquiry moves along the continuum from physical toward social and political topics of research, analysis must increasingly rely on dialogue among scholars" (p. 148). A pluralistic approach also endorses an active stance toward the development of communication theory. As Rosenberg (1986) notes, "Given a range of alternative accounts of knowledge, the only way to decide which will really be fruitful for social science, which will make the potentials for knowledge considerable, is by actually employing them in the work of social scientists" (p. 341).

Perhaps the most persuasive case made for such an approach is presented by Fay and Moon (1977) when they ask the question "What would an adequate philosophy of social science look like?" They compare traditions in social research that value science and causal explanation, that value interpretation, and that value social change. As we will see, these positions are repre-

> *"The view of communication theory adopted in this book suggests that the development of theory within the communication discipline can best be viewed as a pluralistic process in which a variety of viewpoints make valued contributions."*

sentative of the post-positivist, interpretive, and critical approaches to theory. Fay and Moon argue that none of these approaches—in isolation—provides a satisfying approach to social research. Instead, they present an argument for the importance of social research that deals effectively with questions of interpretation, explanation, and critique. Similarly, a volume in the subdiscipline of organizational communication (Corman & Poole, 2000) takes on the explicit goal of finding common ground among the approaches to theory and research presented in this book. As Poole and Lynch (2000) note in the final paragraph of this book,

> While it seems unlikely that any position will win the day, the many options discussed can give us guidance in the practice of scholarship, as we are confronted with problems that indicate the need to combine, work between, or even integrate perspectives. This rich set of approaches greatly increases the possibility that the fruits of research . . . will be substantial, rather than just a smile hanging in the air, with no cat at all behind it. (p. 223)

The remainder of this book, then, will be spent in an examination of the pluralistic field of communication theory. In Chapter 1, we briefly reviewed upcoming chapters and considered the criteria used to select the theories covered in Parts 2 and 3. Here, however, we briefly discuss the perspectives on theory development that will be considered in the remaining three chapters of Part 1. The first of these, the post-positivist perspective on theory development considered in Chapter 3, maintains many ideals of theory development that have flourished in the physical sciences but adapts these ideals in ways that take into account the role of values in theory and social construction processes. The interpretivist perspective on theory development considered in Chapter 4 takes a stance encompassing a nominalist—or social constructionist—ontology and a subjectivist epistemology. Because this perspective emphasizes the situated nature of social life, theory development is most likely to proceed in a way that is grounded in the insider's experi-

ence. Finally, in Chapter 5 we examine the critical perspective on theorizing. This perspective shares some of the ontological and epistemological commitments of the interpretivist school but embraces an activist stance with regard to the role of values in social theory. These three perspectives were chosen for consideration because—under various labels—they are consistently seen as the most dominant approaches to theory development within the philosophy of social science (e.g., Braybrooke, 1987; Fay & Moon, 1977), within other fields of social research (e.g., Guba, 1990b), and within the field of communication (e.g., Bochner, 1985).

Within each of these three chapters, historical background is provided regarding the perspective under consideration and its ontological, epistemological, and axiological entailments. Then, the structure and function of theories within each perspective is considered, and we discuss how theory can be evaluated within that particular approach to theory building. Finally, each of these chapters introduces founding theoretical perspectives that have informed the development of communication theory within each tradition. In discussing each of these approaches to theory development, an effort is made to avoid caricatures of the perspectives. It is easy to present any of these metatheoretical approaches simplistically and in ways that set them up as "straw person" approaches for subsequent critique (see K. I. Miller, 2000, for development of these ideas). These temptations are assiduously avoided as we explore the various perspectives that contribute to the pluralistic enterprise we call communication theorizing.

Key Terms

abstraction
deductive approach
inductive approach
empirical problem
conceptual problem
practical problem
practical theory

INTO YOUR WORLD

We are faced every day with "problems" in our social world. According to this chapter, theory can serve as a way of addressing some of these problems, as well as some of the more academic problems that we often associate with theory. Consider, for example, the strategies that teens can use to resist offers of drug use from other teens. What kind of "theory" would help address this issue? What kind of "abstract" understanding or explanation would be needed to help teens in their drug-resistance attempts? Think about this communication situation, and propose an initial theoretical understanding that addresses some of the questions of *how, why, when,* and *who* regarding teens and drug-resistance strategies.

metatheory
ontology
realist position
nominalist position
social constructionist position
epistemology
objectivist position
subjectivist position
axiology

Discussion Questions

1. Of ontology, epistemology, or axiology, which is the most important to consider when examining a theorist's metatheoretical assumptions? Justify your position.

2. Do positions along the ontological map correspond with certain positions on epistemological or axiological maps? In what ways? Or can these various metatheoretical positions be seen as independent? What are the implications of relationships among ontology, epistemology, and axiology?

3. What are the most crucial differences between the naive theories we construct about everyday life and the theories that social researchers develop?

4. In your own communication experiences, what would you say are some practical problems and some empirical problems that theory could usefully address? What might a theory addressing those problems look like?

42277278-1

Customer Copy

Sold To

Colleen Petersen

9 Paige Trail, Address Line 2

PERKASIE, PA - 18944, US

Phone: (267)424-3810

E-Mail: tuf37242@temple.edu

Ship To

Rachael Petersen

Shipping Method : Store Pickup

Pickup Location: AT STORE

Pickup by   Rachael Petersen

Ship from

Temple University - Main Campus Bookstore

13th and Montgomery Sts, Gittis
Philadelphia, PA - 19122, US

E-Mail: SM693@bncollege.com

Website
http://temple.bncollege.com

Phone: (215)204-5578

1 Your Order

Item #	Description	Price	QTY	Discount	Total
1	MSP 1011: INTRO. TO MEDIA THEORY <P>, New	$56.80	1	$0.00	$56.80

Sub-total		$56.80
+ Shipping		$0.00
+ Tax		$0.00
Total Amount	1 Item(s)	$56.80

2 Processed

Payment Type	Account No.	Date	Amount
Visa	XXXXXXXXXXXX9419	29-Aug-2014	$56.80
		Total Payments	$56.80
		Order Total	$56.80
		Outstanding	$0.00

3 Backordered and Pending Items

Item	Description	Price	QTY	Total
1	FALL 2014 , ENG , 0802 , 011	$0.00	1	$0.00
2	FALL 2014 , FMA , 0843 , 007	$0.00	1	$0.00
3	FALL 2014 , MSP , 1701 , 003	$0.00	1	$0.00
4	MEANING OF MADNESS, used	$47.95	1	$47.95

Sub-total		$47.95
+ Shipping		$0.00
+ Tax		$0.00
Total Amount	4 Item(s)	$47.95

CHAPTER **3**

Thinking About Theory and Research

Rolanda Nash

Rolanda Nash had to hurry to class from work. She always seemed to be running late these days. She had a lot on her mind since she had decided to divorce Anton and move from Sheridan, Wyoming, to Chicago. She was pretty sure Anton was going to leave her alone now and just cooperate with the divorce. After her relationship with him, she felt she would never trust another man again. Meanwhile, she had to complete six credits to graduate and keep the new job she had secured in Chicago. In addition to doing her schoolwork, Rolanda was working thirty hours a week for one of her professors, Dr. Stevens. Dr. Stevens was testing a theory about communication behaviors, and so far it had been a fun job for Rolanda. The theory Dr. Stevens was interested in was called Communication Accommodation Theory. Dr. Stevens had told Rolanda that communication accommodation focused on how and when people made their own communication sound like their conversational partner's (a process of accommodation). According to the theory, when someone wants to get another's approval, there is a higher chance for them to mirror this person's talk. Dr. Stevens wanted to observe communication accommodation in an organizational setting. The professor had sent Rolanda into two different organizations with a tape recorder. Rolanda's task was to tape naturally occurring conversations between subordinates and managers. Stevens called it water cooler conversations, but so far Rolanda had not seen a single water cooler!

Rolanda thought it was very challenging to capture natural conversations. Although Stevens had obtained permission for her to record conversations in the organizations, some people recognized Rolanda and were self-conscious about talking around her. In addition, neither of the two organizations employed many African Americans. Rolanda felt she stuck out as she walked through the hallways. But she was used to that. In most of her university classes she was the only African American woman. At first it really bothered her, but she was used to it by now. She was hoping Chicago would be a better experience.

Now, if she could only get enough conversations to satisfy Dr. Stevens, she could go home to tackle her English assignment. Stevens hadn't really told her how many conversations she needed. Rolanda was hoping ten would be enough. That's all she had gotten in five days of taping. Dr. Stevens had mentioned last week that when Rolanda was finished taping, she would probably be sending her back to the organizations to do some follow-up interviews with the people she had taped. Rolanda wondered how that would work out. She hoped she could get what Dr. Stevens wanted.

Rolanda is involved in theorizing and researching about complex communication interactions both in her work and in her personal life. Although not everyone does research for a living, often people wonder to themselves, or ask one another, Why do we act the way we do? Why do we argue about some things and not others? Why are we successful in communicating sometimes and not at other times? How can we be better communicators? Scholars believe that we can provide answers to these kinds of questions with theory, because as Robert Craig and Heidi Muller (2007) observe, "theorizing is a formalized extension of everyday sense-making and problem solving" (p. ix). Furthermore, when we make observations and compare them to theory, we're doing research to help us in our efforts to make sense of situations and solve problems. Theory and research are inextricably linked. Paul Reynolds (2007) points out that some researchers begin with theory (theory-then-research) whereas others begin with research (research-then-theory), but all researchers need to think about both.

In this book we are discussing theory and research as professionals use them in their work; yet all of us in daily life think like researchers, using implicit theories to help us understand those questions we mentioned previously. Fritz Heider (1958) referred to everyday interactors engaging in theoretical thinking as "naïve psychologists." Whenever we pose an answer to one of our questions (for example, if we suggest that maybe we are really fighting over power and control and not what color to paint the living room), we are engaging in theoretical thinking.

In many ways, this text points out the similarities and differences between thinking as a "naïve" theorist and thinking as a professional theorist. First, as we have just mentioned, they are similar because both puzzle over questions encountered through observations and both seek answers for these questions. Both also set up certain criteria that define what an acceptable answer might be. For instance, when Ely, a student, wonders why his roommate talks so much more than what is comfortable for him, he might decide on the following criteria for an answer: The answer has to apply to all communication contexts (phone, face-to-face, and so forth); and the answer has to make sense (Ely wouldn't accept for an answer that his roommate comes from another planet where talk is more highly valued than here on Earth). When Ely and social scientists find answers that satisfy their criteria, they generalize from them and may apply them to other situations that are similar. If Ely concludes that his roommate is insecure and talks to cover up his insecurity, he may determine that others he meets who talk more than he does are also insecure.

In all those processes, everyday communicators follow the basic outline advanced by social science. However, there are very clear differences apparent in this description as well. First, social scientists systematically test theories whereas nonscientists test selectively. For instance, Ely will accept evidence that agrees with his theory about the relationship of insecurity and talking and tend to ignore evidence that contradicts it. Researchers are more rigorous in their testing and more willing to amend theories, incorporating information arising from inconsistencies in the original formulation of the theory. In the text, many of the theories we present have undergone extensive revisions as

T*I*P

Theory Into Practice

Martina

When we first started talking about the "naïve theorist" idea, I thought it was kind of weird. I was pretty sure I wasn't a theorist, naïve or not! Then I started keeping track of how I was thinking like a theorist in my everyday life. It was amazing how many times I did make a theory and then tried to test it. It seemed like it happened a lot at work. When I was being considered for a promotion, I watched carefully to see what the "higher ups" in my office did and how they reacted to my work. I developed a "theory" that the men in positions of power needed to think of me as their daughter but the women wanted me to perform as an equal. So, when I presented my work to the men, I was more deferential and asked them for advice. I never did that with the women. I decided my theory was correct when I got the promotion!

testing has posed challenges to the original theoretical principles or a need for expansion of them.

Now that you know that theory and research operate in some ways like the way we think already, we're ready to move on to an in-depth examination of our basic terms. In this chapter, we prepare you for reading about the twenty-five theories to follow by providing the following: (1) a definition of theory that maps the term onto intellectual traditions and explains how scholars' assumptions affect the process of theorizing, and (2) a brief description of the research process.

Defining Theory: What's in a Name?

theory
an abstract system of concepts and their relationships that help us to understand a phenomenon

Generally speaking, a **theory** is an abstract system of concepts with indications of the relationships among these concepts that help us to understand a phenomenon. Stephen Littlejohn and Karen Foss (2008) suggest this abstract system is derived through systematic observation. Jonathan H. Turner (1986) defined *theory* as "a process of developing ideas that can allow us to explain how and why events occur" (p. 5). This definition focuses on the nature of theoretical thinking without specifying exactly what the outcome of this thinking might be. William Doherty and his colleagues (1993) have elaborated on Turner's definition by stating that theories are both process and product: "Theorizing is the process of systematically formulating and organizing ideas to understand a particular phenomenon. A theory is the set of interconnected ideas that emerge from this process" (p. 20). In this definition, the authors attempt to be inclusive. They do not use Turner's word *explain* because the goals of theory can be more numerous than simply explanation, a point we explore later in this chapter.

In this brief discussion, you have probably noticed that different theorists approach the definition of *theory* somewhat differently. The search for a

DILBERT © Scott Adams/Distributed by United Feature Syndicate Inc.

universally accepted definition of *theory* is a difficult, if not impossible, task. When defining the term *theory,* as D. C. Phillips (1992) observes, "there is no divinely ordained *correct* usage, but we can strive to use the word consistently and to mark distinctions that we feel are important" (p. 121).

In part, the difficulty in defining *theory* is due to the many ways in which a theory can be classified or categorized. Here we refine our definition by examining the following features and attributes of theories: level of generality, components, and goals.

Level of Generality

One way to understand differences among theories pertains to their level of generality. Level of generality refers to how widely the theory can be applied. Theories can be grand (universal), mid-range (moderately general), or narrow (very specific). **Grand theories** purport to explain all of communication behavior in a manner that is universally true. Outside the discipline of communication, Marxism, an approach we mentioned in Chapter 2, is an example of a grand theory. A grand theory would have the ability to unify all the knowledge we have about communication into one integrated theoretical framework. This may or may not be a worthy goal (Craig, 1999), but most would agree that no grand theory of communication exists. There are too many instances where communication differs from group to group or when communication behavior is modified by changes in context or time to create a grand theory.

A **mid-range theory** explains the behavior of a specific group of people rather than all people, as a grand theory would do. A mid-range theory might try to explain the behavior of all people within a specified time or context.

grand theories
theories that attempt to explain all of a phenomenon such as communication

mid-range theory
a theory that attempts to explain a specified aspect of a phenomenon such as communication

Many theories of communication fall into the mid-range category. Mid-range theories explain a focused aspect of communication behavior, such as how people behave in initial encounters with strangers (see, for example, Chapter 9 describing Uncertainty Reduction Theory), how people agree on decisions in groups (see, for example, Chapter 14 describing Groupthink), or how people from different cultures engage in conflict (see, for example, Chapter 26 describing Face-Negotiation Theory). These theories are bounded by considerations such as time (the initial encounter between strangers explained by Uncertainty Reduction Theory), context (communication in small groups explained by Groupthink), or type of communication behavior (conflict behavior explained by Face-Negotiation Theory). In the case of Face-Negotiation Theory, the boundaries also include the context of cultural communication.

narrow theory
a theory that attempts to explain a very limited aspect of a phenomenon such as communication

Finally, a **narrow theory** "concerns only certain people in certain situations— for example, the communication rules pertinent to standing in an elevator" (Stacks, Hill, & Hickson, 1991, p. 284). Often theories are criticized for claiming to be grander than they really are. For instance, some critics of Standpoint Theory (Chapter 29) argue that it makes claims about all women, but these assertions have to be modified by other identifiers such as class and race.

Theories differ in their level of generality due to their difference in focus or what they try to explain. Some theories focus on the entire communication process (e.g., Symbolic Interaction Theory), whereas others focus more specifically on a given aspect of the process, such as the message or the sender (e.g., Rhetorical Theory). Still others attend to communication as a means for relationship development (e.g., Social Penetration Theory). Knowing a variety of ways to classify theories helps us see how very dissimilar works (such as Uncertainty Reduction, Uses and Gratifications, and Muted Group) can all be defined as theory.

Components

To understand *theory,* we also need to understand the components of theories. Theories are composed of several key parts, the two most important of which are called concepts and relationships. **Concepts** are words or terms that label the most important elements in a theory. Concepts in some of the theories we will discuss include *cohesiveness* (Groupthink), *dissonance* (Cognitive Dissonance Theory), *self* (Symbolic Interaction Theory), and *scene* (Dramatism). As you can see, sometimes theories are named using one of their key concepts, although this is not always the case.

concepts
labels for the most important elements in a theory

A concept often has a specific definition that is unique to its use in a theory, which differs from how we would define the word in everyday conversation. For example, the concept "cultivation" used in Cultivation Analysis (see Chapter 22) refers specifically to the way media, especially television, create a picture of social reality in the minds of media consumers. This use of the term differs somewhat from using it to mean hoeing your garden or developing an interest, skill, or friendship. In the theory, cultivation has a unique and relatively narrow definition. It is always the task of the theorist to provide a clear definition of the concepts used in the theory.

Concepts may be nominal or real. **Nominal concepts** are those that are not observable, such as democracy or love. **Real concepts** are observable, such as personal rituals or spatial distance. As we'll discuss later in the chapter, when researchers use theory in their studies, they must turn both nominal and real constructs into something concrete so that they can be observed. It is much easier to do this for real concepts than for nominal ones.

Relationships specify the ways in which the concepts in the theory are combined. For example, in Chapter 1 we presented three different models of the process of communication. In each model, the concepts are very similar. What is different is the relationship specified among them. In the first model, the relationship is a linear one where one concept relates to the second, which then relates to the next, and so forth. In the second model, the posited relationship is interactive, or two-way. The third model illustrates mutual influence (transaction), where all the concepts are seen as affecting one another simultaneously.

nominal concepts
concepts that are not directly observable

real concepts
concepts that are directly observable

relationships
the ways in which the concepts of a theory relate to one another

Goals

We can also clarify the definition of theory by understanding its purposes. In a broad, inclusive sense, the goals of theory can include explanation, understanding, prediction, and social change; we are able to *explain* something (why Anton behaved so badly in his relationship with Rolanda, for example) because of the concepts and their relationships specified in a theory. We are able to *understand* something (Rolanda's distrust of men) because of theoretical thinking. In addition, we are able to *predict* something (how Rolanda will respond to other men she meets) based on the patterns suggested by a theory. Finally, we are able to effect *social change* or empowerment (altering the institution of marriage so that it more completely empowers both partners, for example) through theoretical inquiry.

Although some theories try to reach all these goals, most feature one goal over the others. Rhetorical theories, some media theories, and many interpersonal theories seek primarily to provide explanation or understanding. Others—for example, traditional persuasion and organizational theories—focus on prediction. Still others—for instance, some feminist and other critical theories—have as their central goal to change the structures of society. As you learned in Chapter 2, for critical theorists, this means effecting social change, not simply improving individual lives. For instance, a theory about conflict management may help people understand how to engage in conflict more productively, thus enriching their lives. Yet it may do nothing to change the underlying structures that promoted the conflict in the first place.

Now we have a working definition for theory: an abstract system of concepts with indications of the relationships among these concepts that helps us to explain, understand, predict, or change a phenomenon (i.e., some aspect of communication). In addition, we can see that theories can be broadly generalized or more narrowly applied. Most theories have the ability to generalize moderately, called mid-range. From this discussion of the definition of theory, it should be clear that experience and theory are related, although experience is concrete and theory is abstract. We'll now address this relationship.

Relationship Between Theory and Experience

In 1952, Carl Hempel compared a scientific theory to a complex spatial network, saying that a theory's "terms are represented by the knots, while the threads connecting the latter correspond, in part, to the definitions and, in part, to the fundamental and derivative hypotheses included in the theory" (p. 36). Hempel then noted that this theory/network

> floats, as it were, above the plane of observation and is anchored to it by rules of interpretation. These might be viewed as strings which are not part of the network but link certain points of the latter with specific places in the plane of observation. . . . From certain observational data, we may ascend, via an interpretive string, to some point in the theoretical network, then proceed, via definitions and hypotheses, to other points, from which another interpretive string permits a descent to the plane of observation. (p. 36)

Hempel suggests that although a theory is abstract, it enables us to understand concrete experiences and observations, and that a theory itself is capable of being modified by observations. In addition, his statement asserts that our concrete experiences and observations are interpreted by us through the lens offered by the theory we are using.

Janet Yerby (1995), commenting on the notion that theories act as a lens, allowing us to see some things while ignoring others, refers to theories as "the stories we have developed to explain our view of reality" (p. 362). The strings of interpretation that Hempel mentions can be seen as the elements in the story we have chosen as satisfactory explanations for communication behaviors. In taking this approach, we have to be aware, as Yerby suggests, that theories, like stories, change and evolve over time as new information modifies and refines them.

This line of thinking prompts us to ask what motivates a scholar to choose one theory (or lens) over another in their work. The answer to this question comes in an examination of the varying approaches to knowing that scholars bring to their work before they even begin to do any research.

Approaches to Knowing: How Do You See (and talk about) the World?

Many scholars (Baxter & Babbie, 2004; Baxter & Braithwaite, 2008; White & Klein, 2008) have discussed how researchers think and talk about the world and their work. Most of these scholars have identified three general approaches: positivistic or empirical, interpretive, and critical. We will discuss each of these in turn, but remember that we're presenting each approach in its extreme form, and many researchers would not identify themselves as subscribing to the extremes. Most people find some way to adapt one of these approaches to fit the particular way they see the world.

The Positivistic, or Empirical, Approach

The **positivistic,** or **empirical, approach** assumes that objective truths can be uncovered and that the process of inquiry that discovers these truths can be, at least in part, value-neutral. This tradition advocates the methods of the natural sciences, with the goal of constructing general laws governing human interactions. An empirical researcher strives to be objective and works for **control,** or direction over the important concepts in the theory. In other words, when the researcher moves to the plane of observation, he or she carefully structures the situation so that only one element varies. This enables the researcher to make relatively definitive statements about that element.

> **positivistic/ empirical approach**
> an approach assuming the existence of objective reality and value-neutral research
>
> **control**
> direction over the important concepts in a theory

As Leslie Baxter and Dawn Braithwaite (2008) observe, the researcher's task in the empirical approach is "to deduce testable hypotheses from a theory" (p. 7). In other words, the positivistic approach moves along the theory-then-research model to which Reynolds (2007) referred.

The Interpretive Approach

The **interpretive approach** views truth as subjective and co-created by the participants, with the researcher clearly one of the participants. There is less emphasis on objectivity in this approach than in the empirical approach because complete objectivity is seen as impossible. However, this does not mean that research in this approach has to rely totally on what participants say with no outside judgment by the researcher. Martyn Hammersley (1992), for example, advocates a "subtle realism" that suggests that researchers "monitor [their] assumptions and the inferences [they] make on the basis of them" (p. 53). In this subtle realism, Hammersley suggests that research can find a way to be reasonably objective. The interpretive researcher believes that values are relevant in the study of communication and that researchers need to be aware of their own values and to state them clearly for readers, because values will naturally permeate the research. These researchers are not concerned with control and the ability to generalize across many people as much as they are interested in rich descriptions about the people they study. For interpretive researchers, theory is best induced from the observations and experiences the researcher shares with the respondents. This means that the interpretive approach is likely to follow Reynolds' (2007) research-then-theory model.

> **interpretive approach**
> an approach viewing truth as subjective and stressing the participation of the researcher in the research process

The Critical Approach

In the **critical approach,** an understanding of knowledge relates to power. As Art Bochner (1985) notes, this approach "assumes that science cannot exist without ideology" (p. 46). Critical researchers believe that those in power shape knowledge in ways that work to perpetuate the status quo. Thus, powerful people work at keeping themselves in power, which requires silencing minority voices questioning the distribution of power and the power holders' version of truth. Patricia Hill Collins (1991) speaks from this approach when she says that "the tension between the suppression of Black women's ideas and our intellectual activism in the face of that suppression, comprises the politics of Black feminist

> **critical approach**
> an approach stressing the researcher's responsibility to change the inequities in the status quo

Table 3.1 Three Approaches to Knowing

	EMPIRICAL	INTERPRETIVE	CRITICAL
Goal	Explanation of world	Probe the relativism of world	Change the world
Engagement of researcher	Separate	Involved	Involved
Application of theory	To generalize about many like cases	To illuminate the individual case	To critique a specific set of cases

thought" (pp. 5–6). Black feminists are not the only researchers who are comfortably rooted in the critical approach Marxists and feminists of all types, among others, also work from this intellectual tradition. For critical researchers, it is generally important to change the status quo to resolve power imbalances and to give voice to those who have been silenced by the power structure.

Some critical theorists, notably Stuart Hall (1981), whose work we feature in Chapter 21, have commented that power imbalances may not always be the result of intentional strategies on the part of the powerful. Rather, ideology, or "those images, concepts, and premises which provide the frameworks through which we represent, interpret, understand and 'make sense' of some aspect of social existence" (Hall, 1981, p. 31), is often "produced and reproduced" accidentally. For example, this may come about when certain images of masculinity work to sell a product. When advertisers observe this success, they continue creating ads with these images. In this fashion, the images of masculinity become entrenched in society. Thus, although the powerful are interested and invested in staying in power, they may not be fully aware of what they do to silence minority voices (Table 3.1).

Approaches to Knowing: What Questions Do You Ask About the World?

ontology
a branch of knowledge focused on the nature of reality

epistemology
a branch of knowledge focused on how we know things

axiology
a branch of knowledge focused on what is worth knowing

Implicit in the three approaches to knowing are answers to questions about the nature of reality (researchers call this **ontology**), questions about how we know things (researchers call these questions **epistemology**), and questions about what is worth knowing (or what researchers call **axiology**). It's important to recognize that each of the three approaches to knowing (empirical, interpretive, and critical) answers questions about ontology, epistemology, and axiology differently. We'll briefly address each of these terms and suggest how the three approaches to knowing treat them differently.

Ontology is the study of being and nonbeing, or in other words, the study of reality. The word *ontology* comes from the Greek language and means the science of being or the general principles of being. The What Is Ontology? website (www.formalontology.it/section_4.htm) provides the following definition for ontology: "a science or study of being: specifically, a branch of metaphysics relating to the nature and relations of being; a particular system according to which problems of the nature of being are investigated; first philosophy." This definition focuses on the idea that ontology gives us a certain vision of the world and on what constitutes its important features. It is called the first philosophy because it is not possible to philosophize until the nature of reality is determined. Often questions of ontology cluster around how much free will people have. Researchers who subscribe to an empirical approach believe that general laws govern human interactions. Thus they also believe that people don't have a lot of free choice in what they do—people are predictable because they follow the laws of human behavior which, to a large extent, determine their actions. A researcher's job is to *uncover* what is already out there in reality. This differs from researchers with an interpretive bent, who would allow that people do have free choice, and see a researcher's job as to co-create reality with research participants. Finally, critical researchers see choice and constraint in the power structures they wish to change.

The questions surrounding epistemology focus on how we go about knowing; what counts as knowledge is intimately related to ontology. How researchers see the world, truth, and human nature necessarily influences how they believe they should try to learn about these things. The approach (positivistic, interpretive, or critical) Dr. Stevens took in our opening example would affect her way of collecting information, an epistemologic choice. For instance, if Dr. Stevens researched as a positivist, she would institute many more controls than we described in our opening case study. Furthermore, the number of observations would not be left to chance or to Rolanda's schedule. Dr. Stevens would have calculated the number of conversations she needed to support statistics testing relationships among status and communication accommodation. If Dr. Stevens operated in the interpretive tradition, she would not be content with her own analysis of the conversations. She might invite the participants to read the transcripts of their conversations so that they could tell her whether they were trying to accommodate to their partners. Stevens would probably be interested in the participants' explanations for why they changed (or did not change) their speech patterns as they conversed with superiors or subordinates in the workplace. Using a critical approach, Dr. Stevens might bring some of the following questions to her research: How is the relationship between workers of differing statuses communicatively constructed? Does convergence happen unequally based on status? Are there status differences other than occupation that impact communication accommodation? How can we change the prevailing power structures to improve the inequities we observe in the workplace?

The final set of questions focuses on the place of values in theory and research. The empirical position on axiology is that science must be value-free. However, most researchers do not take this extreme position and accept that some subjectivity, in the form of values, informs the research process (Bostrom, 2003). The question that is still debated concerns not *whether* values should permeate theory and research but *how* they should.

Here we briefly present three positions on this debate that correspond to the three ways of knowing: avoiding values as much as possible in research (empirical), recognizing how values influence the entire research process (interpretative), and advocating that values should be closely intertwined with scholarly work (critical). The first stance argues that the research process consists of many stages and that values should inform some of these stages but not others. For example, the part of the research enterprise that focuses on theory choice must be informed by the values of the researcher. Scholars choose to view a research problem through the lens that they believe most accurately describes the world. Thus, some researchers choose theoretical frameworks that are consistent with an ontology of free choice, whereas others choose frameworks that are more "lawlike" and deterministic. Yet, when they test these theories (the verification stage), they must eliminate "extra-scientific values from scientific activity" (Popper, 1976, p. 97). As you can see, this stance proposes a very limited role for values.

The second position argues that it is not possible to eliminate values from any part of theorizing and research. In fact, some values are so embedded in researchers' culture that researchers are unconscious that they even hold them. Sandra Bem (1993), for instance, observes that much of the research on differences between women and men was influenced by biases existing at the time. Many feminist scholars argue that social science itself suffers from a male bias (Harding, 1987). Some African American scholars make the same observations about the European American biases that exist in much social scientific research (Allen, 2007; Houston, 1992). Thomas Nakayama and Robert Krizek (1995) point out that communication researchers often take White for granted as the default race. Thus, the values and assumptions held by those with a European American perspective are never highlighted, questioned, or acknowledged; they simply inform a scholar's process. Yoshitaka Miike (2007) takes this one step further to advocate theories that would be Asiacentric (meaning rooted in Asian thinking).

The final position argues that not only are values unavoidable, but they are a desirable aspect of the research process. Earlier in this chapter we referred to the goals of theory as including social change. Those who embrace this goal are called critical theorists. Critical theorists advocate seeing theory and research as political acts that call on scholars to change the status quo. Thus, scholars must contribute to changing conditions rather than simply reporting conditions (Table 3.2).

Table 3.2 Answers Supplied by the Three Approaches to Knowing

	EMPIRICAL	INTERPRETIVE	CRITICAL
Ontology	No free choice	Free choice	Choice restrained by power
Epistemology	Theory first. Control study	Research first. Co-create study	Critique power. Seek change
Axiology	Reduce role of values	Acknowledge values	Celebrate values

Approaches to Knowing: How Do You Go About Theory Building?

When researchers seek to create theory, they are guided by all of the issues we've just discussed: their general approach to knowing things (empirical, interpretive, or critical) and the answers to questions about truth or reality, gathering information, and values (ontology, epistemology, and axiology). In addition, they have some guidelines about how to create theory (Craig, 1999). We will review three traditional guidelines: covering law, rules, and systems. The covering law approach and the rules approach represent two extremes, whereas the systems approach provides an intermediate position between the extremes. We must caution that few scholars take the extreme positions sketched out here. Rather, these positions form benchmarks from which researchers anchor their own stances on questions of communication.

The **covering law approach** seeks to explain an event in the real world by referring to a general law. Researchers applying a covering law approach believe that communication behavior is governed by forces that are predictable and generalizable. The **rules approach,** at the other end of the ontological continuum, holds that communication behavior is rule governed, not lawlike. The rules approach differs from the covering law approach in that researchers holding the rules approach admit the possibility that people are free to change their minds, to behave irrationally, to have idiosyncratic meanings for behaviors, and to change the rules. Ultimately, their differences focus on the concept of choice. The covering law model explains human choices by seeking a prior condition (usually a **cause**) that determines the choice that is made (usually an **effect**). From the rules model, rule following results from a choice made by the follower but does not necessarily involve antecedent conditions or any aspect of the cause–effect logic of the covering law approach.

A third view, the **systems approach,** subscribes somewhat to the beliefs of the rules approach while also suggesting that people's free will may be constrained by the system in which they operate. Further, this approach acknowledges the impossibility of achieving what the covering law approach requires: laws about human communication that are invariant and general. The systems approach proposes assumptions that are more easily met than those of the covering law approach (Monge, 1973). We now examine each of the three approaches in more detail and provide an overview in Table 3.3.

Covering Law Approach

This term was first introduced by William Dray (1957), a historian who defined *covering law* as that "explanation is achieved, and only achieved, by *subsuming what is to be explained under a general law*" (p. 1 [emphasis in original]). Some covering law explanations refer to universal laws that state all *x* is *y*. These laws are not restricted by time or space. However, as new information comes to light, even laws have to be modified. Covering law explanations do not always have to be cause–effect. They may also specify relationships of coexistence. We have a causal relationship when we say that self-disclosures by

covering law approach
a guideline for creating theory suggesting that theories conform to a general law that is universal and invariant

rules approach
a guideline for creating theory that builds human choice into explanations

cause
an antecedent condition that determines an effect

effect
a condition that inevitably follows a causative condition

systems approach
a guideline for creating theory that acknowledges human choice and the constraints of the systems involved

Table 3.3 Guidelines to Communication Theory Construction

APPROACH	DESCRIPTION/EXAMPLE
Covering law	Covering law theorists hold that there are fixed relationships between two or more events or objects. Example: Whenever Linda speaks, Bob interrupts her; this is a lawlike statement that expresses a relationship between Linda and Bob. These statements are commonly referred to as if-then statements.
Rules	Rules theorists contend that much of human behavior is a result of free choice. People pick the social rules that govern their interactions. Example: In an interaction between co-workers, much of their conversation will be guided by rules of politeness, turn taking, and so on.
Systems	Systems theorists hold that human behavior is part of a system. Example: Think of a family as a system of family relationships rather than individual members. This illuminates the complexity of communication patterns within the family.

one person cause self-disclosures from a relational partner. A claim of coexistence merely asserts that two things go together—that is, when one person self-discloses, the other does, too—but it does not claim that the first self-disclosure causes the second. It's possible that social norms of reciprocity cause the second self-disclosure or that both disclosures are caused by the environment (an intimate, dimly lit bar or consuming more alcohol than usual).

hypotheses
testable predictions of relationships between concepts that follow the general predictions made by a theory

Critical attributes of covering law explanations are that they provide an explicit statement of a boundary condition and that they allow **hypotheses,** testable predictions of relationships, of varying levels of specificity, to be generated within this boundary condition. Furthermore, because the system is deductive, complete confirmation of theories is never possible. There will always be unexamined instances of the hypothesis.

The type of covering law that we have just described is considered outdated by most social scientists (Bostrom, 2004). Most researchers today recognize that this type of universal law is unrealistic. Instead, researchers might strive for "probabilistic laws," or statements we can predict with a certain degree of probability. For example, as Berger (1977) asserts, "We can predict with a certain probability that if males and females with certain eye colors have large numbers of children, a certain proportion of those children will have a certain eye color. However, we are *not* in a position to predict what the eye color of a *particular* child will be" (p. 10).

Overall, a covering law approach instructs researchers to search for lawlike generalizations and regularities in human communication. These lawlike generalizations may be culturally bound or may have some other complex relationship with culture. Covering law offers a theory-generating option that aims for complete explanation of a phenomenon. The law, in effect, governs the relationships among phenomena.

Table 3.4 Rules Governing Initial Peer Encounters

In the first fifteen minutes of an encounter:	*In the second fifteen minutes:*
Politeness should be observed.	Politeness should be observed.
Demographics should be exchanged.	Likes and dislikes can be discussed.
Partners should speak in rough equivalence to each other.	One partner can speak more than another, but avoid dominance.
Interruptions and talk-overs should be minimal.	More interruptions can be tolerated, but avoid dominance.

Rules Approach

This approach assumes that people are typically engaged in intentional, goal-directed behavior and are capable of acting rather than simply being acted upon. We can be restricted by previous choices we have made, by the choices of others, and by cultural and social conditions, but we are conscious and active choice makers. Further, human behavior can be classified into two categories: activities that are stimulus–response behaviors (termed **movements**) and activities that are intentional choice responses (termed **actions**) (Cushman & Pearce, 1977). Rules theorists contend that studying actions is most relevant to theorists.

Rules theorists look inside communities or cultures to get a sense of how people regulate their interaction with others (Shimanoff, 1980). Rules do not require people to act in a certain way; rather, rules refer to the standards or criteria that people use when acting in a particular setting (Cushman & Cahn, 1985). For example, when two people meet, they normally do not begin at an intimate level of exchange. Rather, there is an agreed-upon starting point, and they will delve further into intimacy if the two see the relationship as having a future. The process of meeting another is guided by rules, although these rules are rarely verbally identified by either person. Don Cushman and Barnett Pearce (1977) believed that if the relationship evolves, the rules guiding interactions change. Rules, then, are important benchmarks for the direction of an interaction. Table 3.4 illustrates how rules guide initial encounters of many peers in the United States.

Several researchers (Lull, 1982; Wolf, Meyer, & White, 1982) have used a rules-based theoretical framework to study family television viewing behaviors. James Lull (1982) identified three types of rules that govern family television watching. First are **habitual rules,** which are nonnegotiable and are usually instituted by the authority figures in the family. When Roger and Marie tell their children that there can be no television until all homework is checked over by one of them and declared finished for the night, they are establishing a habitual rule.

Parametric rules are also established by family authority figures, but they are more negotiable than habitual rules. For example, the Marsh family may have a rule that members can engage in extended talk only during commercial breaks when they are viewing television. Yet, if something exciting has happened to one member, they may negotiate to talk about it during the program itself.

Finally, Lull identified **tactical rules,** or rules that are understood as a means for achieving a personal or interpersonal goal, but are unstated. For example,

movements
activities based on stimulus–response

actions
activities based on intentional choice responses

habitual rules
nonnegotiable rules that are usually created by an authority figure

parametric rules
rules that are set by an authority figure but are subject to some negotiation

tactical rules
unstated rules used to achieve a personal or interpersonal goal

if Rob and Jeremy are watching television together and Rob likes Jeremy, he may tune in to Jeremy's favorite show even though he himself would not have chosen that program. He follows the tactical rule of maintaining relational harmony with his partner.

Overall, a rules approach instructs researchers to discover the rules that govern particular communication contexts and construct theoretical statements around these rules. The rules perspective offers a theory-generating option that aims for a satisfying explanation of a specific communication situation. The theorist would normally begin with a typology of the rules that govern the situation and move from those to statements connecting the rules and specifying the conditions affecting the rules.

Systems Approach

Systems thinking in communication is derived from General Systems Theory (GST), which is both a theory of systems in general—"from thermostats to missile guidance computers, from amoebas to families" (Whitchurch & Constantine, 1993, p. 325)—and a program of theory construction. Systems thinking captured the attention of communication researchers because it changed the focus from the individual to an entire family, a small group, or an organization. This shift reconceptualized communication for scholars and helped them to think innovatively about experience and interaction in groups. Further, systems thinking replaced the stringent assumptions of covering law with more realistic ones. Systems theorists (Monge, 1973) agreed with the rules assertion that "human communication is not characterized by universal patterns" (p. 9). Systems thinking requires systemic, nonuniversal generalizations, does not depend on inductive reasoning, separates the logical from the empirical, allows alternative explanations for the same phenomenon, and permits partial explanations (Monge, 1973).

Systems thinking rests on several properties, including wholeness, interdependence, hierarchy, boundaries, calibration/feedback, and equifinality. We will explain each of these properties briefly.

wholeness
a fundamental property of systems theory stating that systems are more than the sum of their individual parts

Wholeness   The most fundamental concept of the systems approach is **wholeness**. It refers to the idea that a system cannot be fully comprehended by a study of its individual parts in isolation from one another. In order to understand the system, it must be seen as a whole. Wholeness suggests that we learn more about a couple, for example, by analyzing their interactions together than we do by simply analyzing one partner's motivations or statements alone.

interdependence
a property of systems theory stating that the elements of a system affect one another

Interdependence   Because the elements of a system are interrelated, they exhibit **interdependence**. This means that the behaviors of system members co-construct the system, and all members are affected by shifts and changes in the system. Virginia Satir (1988) compares the family to a mobile to illustrate how this principle applies to families. We might expect that when elderly parents decide to sell the family home and move to a small condo, their decisions will affect all of their children.

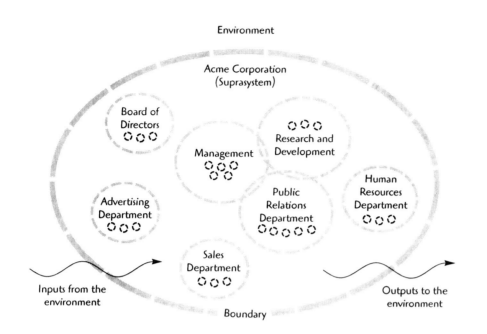

**Figure 3.1
Suprasystems,
Systems, and
Subsystems in the
Acme Corporation**

Hierarchy   All systems have levels, or **subsystems**, and all systems are embedded in other systems, or **suprasystems**. Thus, systems are a **hierarchy**, a complex organization. Each of the subsystems can function independently of the whole system, but each is an integral part of the whole. Subsystems generally shift and change over time, but they may potentially become extremely close and turn into alliances or coalitions that exclude others. For example, if one parent confides a great deal in a son whereas the other talks to one of their daughters, two coalitions may form in the family, making interactions more strained and troubled. This property is mapped in Figure 3.1.

Boundaries   Implicit in the preceding discussion about hierarchy and complexity is the notion that systems develop **boundaries** around themselves and the subsystems they contain. Because human systems are open systems (it is not possible to completely control everything that comes into or goes out from them), these boundaries are relatively permeable: They have **openness**. Thus, although the managers of a General Motors plant in Ohio may wish that their employees did not know about the strike at a General Motors plant in Michigan, they will be unable to prevent information and communication from passing through the boundary around their organizational system.

Calibration/Feedback   All systems need stability and constancy within a defined range (Watzlawick, Beavin, and Jackson, 1967). **Calibration**, or checking the scale, and subsequent **feedback** to change or stabilize the system, allow for control of the range. The thermostat provides a common example illustrating this process. Home heating is usually set at a certain temperature, say 65 degrees. The thermostat will allow a temperature range around 65 before changing anything. Therefore, if the thermostat is set for 65 and the temperature is 65 plus or minus 3 degrees, nothing happens. If the temperature drops below

subsystems
smaller systems that
are embedded in
larger ones

suprasystems
larger systems that
hold smaller ones
within them

hierarchy
a property of systems
theory stating that
systems consist of
multiple levels

boundaries
a property of systems
theory stating that
systems construct
structures specifying
their outer limits

openness
the acknowledgment
that within all human
systems the boundaries
are permeable

calibration
a property of systems
theory stating that
systems periodically
check the scale of
allowable behaviors
and reset the system

feedback
a subprocess of
calibration;
information allowing
for change in the
system

62 degrees, the heat goes on; if it rises above 68 degrees, the furnace shuts off. In this way, the heating system remains stable. However, if conditions change in the house (for example, the family insulates the attic), the thermostat may need to be recalibrated or set at a slightly lower temperature to accommodate the change. After insulating, the house may feel comfortable if the temperature is set at 63 degrees.

Changing the standard (moving the temperature from 65 to 63 degrees) is accomplished through feedback. Feedback, in systems thinking, is positive when it produces change (the thermostat is set differently) and negative when it maintains the status quo (the thermostat remains at 65). When systems change they are called **morphogenic,** and when they stay the same they are called **homeostatic.**

morphogenic
a term for when a system recalibrates (or changes)

homeostatic
a term for a stable system that isn't changing

equifinality
a property of systems theory stating that systems can achieve the same goals through different means

Equifinality   Open systems are characterized by the ability to achieve the same goals through different means, or **equifinality** (von Bertalanffy, 1968). This principle applies to human groups in two ways. First, a single group can achieve a goal through many different routes. For example, if a manager wants to increase productivity, he can raise wages, threaten the workers with firing, hire a consultant, or do some combination of these. There are several ways the manager can reach the goal. Additionally, equifinality implies that different groups can achieve the same goal through multiple pathways. For instance, PK Computer Systems may achieve profitability by adopting a casual organizational culture, whereas Western Communication Systems may achieve profitability by demanding a more formal workplace.

Overall, a systems approach instructs researchers to search for holistic explanations for communication behavior. Systems offers a theory-generating option that aims to model the phenomenon as a whole, admitting the possibility for change from a variety of outside influences.

The Research Process

scientific method
the traditional method for doing research involving controlled observations and analysis to test the principles of a theory

deductive logic
moving from the general (the theory) to the specific (the observations)

inductive logic
moving from the specific (the observations) to the general (the theory)

In the example at the beginning of the chapter, we illustrated how interrelated theory and research processes are. Now we'll briefly discuss the research process. Our discussion will necessarily be brief here; we know many of you will take an entire class devoted to the study of research methods, so here we simply give you an idea of how important theory and research are to one another. At the beginning of this chapter, Dr. Stevens's study illustrated the theory-then-research model. Rolanda's transcripts are used to test what Communication Accommodation Theory predicts about communication behaviors in the workplace. Dr. Stevens will see if the speculations she made based on the theory's logic hold true in the conversations that Rolanda taped. This traditional process, known as the **scientific method,** follows **deductive logic** in that Stevens moved from the general (the theory) to specific instances (the actual conversations gathered in two workplaces). If Stevens had used **inductive logic,** she would have asked Rolanda to record many more conversations. Stevens would have refrained from hypothesizing, or guessing, about what she might find in advance of the data collection. Then she and Rolanda would have listened to their tapes, trying to find some type of pattern that best explained what they heard. Finally, Stevens would have generalized based on her observations.

After Stevens has hypothesized about what she will find in the workplace regarding accommodations between workers and managers based on the theory, she then must **operationalize** all the concepts. This means she needs to specify how she will measure the concepts that are important to her study. In this process, Dr. Stevens turns the abstract concepts of the theory into concrete variables that can be observed and measured. For example, status difference is a critical notion in the theoretical framework, so Stevens specifies to Rolanda how she should measure this. In this case, measurement will be based on job title. Rolanda has to discover the job title for each of the people she observes and then compare those titles to a chart Stevens has given her classifying job titles into the two categories of "supervisor" and "subordinate." This seems like a fairly straightforward means to operationalize the notion of status, but there may be instances where it is not a perfect operationalization. For instance, a lower-level employee who has worked for the company for many years might hold more status than a middle manager who has only recently arrived and is just learning the corporate culture. Additionally, women managers often report some problems with achieving the status expected from their job title. You can see how concepts that are more complex and abstract, such as love and intimacy, would be even more difficult to operationalize than occupational status.

> **operationalize**
> making an abstract idea measurable and observable

The next step in the traditional scientific model sends Rolanda into the two organizations to make **observations** and collect **data** (in this case, the conversations and the job titles). When Rolanda returns with the tapes, Dr. Stevens will have to **code** the conversations, again using operationalizations for terms such as *convergence* (making your speech patterns similar to your partner's) and *divergence* (making your speech patterns dissimilar to your partner's). Some types of data do not need extensive coding to analyze. For example, if Dr. Stevens operationalized status based on income and then provided respondents with a survey asking them to indicate the category for their salary, these data would not need the same type of coding required in the taped conversations. The income categories could simply be numbered consecutively. In contrast, the conversations have to be listened to repeatedly to determine whether a given comment converges with or diverges from the comment preceding it.

> **observations**
> focused examination within a context of interest; may be guided by hypotheses or research questions
>
> **data**
> the raw materials collected by the researcher to answer the questions posed in the research or to test a hypothesis
>
> **code**
> converting raw data to a category system

The deductive approach allows Stevens to test a specific prediction, or hypothesis, generated from a generalization, or theory. The results of this testing allow modifications and corrections to the theory.

The inductive approach operates in the opposite direction and enables Stevens first to gather many specific instances in the hopes of then being able to generalize, or create, theory. This approach is called **grounded theory**. The grounded theory approach does not seek to test hypotheses to support theory; instead, theory "is discovered, developed, and provisionally verified through systematic data collection and analysis of data" (Young, 1998, p. 26) relating to the phenomenon of interest. In this manner, the components of the research process (theory, data collection, and data analysis) are in reciprocal relationship with one another.

> **grounded theory**
> theory induced from data and analysis

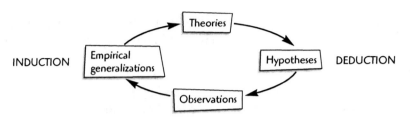

Figure 3.2 The Wheel of Science

Source: Loosely adapted from several conceptual drawings and reduced from the concept on page 18 of Walter L. Wallace, THE LOGIC OF SCIENCE IN SOCIOLOGY (New York: Aldine de Gruyter, 1971). Copyright © 1971 by Walter L. Wallace. Renewed 1999. Reprinted by permission of Transaction Publishers.

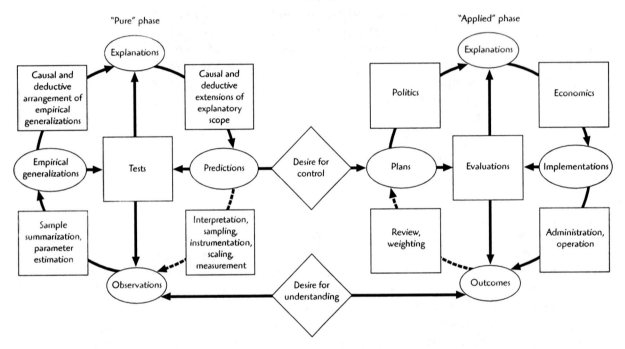

Figure 3.3 The Procedures of Scientific Analysis

Source: From Walter L. Wallace, PRINCIPLES OF SCIENTIFIC SOCIOLOGY (New York: Aldine de Gruyter, 1983), page 359. Copyright © 1983 by Walter L. Wallace. Reprinted by permission of Transaction Publishers.

Although some researchers approach their work strictly as hypothesis testers and some approach it more as theory generators, in practice most weave back and forth between the two. Walter Wallace (1971) suggests that the research process is circular, moving continuously between induction and deduction. Researchers refer to this as the wheel of science (Figure 3.2). Additionally, as Wallace (1983) noted elsewhere, this process is endless: "Each step presupposes that all the others have been taken before it—presumably at lower levels of understanding and control. Thus, although one may *consciously* start a given analysis by making certain predictions, one always has in mind (as largely unconscious background assumptions) certain prior explanations, empirical generalizations, tests, outcomes, implementations, and so on" (p. 358).

Furthermore, Wallace (1983) has expanded this wheel of science to include two types of research: pure and applied (Figure 3.3). In **pure research**, researchers

pure research
research to generate knowledge

Theory Into Practice

Damien

I just got engaged, and I have a lot of questions about engagement and marriage rituals in the United States. I am kind of in conflict because I want to just jump in and celebrate this time in my life, but I am also analyzing it (a hazard of being a communication studies major, I guess). Some of the wedding ceremony strikes me as troubling. Do I really want my fiance's father to "give her away" to me? After thinking about some of the issues we've discussed about the research process, I now want to conduct a study to see if any men my age feel this way after getting engaged. I have a hunch what I would find, but I would like to approach it from a grounded theory approach and let my respondents tell me what they think.

---

are guided by knowledge-generating goals. They are interested in testing or generating theory for its own sake and for the sake of advancing our knowledge in an area. In **applied research,** researchers wish to solve specific problems with the knowledge they or other researchers have generated. Figure 3.3 illustrates the relationship between these two types of research goals and processes. In our example of Dr. Stevens's research, we see her performing pure research. If a specific organization hired Dr. Stevens to consult with them to improve employee morale, however, her research would become applied. Theory and practice are intertwined, and pure and applied research are not unrelated processes. As Larry Frey and his colleagues observe (2000), "the interrelationship of theory and application is especially important in a 'practical discipline' such as communication that has enormous potential to make a difference in people's lives" (p. 36). In Figure 3.2, you can see the arrows running between the two types of research showing this interrelationship.

applied research
research to solve a problem or create a policy

In the example of Rolanda and Dr. Stevens, we have seen how Rolanda's job utilizes theory and how theory and research relate in Dr. Stevens' study. In addition, Rolanda operates as an intuitive or naïve scientist in her daily life. An intuitive scientist follows many of the same processes and reasoning patterns that trained scientists do, just not in as explicit or rigorous a fashion. Usually, intuitive scientists follow inductive logic: They experience something and then generalize from that. So when Rolanda concludes that all men are untrustworthy, she is inducing a general statement about all men from her experiences with one man, Anton. This is similar to the process a researcher might follow; however, a social scientist would not make hasty generalizations, or move to theory, on the basis of one observation. Intuitive science proceeds on the basis of deductive logic as well, as Rolanda's theory about cities demonstrates. She believes that larger cities are more diverse than smaller ones. As she moves from Sheridan to Chicago, she will test that theory with her observations about life in Chicago. Here again, the issue of numbers of observations is important. How long does Rolanda have to live in Chicago before she can be satisfied that her theory is correct? Does she have to sample life in other large cities to substantiate her theory, or is Chicago alone a sufficient observation? This is very similar to Dr. Stevens's concerns in her study. When Rolanda wonders about the number of conversations that she is collecting for Dr. Stevens, she focuses on a key point: How many instances do you need to observe before you can come to a conclusion? There are no absolute answers to this question, although there are some standards that are often accepted by practicing researchers.

In conducting research, one key difference between professional researchers and naïve ones rests on the definition of two terms: reliability and validity. Researchers say that something has **reliability** when you can get the same results over time. For example, if Rolanda visited the organizations in two years and her observations there yielded the same results that they do now, her observations would be called reliable. You can imagine many reasons reliability is difficult to obtain. For instance, if there had been a big turnover in personnel at one of the organizations, reliability would be difficult. Professional researchers conduct statistical tests to judge reliability, or they may return to ask participants if they still feel the same way they did when they were first questioned or observed. Naïve scientists usually operate as though their observations are reliable without ever testing for it.

Reliability is important, but validity is even more critical to the research process. This is the case because observations can be reliable even if they are not valid, but the opposite is not true. To draw useful conclusions from research, observations must be both reliable and valid. **Validity** refers to the fact that the observation method actually captures what it is supposed to. For instance, Dr. Stevens is interested in communication accommodation, so she is having Rolanda listen to workplace conversations in hallways to find it. If people engage in extensive conversations where Rolanda can tape them, then probably the observations are able to measure the concept of interest. But what if people in these organizations don't talk much in the public spaces of the office? What if Rolanda tapes a lot of casual greetings that don't show much of anything important to the notion of communication accommodation? Would Dr. Stevens be correct in concluding that people do not accommodate their communication according to status? Maybe not, if a lot of accommodating is going on behind closed doors where Rolanda didn't go. In that case, the measurement (taped hallway conversations) was not valid because it didn't capture what the researcher was interested in. Again, professional researchers are concerned about the validity of their observations and work diligently to demonstrate validity. Naïve researchers don't think too much about validity unless they somehow discover that they have been basing their generalizations on a mistaken notion.

Overall, the research process is similar for naïve and professional researchers, but professional researchers are more rigorous at every step of the process. Both draw conclusions based on their findings, and ultimately we are convinced by the arguments each advances about the strength of their process. When we believe that the results are based on good (reliable and valid) observations and careful logic, we accept the findings.

reliability
the stability and predictability of an observation

validity
the truth value of an observation

Observations and logic combine in many patterns beyond the deductive and inductive that we have outlined here. There are almost as many research methods as there are researchers, and there is room for a great deal of creativity in the research process.

Conclusion

This chapter introduced the concepts of theory and research and discussed their usefulness for examining communication behaviors. We have provided an initial definition of *theory* as well as explored some of the goals of theory and the relationship between theory and experience. We discussed the frameworks for theories, or three approaches to knowing: empirical, interpretive, and critical. Each of these approaches answers questions about truth (ontology), gathering information (epistemology), and values (axiology) somewhat differently. Further, we discussed how theories can be created using three different guidelines: covering law, systems, and rules. We explained the research process briefly, discussing issues of induction (grounded theory) and deduction (scientific method) and we suggested that researchers differ from naïve theorists in their application of reliability and validity. As we seek to understand communication, we turn to theory to help us organize the information that research provides.

Yet we must realize the limitations of theory and research. Communication interactions consist of multiple perspectives. Theories are, at best, only partial explanations of the multiplicity of social life. Research methods are limited by the assumptions guiding them. We can overcome these limits to an extent by acknowledging the partiality of our theories and research and opening ourselves to diverse points of view. As Yerby (1995) states, our ability to listen to the perspectives of others while at the same time voicing our own perspectives ultimately contributes to our ability to understand how we are connected to others.

Discussion Starters

1. Do you think a theory can help us understand the communication behavior of subordinates and superiors in an organization? Why or why not? Use examples in your response.

2. Provide some examples of ways you think like a theorist in your daily life.

3. What is the difference between inductive and deductive logic? Give some examples of your everyday use of both induction and deduction.

4. Do you see communication behavior as being lawlike, like a system, or rule governed? Explain your answer.

5. How would you characterize your own intellectual traditions? How do these traditions affect your theoretical thinking? Be specific.

6. How do a researcher's belief's about the world actually affect the research process? Be specific.

7. How is a critical theory different from an empirical or humanistic theory? What do we learn about a theory by classifying it in terms of its approach to knowing?

Online Learning Center (www. mhhe.com/west4e)

Visit the Online Learning Center at www.mhhe.com/west4e for chapter-specific resources, such as story-into-theory and multiple-choice quizzes, as well as theory summaries and theory connection questions.

Theories on Thought and Media

CHAPTER 7

Cognitive Dissonance Theory

*Based on the research of **Leon Festinger***

Ali Torres

Ali Torres shuffled the papers on her desk and looked out the office window. She was really bored with this job. When she initially signed on to work with the Puerto Rican Alliance in Gary, Indiana, she was so excited. The job seemed to be a dream come true. First, it offered her a chance to give back to her community—both the city of Gary and the Puerto Rican community within the city. She had grown up in Gary, Indiana, and knew firsthand how difficult it was to get ahead for people of color, especially Latinos. Latinos were a minority among minorities in this city, and it was tough to make much progress. Despite that, Ali had gotten a lot from growing up in Gary. When she was in high school, a friendly guidance counselor had offered her a helping hand and suggested that Ali consider college. Without Ms. Martinez's support, she never would have thought about college, much less actually graduated. But Ali had finished college and now she felt strongly about giving something back. So the job had seemed perfect; it would be a way for her to give back to the community and at the same time use her major in public relations.

Yet, in the six months Ali had worked in the Alliance office, her sole responsibilities had centered on typing and running errands. She felt like a gofer, with no chance to do anything she considered important. Actually, she was beginning to question whether the Alliance itself was doing anything worthwhile. Sometimes she thought the whole operation was just a front so politicians could say something was being done to help the Latino population in the city.

Her co-workers didn't seem to mind that they didn't do much all day, so Ali wasn't getting much support from them. But it was her boss's attitude that bothered Ali the most. He was a respected leader in the Latino community; she remembered him from when she was growing up. When she found out she would be working for him, she had been delighted. But as far as Ali could tell, he hardly ever worked at all. He was rarely in the office, and when he did come in, he took long lunch hours and many breaks. He spoke to Ali very infrequently and never gave her assignments.

Ali was feeling extremely frustrated. She was on her own to develop projects or, more likely, simply to put in eight hours doing a lot of nothing. Ali had decided that she would quit this job and start looking for something where she could feel more useful, but she was having a hard time giving up on her dream of contributing to her community. She had begun this job with such high hopes. She had expected to work to persuade funding agencies to sponsor programs to strengthen opportunities for the Latino community. Ironically, now she found that the only person she was persuading was herself, as she wrestled with the decision of whether to keep working or give up on this job. Ali spoke to some of her friends, who encouraged her to do what she thought was right and quit the Alliance if she wanted to. That made her feel better, but she couldn't completely shake her memories of the auspicious beginning of the job and all her high hopes.

Suppose you are Ali Torres's friend and are interested in knowing how she feels about her job. You notice that she seems a little depressed when she talks about work, and lately she hasn't brought up the subject at all. Her silence about her work is especially obvious to you compared with how enthusiastically she spoke about the position when she first started at the Alliance. You could ask Ali directly how she feels, but you wonder how honest she will be with you. You know Ali doesn't want you to worry about her. You also know that Ali cares a great deal about the ideals of the Alliance and that she might not want to tell you if she is disappointed. Your problem in this situation is inferring Ali's attitudes.

The problem faced by Ali's friend is a common one because people's attitudes cannot be directly observed; yet attitudes are believed to be excellent predictors of people's behaviors (O'Neill & Arendt, 2008). As Susan Fiske and Shelley Taylor (1984) observe, "Attitudes have always been accorded star status in social explanations of human behavior by lay people and professionals alike" (p. 341). Because of their importance, many theories try to explain attitude formation, change, and the interlocking relationship among cognitions, attitudes, affect, and behavioral tendencies. Many psychologists (for example, Rydell, Hugenberg, & McConnell, 2006) assert that the most influential approaches to attitudes come from cognitive consistency theories.

Consistency theories in general posit that the mind operates as an intermediary between stimulus and response. These theories assert that when people receive information (a stimulus), their mind organizes it into a pattern with other previously encountered stimuli. If the new stimulus does not fit the pattern, or is inconsistent, then people feel discomfort. For example, people who supported Barack Obama in the 2008 Democratic primaries found his decision not to take public financing jarring once he had garnered the delegates needed to become the nominee in June 2008. People who supported Obama as an agent of change had to cope with cognitive discomfort when he did something that seemed like "politics as usual." Ali Torres also feels this type of discomfort as she reflects on the discrepancy between her desire to respect her boss and her observations of his seeming indifference to the job. In these cases, consistency theorists note that there is a lack of balance among your **cognitions**, or ways of knowing, beliefs, judgments, and so forth.

Leon Festinger called this feeling of imbalance **cognitive dissonance;** this is the feeling people have when they "find themselves doing things that don't fit with what they know, or having opinions that do not fit with other opinions they hold" (1957, p. 4). This concept forms the core of Festinger's Cognitive Dissonance Theory (CDT), a theory that argues that dissonance is an uncomfortable feeling that motivates people to take steps to reduce it (Figure 7.1). As Roger Brown (1965) notes, the basics of the theory follow rather simple principles: "A state of cognitive dissonance is said to be a state of psychological discomfort or tension which motivates efforts to achieve consonance. *Dissonance* is the name for a disequilibrium and *consonance* the name for an equilibrium" (p. 584). Further, Brown points out that the theory allows for two elements to have three different relationships with each other: They may be consonant, dissonant, or irrelevant.

cognitions
ways of knowing, beliefs, judgments, and thoughts

cognitive dissonance
feeling of discomfort resulting from inconsistent attitudes, thoughts, and behaviors

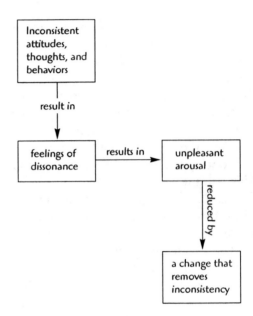

Figure 7.1
The Process
of Cognitive
Dissonance

consonant
relationship
two elements in
equilibrium with
one another

dissonant
relationship
two elements in
disequilibrium with
each other

irrelevant
relationship
two elements that
have no meaningful
relation to each other

A **consonant relationship** exists between two elements when they are in equilibrium with one another. If you believe, for instance, that health and fitness are important goals and you work out three to five times a week, then your beliefs about health and your own behaviors would have a consonant relationship with one another. Ali would have a consonant relationship if she believed that the Alliance was really making a difference in the Latino community and that her work was meaningful. A **dissonant relationship** means that elements are in disequilibrium with one another. An example of a dissonant relationship would be if a practicing Catholic we'll call Rita also believes in a woman's right to choose abortion. In this case, Rita's religious beliefs are in conflict with her beliefs about abortion. In our opening story, Ali Torres is experiencing a dissonant relationship.

An **irrelevant relationship** exists when elements imply nothing about one another. This type of relationship is illustrated by believing that the speed limit should be raised to 65 miles per hour on all freeways and believing that women should have equal rights in the workplace. Although the two beliefs may indicate a general view endorsing individual freedoms, they basically have no relationship to each other. When beliefs are consonant or irrelevant, there is no psychological discomfort. However, if beliefs are dissonant, discomfort results.

The importance of cognitive dissonance for communication researchers rests on Festinger's assertion that the discomfort caused by dissonance motivates

Theory Application in Groups (TAG)

In small groups, create role plays that illustrate a consonant relationship, a dissonant relationship, and an irrelevant relationship.

change. As we see in our opening vignette, Ali Torres is feeling frustrated and uncomfortable in her job. Her initial belief about the opportunities for her to help others through this job and her prior high regard for her boss are inconsistent with her present situation. This is the point at which persuasion can occur. The theory suggests that to be persuasive, strategies should focus on the inconsistencies while providing new behaviors that allow for consistency or balance. Further, cognitive dissonance may motivate communication behavior as people seek to persuade others and as people strive to reduce their dissonant cognitions. For example, when Ali went to her friends to discuss her decision, she was seeking help in reducing dissonance. Her conversations with friends and her efforts at self-persuasion are examples of communication being used in the dissonance reduction process.

Cognitive Dissonance • *Theory at a Glance*

The experience of dissonance—incompatible beliefs and actions or two incompatible beliefs—is unpleasant, and people are highly motivated to avoid it. In their efforts to avoid feelings of dissonance, people will ignore views that oppose their own, change their beliefs to match their actions (or vice versa), and/or seek reassurances after making a difficult decision.

Assumptions of Cognitive Dissonance Theory

As we have indicated, Cognitive Dissonance Theory is an account of how beliefs and behavior change attitudes. Its focus is on the effects of inconsistency among cognitions. Our introductory material suggested a number of assumptions that frame CDT. Four assumptions basic to the theory include:

- Human beings desire consistency in their beliefs, attitudes, and behaviors.
- Dissonance is created by psychological inconsistencies.
- Dissonance is an aversive state that drives people to actions with measurable effects.
- Dissonance motivates efforts to achieve consonance and efforts toward dissonance reduction.

The first assumption portrays a model of human nature that is concerned with stability and consistency. When we discuss Uncertainty Reduction Theory in Chapter 9, you will see a similar conceptualization of human nature. Cognitive Dissonance Theory suggests that people do not enjoy inconsistencies in their thoughts and beliefs. Instead, they seek consistency. This is why Ali feels uncomfortable in her job and unhappy with her thoughts about quitting the job. She is seeking consistency, yet her perceptions of her job provide her with inconsistency.

The second assumption speaks to the kind of consistency that is important to people. The theory is not concerned with a strict logical consistency. Rather, it refers to the fact that cognitions must be psychologically inconsistent (as opposed to logically inconsistent) with one another to arouse cognitive dissonance. For example, if Ali Torres holds the cognition that "I want to contribute to my community," it is *not* logically inconsistent to also believe that the Alliance is not contributing much to the community. The two beliefs are not logically contradictory. Yet it is psychologically inconsistent for Ali to continue to work for the Alliance when she believes it is doing little to help Latinos in Gary, Indiana. That is, Ali will feel psychologically inconsistent by continuing to do nothing when she wishes to be of help. Ali also is stressed by her thoughts of quitting and her lingering hopes for what she might have accomplished in this job.

The third assumption of the theory suggests that when people experience psychological inconsistencies, the dissonance that is created is aversive. Thus, people do not enjoy being in a state of dissonance; it is an uncomfortable state. Festinger asserted that dissonance is a drive state possessing arousal properties. Since Festinger's initial conceptualization of the theory, a significant amount of research has supported this assumption (Rydell, McConnell, & Mackie, 2008; Zanna & Cooper, 1976). Another study (Elkin & Leippe, 1986) found that physiological arousal was related to dissonance. Cognitive Dissonance Theory would assume that Ali would feel uncomfortable as a result of the psychological dissonance that she is experiencing.

Finally, the theory assumes that the arousal generated by dissonance will motivate people to avoid situations that create inconsistencies and strive toward situations that restore consistency. Thus, the picture of human nature that frames the theory is one of seeking psychological consistency as a result of the arousal caused by the aversive state of inconsistent cognitions (Figure 7.2).

Figure 7.2
Consistency in Beliefs, Attitudes, and Behaviors

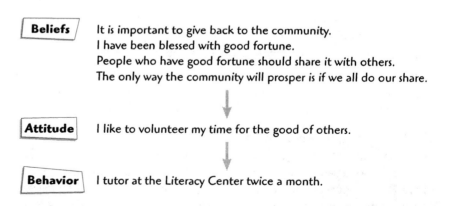

Beliefs — It is important to give back to the community.
I have been blessed with good fortune.
People who have good fortune should share it with others.
The only way the community will prosper is if we all do our share.

Attitude — I like to volunteer my time for the good of others.

Behavior — I tutor at the Literacy Center twice a month.

Concepts and Processes of Cognitive Dissonance

As the theory developed over the years, certain concepts were refined. For example, the following scenario illustrates a situation where dissonance would arise: If Juan believes that relationships should be completely harmonious (a cognition) and yet he argues a great deal with his partner (a conflicting cognition), the theory predicts that Juan will become tense and suffer discomfort. When dissonance theorists seek to predict how much discomfort or dissonance Juan will suffer, they invoke many concepts, which we will discuss in some detail.

Magnitude of Dissonance

The first concept is **magnitude of dissonance,** which refers to the quantitative amount of dissonance a person experiences. Magnitude of dissonance will determine actions people may take and cognitions they may espouse to reduce the dissonance. The theory differentiates between situations producing more dissonance and those producing less dissonance.

> **magnitude of dissonance**
> the quantitative amount of discomfort felt

Three factors influence the magnitude of dissonance a person will feel (Zimbardo, Ebbesen, & Maslach, 1977). First, the degree of **importance,** or how significant the issue is, affects the degree of dissonance felt. If, for example, Juan has many friendships and activities outside his relationship and his partner is not critically important to him, the theory predicts that his magnitude of dissonance will be small. But if Juan finds much of his identity and social interaction in his relationship with his partner, then the magnitude of dissonance should be greater. The same could be said for Ali Torres. If she does a great deal of volunteer work in the community and her job is not the main source of her identity, then the magnitude of her dissonance is not as great as if her job is critically important to her.

> **importance**
> a factor in determining magnitude of dissonance; refers to how significant the issue is

Second, the amount of dissonance is affected by the **dissonance ratio,** or the amount of dissonant cognitions relative to the amount of consonant cognitions. Given Juan's propensity to argue with his partner, he probably has many cognitions that are relevant to that behavior. Some of these cognitions are consistent with his behavior; for example, "It is good to get feelings out in the open." "It is positive to feel you can really be yourself with your partner." "Sometimes arguing allows you both to see problems in a creative way." Several of his cognitions are dissonant with conflict behavior, however. For example, consider: "If we really loved each other, we wouldn't argue so much." "We spend so much time fighting, we never have any fun." "Our fights are so repetitive, we never solve anything." "My parents never argued with each other; we must not be very sensitive to each other." "I didn't picture my relationship like this." Because Juan has more dissonant cognitions than consonant ones, the ratio is negative. Thus, Juan is likely to feel that there is inconsistency, and dissonance will result. If the ratio were more balanced, Juan would feel less dissonance.

> **dissonance ratio**
> a factor in determining magnitude of dissonance; the amount of consonant cognitions relative to the dissonant ones

Finally, the magnitude of dissonance is affected by the rationale that an individual summons to justify the inconsistency. The **rationale** refers to the

> **rationale**
> a factor in determining magnitude of dissonance; refers to the reasoning employed to explain the inconsistency

reasoning employed to explain why an inconsistency exists. The more reasons one has to account for the discrepancy, the less dissonance one will feel. For instance, if Juan and his partner have just moved, changed or lost a job, purchased a home, or experienced any other stressor, Juan may be able to justify the conflicts as being a result of the stress he is feeling and thus probably a temporary situation. In this case, it is likely that the dissonance he feels will be much less than if he is unable to come up with any rationale explaining his behaviors (Matz & Wood, 2005).

Coping With Dissonance

Although Cognitive Dissonance Theory explains that dissonance can be reduced through both behavioral and attitudinal changes, most of the research has focused on the latter. Many ways to increase consistency are cognitively based, and the theory suggests several methods Juan may use to reduce his dissonance. First, Juan could add or subtract cognitions to change the ratio of consonant to dissonant cognitions. In Juan's case, this might mean adding the fact that his friends Jeff and Don fight a lot but seem to be happy, and subtracting the idea that he didn't picture his relationship as full of conflict. Alternatively, Juan might try to reduce the importance of the dissonant cognitions. He might think about the fact that children do not know much about their parents' relationship, so the fact that he did not think his parents fought a lot might not weigh too heavily in the equation. Finally, Juan could seek out information that advocates conflict in relationships and stresses the benefits of open communication between partners. He might discredit the information that suggests conflict is not good for a relationship by believing that it comes from an unrealistic, overly optimistic point of view. In sum, we can cope with dissonance by (1) adding to our consonant beliefs, (2) reducing the importance of our dissonant beliefs, or (3) changing our beliefs to seemingly eliminate the dissonance in some way.

Cognitive Dissonance and Perception

selective exposure
a method for reducing dissonance by seeking information that is consonant with current beliefs and actions

selective attention
a method for reducing dissonance by paying attention to information that is consonant with current beliefs and actions

As Juan engages in any of these strategies to change his cognitions and reduce his feelings of dissonance, perceptual processes come into play. Specifically, Cognitive Dissonance Theory relates to the processes of selective exposure, selective attention, selective interpretation, and selective retention because the theory predicts that people will avoid information that increases dissonance. These perceptual processes are basic to this avoidance.

Selective exposure, or seeking consistent information not already present, helps to reduce dissonance. CDT predicts that people will avoid information that increases dissonance and seek out information that is consistent with their attitudes and behavior. In the example of the conflictual relationship, Juan might seek friends who also fight a great deal yet seem to be happy in their relationships.

Selective attention refers to looking at consistent information once it is there. People attend to information in their environment that conforms to their attitudes and beliefs while ignoring information that is inconsistent. Thus, Ali

Torres might read favorable articles about the Alliance in the newspaper while overlooking articles that suggest contrary views.

Selective **interpretation** involves interpreting ambiguous information so that it becomes consistent. Utilizing selective interpretation, most people interpret close friends' attitudes as more congruent with their own than is actually true (Berscheid & Walster, 1978). Elaine Showalter (1997) discusses the seeming inconsistency of being a feminist critic while also loving to shop and wear feminine clothing and accessories. She interprets advice given to her by an academic about dressing conservatively as actually agreeing with her position that we should put "the *femme* back into feminist" (p. 80). People use selective interpretation to avoid potential dissonance.

Finally, **selective retention** refers to remembering and learning consistent information with much greater ability than we do inconsistent information. Cognitive Dissonance Theory predicts that if a couple were arguing about whether to spend a vacation camping or on a cruise, the partner who wished to camp would not remember the details of the cruise package and the one desiring the cruise would not remember much about the camping plans. If Juan heard a lecture once about how important conflict can be in close relationships, he may well remember that in his current situation of frequent fighting with his partner. Similarly, Ali might focus on stories she heard in the past about good works that the Alliance has done.

Attitudes seem to organize memory in this selective retention process (Lingle & Ostrom, 1981). When thinking about someone as your teacher, you will remember her ability to lecture, her command of the subject, her ability to get a discussion started, and her accessibility to help you with assignments. If, on the other hand, you were thinking about the same person as an actor, you would recall her ability to project a character and to gain your interest. Once you have formed an attitude about someone as a teacher rather than an actor, that influences your recall about that person.

Minimal Justification

One of the interesting and counterintuitive assertions that Festinger advances in this theory has to do with what he calls minimal justification. **Minimal justification** has to do with offering only the minimum incentive required to get someone to change. Festinger (1957) argues that "if one wanted to obtain private change in addition to mere public compliance, the best way to do this would be to offer just enough reward or punishment to elicit compliance" (p. 95).

The experiment that Festinger and his colleague James Carlsmith performed that established the principle of minimal justification is the now-famou' one dollar/twenty dollars study. Festinger and Carlsmith (1959) recruited ma' students at Stanford University and assigned them to do a boring, repetit' task consisting of sorting spools into lots of twelve and giving square pe' quarter turn to the right. At the end of an hour of this monotonous assignr' the experimenter asked the research participants to do him a favor. The rese' explained that they needed another person to continue doing this ta' offered to pay the participants to recruit a woman in the waiting room b'

selective interpretation
a method for reducing dissonance by interpreting ambiguous information so that it becomes consistent with current beliefs and actions

selective retention
a method for reducing dissonance by remembering information that is consonant with current beliefs and actions

minimal justification
~ffering the least
~f incentive
~in

T∗I∗P

Theory Into Practice

Nancy

I certainly have experienced buyer's remorse. And I think I probably handled it in the way Cognitive Dissonance Theory predicts. When my husband and I bought our first house, I was a nervous wreck and the only way I calmed myself down was to think about how bad our other choices were and to spend time talking with Neil about how great this house was. We kind of talked ourselves into believing we made a fabulous choice.

her how enjoyable the task was. This woman was actually a research assistant also, and she was helping the researchers examine how the men tried to persuade her. Some of the men were offered one dollar to recruit the woman, whereas others were offered twenty dollars for the same behavior. Remember, this was 1959, and both these sums were worth a great deal more than they are now. Festinger and Carlsmith found that the men engaged in this study differed in their attitudes at the end. Those who received twenty dollars for recruiting the woman said that they really thought the task was boring, whereas those who received only one dollar stated that they really believed the task was enjoyable.

From these results came the notion of minimal justification. Festinger and Carlsmith argue that doing something a person does not believe in for a minimal reward sets up more dissonance than doing that same thing for a larger reward. If people engage in deception for a lot of money, they will acknowledge that they did it for the money. If they engage in deception for only one dollar, they do not have a ready explanation that will make their attitudes and behaviors form a consonant relationship. To reduce their dissonance, they have to make some type of change to bring consistency to their cognitions. Therefore, they may change their opinion of the task to make sense of why they told the woman in the waiting room that it was fun. Now they believe they told her it was fun because, in fact, it *was* enjoyable. Thus, minimal justification sets up more cognitive dissonance and requires more change to reduce it than a more substantial justification would.

Cognitive Dissonance Theory and Persuasion

Much of the research following from Festinger's work focuses on persuasion, especially with regard to decision making. A large amount of research concentrates on cognitive dissonance as a postdecision phenomenon. Several studies examine **buyer's remorse**, which refers to the dissonance people often feel after deciding on a large purchase. An interesting study about buyer's remorse related to automobile purchases (Donnelly & Ivancevich, 1970). In their study, they located people who were waiting for delivery of cars they had signed contracts to buy. These people were divided into two groups. One group was contacted twice to reassure them about the wisdom of their purchase. Another group was not contacted between the contract signing and the delivery of the car. About twice as many in the group that was not contacted canceled the order for the car. This finding supported the theory that dissonance may be activated after making a large purchase. Further, the study showed that providing people with information about the wisdom of their decision can reduce the dissonance. This finding speaks to the importance of the decision and to manipulating the dissonance ratio, factors we discussed earlier in the chapter.

Another study (Knox & Inkster, 1968) investigated this regret period after a decision in a different context. This study had experimenters approach people either shortly before or shortly after they had placed a two-dollar bet at a Canadian racetrack. The bettors were asked how confident they felt about their horse's chances. Their findings indicated that people were more confident that their horse would win after they had placed the bet than they were before they placed the bet. They interpreted these findings as consistent with CDT because they reasoned that after the bet has been placed, people feel dissonance. The decision to choose one particular horse is dissonant with the belief that the horse has flaws that could prevent it from winning the race. A simple coping mechanism for reducing this dissonance is to increase the beliefs about the attractiveness of the horse that you bet on, or the chosen alternative. Thus, the theory would predict, and Knox and Inkster found, bettors expressing more confidence after making their decision than before. As Robert Wicklund and Jack W. Brehm (1976) point out, when a decision is irrevocable, as in a bet placed, people have to work quickly to reduce the inevitable dissonance that results.

A more recent study (Brownstein, Read, & Simon, 2004) also looked at cognitive dissonance at the racetrack. Participants were given information about horses and then were asked to rate each horse's chance of winning the race. The respondents rated the horses three times before placing their bets and one time afterward. Consistent with Cognitive Dissonance Theory's predictions, the researchers found that the ratings of the chosen horse increased after the choice had been made.

Vani Simmons, Monica Webb, and Thomas Brandon (2004) studied whether cognitive dissonance principles could help college students stop smoking. They tested an experimental learning intervention based on the theory. One hundred forty-four college students who smoked were asked to create educational videos about the risks of smoking or about quitting smoking. They found that intentions to quit smoking were increased by making the videos.

Festinger and two colleagues also examined postdecision dissonance in a pioneering case study (Festinger, Riecken, & Schachter, 1956). Festinger and his colleagues joined a doomsday cult based in Chicago in the 1950s. The group was led by a middle-aged man and woman. The woman, whom the researchers named Mrs. Keech, began to receive messages from spiritual beings who seemed to be predicting a great disaster, a flood that would end the world. Then the spiritual beings transmitted information to Mrs. Keech that the members of the cult would be saved before the flood. The group was instructed that spacemen would arrive and transport the believers to safety on another planet. The believers began to make preparations for the end of their world and their departure to another world. The appointed time for departure was midnight, and the group gathered in Mrs. Keech's living room to await the spaceship that would take them to safety. As the moments slipped by, it became apparent that no one was coming to rescue the believers, and, in fact, they did not need to be rescued because the world was not under water. At first, the cult seemed on the verge of disintegration as a result of the extreme dissonance everyone was feeling. Yet the group was so committed to their beliefs that they found ways to reconcile the dissonance.

The group reconciled their dissonance in two specific ways. First, Mrs. Keech claimed a new message came from the spiritual beings telling the group that their faith had caused God to save the world from destruction. Thus, the group used selective interpretation and allowed new information through selective attention. Second, Mrs. Keech said she had received an additional message telling the group to publicize the situation. The group became energized again, reduced their dissonance, and confirmed themselves in their decision to be members of the group.

Some researchers have observed the relationship of dissonance and communication strategies in situations other than decision making. Patrice Buzzanell and Lynn Turner (2003) examined family communication in families where the major wage earner had lost his or her job within the past eighteen months. Buzzanell and Turner interviewed family members to assess the communication issues created by the job loss.

Buzzanell and Turner found that job loss did create feelings of dissonance in most family members, and the researchers argued that family members reduced their dissonance about job loss by using three interesting strategies. First, families adopted a tone of normalcy, telling the interviewers that nothing had really changed after the job loss. Second, families deliberately foregrounded positive themes and backgrounded negative ones. Finally, families maintained gendered identity construction, working to assure the man who had lost his job that he was still the man of the family. In all of these strategies, family members worked to reduce the dissonance created by job loss.

In yet another context, Patricia Sullivan and Lynn Turner (1996) examined strategies used by female politicians to cope with assumptions about women in the public domain. Sullivan and Turner profiled several women in public life in the 1990s. One of their case studies was of Lani Guinier, who was nominated by President Clinton to be the Assistant Attorney General for Civil Rights. Guinier withdrew her nomination before the confirmation hearings after suffering scathing treatment in the press concerning her views on affirmative action and voting rights. Sullivan and Turner argue that Guinier did not speak out during this time because she believed that the truth would vindicate her. Sullivan and Turner imply that Guinier sought to play by the rules, because to do otherwise would have caused her too much dissonance. Her strategy for coping and keeping consistency ultimately cost her the chance to defend herself in confirmation hearings.

Research Notes

DeSantis, A. D., & Morgan, S. E. (2003). Sometimes a cigar [magazine] is more than just a cigar [magazine]: Pro-smoking arguments in *Cigar Aficionado, 1992–2000. Health Communication, 15,* 457–480.

This study examines the magazine *Cigar Aficionado* from a rhetorical approach to analyze the pro-smoking arguments it advances. The authors analyzed the forty-one issues of the magazine from its inception in 1992 to the last issue of the 2000 calendar year. They found more than 380 pro-smoking arguments, which they defined as "any assertion made in the periodical that defended smoking against anti-smoking health claims" (p. 461).

Each of the arguments was organized into one of the following seven categories:

1. Cigars are not cigarettes.

2. Life is dangerous.

3. Cigars have health benefits.

4. The moderation argument

5. The old-smokers argument

6. The bad-science argument

7. The good-science argument

After a brief review of the evidence, the authors assert that cigar smoking is quite hazardous to health, and they note that many health professionals and nonsmokers cannot understand why people continue to smoke cigars. They argue that the reason, at least in part, may be that these pro-smoking arguments offered by *Cigar Aficionado* provide a major source of cognitive dissonance reduction.

They note that people can experience cognitive dissonance from a variety of sources, such as inconsistency (saying smoking is no problem, but experiencing a hacking cough), cultural mores (noticing the many places where a person can no longer smoke in public), opinion generality (believing oneself to be logical but continuing to

smoke in the face of evidence that says it's harmful), or past experience (knowing someone who died from a disease attributed to smoking). They observe that smokers likely feel dissonance from all of these sources.

The authors proceed to illustrate each of the seven arguments advanced in the magazine as methods offered to readers to reduce this dissonance. For instance, in detailing the cigars are not cigarettes argument, the authors note that the magazine creates a "cognitive buffer" between the established health risks of cigarettes and cigar smoking.

The authors conclude with suggestions for countering these pro-smoking arguments based on an understanding of the cognitive processes detailed in Cognitive Dissonance Theory. They note that "until prevention agencies begin to take *Cigar Aficionado* more seriously, view the magazine as a diligent pro-smoking force, and become more strategic and dynamic in their message construction, cigar smokers will continue to light up, dissonance-free" (p. 479).

Matz, D. C., & Wood, W. (2005). Cognitive dissonance in groups: The consequences of disagreement. *Journal of Personality and Social Psychology, 88,* 1–22.

This article begins with the premise, adopted from Festinger's work, that social groups are both vehicles for reducing cognitive dissonance and sources for generating it. The authors conduct three studies demonstrating group-generated dissonance. Their findings are consistent with the predictions of Cognitive Dissonance Theory. Participants in groups with others who disagreed with them experienced more dissonance than those in groups with others who agreed with them. Participants who believed they had little to no choice in the group they were in experienced less dissonance from disagreements than those who thought they had chosen their group.

(continued)

Sun, C. F., & Scharrer, E. (2004). Staying true to Disney: College students' resistance to criticism of *The Little Mermaid*. *The Communication Review*, 7, 35–55.

This article reviews a media literacy program employed in a college classroom. The program included an extended analysis and critique of the Disney movie, *The Little Mermaid*, combined with a reading of the Hans Christian Andersen tale on which the movie was based. One hundred three written samples from the final project for the class were analyzed for this study.

The authors found that students resisted a critical analysis of the Disney film. In the end, the media literacy program was largely unsuccessful in get-ting students to be more critical consumers of media that challenge the dominant ideology surrounding the mediated images and messages. To explain this result, the authors draw on Cognitive Dissonance Theory stating that this theory provides important insights into students' resistance. The authors argue that dissonance was created when the students had to weigh their past favorable experience with Disney against the material of the class, which was largely negative and pointed out the problematic issues in the film. Therefore, the students were motivated to reduce their dissonance. Their written work at the end of the program revealed several strategies aimed at doing just that.

As this brief review indicates, CDT has been employed in countless studies examining decision making. Recent studies have explored the processes of dissonance and dissonance reduction in contexts such as family (Buzzanell & Turner, 2003), friendships (G. B. White, 2006), business (Shinnar, Young, & Meana, 2004), political communication (Sullivan & Turner, 1996), and the classroom (Boysen, 2008; Sun & Scharrer, 2004). Thus, CDT continues to be a theoretical force for explaining communication behaviors.

Integration, Critique, and Closing

Although researchers have been using and revising Festinger's theory since 1957, and some scholars point to the theory as the primary achievement of social psychology (Aron & Aron, 1989), the theory does have weaknesses and detractors. Most of the criticisms have to do with the utility and testability of the theory.

Integration

Communication Tradition	Rhetorical	Semiotic	Phenomenological	Cybernetic	**Socio-Psychological**	Socio-Cultural	Critical

Communication Context	**Intrapersonal**	Interpersonal	Small Group	Organizational	Public/Rhetorical	Mass/Media	Cultural

Approach to Knowing	**Positivistic/Empirical**	Interpretive/Hermeneutic	Critical

Critique

Evaluation Criteria	Scope	Logical Consistency	Parsimony	**Utility**	**Testability**	Heurism	Test of Time

Utility

One concern of CDT relates to critics' complaints that that the theory may not possess utility because other theoretical frameworks can explain the attitude change found in the one dollar/twenty dollars experiment better than cognitive dissonance.

Irving Janis and Robert Gilmore (1965) argue that when people participate in an inconsistency, such as arguing a position they do not believe in, they become motivated to think up all the arguments in favor of the position while suppressing all the arguments against it. Janis and Gilmore call this process biased scanning. This biased scanning process should increase the chances of accepting the new position—for example, changing one's position from evaluating the spool-sorting task as dull to the position that it really was an interesting task.

Janis and Gilmore (1965) note that when a person is overcompensated for engaging in biased scanning, suspicion and guilt are aroused. Thus, they are able to explain why the large incentive of twenty dollars does not cause the students in Festinger and Carlsmith's (1959) experiment to have an increased attitude change.

Other researchers (Cooper & Fazio, 1984) argue that the original theory of cognitive dissonance contains a great deal of "conceptual fuzziness." Some researchers note that the concept of dissonance is confounded by self-concept or impression management. Impression management refers to the activities people engage in to look good to themselves and others. For example, Elliot Aronson (1969) argues that people wish to appear reasonable to themselves and suggests that in Festinger and Carlsmith's (1959) experiment, if "dissonance exists, it is because the individual's behavior is inconsistent with his self-concept" (p. 27). Aronson asserts that the Stanford students' dissonance resulted from seeing themselves as upright and truthful men contrasted with their behavior of deceiving someone else because they were being paid to do so.

In the study we discussed earlier by Patrice Buzzanell and Lynn Turner (2003) concerning family communication and job loss, we could conceive of the strategies the families adopted as employing impression management rather than reducing dissonance. When fathers reported that nothing had changed in their family despite the job loss, they may have been rationalizing to continue to seem reasonable to themselves, just as Aronson suggests.

In the preceding critiques, researchers disagree about what cognitive state is at work: dissonance, biased scanning, or impression management. Daryl Bem (1967) argues that the central concept of importance is not *any* type of cognition but, rather, is behavioral. Bem states that rather than dissonance in cognitions operating to change people, self-perception is at work. Self-perception simply means that people make conclusions about their own attitudes the same way others do—by observing their behavior. Bem's alternative explanation allows more simplicity in the theory as well.

In Bem's conceptualization, it is not necessary to speculate about the degree of cognitive dissonance that a person feels. People only need to observe what they are doing to calculate what their attitudes must be. For instance, if I am not working out regularly, but I believe fitness and health are important goals, I must not really believe working out is so important to good health. In our chapter opening story about Ali Torres, Bem would argue that the longer Ali works at the Alliance, the more likely she is to come to believe that she is doing something worthwhile. Bem's argument suggests that if Ali's mother asks her if she likes her job, she might reply, "I guess I do. I am still there."

Claude Steele's work (Steele, 1988; Steele, Spencer, & Lynch, 1993) also offers a behavioral explanation for dissonance effects: self-affirmation. However, unlike Bem, Steele and his colleagues argue that dissonance is the result of behaving in a manner that threatens one's sense of moral integrity. You can see how this explanation might work quite well in Ali Torres's situation. Her discomfort might not be because she holds two contradictory beliefs but because she doesn't respect herself for staying in a job where she is not accomplishing anything of significance.

Other scholars believe that Cognitive Dissonance Theory is basically useful and explanatory but needs some refinements. For example, Wicklund and Brehm (1976) argue that CDT is not clear enough about the conditions under which dissonance leads to change in attitudes. They believe that choice is the missing concept in the theory. Wicklund and Brehm posit that when people believe they have a choice about the dissonant relationship, they will be motivated to change that relationship. If people think they are powerless, then they will not be bothered by the dissonance, and they probably will not change. Regarding our beginning scenario about Ali Torres, Wicklund and Brehm would argue that we could predict whether she will leave her job based on how much choice she believes she has in the matter. If, for instance, she is tied to Gary, Indiana, because of family responsibilities or if she believes she would have trouble locating a new job in the city, she may not be motivated to act on her dissonant cognitions. On the other hand, if nothing really ties her to Gary, or there are plenty of other job opportunities, she will be motivated to change based on those same cognitions.

Another refinement is suggested by the work of Joel Cooper and Jeff Stone (2000). Cooper and Stone point out that in the more than 1,000 studies using CDT, only rarely has the group membership of the person experiencing dissonance been considered. Cooper and Stone believe that group membership plays an important role in how people experience and reduce dissonance. For example, they found that social identity derived from religious and political groups had an impact on how people responded to dissonance.

Other critics note that CDT is not as useful as it should be because it does not provide a full explanation for how and when people will attempt to reduce dissonance. First, there is what has been called the "multiple mode" problem. This problem exists because, given a dissonance-producing situation, there are multiple ways to reduce the dissonance. As we discussed earlier in the chapter, there are several ways to bring about more consonance (such as changing your mind or engaging in selective exposure, attention, interpretation, or retention). The weakness in the theory is that it doesn't allow precise predictions.

This prediction problem is also apparent in the fact that the theory does not speak to the issue of individual differences. People vary in their

Theory Into Practice

Amelia

T∗I∗P

This theory makes so much sense, and I can apply it to my own struggle to quit smoking. I know smoking isn't good for me, and I have tried to quit. Everyone tells me I should; and I know it's true. It makes me feel like an idiot that I continue to do something that's harmful to my health. But it's so hard to quit. I have noticed that I use some of the ways to reduce dissonance that the theory talks about. Like I've said that everyone has to die of something, so I've tried to reduce the importance of the dissonance. And I've also mentioned that I smoke low tar cigarettes, and I don't smoke as much as some of my friends—trying to add to the consonant beliefs. The only technique I haven't actually used is to quit, which would remove the dissonance completely!

tolerance for dissonance, and the theory fails to specify how this factors in to its explanation.

Testability

Another weakness that scholars point out relates specifically to our criterion of testability. As you recall, testability refers to the theory's likelihood of ever being proven false. Theories that have a seeming escape clause against being falsified are not as strong as those that do not. Researchers have pointed out that because Cognitive Dissonance Theory asserts that dissonance will motivate people to act, when people do not act, proponents of the theory can say that the dissonance must not have been strong enough, rather than concluding that the theory is wrong. In this way it is difficult to disprove the theory.

Although Cognitive Dissonance Theory has its shortcomings, it does offer us insight into the relationship among attitudes, cognitions, affect, and behaviors, and it does suggest routes to attitude change and persuasion. Social cognition researchers as well as communication scholars continue to use many of the ideas from CDT. As Steven Littlejohn and Karen Foss (2008) observe Festinger's theory is not only the most important consistency theory, it of the most significant theories in social psychology. CDT has been the work for over a thousand research studies (Perloff, 1993), most of whic supported the theory. Additionally, numerous critiques and interpre have refined and revised the theory. And some researchers (Harmon 2000) believe that continuing to refine the theory by examining cog more specifically, for example, will yield rich theoretical insights.

Cognitive Dissonance Theory has contributed greatly to our unde ing of cognitions and their relationship to behaviors. The concept o nance remains a powerful one in the research literature, informing st psychology, cognitive psychology, communication, and other related fi

128 Chapter 7 · Cogn

Inte

Discussion Starters

1. Explain the relationship of selective attention, exposure, interpretation, and retention to cognitive dissonance. Provide examples where appropriate. How do you think Ali Torres might use these processes, given her situation?

2. Give an example of two attitudes you hold that have an irrelevant relationship to each other. Cite two consonant attitudes you hold. Do you have any attitudes that are dissonant with each other? If so, have you done anything about them? Explain how your actions fit with the theory.

3. What do you think about the problem of CDT's testability suggested in this chapter? Could the theory be revised to make it testable?

4. Suppose you want some friends to change their drinking and driving behaviors. How could you apply the theory in persuading your friends?

5. Do you agree with the minimal justification notion? Provide an example in which minimal justification seemed to work to persuade someone.

6. How do you think group membership affects dissonance and what role do you believe it plays in dissonance reduction?

7. Besides persuasion, what other communication applications might you have for CDT?

Online Learning Center [www. mhhe.com/west4e]

Visit the Online Learning Center at www.mhhe.com/west4e for chapter-specific resources, such as story-into-theory and multiple-choice quizzes, as well as theory summaries and theory connection questions.

Theories on the Social Effects of Media Messages and Technologies

History of the Scientific Study of Media Effects

Tantalized fascination surrounds all efforts to study the effects of mass media.
—Paul F. Lazarsfeld, 1949

If one were to judge from the preceding chapter, effects from media communications would appear to be rather powerful. The reason for this is obvious: History is biased toward recording instances when mediated communications seem to provoke action. Major reactions that can be traced to mediated communication are much easier to locate. Except for the existence of a very detailed personal diary or some other trustworthy personal account, instances of limited media effects are difficult for the historian to identify.[1]

Several late 19th-century studies in psychology and sociology involved research on mass media and presaged the theoretical bases for more sophisticated and numerous studies in the decades to follow, but media effects research emerged categorically in the 20th century. In the past half century, graduate programs in mass communication have sprung to life at major research universities throughout the country, and the study of media effects has quickly matured and diversified. Researchers now search for evidence of media effects in a number of distinct research branches such as persuasion, media violence, sexually explicit material, fright reactions, agenda setting, new media technologies, uses and gratifications, cultivation research, and other areas.

Several communication scholars have acknowledged chinks in the armor of the established history and have offered excellent revisionary works, but their accounts either have focused more upon the history of communication studies than on media effects research and thought per se (Dennis & Wartella, 1996; Rogers, 1994) or they have concentrated on the history of communication theories (Heath & Bryant, 2000). E. Katz (1980, 1983) examined the media effects research tradition from a conceptual standpoint, offered an interesting analysis of media effects research issues, and suggested significant points of connection among the various theories of media effects. In our reexamination of the standard history of media effects research for this chapter, we employed historical research methods rather than conceptual analysis alone to note several key points of contention and identify important issues that should be addressed in the future.

35

The chapter first relates the "established" history of media effects research, then provides our view of the actual history, which differs somewhat from the standard version. We identify some neglected pioneers and more recent scholars of media effects who contributed significantly to our knowledge of media effects. We then point out several issues that have been obscured by the established rendition of history and offer suggestions for advancing the knowledge of media effects in the future.

THE "ESTABLISHED" HISTORY

Because of the historical bias toward chronicling powerful media effects and the concern about media's impact, it should not be surprising that in the early days of scientific effects studies, powerful effects were assumed by many. The study of media effects began during World War I in response to concerns about propaganda spread by the military and after the war by corporations (in the form of advertising and public relations efforts). At first, social scientists and the public believed that mass media produced powerful effects upon their unsuspecting audiences.

Thus begins the "established" history of media effects study in the United States. This standard history has been told and retold in countless lectures, articles, and chapters. J. W. Carey (1996) provided an eloquent summary of the established history, which we quote from time to time to enrich this discussion.

> As the "jazz age" turned into the Great Depression, the fears of propaganda and the media were confirmed by the mass movements in politics and culture typical of that period and by a series of specific and startling events of which Orson Welles' radio broadcast "The War of the Worlds" stood as an archetype. In the standard history, this random assortment of fears, alarms, jeremiads, political pronouncements, and a few pieces of empirical research were collapsed into the "hypodermic-needle model" or "bullet theory" or "model of unlimited effects" of the mass media, for they converged on a common conclusion: The media collectively, but in particularly the newer, illiterate media of radio and film, possessed extraordinary power to shape the beliefs and conduct of ordinary men and women. (p. 22)

According to the standard history, most people in the United States (including most social scientists) believed that mass media, especially electronic media such as film and radio, had incredible powers to influence their audiences. The immense power of media messages on unsuspecting audiences was described in colorful ways: Mass media supposedly fired messages like dangerous bullets, or shot messages like strong drugs pushed through hypodermic needles. These descriptions gave rise to the "bullet" or "hypodermic-needle" theory of powerful media effects.

The standard history typically attributed the rise of the bullet theory as a response to the development of a mass society of fragmented individuals receiving similar messages from the mass media of communication. Early theorists focused on the phenomenal changes in society from the late 19th to early 20th century and the resulting influences on the masses. H. Blumer (1951), noting the importance of mass behavior, wrote that due to urbanization and industrialization of the early 20th century,

> mass behaviour has emerged in increasing magnitude and importance. This is due primarily to the operation of factors which have detached people from their local cultures and local group settings. Migrations, changes of residence, newspapers, motion pictures, the radio, education—all have operated to detach individuals from customary moorings and thrust them into a wider world. In the face of this world, individuals have had to make adjustments on the basis of largely unaided selections. The convergence of their selection has made the mass a potent influence. At times its behaviour comes to approximate that of a crowd, especially under conditions of excitement. At such times it is likely to be influenced by excited appeals as these appear in the press or over the radio—appeals that play upon primitive impulses, antipathies and traditional hatreds.[2] (pp. 187–188)

A number of early books were written with an underlying acceptance of the bullet or hypodermic-needle theories;[3] that is, the immense power of mass communication messages on their audiences. These included, to name a few, Walter Lippmann's *Public Opinion* (1922), Harold Lasswell's *Propaganda Technique in the World War* (1927), and G. G. Bruntz's *Allied Propaganda and the Collapse of the German Empire in 1918* (1938). Also, the standard history relates that the bullet theory served as the basis for a series of studies sponsored by the Payne Fund in the 1920s. These studies sought to determine the influence of the motion picture on children and found that

> as an instrument of education it has unusual power to impart information, to influence specific attitudes toward objects of social value, to affect emotions either in gross or in microscopic proportions, to affect health in a minor degree through sleep disturbance, and to affect profoundly the patterns of conduct of children. (Charters, 1950, p. 406)

One media historian called journalist Walter Lippmann's *Public Opinion* "the originating book in the modern history of communication research"[4] (Carey, 1996, p. 28). Another prominent media scholar viewed it as a founding work for agenda-setting research (Rogers, 1994). In this classic work, Lippmann called upon his experiences with propaganda during World War I. The book became "a key intellectual influence in creating public apprehension about the role of propaganda in a democratic society" (Rogers, 1994, p. 236). Lippmann emphasized the role of the news media in influencing the perceptions of audiences about issues of importance.

The standard history states that the hypodermic-needle theory remained dominant until after the Depression, when empirical studies began to indicate that effects from mass media were not as powerful as originally thought. Rather than a society of fragmented individuals receiving all-powerful messages from mass media, the view shifted to one of a society of individuals who interacted within groups and thus limited the effects of media messages. Studies by Paul

Early studies such as those sponsored by the Payne Fund examined the effects of movies on children.
Source: © Sean Sexton Collection/Corbis

Lazarsfeld at Columbia University's Bureau of Applied Social Research and by other social scientists such as Carl Hovland working for the U.S. War Department, indicated that mass media had only limited effects on individuals in their audiences.

> What was also discovered, in the standard rendition, was that individuals, the members of the audience, were protected from the deleterious possibilities inherent in the mass media by a group of predispositional or mediating factors . . . Some individuals (a few) under some circumstances (rare) were directly affected by the mass media. Otherwise, media propaganda and mass culture were held at bay by an invisible shield erected by a universally resistant psyche and a universally present network of social groups. (Carey, 1996, p. 23)

The limited effects model became thoroughly established in 1960 with the publication of Joseph Klapper's *The Effects of Mass Communication.* This classic work, based on his doctoral dissertation at Columbia University, reviewed hundreds of media effects studies from the 1920s through the 1950s and attempted to make blanket generalizations on the subject of mass media effects. Klapper called for a new approach to research in the field, a "phenomenistic approach," which emphasized particular factors that limited the effects of mass media messages on individuals.

Klapper concluded that the fears of propaganda, of manipulative elites, of media-induced extremist behavior, were misplaced and hysterical . . . Given the conservative bias of the media and of social life generally, Klapper concluded that the preponderant effect was the reinforcement of the status quo . . . With the conclusion firmly established that the media had but limited effects, the research agenda was largely a mopping-up operation: the closer and more detailed specification of the specific operation of mediating and intervening factors . . . In a well-known line, interest shifted from what it was that the media did to people toward what it was people did with the media. This was then a shift in interest and attention from the source to the receiver and a relocation of the point of power in the process: The audience controlled the producers. Except for some special problems (violence and pornography are the best-known examples) and some special groups (principally children), interest in direct effects and propaganda withered away. (Carey, 1996, pp. 23–24)

In the decades following the 1960s, mass media research thrived as the field of mass communication became firmly established at research universities throughout the nation. Certain new theories and research findings did not fit neatly into the limited effects paradigm; therefore, the history was amended to include new studies that indicated moderate to powerful media effects were indeed possible (Ball-Rokeach, Rokeach, & Grube, 1984a, 1984b; Blumler & McLeod, 1974; Maccoby & Farquhar, 1975; Mendelsohn, 1973; Noelle-Neumann, 1973).

A marvelous graphic representation of the established history of media effects is included in W. J. Severin and J. W. Tankard, Jr. (1992) and reproduced here as Figure 3.1. This linear model indicates some of the major studies and research programs in mass communication—some that supposedly caused drastic shifts in scholarly thought regarding the power of media effects through the years. Table 3.1 presents a timeline that corresponds to Figure 3.1 and offers brief descriptions of the various studies that contributed to each major model.

This standard scenario of "all-powerful" effects to "limited" effects to "moderate" to "powerful" effects provided a simple and convenient history of the field of communication research. Unfortunately, as many scholars have pointed out (Carey, 1996; Wartella, 1996), the established history is not altogether satisfying. Although it contains accuracies, it also misleads due to its strict adherence to the supposed major shifts in thought about the power of media effects triggered by particular research findings. Moreover, certain research findings from these major studies (and others) that run contrary to the established picture are simply ignored. Additionally, the standard history emphasizes the importance of some scholars but neglects to mention other individuals and their studies.

In the following section, we offer a new approach for describing the history of research on mass media effects. Although the old history remains attractive because of its ease of description and topical divisions, the revised history we now relate includes additional evidence and a fresh perspective. We hope that what is lost in convenience will be gained in greater accuracy.

39

CHAPTER 3
History of the
Scientific Study
of Media Effects

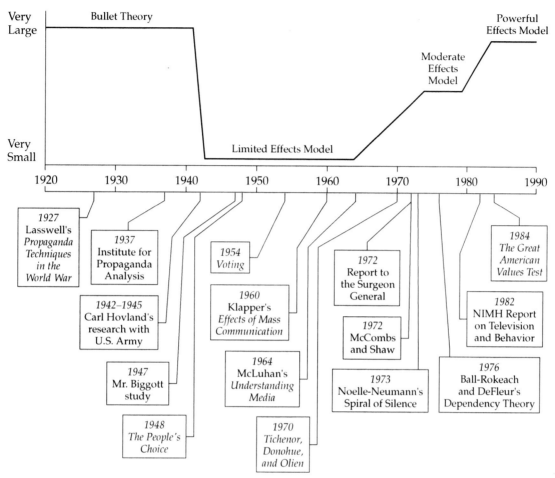

FIGURE 3.1. Size of Effect Due to Mass Communication, for Various Theories.
Source: From W. J. Severin and J. W. Tankard, Jr., *Communication Theories: Origins, Methods, and Uses in the Mass Media*, 3e. Copyright © 1992 by Allyn & Bacon. Reprinted/adapted with permission.

A REVISED HISTORY

A more accurate history of mass media effects research shares some similarities with established history but differs in important ways as well. The two versions have in common the many research studies that indicated different levels of media effects. (Moreover, the "established" history is always recounted in the improved history because that version has been accepted as gospel for so many years.) The new history differs from the standard version in these ways: the acknowledgment of early, precursory media effects studies by psychologists, sociologists, and other investigators; the reevaluation of summary findings from some of the major studies; the inclusion of particular studies through the years that did not fit neatly into the "standard" scenario; the importance attributed to particular scholars; the emphasis on the advances in effects research through the

Table 3.1   Timeline

BULLET THEORY MODEL

1927	Lasswell's *Propaganda Technique in the World War* (Lasswell, 1928). Based upon his doctoral dissertation, this qualitative work analyzed the content of propaganda messages of World War I, identifying various propaganda techniques.
1937	Institute for Propaganda Analysis. This research institute was formed in response to public fear regarding the persuasive power of propaganda via mass media. Many worried that an evil tyrant like Hitler could gain power in the United States by flooding mass communication media with propaganda messages. Studies were conducted in an effort to understand the effects of propaganda.

LIMITED EFFECTS MODEL

1942–1945	Carl Hovland's research with the U.S. Army. Hovland and his associates conducted persuasion research for the Research Branch of the U.S. Army's Information and Education division. Hovland's controlled experiments measured attitude changes among soldiers who viewed training or motivational films. They found that the films did not increase soldiers' motivations.
1947	Mr. Biggott study. This study by Cooper and Jahoda (1947) examined the effects of cartoons that poked fun at prejudice. Rather than changing any attitudes, the cartoons only strengthened or confirmed preexisting attitudes, whether prejudiced or unprejudiced.
1948	*The People's Choice.* Lazarsfeld, Berelson, and Gaudet (1948) studied voting decisions among voters in Erie County, Ohio, during the 1940 election campaign of Franklin D. Roosevelt and Wendell Wilkie. They found that interpersonal contacts were more powerful than mass media in influencing voting decisions. Mass media messages reached influential citizens called "opinion leaders," who in turn passed along information to others. This process was labeled the "two-step flow" of communication.
1954	*Voting.* Berelson, Lazarsfeld, and McPhee (1954) conducted panel surveys among voters in Elmira, New York, during the 1948 campaign that pitted Harry Truman against Thomas E. Dewey. The studies found that mass media influence played a small part in affecting voting decisions. Personal influence (interpersonal communication) was found to be the most important factor determining a person's voting decision.
1960	Klapper's *Effects of Mass Communication.* This classic work surveyed several hundred media effects studies and concluded that the effects of mass communication were limited.

MODERATE EFFECTS MODEL

1964	McLuhan's *Understanding Media.* Canadian Marshall McLuhan (1964) offered a new view toward mass media communications. He believed that media effects did not result from media content, but from the form of the medium itself. In other words, the effects occurred at a very base level, altering patterns of perception and thought.
1970	Tichenor, Donohue, and Olien. These researchers posited the "knowledge gap hypothesis," which states that "as the infusion of mass media information into a social system increases, segments of the population with higher socioeconomic status tend to acquire this information at a faster rate than the lower status segments, so that the gap in knowledge between these segments tends to increase rather than decrease" (Tichenor, Donohue, & Olien, 1970, pp. 159–160).

(continued)

Table 3.1　Timeline (concluded)

MODERATE EFFECTS MODEL (CONCLUDED)

1971	Report to the Surgeon General. This report found that a causal relationship existed between viewing televised violence and subsequent aggressive behavior, but "any such causal relation operates only on some children (who are predisposed to be aggressive)" and "operates only in some environmental contexts" (Surgeon General's Scientific Advisory Committee on Television and Social Behavior, 1972, p. 11).
1972	McCombs and Shaw (1972). These researchers conducted the first study of the agenda-setting hypothesis, which posits that news media coverage of particular issues influences their audiences' views about what issues are important.
1973	Spiral of Silence. Noelle-Neumann's (1973) theory of rather powerful media effects suggests that people become reluctant to speak an opinion that is counter to the majority opinion in society. Mass media are instrumental in shaping impressions about public opinions that are dominant or becoming dominant.
1976	Ball-Rokeach and DeFleur's Dependency Theory (1976). This theory stresses a relationship between societal systems, media systems, and audiences. It states that the degree to which audiences depend upon mass media information varies based on individual differences, the amount of disorder or conflict present in society, and the number and centrality of information functions that they serve.

POWERFUL EFFECTS MODEL

1983	NIMH Report on Television and Behavior. This report, sponsored by the National Institute of Mental Health, surveyed the research on effects of TV violence and found positive correlations between TV violence viewing and subsequent aggression among children and teens. "Not all children become aggressive, of course, but the correlations between violence and aggression are positive. In magnitude, television violence is as strongly correlated with aggressive behavior as any other behavioral variable that has been measured" (1983, p. 28).
1984	*The Great American Values Test.* Ball-Rokeach, Rokeach, and Grube's (1984b) elaborate study showed that when people are confronted with inconsistencies in their basic beliefs or values, they modify their values, attitudes, and behaviors accordingly. The effects of viewing a 30-minute television program on values were rather powerful.

years; and the identification of some sorely needed but missing classification rules that are fundamentally necessary for particular systematic inquiries that will advance overall knowledge and allow generalizations regarding media effects.

The history of mass media effects research does not move in pendulum swings from "all-powerful" to "limited" to "moderate" to "powerful" effects (again, except for the recounting of the established version). Instead, our history emphasizes the body of research that has, from the beginning, found overwhelming evidence for *significant* effects from mass media communications on audiences, based for the most part upon scientific methods and traditional statistical models. Additionally, the recounting of the history makes apparent an immediate need for clarifications, standardizations, and much additional research in the field of mass media effects (Thompson & Bryant, 2000).

Political Agendas in Research on Effects of Violence: Historical Perspectives

In his classic work *The Politics of TV Violence*, W. D. Rowland (1983) also offers a revised version of the history of media effects research, focusing on television violence, from the standpoint of the underlying political motives of various groups with a stake in the results (e.g., the networks, politicians, the concerned public). In the 1950s, public pressure to know more about the effects of television grew particularly intense after it became apparent that the new medium was becoming an essential part of U.S. society and culture. Through the years, elected officials have responded with major inquiries whenever public concern about the ill effects of television violence was on the rise. A number of groups have particular stakes in the results of research on media violence: politicians, the general public, industry executives, reformers, and media effects researchers.

For their part the politicians may be depicted as having found in the effects research efforts the vehicle necessary for them to project an image of concerned inquiry, while ensuring that that inquiry would force them into little, if any, legislative action. (p. 30)

Building on the prior relationships with university-based research centers and joint governmental funding, the industry continued to support and promote selected research efforts while overlooking or avoiding others . . . Throughout this process of development, the broadcasting industry alternately supported and opposed the research enterprise, carefully cultivating—and thereby shaping—certain aspects and allowing others to wither. (pp. 29–30)

The mass communication research community found the vehicle necessary for it to begin to obtain identity and ultimately to achieve legitimacy in the academy. The struggles therein for supremacy among competing social sciences carried over into the effort to interpret the new medium. A liberal, optimistic, and newly retooled American social psychology proved to be a highly attractive competitor for research funds and public recognition. (p. 27)

Source: W. D. Rowland (1983), *The politics of TV violence*, Beverly Hills: Sage, pp. 27, 29–30.

Without standard lines of demarcation, media effects researchers have often made qualitative judgment calls about the power of effects. Based upon these qualitative verdicts, what emerges is a history of research that states conclusively that, yes, various kinds of mass media effects do occur, but the levels of influence have been assumed to vary from limited to rather powerful; furthermore, researchers have recognized this—mostly they have argued this—from the beginning.

The intense debate about the power or limits of media effects still rages to this day, but knowledge in the field continues to advance. For example, as is delineated in subsequent chapters, we have discovered that media effects may be cognitive (affecting thoughts or learning), behavioral (affecting behavior), or affective (affecting attitudes and emotions). Effects may be either direct or indirect, and they may be short term, long term, or delayed. They may be self-contained or cumulative. We have learned much about individual differences, psychological factors, environmental factors, and social group characteristics that cause audience members to perceive and react to media messages in specific ways. Still, much remains to be discovered, and in the final part of this section we will take a look at some of the interesting landscapes waiting to be painted by media effects researchers in the 21st century.

Precursors

Several 19th- and early 20th-century studies in psychology, sociology, and social psychology involved the examination of particular mass media effects. Some studies were philosophical in nature and offered comments on the suspected influence of mediated communications on audiences and public opinion, rather than isolating particular social effects on mass media audiences in a controlled design or a laboratory setting. The handful of experimental studies conducted usually focused on the measure of very specific physical or psychological effects from media exposure.

We cite these studies for two reasons. Because of their emphasis on mass media and their introduction of ideas that would later become the theoretical bases of particular media effects studies, they should be considered precursors to the mass media effects studies that would arise in the 20th century. Additionally, two of these precursory studies reveal that the models for suspected powerful and limited effects from mass media communications developed almost simultaneously, contrary to the established version and its representative studies.

Two articles in the *American Journal of Sociology* in the late 19th century illustrate early differing views on the power mediated communications exerted on audiences. They introduced ideas that other social scientists would explore more fully in theoretical formations and controlled experiments during the next century. It is interesting that of these two articles, the "limited effects" view preceded the "powerful effects" view. J. W. Jenks (1895) doubted the influence of newspapers of the period on the formation of public opinion, and he proposed that the individual differences of audience members modified the influential power of communications:

> One chief reason, perhaps, of the comparatively small influence of our press is that the people know the fact that the papers are run from motives of personal profits, and that the policy of the paper is largely determined by the amount to which its opinions will affect its sales and advertising . . . [W]e all of us doubtless have our opinions formed from former prejudices, we ourselves unconsciously selecting the facts and statements that fit into these former prejudices, and thus tend to conform to our own beliefs . . . It is probably not too much to say that not 25 percent of our adult voting population have deliberately made up an opinion on a public question after anything like a reasonably full and fair study of the facts in the case. Public opinion, then, seems to be a mixture of sense and nonsense, of sentiment, of prejudice, of more or less clearly defined feelings coming from influences of various kinds that have been brought to bear upon the citizens, these influences perhaps being mostly those of sentiment rather than those acting upon the judgment. (p. 160)

V. S. Yarros took the opposite view by emphasizing the power of the newspaper as an organ of public opinion; however, he bemoaned the "mendacity, sensationalism, and recklessness" (1899, p. 374) that characterized most of the newspapers of his day. He also regretted that so many editors of the day were so incompetent yet wielded so much power over an unsuspecting public:

> The editor is glad to have the support of authority, but he is not daunted or disturbed at finding recognized authority against his position. The mature opinions

of scholars and experts he treats with a flippancy and contempt which the slightest degree of responsibility would render impossible. But the editor is irresponsible. The judicious and competent few may laugh at his ignorance and presumption, but the cheap applause of the many who mistake smartness for wit and loud assertion for knowledge affords abundant compensation. Controversy with an editor is a blunder. He always has the last word, and his space is unlimited. He is a adept at dust-throwing, question-begging, and confusing the issue. In private life he may be intellectually and morally insignificant, but his readers are imposed upon by the air of infallibility with which he treats all things, and the assurance with which he assails those who have the audacity to disagree with him. The average newspaper reader easily yields to iteration and bombast. He believes that which is said daily in print by the august and mysterious power behind the editoral "we." His sentiments and notions are formed for him by that power, and he is not even conscious of the fact. (p. 375)

The debate about the power of newspapers to either direct or reflect public opinion, which is the forerunner of the mirror/lamp metaphor of the popular culture debate of the 1950s, as well as an antecedent of the modern-day argument for and against the agenda-setting hypothesis, continues to this day. In the 20th century, articles in the *American Journal of Sociology* and elsewhere kept the debate alive before and after the publication of Lippmann's *Public Opinion* (Angell, 1941; Orton, 1927; Park, 1941; Shepard, 1909).

Several early experimental studies deserve mention as precursors to modern-day media effects, especially in the area of entertainment. These include a study of the effects of music on attention (Titchener, 1898), the effects of music on thoracic breathing (Foster & Gamble, 1906), and a study of musical enjoyment as measured by plethysmographic and pneumographic records of changes in circulation and respiration (Weld, 1912). Another early study, more theoretical than experimental, examined the nature and origin of humor as a mental process and the functions of humor (Kline, 1907).

Frances Fenton

One of the earliest (perhaps the first) studies of the effects of consumption of media violence on behavior was a doctoral dissertation by Frances Fenton. The partial and summary findings of her study appeared in two issues of the *American Journal of Sociology* in November 1910 and January 1911. Fenton pointed out that the popular notion that newspaper accounts of antisocial activities had suggestive powers on readers was well established prior to her thesis (see Fenton, 1910, pp. 345 and 350 for lists of articles). She defined *suggestion* as

the process by which ideas, images, impulsive tendencies, or any sort of stimulus, enter from without into the composition of the neural make-up or disposition and, at times more or less in the focus of consciousness, at other times not in the focus at all, are transformed into activity by the agency of a stimulus which bears an effective though unrecognized relation or similarity to the image or neural set, and in which there is in large part, or wholly, failure to anticipate the results of the suggested act. (pp. 364–365)

Fenton argued "on the basis of the psychology of suggestion" that a direct causal relationship could be assumed between reading newspaper articles on crime and on antisocial activities and subsequent criminal or antisocial acts. In her dissertation, she identified numerous cases in which individuals were known to have committed copycat-type crimes or other antisocial acts after getting ideas from a newspaper article. Due to lack of available space, the journal articles included only summary headings to describe the nature of the cases, but these headings were said to represent

> a mass of both direct and indirect evidence of the suggestive influence of the newspaper on anti-social activity gathered from a wide range of territory and from many different sources. (pp. 557–558)

She also measured the amount of such material appearing in several large-circulation newspapers of the "yellow" variety, although she emphasized that

> this was undertaken not because the actual amount of anti-social matter in a newspaper is known to bear a direct relation to the growth of crime, or because we have any evidence to show that changes in the two bear a constant relation to one another. (p. 539)

Gabriel Tarde

At about the same time that Fenton produced her study, Gabriel Tarde was undertaking his own study of crime. In *Penal Philsophy* (1912), Tarde offered a quote from A. Corre's *Crime et suicide* regarding the effects of reading about hideous crimes such as the Jack-the-Ripper murders. Corre observed that "pernicious influence" from publicity of such crimes led to "suggesto-imitative assaults," or copycat crimes. "Infectious epidemics spread with the air or the wind; epidemics of crime follow the line of the telegraph," Corre wrote (Tarde, 1912, pp. 340–341).

SOME PIONEERS IN MEDIA EFFECTS RESEARCH

In the years following World War I, innovative scholars from various disciplines at several particular institutions of learning conducted pioneering studies to examine the fledgling domain of scientific research on the effects of mass communication. These scholars, who came from disciplines outside journalism or mass communication, hailed principally from the University of Chicago, Columbia University, and Yale University. They included (among a number of others) the following: Carl Hovland, an experimental psychologist from Yale University; Paul F. Lazarsfeld, a sociologist at Columbia University; Harold Lasswell, a political scientist at the University of Chicago and, later, Yale University; Kurt Lewin, a social psychologist at the University of Iowa and, later, MIT; Samuel A. Stouffer, a sociologist from the University of Chicago; and Douglas Waples, a "professor of researches in reading" (Waples, 1942, p. xi) at the University of Chicago.[5] The importance of the first four of these scholars to the history of mass communication research has been firmly established by Wilbur Schramm prior to his death in 1987 (Rogers & Chaffee, 1997) and reiterated by Rogers (1994), and for this reason alone we greatly condense our discussion of them. We concentrate more on the final two scholars who have not received much recognition in either the standard or other revised versions of communications history, even though they made significant contributions to the media effects tradition.

Carl Hovland

Carl Hovland studied the effects of training films on the attitudes of American soldiers during World War II (Hovland, Lumsdaine, & Sheffield, 1965), and later directed experimental research that explored media effects on attitude change.[6] The tight design of the experiments conducted by Hovland became the model for much future research in media effects. Wilbur Schramm, a principle "mover and shaker" of mass communication research in the United States, said that Carl Hovland's body of research from 1945 to 1961 constituted "the largest single contribution . . . to this field any man has made" (Schramm, 1997, p. 104).

Paul Lazarsfeld

Paul F. Lazarsfeld earned a PhD in mathematics, but his diverse research interests included social psychology, sociology, and mass communication. Lazarsfeld and his research institute at Columbia University pioneered research in the effects of radio and introduced the notion that interpersonal communication was an important mediating factor in certain mass media effects. In the 1940s Lazarsfeld and his colleagues examined the influences of mass media on public opinion during a presidential campaign. They found that most people were influenced primarily through interpersonal contacts rather than by what they read in newspapers and magazines or heard on the radio, although those media were found to have some influence in and of themselves.[7] Particular individuals whom the researchers called "opinion leaders," who were often rather heavy users of mass media, were found to pass along information to others in the community who looked to them for guidance. This finding led to establishment of a two-step flow model of mass communication, in which media effects were perceived as being modified by interpersonal communication about those media messages. Subsequent research expanded the two-step flow model into one of multistep flow:

> Later studies concluded that the influence of opinion leaders was not always "downward," as in the interpretation of news events for a less informed audience. Opinion leaders were found to communicate "upward" to the media gatekeepers (i.e., newspaper editors and radio programmers) as well as share information "sideways" with other opinion leaders. Further studies of interpersonal communication showed that an individual's personal identification with an organization, religion, or other social group has a strong influence on the type of media content selected . . . Group norms apparently provide a type of "social reality" check built on similar and shared beliefs, attitudes, opinions, and concerns that tend to form barriers against mediated messages contrary to the group's point of view. Likewise, mediated messages in agreement with the group or provided by the group are usually attended to and utilized to reinforce the status quo. (Heath & Bryant, 2000, pp. 349–350)

Harold Lasswell

Harold D. Lasswell made many contributions to the study of media effects, the most notable being his five-question model—"Who says what in which channel to whom with what effects?" (Lasswell, 1948)—his studies of propaganda, and his identification of three important functions that mass communications serve in society: surveillance of the environment, correlation of society's response to events in the environment, and transmission of the cultural heritage.[8] E. M. Rogers (1994) listed five major contributions that he believed Lasswell made to communication study:

1. His five-questions model of communication led to the emphasis in communication study on determining effects. Lasswell's contemporary, Paul F. Lazarsfeld, did even more to crystallize this focus on communication effects.
2. He pioneered in content analysis methods, virtually inventing the methodology of qualitative and quantitative measurement of communication messages (propaganda messages and newspaper editorials, for example).
3. His study of political and wartime propaganda represented an important early type of communication study. The word *propaganda* later gained a negative connotation and is not used much today, although there is even more political propaganda. Propaganda analysis has been absorbed into the general body of communication research.
4. He introduced Freudian psychoanalytic theory to the social sciences in America. Lasswell integrated Freudian theory with political analysis, as in his psychoanalytic study of political leaders. He applied Freud's id-ego-superego via content analysis to political science problems. In essence, he utilized intraindividual Freudian theory at the societal level.
5. He helped create the policy sciences, an interdisciplinary movement to integrate social science knowledge with public action. The social sciences, however, generally resisted this attempt at integration and application to public policy problems. (pp. 232–233)

Kurt Lewin

Social psychologist Kurt Lewin did pioneering studies in the dynamics of group communication. While at the University of Iowa, he conducted a famous group of communication experiments to explore the differences in persuasive power on audiences in different group conditions. In the best known of these experiments, "the sweetbreads study," groups of housewives reluctant to serve glandular meats to their families learned about the benefits of beef hearts, thymus (sweetbreads), liver, and kidneys by either attending a lecture or a discussion group. The discussion group situation proved far more effective in changing the behavior of the housewives (making them more likely to serve glandular meats to their families).

According to Rogers, Lewin's "greatest academic influence was through the brilliant students whom he trained" (1994, p. 354). One of his students, Leon Festinger, directed a study to identify communication network links among married students living in a set of apartments (Festinger, Schachter, & Bach, 1950).

Later, Festinger advanced his famous theory of cognitive dissonance, which proposes that whenever an individual's attitudes and actions are in conflict, the person will adjust cognitions in an attempt to resolve the conflict.[9]

Samuel Stouffer

Paul Lazarsfeld dedicated to Stouffer his report of the Columbia University voting studies, "which profited from his skillful procedures of survey analysis" (1962, p. xxxi). He also cited Stouffer's influence on Carl Hovland's studies on attitudes and communications conducted at Yale University after World War II. Stouffer pioneered the use of empirical research, especially survey research, for social enquiries, and the use of precise statistical methods. He directed research for the Division of Information and Education of the United States Army during World War II.

After the war, Stouffer conducted several studies of communications media, but these studies deal more with the effectiveness of media and often are not labeled as effects studies.[10] His importance to the history of media effects research lies in his empirical expertise, his influence on early communication researchers such as Hovland and Lazarsfeld, and his insistence that communication research adhere to strict empirical standards. In a 1942 chapter called "A Sociologist Takes a Look at Communications Research," Stouffer applauded the careful methods of the investigation by R. C. Peterson and L. L. Thurstone (1933), one of the famous Payne Fund Studies that examined the effects of movies on children.

> A classic example of a complete experimental study in communications research was Thurstone and Peterson's study of the effects of specific motion pictures on social attitudes . . . Subsequently there have been several other studies more or less similar to Thurstone's and Peterson's, but it is surprising that there have not been more . . . This experiment demonstrated that a single movie has measurable and relatively lasting effects on children—but did anybody doubt that? Why spend a lot of money and time to demonstrate the obvious? There are two answers to this. In the first place, Thurstone showed that the direction of the effect (whether toward or against a given set of values) was not always predictable on a common-sense basis. A film glorifying a gambler had the unpredicted effect of making children feel more than ever that gambling was an evil. In the second place, Thurstone and Peterson were able to prove that effects of single films lasted over a long period of time and also that certain combinations of films had mutually reinforcing effects. It is true that they left hundreds of interesting questions unanswered. What types of children were affected most? What types of scenes within a given picture had the most effect? Were there differences in the kind of effect which would require a multidimensional rather than unidimensional attitude continuum for description? Such questions call for further research, and the Thurstone-Peterson method shows a way of answering them. (pp. 138–141)

Stouffer emphasized the importance of controlling for variables such as educational status, age, or other differences among audiences that could account for differences between the groups tested—variables that might mediate media effects. When the researcher does not control for confounding variables, he warned, "we can only hope and pray that we are controlling all the factors which would tend to differentiate" (p. 139) the control and experimental groups.

Finally, Stouffer's empirical expertise and prescience allowed him to identify problems in 1942 that continue to plague communication researchers in the 21st century—namely, the accurate measure of cumulative effects of mass media communications:

> It is a difficult matter to design an experiment which will measure the cumulative effect of, say, a year's exposure to a given medium of communication . . . The difficulty of evaluating cumulative effects of many small stimuli in the field of communications is all the more serious because there is good basis for the belief that it is in just this way that communications have their principal effect. One soft-drink ad may not invite the pause that refreshes, but hundreds, and even thousands of them, confronting the consumer in as many different social situations evidently help sell the product. (pp. 141–142)

Douglas Waples

Douglas Waples was a professor in the Graduate Library School at the University of Chicago. His significance to modern media effects research has been ignored by the standard history, but in fact it may be rather substantial. In 1940, at the same time that Lazarsfeld was conducting radio studies at Columbia University, Waples, Bernard Berelson, and F. R. Bradshaw published their work on the effects of print media, *What Reading Does to People*. The work revealed much about print media effects on attitude change.

> The studies have repeatedly shown that reading can change attitudes. They have also shown that certain reader traits and certain content elements will modify the effect of the reading. For example, the effects are modified by differences in what the readers already know about the subject. The less the reader knows about the complexities of and objections to issues discussed in the text, the greater the change in attitude will be. (pp. 108–109)

More significantly, Waples offered the earliest published version of the most famous statement about the process of communication in the history of effects research, and he added an important phrase that the later versions neglected. "Who says what in which channel to whom with what effect?" (Lasswell, 1948, p. 37) has always been credited to Lasswell in the standard—and other revised—histories of communication research. Joseph Klapper (1960) indicated the statement originated with Lasswell in 1946 (Smith, Lasswell, & Casey, 1946), but an article by Waples in the *American Journal of Sociology* in 1942 begins with the following quotation: "*Who* communicates *what* to *whom* by *what medium*, under *what conditions*, and with *what effects?*" (p. 907). Rogers (1994) credited the "who says what" statement to Lasswell, spoken during a Rockefeller Communication Seminar in 1940, a conference also attended by Waples, but the quote is not recorded in the rather detailed conference papers.[11] D. Lerner and L. M. Nelson (1977) said that Lasswell's *Propaganda Technique in the World War* "set forth the dominant paradigm" (p. 1) of the five-question line, but nothing resembling the "who says what" statement appears in that text. As for the Waples quote, whether he was quoting Lasswell, himself, or someone else is unclear; neither scholar provided a citation for the words, either in 1942 or 1948.

The identity of the speaker is less important than the substance of the Waples' quote; namely, the inclusion of the "under what conditions" phrase. This phrase, absent from any of the published Lasswell versions, adds a sophistication to the process that is essential to the sorting out of media effects at their various levels. Waples wrote the following after the quote:

> Reliable answers to this complex question at regular time intervals would greatly clarify the process of social change via communications and would simplify predictions of impending changes. (1942, p. 907)

INTEREST IN MEDIA EFFECTS CONTINUES

The number of scholars drawn to communication inquiry continued to increase throughout the 1940s and 1950s. The innovative studies and the innovators had much influence on the "founder" of the disciplinary approach to mass communication study, Wilbur Schramm (Rogers, 1994).

Wilbur Schramm

Though Schramm did not specialize exclusively in media effects (one of his principal areas of interest was in international communication and the role of mass communication in developing third-world nations), his importance must not be overlooked due to his role as consolidator and legitimizer of mass communication study—including media effects.

> Schramm was the first professor of communication so-designated; his was the first communication research institute and the first doctoral program awarding degrees in communication; and Schramm presided over the first academic unit (a "division") of communication in the world. (Rogers & Chaffee, 1997, p. 7)

Schramm initiated the first PhD program in mass communication in 1943, when he served as director of the journalism school at the University of Iowa. Three years later, he had founded the Bureau of Audience Research at Iowa, one of several communication research institutes that sprang to life during the 1940s and 1950s. These institutes were patterned somewhat after Lazarsfeld's Bureau of Applied Social Research at Columbia.

Mediating Factors

During these decades, researchers began to focus experiments on the different reactions of individuals to the same media presentations. Rather than viewing audiences as passive victims who could be manipulated by mass media messages, scholars soon realized that individual differences and environmental factors were important mediators in the process of mass media effects.

Experiments in behaviorism, motivation, persuasion, and conditioning led researchers to examine the processes of habit formation and learning. Differences among individual personality traits and psychological organization were found to be affected by the social environment in which people were raised. Moreover, studies in human perception showed that an individual's values, needs, beliefs, and attitudes were instrumental in determining how stimuli are selected from the environment and the way meaning is attributed to those stimuli within an individual's frame of reference. (Heath & Bryant, 2000, p. 347)

Studies with theoretical bases in psychology and sociology found that audience members selectively attended to media messages, depending upon their predispositions, interests, attitudes, social category, and a number of other factors. Similar variables were found to influence an individual's perception of a media message and what the person remembered about the message. These concepts were later defined as selective exposure, selective perception, selective retention, and the social categories perspective, which posits that people with similar demographic characteristics react similarly to media messages.

ATTEMPTS TO GENERALIZE ABOUT EFFECTS

Bernard Berelson

Bernard Berelson, another pioneer in media effects research, was a colleague of Waples at the University of Chicago, where Berelson served as dean of the Library School, and later a colleague of Lazarsfeld's at Columbia University and the Bureau for Applied Social Research. He coauthored with Lazarsfeld the classic voting study, *The People's Choice*.

Berelson was perhaps the first researcher to attempt to make umbrella generalizations about mass communication effects when he suggested the following formulation for research. His concern was for the influence of communication effects on public opinion, rather than media effects overall, yet his formulation could be applied to other research in media effects:

> Some kinds of *communication* on some kinds of *issues*, brought to the attention of some kinds of *people* under some kinds of *conditions*, have some kinds of *effects*. This formulation identifies five central factors (or rather groups of factors) which are involved in the process, and it is the interrelationship of these variables which represents the subject matter of theory in this field. At present, students can fill out only part of the total picture—a small part—but the development of major variables and the formulation of hypotheses and generalizations concerning them are steps in the right direction. (1948, p. 172)

Several years later Berelson noted the many complex findings that had emerged from research studies that would have to be considered in the development of any overarching theory of mass communication effects:

> The effects of communication are many and diverse. They may be short-range or long-run. They may be manifest or latent. They may be strong or weak. They may derive from any number of aspects of the communication content. They

may be considered as psychological or political or economic or sociological. They may operate upon opinions, values, information levels, skills, taste, behavior . . . Because of the variety and the complexity of the effects of communications, this topic probably represents the most neglected area in communication research. (Berelson & Janowitz, 1950, p. 395)

Joseph Klapper

Ten years later, one of Lazarsfeld's students, Joseph Klapper, produced his still valuable and classic work, *The Effects of Mass Communication* (1960). In this book, Klapper offered several overarching generalizations "in their bare bones" (p. 7) about the effects of mass media messages. Unfortunately, through the course of history, the ideas in Klapper's book have been greatly reduced to a "limited effects" notion that encouraged a "phenomenistic approach" that would identify mediating factors involved in effects, even though Klapper warned repeatedly about the grave danger in "the tendency to go overboard in blindly minimizing the effects and potentialities of mass communications" (p. 252).

Klapper's generalizations have usually been overlooked or quoted only in partial form. In most cases, only the first two generalizations have been reproduced—the two that, not surprisingly, emphasize the many studies that show limited or indirect effects of media communications. Generalizations 3, 4, and 5—those that emphasize that direct effects from media communications are indeed possible—have been ignored by the standard history. For this reason, we include all five generalizations in Figure 3.2.

FIGURE 3.2. Klapper's Generalizations

1. Mass communication *ordinarily* does not serve as a necessary and sufficient cause of audience effects, but rather functions among and through a nexus of mediating factors and influences.
2. These mediating factors are such that they typically render mass communication a contributory agent, but not the sole cause, in a process of reinforcing the existing conditions. Regardless of the condition in question—be it the vote intentions of audience members, their tendency toward or away from delinquent behavior, or their general orientation toward life and its problems—and regardless of whether the effect in question be social or individual, the media are more likely to reinforce than to change.
3. On such occasions as mass communication does function in the service of change, one of two conditions is likely to exist. Either:
   a. The mediating factors will be found to be inoperative and the effect of the media will be found to be direct; or
   b. The mediating factors, which normally favor reinforcement, will be found to be impelling toward change.
4. There are certain residual situations in which mass communication seems to produce direct effects, or directly and of itself to serve certain psychophysical functions.
5. The efficacy of mass communication, either as a contributory agent or as an agent of direct effect, is affected by various aspects of the media and communications themselves or of the communication situation, including, for example, aspects of textual organization, the nature of the source and medium, the existing climate of public opinion, and the like.

THE 1970S AND BEYOND

In the 1970s, the decade following the appearance of Klapper's (1960) book, psychological theories arose that had strong implications for the understanding of mass media effects. The theories of Albert Bandura (1973; 1991)—social learning theory and, later, social cognitive theory—opened up alternative lines of inquiry for communication researchers.[12] Rather than focus primarily on mass communication's effects upon attitude change, scholars in the 1970s and beyond began for the most part to examine more complex behavioral responses, changes in cognitive patterns, and media effects on learning and knowledge (Becker, McCombs, & McLeod, 1975; Chaffee, 1977; Clarke & Kline, 1974). Many of the most important of these findings are discussed throughout the remainder of this text.

Social learning theory explains how viewers learn and model behaviors they see in the mass media, based upon their environmental and cognitive predispositions. It began to serve as the basis for a bevy of research that examined the effects, especially among children, of viewing violence on film and television, the latter medium fast coming into dominance.

In the years since the 1960s, as the field of mass communication research continued to blossom and attract more scholars interested specifically in media effects, other areas of media effects research were either born or developed into maturity. These included cultivation analysis and other sociological procedures that attempt to measure the cumulative effects of mass communication, research to examine the agenda-setting hypothesis that mass media are responsible for bringing public awareness to particular issues, research to explore the reasons why audience members used particular mass media, and the many other areas of media effects.

FINAL POINTS OF CONTENTION WITH THE STANDARD HISTORY

As mentioned previously, we take issue with several aspects of the established history and, in reviewing the history, we notice the necessity for clarifications, standardizations, and additional research. In this section we identify those points of contention, and in the next section we suggest what we hope will be a productive path for media effects research in the 21st century.

Studies that indicate "limited" and "powerful" effects can be identified in every period of the history of media effects research. Although a number of studies and works during the bullet theory years did indicate that "powerful" media effects were possible (Annis & Meier, 1934; Britt & Menefee, 1939; Bruntz, 1938; Cantril, Gaudet, & Herzog, 1940; Lasswell, 1927), others found that mass media had only limited effects on their audiences. In 1926, for example, G. A. Lundberg found only a slight relationship between the opinions of Seattle residents on four public issues and on stands taken by the newspaper. He concluded that

> A modern commercial newspaper has little direct influence on the opinions of its readers on public questions. It probably seeks to discover and reflect that opinion rather than to make it. (p. 712).

The following year, an essay in the *American Journal of Sociology*, titled "The Limited Social Effect of Radio Broadcasting," questioned the powerful effects of radio on society. M. D. Beuick (1927) believed the effects of the medium would be rather limited, and that its greatest benefits would be to isolated individuals. We previously referred to the study by Waples and his associates on the effects of print media on public opinion and the "limited effects" conclusions they reached. These studies reveal that the limited effects idea was well established long before the standard history recognized its existence.

The same inconsistencies can be found during the "limited effects" years of communication research and beyond (Lazarsfeld & Stanton, 1942/1944; Lerner, 1949; Merton, 1946); furthermore, some of the major studies in the standard history contain mixed findings on the power of media communications, but these findings have been lost beneath the all-encompassing rubrics of powerful or limited effects models. For example, even though Hovland's experiments showed that the army films did not raise the motivational level of the troops, they *did* reveal significant effects in the cognitive dimension—soldiers learned a good deal of factual information by viewing the film (Hovland, Lumsdaine, & Sheffield, 1965). Also, in an even more important example previously reviewed, the findings of Klapper's *The Effects of Mass Communication* (1960) have generally been reduced to supporting only a limited- or indirect-effects scenario, yet Klapper clearly indicated that instances of direct effects were apparent from some of the research findings he reviewed, and he warned of the dangers of underestimating the power of media communications on audiences.

FUTURE OF EFFECTS RESEARCH

The challenges for media effects of the 21st century are great, but they will eventually be met if researchers continue to approach the problems with "tantalized fascination" (Lazarsfeld, 1949, p. 1). First and foremost, if we are to continue to describe media effects as either powerful, moderate, or limited, we must come up with standard, empirical lines of demarcation to separate the levels. In his influential article on "The Myth of Massive Media Impact," W. J. McGuire (1986) based his definition of small effects sizes on the percentage of variance accounted for by several dependent variables of effects; certainly statistical effect sizes would be one basis for delineating the standards. McGuire argued that powerful media effects were exaggerated, based on review of a handful of important studies in a variety of areas.

> A formidable proportion of the published studies (and presumably an even higher proportion of the unpublished studies) have failed to show overall effects sizable enough even to reach the conventionally accepted .05 level of statistical significance. Some respectable studies in several of the dozen impact areas reviewed . . . do have impacts significant at the .05 level, but even these tend to have very small effect sizes, accounting for no more than 2 or 3% of the variance in dependent variables . . . (p. 177)

Although we respect the forcefulness of McGuire's argument, we must point out that a number of studies have shown media effects significant at not only the .05 level, but at the .01 and the .001 level and beyond, and with effects sizes that account for substantial amounts of the variance (Bryant & Zillmann, 1994). Moreover, meta-analyses (statistical studies that make generalizations about effects by examining and comparing findings from many different completed research studies) of media effects reveal relatively robust effects sizes within entire genres of media effects investigations and more modest effect sizes associated with other genres (Carveth & Bryant, in press). Other studies, although recording effects in the small-to-moderate range, gain significance when one considers the vast sizes of media audiences (Andison, 1977; Wood, Wong, & Cachere, 1991). Neither these studies nor their robust effects are "mythical," but in order to classify them as "powerful" effects, a precise classification schema must first be established.

In another example, Hovland (1959) described the divergence in results from correlational studies and experimental studies on attitude change from exposure to mass communication in simple terms of *percentages of people found to be affected*. This represents another method that could be used to classify the appropriate types of studies into the various levels.

> Lazarsfeld, Berelson, and Gaudet . . . estimate that the political positions of only about 5 percent of their respondents were changed by the election campaign, and they are inclined to attribute even this small amount of change more to personal influence than to the mass media . . . Research using experimental procedures, on the other hand, indicates the possibility of considerable modifiability of attitudes through exposure to communication. In both Klapper's survey (1949) and in my chapter in the *Handbook of Social Psychology* (Hovland, 1954) a number of experimental studies are discussed in which the opinions of a third to a half or more of the audience are changed. (p. 440)

Another challenge for media effects researchers will be to identify the circumstances, conditions, or variables that account for media effects at all their various levels and forms and offer generalizations—perhaps very complex ones, even typologies of effects—that will explain the complex phenomenon of mass media effects. These are the theoretical generalizations that will advance understanding in the field of media effects. To advance such theories, communication scholars will need to use either quantitative meta-analysis techniques (when feasible) or more qualitative, intensive examination of studies in the different areas of effects research (such as that employed by Klapper), grouping the studies on the basis of their effects levels (based upon the to-be-established schema or on other theoretical criteria).

In 1960 Klapper insisted that the time for media effects generalizations had arrived. Forty years after Klapper's insistence, we can say that we know much more about the effects of media communications, but precise, blanket generalizations remain elusive, owing to the complex nature of the subject. One obvious omission in the effects literature to date is the conspicuous absence of a "no-effects model." Academic journals are severely biased toward publishing studies that show the occurrence of statistically significant media effects. Studies that find no significant effects do not normally appear—a 1944 study by Mott was a notable exception. Most studies examine a number of factors or variables, and statistically significant relationships are usually found for some but not others. No scholar has yet sifted through the thousands of effects studies to identify those particular variables or instances—reported in many studies—

when no noticable effects occurred. The statistically significant results are the ones that attract the most attention, yet the instances when media effects do not occur should be of as much interest to communication scholars as the instances when effects do occur—the no-effects scenario is, thusfar, a missing piece of the effects puzzle.[13]

In recent years, a research technique known as meta-analysis has been useful in making generalizations about the different genres of media effects. For example, Paik and Comstock (1994) conducted a major review of studies on the effects of television violence and produced a useful meta-analysis by partitioning variables (e.g., viewer attributes and types of antisocial behavior) in their research design. Meta-analysis involves finding common statistical ground among a large number of same-genre studies and then offering summary findings based on all the available evidence. Throughout this book, we include discoveries from recent meta-analyses in the various types of effects research.

Meta-analyses may be the best hope of producing blanket generalizations similar to those proposed by Klapper. If such generalizations are indeed possible, they would need to sufficiently explain the circumstances and conditions necessary for powerful or limited, direct or indirect, short-term or long-term, cumulative, cognitive, affective, or behavioral effects from mass media communications and, if possible, the factors present in a no-effects scenario. The enormity of the task stands apparent when one realizes that Klapper (1960) seems to be the only scholar in the history of media effects research who has even attempted to make such blanket generalizations on media effects across the board. Klapper offered a good starting point for those scholars of the 21st century brave enough to tackle the job of sorting through and studying the thousands of media effects studies that have been conducted through the years.

Klapper emphasized that he was "in no way committed to these particular generalizations, let alone to the exact form in which they here appear" (p. 9). He hoped that additional thought and research on the subject would "modify and perhaps annihilate the schema," and pointed out that he was "far less concerned with insuring the viability of these generalizations" than with "indicating that the time for generalization is at hand" (p. 9). "For certainly these particular generalizations do not usher in the millennium. They are imperfect and underdeveloped, they are inadequate in scope, and in some senses they are dangerous" (p. 251). It seems that, contrary to Klapper's view, his generalizations *do* usher us into the millennium. Forty years after Klapper insisted that generalizations needed to be made, the challenge remains unmet. It is our hope that this text will pique the interest of future media effects scholars who will meet the challenge of developing the long-awaited, overarching theory of media effects.

SUMMARY

The "established" history of media effects research offers a linear model of thought about the relative power of mass media messages on their audiences. In the years following World War I, scholars and the public believed that media possessed great power to influence the beliefs, attitudes, and actions of individuals in their audiences. This was called the "hypodermic-needle" theory or "bullet" theory of media influence. This model remained dominant until after the Depression when empirical studies indicated that the effects from mass media were not as powerful as originally thought. Studies by Lazarsfeld and Hovland indicated that mass media had only limited effects on individuals in their audiences. The limited effects model became firmly established in 1960 with the publication of Joseph Klapper's *The Effects of Mass Communication*. In the decades that followed, certain research findings and new theories did not fit into the limited effects model; therefore, the standard history was amended to include new studies that indicated that moderate to powerful media effects were indeed possible.

The standard scenario of "all-powerful effects to limited effects to moderate effects to powerful effects" provided a simple and convenient history of the field of media effects research. Unfortunately, the established history is neither satisfying nor accurate.

Our revised history of mass media effects research differs from the established version in the following: the acknowledgment of early, precursory media effects studies by psychologists, sociologists, and other investigators; the reevaluation of summary findings from some of the major studies; the inclusion of particular studies through the years that did not fit neatly into the "standard" scenario; the importance attributed to particular scholars; the emphasis on the advances in effects research through the years; and the identification of some sorely needed but still missing operational definitions for studies that will advance overall knowledge and allow generalizations regarding media effects.

This revised history emphasizes a body of research that has, from the beginning, found overwhelming evidence for significant effects from mass media communications on audiences, based for the most part upon scientific methods applying conventional statistical techniques. The history does not move in pendulum swings, due to the nonexistence of operational definitions to indicate the precise empirical ranges of "limited," or "moderate," or "powerful" effects. This history makes apparent the dire need for such operational definitions.

Our revised history acknowledges years of qualitative judgment calls on the part of researchers that label media effects in ranges from limited to powerful. It emphasizes that the debate about the relative power of mass media effects has been active since research on the subject began and remains an issue to this date. It also recognizes considerable advances in knowledge about media effects that have occurred through the years due to empirical investigations. Findings have indicated that media effects may be either cognitive (affecting thoughts or learning), behavioral (affecting behavior), or affective (affecting attitudes and emotions), and that the effects may be either direct, indirect, short-term, long-term, intermittent (e.g., sleeper effects), or cumulative. Findings have also revealed that individual differences, psychological factors, environmental factors, and social group characteristics cause audience members to perceive and react to media messages in specific ways.

In the future, media effects researchers will be challenged to come up with standard, empirical lines of demarcation that will classify effects as either powerful, moderate, or limited. Another challenge will be to identify the circumstances, conditions, or variables that account for media effects at their various levels and forms and make generalizations to explain the complex phenomenon of mass media effects. These generalizations should explain circumstances and conditions necessary for powerful or limited, direct or indirect, short-term or long-term, cumulative, cognitive, affective, and behavioral effects from mass media communications and, if possible, the factors present in a "no-effects" scenario. Despite these needs, we have learned a great deal about media effects through the years. Still, 40 years after Klapper's insistence that the time for media effects generalizations had arrived, we remain dependent upon his five generalizations for any overarching theory of media effects.

REFERENCES

ANDISON, F. (1977). TV violence and viewer aggression: A cumulation of study results 1956–1976. *Public Opinion Quarterly, 41,* 314–331.

ANGELL, J. R. (1941). Radio and national morale. *The American Journal of Sociology, 47,* 352–359.

ANNIS, A. D., & MEIER, N. C. (1934) The induction of opinion through suggestion by means of "planted content." *Journal of Social Psychology, 5,* 65–81.

BALL-ROKEACH, S. J., & DEFLEUR, M. L. (1976). A dependency model of mass-media effects. *Communication Research, 3,* 3–21.

BALL-ROKEACH, S. J., ROKEACH, M., & GRUBE, J. W. (1984a, November). The great American values test. *Psychology Today,* 34–41.

BALL-ROKEACH, S. J., ROKEACH, M., & GRUBE, J. W. (1984b). *The great American values test: Influencing behavior and belief through television.* New York: Free Press.

BANDURA, A. (1965). Vicarious processes: A case of no-trial learning. In L. Berkowitz (Ed.), *Advances in experimental social psychology* (Vol. 2, pp. 1–55). New York: Academic.

BANDURA, A. (1973). *Aggression: A social learning analysis.* Englewood Cliffs, NJ: Prentice Hall.

BANDURA, A. (1991). Social cognitive theory of moral thought and action. In W. M. Kurtines & J. L. Gerwitz (Eds.), *Handbook of moral behavior and development* (Vol. 1, pp. 45–103). Hillsdale, NJ: Erlbaum.

BANDURA, A., ROSS, D., & ROSS, S. A. (1963). Imitation of film-mediated aggressive models. *Journal of Abnormal and Social Psychology, 66,* 3–11.

BANDURA, A., & WALTERS, R. H. (1963). *Social learning and personality development.* New York: Holt, Rinehart and Winston.

BECKER, L. B., McCOMBS, M. E., & McLEOD, J. M. (1975). The development of political cognitions. In S. H. Chaffee (Ed.), *Political communication* (pp. 21–64). Newbury Park, CA: Sage.

BERELSON, B. (1948). Communications and public opinion. In W. Schramm (Ed.), *Communications in modern society* (pp. 168–185). Urbana, IL: University of Illinois Press.

BERELSON, B., & JANOWITZ, M. (1950). (Eds.). *Reader in public opinion and communication.* Glencoe, IL: The Free Press.

BERELSON, B. R., LAZARSFELD, P. F., & McPHEE, W. N. (1954). *Voting: A study of opinion formation in a presidential campaign.* Chicago: University of Chicago Press.

BEUICK, M. D. (1927). The limited social effect of radio broadcasting. *The American Journal of Sociology, 32,* 615–622.

BLUMER, H. (1951). The mass, the public, and public opinion. In A. M. Lee (Ed.). *New outlines of the principles of sociology* (2nd rev. ed.). New York: Barnes & Noble.

BLUMLER, J. G., & McLEOD, J. M. (1974). Communication and voter turnout in Britain. In T. Legatt (Eds.), *Sociological theory and social research* (pp. 265–312). Beverly Hills, CA: Sage.

BRITT, S. H., & MENEFEE, S. C. (1939). Did the publicity of the Dies Committee in 1938 influence public opinion? *Public Opinion Quarterly, 3,* 449–457.

BRUNTZ, G. G. (1938). *Allied propaganda and the collapse of the German empire in 1918.* Stanford: Stanford University Press.

BRYANT, J., & ZILLMANN, D. (1994). (Eds.). *Media effects: Advances in theory and research.* Mahwah, NJ: Erlbaum.

CANTOR, J., SPARKS, G. G., & HOFFNER, C. (1988). Calming children's television fears: Mr. Rogers vs. the Incredible Hulk. *Journal of Broadcasting & Electronic Media, 32,* 271–288.

CANTOR, J., & WILSON, B. J. (1984). Modifying fear responses to mass media in preschool and elementary school children. *Journal of Broadcasting, 28,* 431–443.

CANTRIL, H., GAUDET, H., & HERZOG, H. (1940). *The invasion from Mars: A study in the psychology of panic.* Princeton, NJ: Princeton University Press.

CAREY, J. W. (1996). The Chicago School and mass communication research. In E. E. Dennis & E. Wartella (Eds.), *American communication research: The remembered history* (pp. 21–38). Mahwah, N.J.: Erlbaum.

CARVETH, R. A., & BRYANT, J. (Eds.). (In press). *Meta-analyses of media effects.* Mahwah, NJ: Erlbaum.

CHAFFEE, S. H. (1977). Mass media effects. In D. Lerner & L. Nelson (Eds.), *Communication research* (pp. 210–241). Honolulu: University of Hawaii Press.

CHAFFEE, S. H., & HOCHHEIMER, J. L. (1985). The beginnings of political communication research in the United States: Origins of the "limited effects" model. In E. M. Rogers & F. Balle (Eds.), *The media revolution in America and Western Europe* (pp. 60–95). Norwood, NJ: Ablex.

CHARTERS, W. W. (1950). Motion pictures and youth. In B. Berelson & M. Janowitz (Eds.), *Reader in public opinion and communication* (pp. 397–406). Glencoe, IL: The Free Press.

CLARKE, P., & KLINE, F. G. (1974). Media effects reconsidered. *Communication Research, 1,* 224–240.

COOPER, E., & JAHODA, M. (1947). The evasion of propaganda: How prejudiced people respond to anti-prejudice propaganda. *Journal of Psychology, 23,* 15–25.

DENNIS, E. E., & WARTELLA, E. (Eds.) (1996). *American communication research: The remembered history.* Mahwah, NJ: Erlbaum.

FENTON, F. (1910). The influence of newspaper presentations upon the growth of crime and other anti-social activity. *The American Journal of Sociology, 16,* 342–371.

FENTON, F. (1911). The influence of newspaper presentations upon the growth of crime and other anti-social activity. *The American Journal of Sociology, 16,* 538–564.

FESTINGER, L., SCHACHTER, S., & BACH, K. (Eds.). (1950). *Social pressures in informal groups: A study of human factors in housing.* Stanford: Stanford University Press.

FOSTER, E., & GAMBLE, E. A. (1906). The effect of music on thoracic breathing. *The American Journal of Psychology, 17,* 406–414.

HEATH, R. L., & BRYANT, J. (2000). *Human communication theory and research: concepts, contexts, and challenges.* Mahwah, NJ: Erlbaum.

HOVLAND, C. I. (1954). Effects of the mass media on communication. In G. Lindzey (Ed.), *Handbook of social psychology, 2,* 1062–1103. Cambridge, MA: Addison-Wesley.

HOVLAND, C. I. (1959). Reconciling conflicting results derived from experimental and survey studies of attitude change. *American Psychologist, 14,* 8–17.

HOVLAND, C. I., LUMSDAINE, A. A., & SHEFFIELD, F. D. (1965). *Experiments on mass communication.* New York: Wiley. (Original work published 1949)

JENKS, J. W. (1895). The guidance of public opinion. *The American Journal of Sociology, 1,* 158–169.

KATZ, E. (1980). On conceptualizing media effects. In T. McCormack (Ed.), Studies in communication (Vol. 1 pp. 119–141). Greenwich, CT: JAI Press.

KATZ, E. (1983). On conceptualizing media effects. In S. Oskamp (Ed.), Television as a social issue, *Applied Social Psychology Annual, 8,* 361–374. Newbury Park, CA: Sage.

KLAPPER, J. T. (1949). *The effects of mass media, A report to the director of the public library inquiry.* New York: Columbia University Bureau of Applied Social Research.

KLAPPER, J. T. (1960). *The effects of mass communication.* New York: Free Press.

KLINE, L. W. (1907). The psychology of humor. *The American Journal of Psychology, 18,* 421–441.

LASSWELL, H. D. (1927). *Propaganda technique in the World War.* New York: Knopf.

LASSWELL, H. D. (1948). The structure and function of communication in society. In L. Bryson (Ed.), *The communication of ideas, a series of addresses* (pp. 37–51). Binghamton, NY: Vail-Ballou Press.

LAZARSFELD, P. F. (1940). *Radio and the printed page.* New York: Duell, Sloan and Pearce.

LAZARSFELD, P. F. (1949). Forward. In J. T. Klapper, *The effects of mass media, A report to the director of the public library inquiry* (pp. 1–9). New York: Columbia University Bureau of Applied Social Research.

LAZARSFELD, P. F. (1962). Introduction. In Stouffer, S. A., *Social research to test ideas, Selected writings of Samuel A. Stouffer* (pp. xv–xxxi). New York: The Free Press of Glencoe.

LAZARSFELD, P. F., BERELSON, B., & GAUDET, H. (1948). *The people's choice.* New York: Duell, Sloan, and Pearce. (Original work published 1944)

LAZARSFELD, P. F., & STANTON, F. N. (Eds.). (1942). *Radio research, 1941.* New York: Duell, Sloan, and Pearce.

LAZARSFELD, P. F., & STANTON, F. N. (Eds.). (1944). *Radio research, 1942–43.* New York: Duell, Sloan, and Pearce.

LERNER, D. (1949). *Sykewar; Psychological warfare against Germany, D-Day to VE-Day.* New York: G. W. Stewart.

LERNER, D., & NELSON, L. M. (1977). *Communication research—A half-century appraisal.* Honolulu: The University Press of Hawaii.

LIPPMANN, W. (1922). *Public opinion.* New York: Harcourt Brace.

LOWERY, S. A., & DeFLEUR, M. L. (1995). *Milestones in mass communication research, media effects* (3rd ed.). White Plains, NY: Longman.

LUNDBERG, G. A. (1926). The newspaper and public opinion. *Social Forces, 4,* 709–715.

MACCOBY, N., & FARQUHAR, J. W. (1975). Communication for health: Unselling heart disease. *Journal of Communication, 25,* 114–126.

McCOMBS, M. E., & SHAW, D. L. (1972). The agenda-setting function of mass media. *Public Opinion Quarterly, 36,* 176–187.

McGUIRE, W. J. (1986). The myth of massive media impact: Savagings and salvagings. *Public Communication and Behavior, 1,* 173–257.

McLEOD, J. M., & McDONALD, D. G. (1985). Beyond simple exposure: Media orientations and their impact on political processes. *Communication Research, 12,* 3–33.

McLUHAN, M. (1964). *Understanding media: The extensions of man.* New York: McGraw-Hill.

McQUAIL, D. (1972). *Towards a sociology of mass communications.* London: Collier-Macmillan. (Original work published 1969)

MENDELSOHN, H. (1973). Some reasons why information campaigns can succeed. *Public Opinion Quarterly, 37,* 50–61.

MERTON, R. K. (ASSISTED BY M. FISKE AND A. CURTIS). (1946). *Mass persuasion.* New York: Harper.

MOTT, F. L. (1944). Newspapers in presidential campaigns. *Public Opinion Quarterly, 8,* 348–367.

National Institute of Mental Health. (1983). Television and behavior: Ten years of scientific progress and implications for the eighties. In E. Wartella & D. C. Whitney (Eds.), *Mass communication review yearbook*, (Vol. 4, pp. 23–35). Beverly Hills, CA: Sage.

NOELLE-NEUMANN, E. (1973). Return to the concept of powerful mass media. *Studies of Broadcasting, 9,* 67–112.

ORTON, W. (1927). News and opinion. *The American Journal of Sociology, 33,* 80–93.

PARK, R. E. (1941). News and the power of the press. *The American Journal of Sociology, 47,* 1–11.

PETERSON, R. C., & THURSTONE, L. L. (1933). *Motion pictures and the social attitudes of children.* New York: Macmillan.

RANNEY, A. (1983). *Channels of power.* New York: Basic Books.

ROGERS, E. M. (1994). *A history of communication study: A biographical aproach.* New York: The Free Press.

ROGERS, E. M., & CHAFFEE, S. H. (Eds.) (1997). *The beginnings of communication study in America, A personal memoir by Wilbur Schramm.* Thousand Oaks, CA: Sage.

SCHRAMM, W. (1997). Carl Hovland: Experiments, attitudes, and communication. In S. H. Chaffee & E. M. Rogers (Eds.). *The beginnings of communication study in America: A personal memoir by Wilbur Schramm* (pp. 87–105). Thousand Oaks, CA: Sage.

SEVERIN, W. J., & TANKARD, JR., J. W. (1992). *Communication theories: Origins, methods, and uses in the mass media* (3rd ed.). New York: Longman.

SHEPARD, W. J. (1909). Public opinion. *The American Journal of Sociology, 15,* 32–60.

SMITH, B. L., LASSWELL, H. D., & CASEY, R. D. (1946). *Propaganda, communication, and public opinion: A comprehensive reference guide.* Princeton: Princeton University Press.

STOUFFER, S. A. (1942). A sociologist looks at communications research. In D. Waples (Ed.), *Print, radio, and film in a democracy: Ten papers on the administration of mass communications in the public interest—read before the Sixth Annual Institute of the Graduate Library School, The University of Chicago—August 4–9, 1941,* pp. 133–146. Chicago: The University of Chicago Press.

Surgeon General's Scientific Advisory Committee on Television and Social Behavior. (1972). *Television and growing up: The impact of televised violence.* Washington, DC: U.S. Government Printing Office.

TARDE, G. (1912). *Penal philosophy.* Boston: Little, Brown, and Company.

THOMPSON, S., & BRYANT, J. (2000 June). *Debunking the media effects gospel: A reexamination of media effects research history and directions for researchers of the twenty-first century.* Paper presented at the International Communication Association 50th Annual Conference, Acapulco, Mexico.

TITCHENER, E. B. (1898). Minor studies from the psychological laboratory of Cornell University: Distraction by musical sounds; the effect of pitch upon attention. *The American Journal of Psychology, 99,* 332–345.

TICHENOR, P., DONOHUE, G., & OLIEN, C. (1970). Mass media flow and differential growth in knowledge. *Public Opinion Quarterly, 34,* 159–170.

WAPLES, D. (1942a). Communications. *The American Journal of Sociology 47,* 907–917.

WAPLES, D. (Ed.). (1942b). *Print, radio, and film in a democracy.* Chicago: The University of Chicago Press.

WAPLES, D., BERELSON, B., & BRADSHAW, F. R. (1940). *What reading does to people: A summary of evidence on the social effects of reading and a statement of problems for research.* Chicago: University of Chicago Press.

WARTELLA, E. (1996). The history reconsidered. In E. E. Dennis & E. Wartella (Eds.), *American communication research—The remembered history* (pp. 169–180). Mahwah, NJ: Erlbaum.

WELD, H. P. (1912). An experimental study of musical enjoyment. *The American Journal of Psychology, 23,* 245–309.

WOOD, W., WONG, F. Y., & CACHERE, G. (1991). Effects of media violence on viewers' aggression in unconstrained social interaction. *Psychological Bulletin, 109,* 371–383.

WRIGHT, C. R. (1960). Functional analysis and mass communication. *Public Opinion Quarterly, 24,* 605–620.

YARROS, V. S. (1899). The press and public opinion. *The American Journal of Sociology, 5,* 372–382.

ENDNOTES

1. Difficult but not impossible: F. L. Mott (1944) conducted a historical study and found "no correlation, positive or negative, between the support of a majority of newspapers during a campaign and success at the polls" (p. 356). Another instance of limited effects that could be argued is indicated by Isaiah Thomas's *History of Printing,* which offered state-by-state counts on the number of newspapers for and against ratification of the Constitution. In some cases, newspapers seemed to have little or no effect upon the outcome of the vote. In Delaware, for example, no newspapers favored adoption and two opposed adoption, yet Delaware was the first state to adopt the Constitution—and by unanimous vote at its convention.

2. Blumer's statement, originally written in 1939, was later called by Denis McQuail (1972/1969) "the most influential single statement of the concept of the mass, looked at from the perspective of the sociology of collective behaviour" (p. 100).

3. None used these terms, however. Many have attributed the "hypodermic needle" phrase to Lasswell, but a re-reading of Lasswell's works revealed he used no such phrase (Chaffee & Hochheimer, 1985).

4. Carey wrote: "Lippmann, in fact, redefined the problem of the media from one of morals, politics, and freedom to one of psychology and epistemology. He established the tradition of propaganda analysis and simultaneously, by framing the problem not as one of normative political theory but as one of human psychology, opened up the tradition of effects analysis that was to dominate the literature less than two decades after the publication of *Public Opinion*" (Carey, 1996, p. 30).

5. Rogers (1994) offers information about many others who made important contributions to communication study, including mass media effects research. The student is encouraged to refer to this work.

6. It should be recalled from the standard history that Hovland's U.S. Army studies reportedly showed limited media effects; however, the limits of the effects extended only to attitude change—the films proved to have much stronger effects on learning; that is, the soldiers learned a great deal from the films.

7. More recent findings (Blumler & McLeod, 1974; McLeod & McDonald, 1985; Ranney, 1983) suggest that the influence of mass media may be more powerful in the political communication process than the findings of *The People's Choice* indicated.

8. Wright (1960) added "entertainment" as another important function of mass media.

9. Rogers (1994, p. 352) offered this example of cognitive dissonance: "One effect of dissonance is for an individual to avoid exposure to conflicting messages. For example, once an individual purchases a new car, that individual tends to avoid advertisements for competing makes of cars."

10. One explored the different advantages of radio and newspaper as news sources, and identified preferences for one or the other among various classes and groups of people. Another examined the effect that radio was having on newspaper circulation. Both were included in Lazarsfeld's *Radio and the Printed Page* (1940).

11. The conference proceedings are included in the papers of Lyman Bryson at the Library of Congress (Rockefeller Foundation, "Needed Research in Communication", "Public Opinion and the Emergency", and "Memorandum on Communications Conference," U.S. Library of Congress: Papers of Lyman Bryson, Box 18, October 17, 1940, November 1, 1940, and January 18, 1941).

12. Bandura began studying children and teens and the learning of antisocial behavior by viewing models' actions on films or on television during the 1960s (e.g., Bandura, 1965; Bandura, Ross, & Ross, 1963; Bandura & Walters, 1963).

13. Some of the recent works of Cantor and her associates (Cantor, Sparks & Hoffner, 1988; Cantor & Wilson, 1984) have explored ways in which effects may be diminished, but a "no effects" model has never been advanced.

CHAPTER 22

Cultivation Analysis

*Based on the research of **George Gerbner***

Joyce Jensen

Joyce Jensen was preparing to vote for the very first time. She had been looking forward to this privilege since she was 12 years old. She considered herself a news junkie, and she'd always devoured the morning newspaper, the local TV news, CNN, the national network news, *Time,* and *Newsweek*. She made it a point to watch C-SPAN, a cable station dedicated to the world of politics. She knew that she was one of only a handful in her class who could identify all of the U.S. Supreme Court justices. She was ready to take some flak as a news nerd because the world fascinated her. She always knew that when she turned 18, she'd be prepared for the right and responsibility of voting.

Now she was faced with a decision as she voted for her state's governor. Although undecided, she was leaning toward Roberta Johndrew, the tough-on-crime candidate. Johndrew favored greater use of the death penalty, limits on appeals by people convicted of crimes, and putting more police on the street. Yet Joyce thought that Frank Milnes, the education candidate, had some good ideas as well. Crime—in Joyce's state and in the country as a whole—was down for the sixth consecutive year. The statistics were most impressive, Milnes said, when considering violent crime. All types of violent crime had been in decline for nearly a decade. Milnes argued that money being spent for more police, more prisons, and more executions would be better spent on improving schools. After all, Milnes asserted, more dollars in the state were being spent on incarceration than

on educating young people. Better schools, he argued, would mean even less crime in the future. "What kind of state do we live in," he demanded in his campaign literature, "when we refuse to give raises to our teachers and pay our prison guards more than our teachers?"

Those were powerful arguments, thought Joyce. She regretted that teachers were not getting paid commensurate with their expertise and responsibilities. She knew that she wanted to have children eventually, and she wanted them to get the best education possible. She could see how paying teachers more might help achieve that.

But as a young, single woman, these arguments were secondary to safety considerations. There seemed to be so much crime in the city. Every night when she watched the news on television, there seemed to be more crimes reported. She was often uncomfortable when she was out at night. At times, she even felt uneasy being at home alone. Maybe it is an irrational fear, she thought to herself, but it's there and it feels real.

As Joyce pondered her vote in the booth, so much was going through her mind. She considered her present situation as a single woman as well as her desire for future children. She reflected on both Roberta Johndrew and Frank Milnes and their comments over the past several months. As she contemplated her options for another moment or two, she felt she would be able to make a good decision. So much depended on citizens making informed choices. Joyce was thrilled to exercise her right as a U.S. citizen.

Television is as much a part of the human experience in the United States as family. All across our country, people tune in to a variety of television programs, from soap operas to C-SPAN. We are a society reliant on TV and what it has to offer each day. Television has found its way into our living rooms, our conversations, and even our psyches. This invention from the 1940s has sustained itself well into the new millennium.

Responding to the pervasiveness of television in society over thirty years ago, George Gerbner and his colleague Lawrence Gross (1972) commented that people watch television as though they were attending church, except that they typically watch television more religiously. Focusing their work on the effects of television (a topic we return to later), Gerbner and Gross embarked on the Cultural Indicators Project, conducting regular, periodic examinations of television programming and the "conceptions of social reality that viewing cultivates in child and adult audiences" (p. 174). In initiating what would become known as Cultivation Analysis, they were making a **causal argument** (television cultivates—causes—conceptions of social reality). Cultivation Analysis is a theory that predicts and explains the long-term formation and shaping of perceptions, understandings, and beliefs about the world as a result of consumption of media messages. Gerbner's line of thinking in Cultivation Analysis suggests that mass communication, especially television, cultivates certain beliefs about reality that are held in common by mass communication consumers. As Gerbner observes, "most of what we know, or think we know, we have never personally experienced" (Gerbner, 1999, p. ix). We "know" these things because of the stories we see and hear in the media (Buffington & Fraley, 2008).

causal argument
an assertion of cause and effect, including the direction of the causality

Cultivation researchers can easily explain Joyce Jensen's voting quandary. Official statistics that indicate that violent crime is in steady decline are certainly real enough. But so, too, is Joyce's feeling of unease and insecurity when she is alone. Cultivation Analysis would refer to these feelings of insecurity as her social reality. Moreover, that reality is as real as any other for Joyce, and it is media fueled, if not media created and maintained.

Iver Peterson (2002) made a similar observation about the anthrax scares in the United States post–September 11, 2001. He notes that although the (media-fueled) fears about anthrax are very pervasive and real, the actual cases of anthrax contamination are rare. Peterson quotes Clifton R. Lacy, commissioner of the New Jersey Department of Health and Senior Services, as saying that the risks to the citizens of New Jersey by anthrax spores are "vanishingly small" (p. A21). Dr. Lacy also urged people to take to heart the message that there have been no new cases in the state since October 2001.

In the 1970s, Gerbner's view that media messages alter traditional notions of time, space, and social groupings was a direct challenge to the prevailing thought that media had little, if any, effect on individuals and on the culture. Like Uses and Gratifications Theory, which we discuss in Chapter 23, Cultivation Analysis was developed in response to the beliefs about the media's limited effects that were dominant at the time. More important, however, it reflects media theory's slow transformation from reliance on the transmissional perspective to greater acceptance of the ritual perspective of mass communication.

Calvin and Hobbes   by Bill Watterson

transmissional perspective
a position depicting the media as senders of messages across space

ritual perspective
a position depicting the media as representers of shared beliefs

The **transmissional perspective** sees media as senders of messages—discrete bits of information—across space. This perspective and limited effects theories are comfortable partners. If all media do is transmit bits of information, people can choose to use or not use that information as they wish. In the **ritual perspective**, however, media are conceptualized not as a means of transmitting "messages in space" but as central to "the maintenance of society in time" (Carey, 1975, p. 6). Mass communication is "not the act of imparting information but the representation of shared beliefs" (p. 6).

Developing Cultivation Analysis

Gerbner first used the term *cultivation* in 1969; however, Cultivation Analysis, as a discrete and powerful theory, did not emerge for a number of years. It evolved over time through a series of methodological and theoretical steps by Gerbner and his colleagues and, as such, reflects that development.

During the 1960s, interest in media effects, particularly effects of television, ran very high. The federal government was concerned about media's influence on society, especially media's possible contribution to rising levels of violence among young people. In 1967 President Lyndon Johnson ordered the creation of the National Commission on the Causes and Prevention of Violence. It was followed in 1972 by the surgeon general's Scientific Advisory Committee on Television and Social Behavior. Both groups examined media (especially television) and their impact (especially the effects of aggression and violence). Gerbner, a respected social scientist, was involved in both efforts.

Violence Index
a yearly content analysis of prime-time network programming to assess the amount of violence represented

Gerbner's task was to produce an annual **Violence Index**, a yearly content analysis of a sample week of network television prime-time content that would show, from season to season, how much violence was actually present on television. Its value to those interested in the media violence issue was obvious: If the link between television fare and subsequent viewer aggression was to be made, the presence of violence on television needed to be demonstrated. Moreover, observers would be able to correlate annual increases in the amount of violent television content with annual increases in the amount of real-world violent crime. But the index was immediately challenged by both media industry and limited effects researchers. How was violence defined? Was verbal aggression violence? Was obviously fake violence on a comedy counted the same as more realistically portrayed violence on a drama? Why examine only prime-time network television, because children's heaviest viewing occurs at other times of the day? Why focus on violence? Why not examine other social ills, such as racism and sexism?

Gerbner and his associates continuously refined the Index to meet the complaints of its critics, and what their annual counting demonstrated was that violence appeared on prime-time television at levels unmatched in the real world. The 1982 Index, for example, showed that "crime in prime time is at least 10 times as rampant as in the real world (and) an average of five to six acts of overt physical violence per hour involves over half of all major characters" (Gerbner, Gross, Morgan, & Signorielli, 1982, p. 106).

Cultivation Analysis • Theory at a Glance

Television and other media play an extremely important role in how people view their world. In today's society, most people get their information from mediated sources rather than through direct experience. Therefore, mediated sources can shape a person's sense of reality. This is especially the case with regard to violence. Heavy television viewing cultivates a sense of the world as a violent place, and heavy television viewers perceive that there is more violence in the world than there actually is or than lighter viewers perceive.

Assumptions of Cultivation Analysis

In advancing the position that mediated reality causes consumers to cultivate their own social reality, Cultivation Analysis makes a number of assumptions. Because it was and still remains primarily a television-based theory, these three assumptions speak to the relationship between that medium and the culture:

- Television is essentially and fundamentally different from other forms of mass media.
- Television shapes our society's way of thinking and relating.
- The influence of television is limited.

The first assumption of Cultivation Analysis underscores the uniqueness of television. Television is in more than 98 percent of all U.S. homes. It requires

Research Notes

Glascock, J., & Ruggerio, T. E. (2004). Representations of class and gender of primetime Spanish-language television in the United States. *Communication Quarterly, 52,* 390–402.

This study examines Spanish-language television available in the United States on three networks (Univision, Telemundo, and TV Azteca) through a content analysis. Six telenovelas and one drama were analyzed for gender roles, class, sexual talk, and physical and verbal aggression. The findings included that women were shown almost as often as men, and that they were more likely to play lead roles than men. Similar to U.S. television, women were depicted as having more household and child care responsibilities and having less job status. Gender-role stereotypes were more pronounced on the Spanish-language shows than on U.S. network prime-time programming, and men were more physically and verbally aggressive (although the overall amount of physical aggression was less than on U.S. TV).

The authors reflect on the sense of reality that is being cultivated in the minds of viewers by this type of programming.

Wilson, B. J., Martins, N., & Marske, A. L. (2005). Children's and parents' fright reactions to kidnapping stories in the news. *Communication Monographs, 72,* 46–70.

This study is based on a random telephone survey of 182 parents of children between the ages of 5 and 18 who were asked to report on their own, and their perception of their children's, fears about kidnapping. Respondents were also asked about

their own and their children's exposure to television and other media. The phone interviews lasted approximately 20 minutes.

In general, they found that children's fears were reduced with age, as the parents reported that their older children had fewer fears about kidnapping than did their younger children. Parents also reported that they were more fearful than were their children. In terms of the relationship of media exposure and fear, the study revealed a pattern that "poses a challenge to cultivation theory . . . [because the] data suggest that heavy viewing of news can cultivate fear of abduction in children, but that TV viewing in general does not" (p. 63).

Partial support was obtained for CA in the parents' responses about their own fears and media habits. Parents who paid close attention to media reports about kidnapping were more afraid than those who did not, but the sheer amount of TV viewing did not predict parents' fear or perception of kidnapping. Further, the authors found that parents who read newspapers regularly "tended to estimate *fewer* child kidnappings each year and also tended to be less frightened by the kidnapping stories, even after controlling for education" (p. 65).

In conclusion, the authors observe that their study was conducted in a small town with a very low level of violent crime. Yet 30 percent of their respondents said the news stories about kidnapping had caused them to forbid their children to be outside alone, and 12 percent noted that they'd bought protection devices for their children as a result of the media reports. These results lend some support to Cultivation Analysis.

---

no literacy, as do print media. Unlike the movies, it can be free (beyond the initial cost of the set and the cost of advertising added to the products we buy). Unlike radio, it combines pictures and sound. It requires no mobility, as do church attendance and going to the movies or the theater. Television is the only medium ever invented that is ageless—that is, people can use it at the earliest and latest years of life, as well as all those years in between.

Theory Application in Groups (TAG)

In small groups, research the actual number of violent crimes in your community from a governmental source. Compare that number to a night of prime-time television's representation of violent crimes. Use the following definition of violent crimes from the U.S. Department of Justice: murder, rape, robbery, and aggravated assault.

Because of this accessibility and availability to everyone, television is the "central cultural arm" of our society (Gerbner, Gross, Jackson-Beeck, Jeffries-Fox, & Signorielli, 1978, p. 178). Television draws together dissimilar groups and can show their similarities. For instance, during the initial attacks of the war in Iraq, television transmitted live signals from Baghdad. Those in support of the bombings pointed to the importance of hitting key military targets, whereas those opposed to the war noted the number of civilian casualties. It was television that allowed both sides to invoke disparate images of the war. In other words, television is the culture's primary storyteller and has the ability to gather together different groups. In addition, who can doubt the role that television has played in working through the nation's story about the tragedy of September 11, 2001? Hurricane Katrina? California brush fines?

The second assumption pertains to the influence of television. Gerbner and Gross (1972) comment that "the substance of the consciousness cultivated by TV is not so much specific attitudes and opinions as more basic assumptions about the 'facts' of life and standards of judgment on which conclusions are based" (p. 175). That is, television doesn't so much persuade us (it didn't try to convince Joyce Jensen that the streets are unsafe) as paint a more or less convincing picture of what the world is like. Gerbner (1998) observed that television reaches people, on average, more than seven hours each day. During this time, television offers "a centralized system of story-telling" (p. 177). Gerbner agrees with Walter Fisher, whom we discussed in Chapter 20, that people live in stories. Gerbner, however, asserts that most of the stories in modern society now come from television.

Television's major cultural function is to stabilize social patterns, to cultivate resistance to change. Television is a medium of socialization and enculturation. Gerbner and his cohorts eloquently state that

> the repetitive pattern of television's mass-produced messages and images forms the mainstream of the common symbolic environment that cultivates the most widely shared conceptions of reality. We live in terms of the stories we tell—stories about what things exist, stories about how things work, and stories about what to do—and television tells them all through news, drama, and advertising to almost everybody most of the time. (Gerbner et al., 1978, p. 178)

Where did Joyce Jensen's—and other voters'—shared conceptions of reality about crime and personal safety come from? Cultivation researchers would immediately point to television, where, despite a nationwide 20 percent drop in the homicide rate between 1993 and 1996, for example, the number of murder stories on the network evening news soared 721 percent (Kurtz, 1998). This distortion has continued in ways that the theory would predict. Barbara Wilson and her colleagues (Wilson, Martins, & Marske, 2005) found that parents who paid a great deal of attention to television news thought their children were more at risk for kidnapping than those parents who watched less TV. Yet the Bureau of Justice Statistics rates of violent crimes among 12- to 19-year-olds since 1973 does not support this belief. The findings indicate that in 1973 the rate of violent crimes against children ages 12–19 was approximately eighty cases per 1,000 children. Thirty years later, in 2003, the rate had dropped to approximately fifty per 1,000 youth (Bureau of Justice statistics, 2004). Further, kidnapping makes up less than 2 percent of all violent crimes against youth (Finklehor & Ormrod, 2000).

Based on this assumption, Cultivation Analysis supplies an alternative way of thinking about TV violence. Some theories, like Social Learning Theory (Bandura, 1977), assume that we become more violent after being exposed to violence. Other approaches, like the notion of catharsis, would suggest that watching violence purges us of our own violent impulses and we actually become less violent. Cultivation Analysis does not speak to what we will do based on watching violent television; instead, it assumes that watching violent TV makes us feel afraid because it cultivates within us the image of a mean and dangerous world.

The third assumption of Cultivation Analysis states that television's effects are limited. This may sound peculiar, given the fact that television is so pervasive. Yet the observable, measurable, and independent contributions of television to the culture are relatively small. This may sound like a restatement of minimal effects thinking, but Gerbner uses an ice age analogy to distance Cultivation Analysis from limited effects. The **ice age analogy** states that "just as an average temperature shift of a few degrees can lead to an ice age or the outcomes of elections can be determined by slight margins, so too can a relatively small but pervasive influence make a crucial difference. The 'size' of an 'effect' is far less critical than the direction of its steady contribution" (Gerbner, Gross, Morgan, & Signorielli, 1980, p. 14). The argument is not that television's impact is inconsequential. Rather, although television's measurable, observable, and independent effect on the culture at any point in time might be small, that impact is nonetheless present and significant. Further, Gerbner and his associates argue that it is not the case that watching a specific television program causes a specific behavior (e.g., that watching *Without a Trace* will cause someone to kidnap another person) but rather that watching television in general has a cumulative and pervasive impact on our vision of the world.

ice age analogy
a position stating that television doesn't have to have a single major impact, but influences viewers through steady limited effects

Processes and Products of Cultivation Analysis

Cultivation Analysis has been applied to a wide variety of effects issues, as well as to different situations in which television viewers find themselves. In doing so, researchers have developed specific processes and products related to the theory.

The Four-Step Process

To empirically demonstrate their belief that television has an important causal effect on the culture, Cultivation researchers developed a four-step process. The first step, *message system analysis*, consists of detailed content analyses of television programming in order to demonstrate its most recurring and consistent presentations of images, themes, values, and portrayals. For example, it is possible to conduct a message system analysis of the number of episodes of bodily harm on such shows as *Laws & Order* and *CSI*.

The second step, *formulation of questions about viewers' social realities*, involves developing questions about people's understandings of their everyday lives. For example, a typical Cultivation Analysis question is, "In any given week, what are the chances that you will be involved in some kind of violence? About 1 in 10 or about 1 in 100?" Another is, "Of all the crime that occurs in the United States in any year, what proportion is violent crime like rape, murder, assault, and robbery?"

The third step, *surveying the audience*, requires that the questions from step two be posed to audience members *and* that researchers ask these viewers about their levels of television consumption.

Finally, step four entails *comparing the social realities of light and heavy viewers*. For Gerbner, a "cultivation differential" exists between light and heavy viewers and perceptions of violence. **Cultivation differential** can be defined as the percentage of difference in response between light and heavy television viewers. Gerbner (1998) explains that amount of viewing is used in relative terms. Thus, heavy viewers are those who watch the most in any sample of people that are measured, whereas light viewers are those who watch the least.

cultivation differential
the percentage of difference in response between light and heavy television viewers

Mainstreaming and Resonance

How does television contribute to viewers' conceptions of social reality? The process of cultivation occurs in two ways. One is mainstreaming. **Mainstreaming** occurs when, especially for heavier viewers, television's symbols dominate other sources of information and ideas about the world. As a result of heavy viewing, people's constructed social realities move toward the mainstream—not a mainstream in any political sense, but a culturally dominant reality that is more similar to television's reality than to any measurable, objective external reality. Heavy viewers tend to believe the mainstreamed realities that the world is a more dangerous place than it really is, that all politicians are corrupt, that teen crime is at record high levels, that African American families are all on welfare, that illegitimate births are skyrocketing, and so forth.

Mainstreaming means that heavy television viewers of different co-cultures are more similar in their beliefs about the world than their varying group membership might suggest. Thus, African Americans and European Americans who are heavy television viewers would perceive the world more similarly than might be expected. As Gerbner (1998) states, "Differences that usually are associated with the varied cultural, social, and political characteristics of these groups are diminished in the responses of heavy viewers in these same groups" (p. 183).

mainstreaming
the tendency for heavy viewers to perceive a similar culturally dominant reality to that pictured on the media although this differs from actual reality

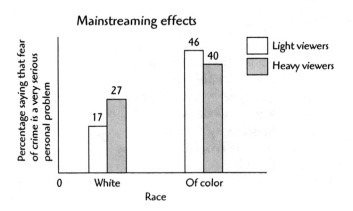

Mainstreaming effects

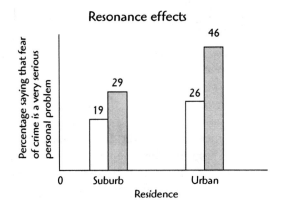

Resonance effects

Figure 22.1
Effects of Mainstreaming and Resonance
Source: Adapted from "The Mainstreaming of America: Violence Profile No. 11" by Gerber et al. in *Journal of Communication,* vol. 7 (1980), p. 16, Figure 2. Reprinted by permission of John Wiley & Sons Ltd.

resonance
occurs when a viewer's lived reality coincides with the reality pictured in the media

first order effects
a method for cultivation to occur; refers to learning facts from the media

second order effects
a method for cultivation to occur; refers to learning values and assumptions from the media

The second way cultivation operates is through resonance. **Resonance** occurs when things on television are, in fact, congruent with viewers' actual everyday realities. In other words, people's objective external reality resonates with that of television. Some urban dwellers, for example, may see the violent world of television resonated in their deteriorating neighborhoods. As Gerbner (1998) notes, this provides "a 'double dose' of messages that 'resonate' and amplify cultivation" (p. 182). The social reality that is cultivated for these viewers may in fact match their objective reality, but its possible effect is to preclude the formation of a more optimistic social reality; it denies them hope that they can build a better life. See Figure 22.1 for a representation of the effects of mainstreaming and resonance.

Cultivation, either as mainstreaming or as resonance, produces effects on two levels. **First order effects** refer to the learning of facts such as how many employed males are involved in law enforcement or what proportion of marriages end in divorce. For example, Joyce Jensen knew from candidate Milnes's television spots that the amount of crime in her state was in decline. **Second order effects** involve "hypotheses about more general issues and assumptions" that people make about their environments (Gerbner, Gross, Morgan, & Signorielli, 1986, p. 28). Questions like, Do you think people are basically honest? and Do you think police should be allowed to use greater force to subdue criminals? are aimed at these second order effects.

The Mean World Index

A product of Cultivation Analysis is the Mean World Index (Gerbner, Gross, Morgan, & Signorielli, 1980), which consists of a series of three statements:

- Most people are just looking out for themselves.
- You can't be too careful in dealing with people.
- Most people would take advantage of you if they got the chance.

Cultivation Analysis predicts that agreement with these statements from heavy and light viewers will differ, with heavy viewers seeing the world as a meaner place than light viewers. It also predicts that the amount of television viewing is the best predictor of people's answers, overwhelming other kinds of distinctions among different people—for example, income and education.

Gerbner and his colleagues (1980) demonstrated the efficacy of their Mean World Index in a study that showed heavy viewers were much more likely to see the world as a mean place than were light viewers. Better-educated, financially better-off viewers in general saw the world as less mean than did those with less education and income. But in testing the power of television, the researchers demonstrated that heavy viewers from the better-educated, better-off groups saw the world as being as dangerous as did low-income and less-educated people. In other words, heavy viewers held a mainstreamed perception of the world as a mean place, regardless of factors such as education and income. Cultivation researchers see this as evidence that television content is a factor in the construction of social realities for heavy viewers, regardless of individual or social differences.

Gerbner and his associates identify a number of other areas where the two types of viewers might differ. They include their beliefs about the likelihood of involvement with a violent crime, their fear of walking at night, and their perceptions of law enforcement. The findings are intriguing. First, they found that people with light viewing habits believed that about 1 in 100 will be a victim of violence; heavy viewers of television predicted that about 1 in 10 will be involved in violence. Second, they found that more women than men were fearful of walking alone at night and that heavy viewers overestimated the amount of violent crime. Third, heavy viewers felt that 5 percent of the culture is involved in law enforcement, whereas light viewers felt that 1 percent is involved. Important to the logic of Cultivation Analysis is that the responses of the heavy viewers mirror quite accurately the results of content analyses of television, where violence is usually recorded in heavy doses: Because violence is so common on television, heavy viewers are more likely to be fearful or mistrustful of the real world. Given what we've presented here, Joyce Jensen's viewing habits may be influencing her thinking about her choice between Milnes and Johndrew.

Cultivation Analysis as Critical Theory

Cultivation Analysis has made an important contribution to contemporary thinking about mass communication. Horace Newcomb (1978), an early commentator about Cultivation Analysis, wrote of Gerbner and his colleagues:

Table 22.1 The Three Bs of Television

TERM	DEFINITION	EXAMPLE
Blurring	Traditional distinctions are blurred.	Educated people see the world similarly to those who have less education.
Blending	"Reality" is blended into a cultural mainstream.	We agree on what's real.
Bending	The mainstream reality benefits the elite.	We all want to buy more products.

"Their foresight to collect data on a systematic, long-term basis, to move out of the laboratory and away from the closed experimental model, will enable other researchers to avoid costly mistakes. Their material holds a wealth of information" (p. 281).

But just what is the role of television in our culture uncovered by the Cultivation Analysis researchers? Cultivation theorists would argue that Joyce Jensen's apprehension—and the vote for the tough-on-crime candidate it might produce—is based on a view of the world that is cultivated by television. Learning from television produces not only perceptions of a mean world (which researchers in Cultivation Analysis argue become a self-fulfilling prophecy as people's distrust of others breeds an atmosphere of further distrust) but also a warping of political, social, and cultural discourse. How many political candidates, they ask, have the courage to argue against the building of more prisons or against the death penalty? The issue is not the validity of these positions but the absence of meaningful, objective debate on them. The argument here is similar to that offered by Elizabeth Noelle-Neumann's Spiral of Silence Theory, which we discuss in Chapter 24: People may be less willing to speak out about alternative approaches to crime and crime prevention because the media, especially television, cultivate a dominant social reality that renders these conversations out of step with the voters.

How can television be so powerful a force if its influence occurs as slowly as the coming of the ice age? Gerbner answers this question with his 3 Bs of television. Television, he wrote, blurs traditional distinctions of people's views of their world, blends people's realities into television's cultural mainstream, and bends that mainstream to the institutional interests of television and its sponsors (Table 22.1). Television's power rests in its utilization by powerful industries and elites to meet their, rather than the culture's, interests. Cultivation Analysis is a critical theory, as we described it in Chapter 3, because it is concerned with the way that communication perpetuates the dominance of one group over another (Littlejohn & Foss, 2008). As James Shanahan and Victoria Jones (1999) argue,

> Cultivation is sometimes taken as a return to a strong "powerful effects" view of mass media. This view isn't completely incorrect, but it misses the point that cultivation was originally conceived as a *critical* theory, which

Theory Into Practice

Nelly

I have to say that I have rarely seen a family like mine on TV. But I am not sure that's all bad. I have to see my family all the time so I don't know if I want to watch people that look like us on TV for entertainment. My family is pretty boring and not really funny so I can't imagine anyone would want to watch us. But, now that I think about it, it is annoying that no one on TV looks normal—even the people on so-called reality TV are so much better looking than the average person, I can't believe it. It's not as bad as violence, but it does cultivate the idea that people are supposed to look like super models.

happens to address media issues precisely and only because the mass media (especially television) serve the function of storytelling. (p. 32)

Cultivation Analysis, as a critical theory, examines an important social institution (television) in terms of how it uses its storytelling function to serve ends other than the benefit of the larger society. In 1996, Gerbner helped found the worldwide Cultural Environment Movement to assist people in their struggle against powerful media industries. Its *Viewers' Declaration of Independence* reads, in part, "Let the world hear the reasons that compel us to assert our rights and take an active role in the shaping of our common cultural environment. . . . Humans live and learn by stories. Today they are no longer hand-crafted, home-made, community-inspired. They are no longer told by families, schools, or churches but are the products of a complex mass-production and marketing process" (Cultural Environment Movement, 1996, p. 1). Gerbner (1998) continues to be concerned with the effects created by stories told by agencies that do not aim to teach but rather aim to sell.

In addition, Cultivation Analysis shares another characteristic with other critical theories: It is political; that is, in accepting its assumptions, its proponents must commit to doing something about the situation.

George Gerbner has taken to heart the critical researcher's call to action. In the mid-1990s, he developed the PROD (Proportional Representation of Diversity) index. The goal of the index was to examine the distortion in representation of various co-cultures "across the demography of the media landscape" (Shanahan & Morgan, 1999, p. 223). The index determined how well or poorly groups were represented on television relative to their numbers in the population. The first index Gerbner produced surveyed broadcast network programming and major Hollywood films for 1995–1996. Almost every group (women, African Americans, Latinos, Asians, Native Americans, under age 18, over age 65, gay men and lesbians, disabled, and the poor or lower class) listed in the diversity index was grossly underrepresented in the media. The only group that was not was Native Americans, and this is probably explained by their relatively low population proportionally.

Gerbner took his critical role seriously and stated in a press release associated with the presentation of the index, "Far from being 'quotas' to be imposed on creative people, the Index reflects the limitations on creative freedom in the television and motion picture industries. This is a 'report card' of industry performance. We look forward to steady improvement in the diversity and equity of the cultural environment into which our children are born and in which they come to define themselves and others" (Gerbner, 1997, cited in Shanahan & Morgan, 1999, p. 223). Gerbner believed it is important to highlight how the media industries reflect the needs and perspectives of dominant groups. A more recent report analyzing the 2001 fall session of network programing came to similar conclusions (UCLA Center for African American Studies, 2002).

Integration, Critique, and Closing

Gerbner and his colleagues have been influential in identifying television as a shaping force in society. Cultivation Analysis helps explain the implications of viewing habits, and it has been a very popular theory in mass communication research. In a study conducted by Jennings Bryant and Dorina Miron (2004) surveying almost 2,000 articles published in the three top mass communication journals since 1956, the theory was the third most frequently utilized theory. As you think about Cultivation Analysis, the following criteria for evaluation are addressed: logical consistency, utility, heurism, and test of time.

Integration

Communication Tradition	Rhetorical	Semiotic	Phenomenological	Cybernetic	Socio-Psychological	**Socio-Cultural**	**Critical**
Communication Context	Intrapersonal	Interpersonal	Small Group	Organizational	Public/Rhetorical	**Mass/Media**	Cultural
Approach to Knowing	**Positivistic/Empirical**	Interpretive/Hermeneutic	Critical

Critique

Evaluation Criteria	Scope	**Logical Consistency**	Parsimony	**Utility**	Testability	**Heurism**	**Test of Time**

Logical Consistency

Critics who fault the logical consistency of CA note that the methods employed by CA researchers do not match the conceptual reach of the theory. They note that the research supporting Cultivation Analysis employs social scientific methods typically identified with the transmissional perspective and limited effects findings. Yet Cultivation Analysis examines larger cultural questions most often raised by humanists. Horace Newcomb (1978) writes, "More than any other research effort in the area of television studies the work of Gerbner and Gross and their associates sits squarely at the juncture of the social sciences and the humanities" (p. 265). By asserting cultural effects, Cultivation Analysis offends many humanists, who feel that their turf has been improperly appropriated and misinterpreted. "The question," writes Newcomb, "'What does it all mean?' is, essentially, a humanistic question" (p. 266). Many humanists, quite at ease when discussing the relationship between literature (novels, art, music, theater) and culture, have great difficulty accepting television as the culture's new, dominant "literature."

Utility

Cultivation Analysis is also criticized because its claims are not always useful in explaining the phenomenon of interest: how people see the world. First, Newcomb (1978) argues that violence is not presented as uniformly on television as the theory assumes, so television cannot be reliably responsible for cultivating the same sense of reality for all viewers. In addition, Cultivation Analysis is criticized for ignoring other issues such as the perceived realism of the televised content, which might be critical in explaining people's understanding of reality (Minnebo & Van Acker, 2004). Furthermore, other researchers (Wilson, Martins, & Marske, 2005) found that attention to television might be more important to cultivating perceptions than simply the amount of TV viewing. The fact that the theory seems to ignore cognitive processes such as attention or rational thinking style renders it less useful than is desired (Berger, 2005).

Heurism

When we examine Cultivation Analysis against our criteria from Chapter 4, we find that it measures up quite well with regard to heurism. For example, the theory has been applied to crime (Signorielli, 1990), fear of victimization (Sparks & Ogles, 1990), attitudes toward racism (Allen & Hatchett, 1986), feelings of alienation (Morgan, 1986), anxiety (Zillman & Wakshlag, 1985), gender stereotyping (Carveth & Alexander, 1985; Preston, 1990), affluence (Potter, 1991), the aged (Gerbner et al., 1980), American stereotypes (Tan, 1982), civil liberties (Carlson, 1983), divorce (Potter, 1991), materialism (Reimer & Rosengren, 1990), values (Potter, 1993), health issues (Molitor, 1994; Potter, 1991), perceptions of adolescent drug use (Minnebo & Eggermont, 2007), and Spanish-language TV (Glascock & Ruggerio, 2004).

Test of Time

As we've noted, Cultivation Analysis is heuristic, but two issues may be working against it thirty years after its inception. First, studies based on its tenets are failing to find results consistent with the theory's predictions. Leo Jeffres, David Atkin, and Kimberly Neuendorf (2001), for instance, found that heavy

Theory Into Practice

Bree

I know that the criticisms of Cultivation Analysis make sense. Gerbner came up with his ideas so long ago, and TV is completely different now than it was in the 1960s. Still, I have to think that some of what the theory says is true. I was so surprised to hear that violent crime was falling in the United States. I could have sworn it was on the rise. And I am thinking I get that idea because I do watch a ton of TV. I watch most of the crime shows that were mentioned in the chapter: *CSI*, *Law & Order*, and *Without a Trace* are some of my favorites.

T*I*P

television viewing seemed to be cultivating more diversity of opinion about public issues rather than mainstreaming people's perceptions as Cultivation Analysis predicts. In other words, the three Bs that Gerbner and his colleagues discussed did not obtain in Jeffres, Atkin, and Neuendorf's study. Jeffres and his colleagues called the effect they found "scatter-streaming" and noted that it provided weak support for Cultivation Analysis. Consistent with the Mean World Hypothesis, they did find that heavier users of TV expressed a greater need for gun control than did lighter users.

Second, as James Shanahan and Michael Morgan (1999) observe, times and media use are changing: "As more and more people grow up with TV, it is possible that it will become increasingly difficult to discern differences between light and heavy viewers" (p. 161). In addition, as TiVo, DVDs, digital cable, and other technologies alter our manner of TV viewing, it is likely that some of the theory's contentions will no longer hold true. For instance, if viewers can organize programming for themselves, it is unlikely that heavy viewing will mean the same thing for all viewers. Heavy viewing of cooking shows, for example, would be expected to cultivate a different reality from heavy viewing of soap operas or crime shows.

Cultivation offers responses to these criticisms. First, although there may be many more channels and people may have greater control over selectivity than they once had, television's dramatic and aesthetic conventions produce remarkably uniform content within as well as across genres. Second, because most television watching is ritual—that is, selected more by time of day than by specific program or the availability of multiple channels—heavy viewers will be exposed *overall* to more of television's dominant images. Further, most viewers, even with dozens of channels available to them, primarily select from only five or six, evidencing a very limited range of selection.

Criticism aside, Cultivation Analysis has been and remains one of the most influential mass communication theories of the last two decades. It is the foundation of much contemporary research and, as we've seen, has even become an international social movement. Another source of its influence is that it can be applied by anyone. It asks people to assess their own media use alongside the socially constructed reality of the world they inhabit. Imagine yourself as Joyce Jensen preparing to cast an important vote. You may well undergo the same mental debate as she. Yet think of how even a passing understanding of Cultivation Analysis might help you arrive at your decision and understand your motivations.

Discussion Starters

1. Are you like Joyce Jensen in that you do not feel safe walking in your neighborhood at night? How much television do you watch? Do you fit the profile offered by Cultivation Analysis? Why or why not?

2. Cultivation Analysis is a critical theory and demands action from its adherents. Do you believe researchers and theorists should become politically active in the fields they study? Why or why not?

3. Do you agree with the hypothesis concerning the Mean World Index? Why or why not?

4. How do you define violence on television? Do you think it is possible to calculate violent acts as Gerbner and his colleagues have done? Explain your answer.

5. Do you believe that the world is a mean place? What real-world evidence do you have that it is? What television evidence do you have that it is?

6. How do you respond to the criticism that more television channels and more divisions among viewers mean that the assumptions of Cultivation Analysis are no longer valid?

7. What other variables might affect people's perception of the world in addition to their amount of television viewing?

Online Learning Center   (www. **mhhe.com/west4e**)

Visit the Online Learning Center at www.mhhe.com/west4e for chapter-specific resources, such as story-into-theory and multiple-choice quizzes, as well as theory summaries and theory connection questions.

CHAPTER **28**

Socio-psychological tradition

Agenda-Setting Theory

of Maxwell McCombs & Donald Shaw

For some unexplained reason, in June 1972, five unknown men broke into the Democratic National Committee headquarters looking for undetermined information. It was the sort of local crime story that rated two paragraphs on page 17 of the *Washington Post*. Yet editor Ben Bradlee and reporters Bob Woodward and Carl Bernstein gave the story repeatedly high visibility even though the public initially seemed to regard the incident as trivial.

President Nixon dismissed the break-in as a "third-rate burglary," but over the following year Americans showed an increasing public awareness of Watergate's significance. Half the country became familiar with the word Watergate over the summer of 1972. By April 1973, that figure had risen to 90 percent. When television began gavel-to-gavel coverage of the Senate hearings on the matter a year after the break-in, virtually every adult in the United States knew what *Watergate* was about. Six months after the hearings President Nixon still protested, "I am not a crook." But by the spring of 1974, he was forced from office because the majority of citizens and their representatives had decided that he was.

THE ORIGINAL AGENDA: NOT WHAT TO *THINK*, BUT WHAT TO THINK *ABOUT*

Agenda-setting hypothesis
The mass media have the ability to transfer the salience of issues on their news agenda to the public agenda.

Journalism professors Maxwell McCombs and Donald Shaw regard Watergate as a perfect example of the agenda-setting function of the mass media. They were not surprised that the Watergate issue caught fire after months on the front page of the *Washington Post*. McCombs and Shaw believe that the "mass media have the ability to transfer the salience of items on their news agendas to the public agenda."[1] They aren't suggesting that broadcast and print personnel make a deliberate attempt to influence listener, viewer, or reader opinion on the issues. Reporters in the free world have a deserved reputation for independence and fairness. But McCombs and Shaw say that we look to news professionals for cues on where to focus our attention. "*We* judge as important what the *media* judge as important."[2]

Although McCombs and Shaw first referred to the agenda-setting function of the media in 1972, the idea that people desire media assistance in determining political reality had already been voiced by a number of current events analysts. In an attempt to explain how the United States had been drawn into World War I, Pulitzer Prize–winning author Walter Lippmann claimed that the media act as a mediator between "the world outside and the pictures in our heads."[3] McCombs

360   *MASS COMMUNICATION*

and Shaw also quote University of Wisconsin political scientist Bernard Cohen's observation concerning the specific function the media serve: "The press may not be successful much of the time in telling people what to think, but it is stunningly successful in telling its readers what to think about."[4]

Starting with the Kennedy-Nixon contest in 1960, political analyst Theodore White wrote the definitive account of four presidential elections. Independently of McCombs and Shaw, and in opposition to then-current wisdom that mass communication had limited effects upon its audience, White came to the conclusion that the media shaped those election campaigns:

> The power of the press in America is a primordial one. It sets the agenda of public discussion; and this sweeping political power is unrestrained by any law. It determines what people will talk and think about—an authority that in other nations is reserved for tyrants, priests, parties and mandarins.[5]

A THEORY WHOSE TIME HAD COME

McCombs and Shaw's agenda-setting theory found an appreciative audience among mass communication researchers. The prevailing selective exposure hypothesis claimed that people would attend only to news and views that didn't threaten their established beliefs. The media were seen as merely stroking pre-existent attitudes. After two decades of downplaying the influence of newspapers, magazines, radio, and television, the field was disenchanted with this limited-effects approach. Agenda-setting theory boasted two attractive features: it reaffirmed the power of the press while still maintaining that individuals were free to choose.

McCombs and Shaw's agenda-setting theory represents a back-to-the-basics approach to mass communication research. Like the initial Erie County voting studies,[6] the focus is on election campaigns. The hypothesis predicts a cause-and-effect relationship between media content and voter perception. Although later work explores the conditions under which the media priorities are most influential, the theory rises or falls on its ability to show a match between the media's agenda and the public's agenda later on. McCombs and Shaw supported their main hypothesis with results from surveys they took while working together at the University of North Carolina at Chapel Hill.[7] (McCombs is now at the University of Texas.) Their analysis of the 1968 race for president between Richard Nixon and Hubert Humphrey set the pattern for later agenda-setting research. The study provides an opportunity to examine in detail the type of quantitative survey research that Stuart Hall and other critical theorists so strongly oppose.

MEDIA AGENDA AND PUBLIC AGENDA: A CLOSE MATCH

Media agenda
The pattern of news coverage across major print and broadcast media as measured by the prominence and length of stories.

McCombs and Shaw's first task was to measure the *media agenda*. They determined that Chapel Hill residents relied on a mix of nine print and broadcast sources for political news—two Raleigh papers, two Durham papers, *Time, Newsweek,* the out-of-state edition of the *New York Times,* and the CBS and NBC evening news.

They established *position* and *length* of story as the two main criteria of prominence. For newspapers, the front-page headline story, a three-column story on an inside page, and the lead editorial were all counted as evidence of significant focus on an issue. For news magazines, the requirement was an opening story in the news section or any political issue to which the editors devoted a full column. Prominence in the television news format was defined by placement as one of the first three news items or any discussion that lasted over 45 seconds.

Because the agenda-setting hypothesis refers to substantive issues, the researchers discarded news items about campaign strategy, position in the polls, and the personalities of the candidates. The remaining stories were then sorted into 15 subject categories, which were later boiled down into 5 major issues. A composite index of media prominence revealed the following order of importance: foreign policy, law and order, fiscal policy, public welfare, and civil rights.

Public agenda
The most important public issues as measured by public opinion surveys.

In order to measure the *public's agenda*, McCombs and Shaw asked Chapel Hill voters to outline what each one considered the key issue of the campaign, regardless of what the candidates might be saying. People who were already committed to a candidate were dropped from the pool of respondents. The researchers assigned the specific answers to the same broad categories used for media analysis. They then compared the aggregate data from undecided voters with the composite description of media content. The rank of the five issues on both lists was nearly identical.

WHAT CAUSES WHAT?

McCombs and Shaw believe that the hypothesized agenda-setting function of the media is responsible for the almost perfect correlation they found between the media and public ordering of priorities:

Media Agenda → Voters' Agenda

But as critics of cultivation theory remind us, correlation is not causation. It's possible that newspaper and television coverage simply reflects public concerns that already exist:

Voters' Agenda → Media Agenda

The results of the Chapel Hill study could be interpreted as providing support for the notion that the media are just as market-driven in their news coverage as they are in programming entertainment. By themselves, McCombs and Shaw's findings were impressive, but equivocal. A true test of the agenda-setting hypothesis must be able to show that public priorities lag behind the media agenda. I'll briefly describe three research studies that provide evidence that the media agenda is, in fact, the *cause,* while the public agenda is its somewhat delayed *effect.*

During the 1976 presidential campaign that led to Jimmy Carter's election, McCombs and three other researchers systematically *surveyed* public opinion at three locations across the country. Between February and December, they interviewed voters in Lebanon, New Hampshire; Indianapolis, Indiana; and Evanston, Illinois, on nine occasions. During the same period, they also monitored election coverage over the three major TV networks and in the local newspapers. A correlational time-lag analysis showed that the public agenda reliably trailed the media agenda by about four to six weeks. The correlation was highest during the primary season, but media priorities were later reflected in voters' priorities throughout the campaign.[8]

Is it possible that *both* the media agenda and the public agenda merely reflect current events as they unfold, but that news professionals become aware of what's happening sooner than most of us do? To examine that possibility, communication researcher Ray Funkhouser, now retired from Pennsylvania State University, undertook an extensive *historical* review of stories in news magazines from 1960 to 1970.[9]

362   *MASS COMMUNICATION*

He charted the rise and fall of media attention on issues and compared these trends with annual Gallup poll responses to a question about "the most important problem facing America." Funkhouser's results make it clear that the twin agendas aren't mere reflections of reality. For example, the number of American troops in Vietnam increased until 1968, but news coverage peaked two years before that. The same was true of urban violence and campus unrest. Press interest cooled down while cities and colleges were still heating up. It appears that Walter Lippmann was right—the actual environment and the pictures in our mind are two different worlds.

These survey and historical studies provided strong support for McCombs and Shaw's basic agenda-setting hypothesis. But it took a tightly controlled *experiment* run by Yale researchers to establish a cause-and-effect chain of influence from the media agenda to the public agenda.[10] Political scientists Shanto Iyengar, Mark Peters, and Donald Kinder spliced previously aired news features into tapes of current network newscasts. For four days straight, three groups of New Haven residents came together to watch the evening news and fill out a questionnaire about their own concerns. Each group saw a different version—one version contained a daily story on environmental pollution, another had a daily feature on national defense, and a third offered a daily dose of news about economic inflation. Viewers who saw the media agendas that focused on pollution and defense elevated those issues on their own lists of concerns—definite confirmation of a cause-and-effect relationship between the media agenda and the public agenda. (As it turned out, inflation was already an important topic for most participants, so there wasn't any room for that issue to move up on the third group's agenda.)

WHO SETS THE AGENDA FOR THE AGENDA SETTERS?

In their experiment, Iyengar, Peters, and Kinder gave increased visibility to the issues of economic inflation, national defense, and environmental pollution. Although they could have selected other news topics, they were limited to the extent that they could only pick among stories that actually had been aired. In fact, 75 percent of the stories that come across a news desk are never printed or broadcast. News doesn't select itself. Who sets the agenda for the agenda setters?

One view regards a handful of news editors as the guardians, or "gatekeepers," of political dialogue. Nothing gets put on the political agenda without the concurrence of a few select people—the operation chiefs of the Associated Press, the *New York Times*, the *Washington Post, Time, Newsweek,* ABC, NBC, CBS, CNN, Fox, and MSNBC. Although there is no evidence to support right-wing conservative charges that the editors are part of a liberal, eastern-establishment conspiracy, these key decision makers are undeniably part of a media elite that doesn't represent a cross section of U.S. citizens. The media elite consists of middle-aged Caucasian males who attend the same conferences, banquets, and parties. As Watergate demonstrated, when one of them features an issue, the rest of the nation's media tend to pick up the story. This intermedia effect is especially strong when the *New York Times* takes the lead.

An alternative view regards the candidates themselves as the ultimate source of issue salience. During the 1988 presidential election, George Bush successfully focused media attention on Willie Horton, a convict who raped and murdered a woman while he was on furlough from a prison in Massachusetts. Bush's media handlers (sometimes referred to as "spin doctors") turned the tragedy into a commentary on the Democratic governor's liberalism, and not a day went by without some effort to smear his opponent with Horton's crime. By winning the election, Bush inherited the power that a president has to raise any issue to national prominence with a few remarks. He was able to put the tax issue on the table with his famous statement "Read my lips—no new taxes!" But he was unable to get the issue off the table when he broke that pledge. He also tried to dismiss the economic recession as a "mild technical adjustment." The press and the populace decided it was major.

Current thinking on news selection focuses on the crucial role of public relations professionals working for government agencies, corporations, and interest groups. Even prestigious newspapers with large investigative staffs such as the *Washington Post* and the *New York Times* get more than half of what they print straight from press releases and press conferences.[11]

Interest aggregations
Clusters of people who demand center stage for their one, overriding concern; pressure groups.

Interest aggregations are becoming increasingly adept at creating news that must be reported. Columbia University sociologist Robert Merton coined this term to refer to clusters of people who demand center stage for their one, overriding concern, whatever it might be—antiabortion, antiwar, anticommunism, antipollution, anti-free trade, anti-immigration, anti-gay marriage. As the examples indicate, these groups usually rally around a specific action that they oppose. They stage demonstrations, marches, and other media events so that television and the press will be forced to cover their issue. The net effect is that various power centers are vying for the right to be heard. The media seem to pay attention to those who grab it.

On rare occasions, news events are so compelling that editors have no choice but to feature them for extended periods of time. The monthlong Florida recount in 2000 to determine whether George W. Bush or Al Gore would be president was one such case. And, of course, the 9/11 terrorist attack totally dominated U.S. print and broadcast news, pushing almost every other story off the front page and television screen for the rest of the year. More recently, the 2004 Indian Ocean tsunami that swept over 200,000 people to death also swept everything else off the media agenda. So did the flood waters that engulfed New Orleans when Hurricane Katrina struck in 2005.

WHO IS MOST AFFECTED BY THE MEDIA AGENDA?

Even in their original Chapel Hill study, McCombs and Shaw understood that "people are not automatons waiting to be programmed by the news media."[12] They suspected that some viewers might be more resistant to the media's political priorities than others—that's why they filtered out the responses of voters who were already committed to a candidate. In follow-up studies, McCombs and Shaw turned to the *uses and gratifications* approach, which suggests that viewers are selective in the kinds of TV programs they watch. The theorists sought to discover exactly what kind of person is most susceptible to the media agenda. They concluded that people who have a willingness to let the media shape their thinking have a high *need for orientation*. Others refer to it as an *index of curiosity*.

Index of curiosity
A measure of the extent to which individuals' need for orientation motivates them to let the media shape their views.

Need for orientation arises from high *relevance* and *uncertainty*. For example, because I'm a dog and cat owner, any story about cruelty to animals always catches my attention (high relevance). However, I don't really know the extent to which medical advances require experimentation on live animals (high uncertainty). According to McCombs and Shaw, this combination would make me a likely candidate to be influenced by media stories about vivisection. If the news editors of *Time* and ABC think it's important, I probably will too.

It's hard for me to imagine broadcast and print media providing saturation coverage on the issue of animal welfare. Yet even if they did and I had a high need for orientation on the issue, my response to the coverage would depend on what *aspects* of the story they featured. They might stress dogs in pain, medical breakthroughs, coldhearted scientists, or vivisection as the alternative to human guinea pigs. As discussed in the next two sections of this chapter, that selection process has a powerful effect on readers and viewers.

FRAMING: TRANSFERRING THE SALIENCE OF ATTRIBUTES

Until the 1990s, almost every article about the theory included a reiteration of the agenda-setting mantra—*the media aren't very successful in telling us what to think, but they are stunningly successful in telling us what to think about.* In other words, the media make some issues more *salient.* We pay greater attention to those issues and regard them as more important. By the mid-1990s, however, McCombs was saying that the media do more than that. They do, in fact, influence the way we think. The specific process he cites is one that many media scholars discuss—*framing.*

James Tankard, one of the leading writers on mass communication theory, defines a media frame as "the central organizing idea for news content that supplies a context and suggests what the issue is through the use of *selection, emphasis, exclusion,* and *elaboration.*"[13] The final four nouns in that sentence suggest that the media not only set the agenda for what issues, events, or candidates are most important but also transfer the salience of specific attributes belonging to those potential objects of interest. My own "final four" experience may help explain the distinction.

Framing
The selection of a restricted number of thematically related attributes for inclusion on the media agenda when a particular object or issue is discussed.

I'm writing this section while visiting relatives in St. Petersburg, Florida. The *St. Petersburg Times* is filled with stories about the finals of the NCAA men's basketball tournament that starts here tomorrow. The field of 64 teams has now been narrowed to 4, and it's hard to imagine anything the newspaper or television stations could do to make this Final Four event more prominent for local residents. No one seems to talk about anything else.

What is it about the Final Four extravaganza that captures people's attention? For some it's the high quality of basketball play they expect to see. For others it's a rooting interest for a particular team. But beyond these inherent characteristics of a basketball tournament, there are many other potential features of the event that might come to mind:

Gambling—there's more money bet on this game than on the Super Bowl.

Party scene—a guy leans out the window and yells, "This is where it's at."

Local economy—this is the weekend that could keep Florida green.

Exploitation of players—how many of these guys will ever graduate?

Beach forecast—it will be sunny and warm both today and tomorrow.

The morning paper carried separate stories on all these features, but coverage on benefits to the local economy and the gambling angle were front-page features that ran five times as long as the brief article on player exploitation buried inside.

We see, therefore, that there are two levels of agenda setting. The first level, according to McCombs, is the transfer of salience of an *attitude object* in the mass media's pictures of the world to a prominent place among the pictures in our head. The Final Four becomes important to us. This is the agenda-setting function that survey researchers have traditionally studied.

"Your royal command has been obeyed, Highness. Every town crier in the land is crying: 'Old King Cole is a merry ole soul.' Before nightfall we'll have them all believing it."

Cartoon by Ed Frascino. Reprinted by permission.

The second level of agenda setting is the transfer of salience of a dominant set of *attributes* that the media associate with an attitude object to the specific features of the image projected on the walls of our minds.[14] When I now think of the Final Four, I imagine money changing hands for a variety of reasons. I don't think about GPAs or diplomas. According to McCombs, the agenda setting of attributes mirrors the process of framing that Robert Entman describes in his article clarifying the concept:

> To frame is to select some aspects of a perceived reality and make them more salient in a communication text, in such a way as to promote a particular problem definition, causal interpretation, moral evaluation and/or treatment recommendation for the item described.[15]

NOT JUST WHAT TO THINK ABOUT, BUT HOW TO THINK ABOUT IT

Is there evidence that the process of framing as defined by agenda-setting theorists actually alters the pictures in the minds of people when they read the newspaper or tune in to broadcast news? Does the media's construction of an agenda with a cluster of related attributes create a coherent image in the minds of subscribers, listeners, and viewers? McCombs cites two national election studies in other countries that show this is how framing works. One was conducted in

Japan,[16] the other in Spain.[17] I find compelling evidence in a third study conducted by Salma Ghanem for her doctoral dissertation under McCombs' supervision at the University of Texas.[18]

Ghanem analyzed the changing percentage of Texans who ranked crime as the most important problem facing the country between 1992 and 1995. The figure rose steadily from 2 percent in 1992 to 37 percent of the respondents in 1994 and then dipped back to a still high 21 percent a year later. Ironically, even as public concern about crime was on the rise the first two years, the actual frequency and severity of unlawful acts were actually going down. On the basis of many first-level agenda-setting studies like the Chapel Hill research, Ghanem assumed that the increased salience of crime was driven by media that featured crime stories prominently and often. She found a high correlation (+.70) between the amount of media coverage and the depth of public concern.

Ghanem was more interested in tracking the transfer of salience of specific crime attributes—the second level of agenda setting. Of the dozen or so media frames for stories about crime, two bundles of attributes were strongly linked to the public's increasing alarm. The most powerful frame was one that cast crime as something that could happen to anyone. The stories noted that the robbery took place in broad daylight, or the shooting was random and without provocation.

The second frame was where the crime took place. Out-of-state problems were of casual interest, but when a reported felony occurred locally or in the state of Texas, concern rose quickly. Note that both frames were features of news stories that shrank the psychological distance between the crimes they described and the average citizens who read or heard about them. Many concluded, "I could be next." The high correlations (+.78, +.73) between these media frames and the subsequent public concern suggest that attribute frames make compelling arguments for the choices people make after exposure to the news.

Framing is not an option. Reporters inevitably frame a story by the personal attributes of public figures they select to describe. For example, the media continually reported on the "youthful vigor" of John F. Kennedy while he was alive but made no mention of his extramarital affairs, which were well-known to the White House press corps. The 1988 presidential race was all but over after *Time* framed the contest between George Bush, Sr., and Michael Dukakis as "The Nice Man vs. the Ice Man." And in 1996 Republican spin doctors fought an uphill battle positioning their candidate once media stories focused on Bob Dole's lack of passion—"Dead Man Walking" was the quip of commentator Mark Shields. Media depictions in the 2004 campaign for president focused on conflicting candidate attributes. Senator John Kerry was repeatedly described as "flip-flopping" on the issues. George W. Bush was labeled as "stubborn." Media outlets are constantly searching for material that they regard as *newsworthy*. When they find it, they do more than tell their audiences *what to think about*.

McCombs and Shaw no longer subscribe to Cohen's classic remark about the media's limited agenda-setting role. They now headline their work with a revised and expanded version that describes agenda setting as a much more powerful media function:

The media may not only tell us what to think about,
they also may tell us how and what to think about it,
and perhaps even what to do about it.[19]

BEYOND OPINION: THE BEHAVIORAL EFFECT OF THE MEDIA'S AGENDA

Most of the 400 empirical studies on agenda setting have measured the effect of media agendas on public *opinion*. But some intriguing findings suggest that media priorities also affect people's *behavior*. For example, Alexander Bloj, a graduate student of McCombs, had access to the sales records of a major airline in a large northeastern city.[20] He was also able to find out about the purchase pattern of flight insurance sold at the airport. Bloj predicted that prominent stories of airplane crashes and hijackings in the *New York Times* would both lower ticket sales and increase the purchases of trip insurance the following week. He defined media salience of flight safety as any story running for two days that reported a crash with double-digit fatalities or a skyjacker gaining control of a plane in the air.

Fortunately, disaster-salient weeks over a five-year period in the early 1970s were much less common than were weeks when air safety wasn't an issue. But when the stories appeared, fewer people bought tickets, while more bought flight insurance. Of course, 30 years later no one doubts that saturation media coverage affects travel behavior. Most of us have a televised image of an airliner crashing into the World Trade Center etched in our minds, with the result that the number of people flying plummeted and didn't recover for over two years.

In a similar but more sophisticated study, communication scholar Deborah Blood (University of Connecticut) and economist Peter Phillips (Yale University) also used the *New York Times* to gauge a fluctuating media agenda related to financial news. They sampled headlines every month from 1980 to 1993 to discover whether the newspaper was bullish or bearish on the U.S. economy. They found little relationship between the media agenda and the prevailing economic conditions as measured by the Index of Leading Economic Indicators, a measure tied to business and consumer behavior. They did, however, discover a strong *media malady effect:*

Media malady effect
Negative economic headlines and stories that depress consumer sentiment and leading economic indicators.

> Negative economic headlines were found to have a significant and negative impact on subsequent consumer sentiment [and] an adverse effect on subsequent leading economic indicators up to a five-month time lag. . . . Clearly news organizations hold the power to effect change.[21]

Nowhere is the behavioral effect of the media agenda more apparent than in the business of professional sports. In his book *The Ultimate Assist,* John Fortunato explores the commercial partnership between network television's agenda and the National Basketball Association (NBA).[22] Television dramatically raised the salience of the game (the first level of agenda setting) by consistently scheduling the best teams in prime-time viewing slots. It also grabbed viewer attention by focusing the camera on these teams' premier players. During the peak years of Michael Jordan's playing career, it was "all Michael, all the time."

Television shaped an attractive picture of the NBA in viewers' minds (the second level of agenda setting) through a series of off-court frames. Interviews with select players and coaches, color commentary, graphics, and instant replays of players' spectacular moves all created a positive image of the NBA. As for the rape accusation against L.A. Lakers superstar Kobe Bryant, and later his feud with teammate Shaq O'Neal that split the team, the media cooperated in downplaying those attributes that tarnish the NBA's image.

This 30-year effort to shape the public agenda has not only had a spectacular effect on fan behavior but has also altered the face of popular culture. From 1970 to 2000, the number of NBA teams and the number of games basically doubled. The number of fans going to games quadrupled. But the astronomical difference is in the money. In 1970, television provided $10 million in revenue to the NBA. In 2000, the payout was $20 billion—no small change. McCombs' comment: "Agenda setting the theory, can also be agenda setting the business plan."[23]

Will New Media Continue to Guide Focus, Opinions, and Behavior?

Ironically, the power of agenda setting that McCombs and Shaw describe may be on the wane. In a creative experiment, University of Illinois researchers Scott Althaus and David Tewksbury predicted that traditional print media would be more effective than new electronic media in setting a reader's agenda.[24] They reasoned that people who are reading a newspaper know that editors consider a long, front-page article under a banner headline as more important than a short story buried on an inside page. Not only are these comparative cues absent on the computer screen, but online readers can click on links to similar stories and never see accounts of events that paper readers would see as they thumbed through the pages.

Althaus and Tewksbury recruited students to spend 30–60 minutes a day for 5 days reading either a print version or an online version of the *New York Times* under controlled conditions. For both groups it was their only exposure to news that week. On the sixth day, the researchers tested recognition and recall of the week's stories and assessed which problems facing the country students personally regarded as most important. Not only did those who read the traditional paper remember more content but they also selected a higher percentage of international issues as more important to them, thus aligning them closer to the prioritized agenda of the *Times'* editors. The researchers conclude that "by providing users with more content choices and control over exposure, new technologies may allow people to create personalized information environments that shut them off from larger flows of public information in a society."[25] They might also add that traditional news media may not have as much power to transfer the salience of issues or attributes as they have in the past.

ETHICAL REFLECTION: CHRISTIANS' COMMUNITARIAN ETHICS

Clifford Christians is a professor at the Institute of Communications Research at the University of Illinois at Urbana-Champaign and is lead author of *Good News: Social Ethics and the Press*.[26] Although he values free speech, he doesn't share the near-absolute devotion to the First Amendment that seems to be the sole ethical commitment of many journalists. Christians rejects reporters and editors' insistence on an absolute right of free expression that is based on the individualistic rationalism of John Locke and other Enlightenment thinkers. In our age of ethical relativism where *continue the conversation* is the best that philosophy has to offer,[27] Christians believes that discovering the truth is still possible if we are willing to examine the nature of our humanity. The human nature he perceives is, at root, personhood in community.[28]

Christians agrees with Martin Buber that the relation is the cradle of life. ("In the beginning is the relation."[29]) He is convinced, therefore, that mutuality is the essence of humanness. People are most fully human as "persons-in-relation" who live simultaneously for others and for themselves.

Communitarian ethics
A moral responsibility to promote community, mutuality, and persons-in-relation who live simultaneously for others and for themselves.

> A moral community demonstrates more than mere interdependence; it is character-ized by mutuality, a will-to-community, a genuine concern for the other apart from immediate self-interest. . . . An act is morally right when compelled by the intention to maintain the community of persons; it is wrong if driven by self-centeredness.[30]

Christians understands that a commitment to mutuality would significantly alter media culture and mission. His *communitarian ethics* establish civic transfor-mation rather than objective information as the primary goal of the press. Report-ers' aim would thus become a revitalized citizenship shaped by community norms—morally literate and active participants, not just readers and audiences provided with data.[31] Editors, publishers, and owners—the gatekeepers of the media agenda—would be held to the same standard. Christians insists that media criticism must be willing to reestablish the idea of moral right and wrong. Selfish practices aimed at splintering community are not merely misguided; they are evil.[32]

Agape love
An unconditional love for others because they are created in the image of God.

Christians' communitarian ethics are based on the Christian tradition of *agape love*—an unconditional love for others because they are created in the image of God. He believes journalists have a social responsibility to promote the sacredness of life by respecting human dignity, truthtelling, and doing no harm to innocents.[33] With an emphasis on establishing communal bonds, alien-ated people on the margins of society receive special attention from communi-tarians. Christians ultimately judges journalists on the basis of how well they use the media's power to champion the goal of social justice. For example, Christians asks:

> Is the press a voice for the unemployed, food-stamp recipients, Appalachian min-ers, the urban poor, Hispanics in rural shacks, the elderly, women discriminated against in hiring and promotion, ethnic minorities with no future in North Ameri-ca's downsizing economy?[34]

If the media sets that kind of agenda and features attributes that promote com-munity, he believes they are fulfilling their communitarian responsibility.

CRITIQUE: ARE THE EFFECTS TOO LIMITED, THE SCOPE TOO WIDE?

When McCombs and Shaw first proposed the agenda-setting hypothesis, they saw it as a sharp break from the limited-effects model that had held sway in media research since Lazarsfeld introduced the concept of *selective exposure* (see the introduction to Media Effects). Although not reverting to the old hypodermic needle model or magic bullet conception of media influence, McCombs and Shaw ascribed to broadcast and print journalism the significant power to set the public's political priorities. As years of careful research have shown, however, it doesn't always work. Perhaps the best that could be said until the mid-1990s was that the media agenda affects the salience of some issues for some people some of the time. So in 1994, McCombs suggested that "agenda setting is a theory of limited media effects."[35] That would be quite a comedown from its original promise.

The new dimension of framing reasserts a powerful media effects model. As Ohio State University journalism professor Gerald Kosicki states,

> Media "gatekeepers" do not merely keep watch over information, shuffling it here and there. Instead, they engage in active construction of the messages, emphasizing certain aspects of an issue and not others.[36]

But Kosicki questions whether framing is even a legitimate topic of study under an agenda-setting banner. He sees nothing in McCombs and Shaw's original model that anticipates the importance of interpretive frames.

As McCombs is fond of pointing out, the evidence is there. In the lead article of a 1977 book that he and Shaw edited, they clearly previewed the current "New Frontiers" of agendas of attributes and framing:

> Agenda setting as a concept is not limited to the correspondence between salience of topics for the media and the audience. We can also consider the saliency of various attributes of these objects (topics, issues, persons or whatever) reported in the media. To what extent is our view of an object shaped or influenced by the picture sketched in the media, especially by those attributes which the media deem news-worthy?[37]

McCombs' definition of framing appears to be quite specific: "Framing is the selection of a restricted number of thematically related attributes for inclusion on the media agenda when a particular object is discussed."[38] It doesn't seem to include the emotional connotation of key terms used in ongoing public debate of issues such as abortion. For example, the effect on the audience may be quite different if a story is labeled as *antiabortion forces* versus *freedom of choice* rather than *right-to-life advocates* versus *proabortion advocates*. The definition also seems to exclude presentational factors such as a broadcaster's raised eyebrow while saying one of these phrases.

In contrast, the popularity of framing as an *interpretive* construct in media studies has resulted in diverse and ambiguous meanings. The way that Stuart Hall and other critical theorists use the term is so elastic that the word seems to refer to anything they don't like. Thus, I regard a narrow view of framing as a distinct advantage for empirically based media effects research.

Whether or not we accept a restricted definition of framing, the agenda-setting function of the mass media has earned a firm place in media effects literature. McCombs and Shaw have established a plausible case that some people look to print and broadcast news for guidance on which issues are really important. Agenda-setting theory also provides a needed reminder that news stories are just that—stories. The message always requires interpretation. For these reasons, McCombs and Shaw have accomplished the function they ascribe to the media. Agenda-setting theory has a priority place on the agenda of mass communication theory and research.

QUESTIONS TO SHARPEN YOUR FOCUS

1. If the media aren't telling you what to think, why is their ability to tell you *what to think about* so important?

2. What *type of person* under what *type of circumstances* is most susceptible to the media's *agenda-setting function?*

3. Hillary Clinton continues to be one of the most controversial public figures in America. What *dominant set of attributes* could you use to *frame* her visit to a children's hospital to make her look good? How could you make her look bad?

4. Is there a recent issue that *news reporters and commentators* are now talking about daily that you and the people you know don't care about? Do you think you'll still be unconcerned two months from now?

CONVERSATIONS

View this segment online at www.mhhe.com/griffin7 or www.afirstlook.com.

In our conversation, Max McCombs discusses the process of framing and how this concept has changed the scope of his theory. He also answers questions posed by my students. How many issues can a person focus on at one time? If he ran the classic Chapel Hill study today, would he use CNN as a media outlet that sets the public agenda? Do TV entertainment shows have an agenda-setting function? I wanted to know how he saw potential media bias. Are all news stories delivered with a spin? Does he see anything sinister about intentionally framing a story? Is there a liberal bias in the national media? I think you'll be surprised by his direct responses.

A SECOND LOOK

Recommended resource: Maxwell McCombs and Amy Reynolds, "News Influence on Our Pictures of the World," in *Media Effects: Advances in Theory and Research,* Jennings Bryant and Dolf Zillmann (eds.), Lawrence Erlbaum, Mahwah, NJ, 2002, pp. 1–18.

Comprehensive summary of theory and research: Maxwell McCombs, *Setting the Agenda,* Polity, Cambridge, UK, 2004.

Historical development: Maxwell McCombs and Tamara Bell, "The Agenda-Setting Role of Mass Communication," in *An Integrated Approach to Communication Theory and Research,* Michael Salwen and Donald Stacks (eds.), Lawrence Erlbaum, Hillsdale, NJ, 1996, pp. 93–110.

Five stages of agenda-setting research and development: Maxwell McCombs, "A Look at Agenda-Setting: Past, Present and Future," *Journalism Studies,* Vol. 6, 2005, pp. 543–557.

Prototype election study: Maxwell McCombs and Donald Shaw, "The Agenda-Setting Function of the Mass Media," *Public Opinion Quarterly,* Vol. 36, 1972, pp. 176–187.

Framing: Maxwell McCombs and Salma Ghanem, "The Convergence of Agenda Setting and Framing," in *Framing Public Life,* Stephen Reese, Oscar Gandy, Jr., and August Grant (eds.), Lawrence Erlbaum, Mahwah, NJ, 2001, pp. 67–81.

Relationship of agenda setting, framing, and priming: Dietram Scheufele and David Tewksbury, "Framing, Agenda Setting, and Priming: The Evolution of Three Media Effects Models," *Journal of Communication,* Vol. 57, 2007, pp. 9–20.

Bundles of attributes: Maxwell McCombs, "New Frontiers in Agenda Setting: Agendas of Attributes and Frames," *Mass Comm Review 24,* 1997, pp. 4–24.

Sophisticated election study: Maxwell McCombs, Esteban Lopez-Escobar, and Juan Pablo Llamas, "Setting the Agenda of Attributes in the 1996 Spanish General Election," *Journal of Communication,* Vol. 50, No. 2, 2000, pp. 77–92.

Anthology of earlier agenda-setting research: David Protess and Maxwell McCombs, *Agenda Setting: Readings on Media, Public Opinion, and Policymaking,* Lawrence Erlbaum, Hillsdale, NJ, 1991.

Later scholarship: Maxwell McCombs, Donald Shaw, and David Weaver, *Communication and Democracy: Exploring the Intellectual Frontiers in Agenda-Setting Theory,* Lawrence Erlbaum, Mahwah, NJ, 1997.

Focus on the theorist: William Davie and T. Michael Maher, "Maxwell McCombs: Agenda-Setting Explorer," *Journal of Broadcasting and Electronic Media,* Vol. 50, 2006, pp. 358–364.

Critique: Gerald Kosicki, "Problems and Opportunities in Agenda-Setting Research," *Journal of Communication,* Vol. 43, No. 2, 1993, pp. 100–127.

CHAPTER 24

Spiral of Silence Theory

*Based on the research of **Elisabeth Noelle-Neumann***

Carol Johansen

Each morning, Carol Johansen attends the seniors' breakfast at the local senior center. She can afford to go out to a restaurant for breakfast, but she goes to the center because she enjoys the company. She encounters a rambunctious cast of characters, including Earl, a World War I veteran who sings Broadway songs; Nancy, a former nurse who tells lively stories about former patients; and Nick, a New England lobsterman who is an avid newspaper reader. This morning's breakfast was especially interesting because the conversation quickly turned to a newspaper article on spanking children.

Nick read the article to the group, and after he was done, he offered his opinion on the topic: "I agree with this writer. I don't see anything wrong with spanking a kid. Look at this survey in the paper. Over 60 percent of the state believes it's okay to spank, but only 40 percent of the country does. Nowadays, though, you can't lay a hand on a kid. They're ready to sue you, or you'll get some state worker to come into your own house and take your kid away. It's not right."

"I agree," said Nancy. "I can tell you that my neighbor's daughter is almost 8 and a holy terror. But her mother won't touch her! I don't get it. If that was my child, I wouldn't mind putting her over my knee and giving her a good wallop! The girl's mom and dad don't want to send 'the wrong message' to her so she gets away with a lot."

Earl became more interested in the subject as Nancy spoke. Like the others, Earl had a strong opinion on the subject: "Look. How many people at this table were spanked when they were little?" All seven raised their hands. "And how many of you think that you're violent people?" None showed any response. "There. That's my point. Today, they tell you that if you spank your own kid, then that kid is going to end up violent. But look at us. We aren't violent. We don't hurt anyone. There's just too much of this political correctness out there, and too many parents simply have no rights anymore."

Carol continued glancing at one of Nick's newspapers. She, like the others, had an opinion on the subject. But her thoughts differed from those of the others. She did not believe in spanking a child at all. She had been spanked like the rest of her friends, but her dad had not known when to stop. Carol had often been physically abused. She thought about the number of parents who are not able to stop at just one slap on the behind. She also thought about what hitting accomplished. Children can be taught right and wrong, she felt, without being hit.

"Hey, Carol," Nick interrupted, "you're pretty quiet. What's your take on all this?"

Carol thought for a quick moment. Should she disagree with the rest of them? What about all the people in her community who also agree with spanking? Carol recalled seeing a news program on the topic about a week ago, and the reporter had interviewed several adult children who had been spanked and who felt that spanking was the only discipline to use on them during their childhood.

She knew that she disagreed with her breakfast colleagues, but how could she begin to explain all of her thoughts? They wouldn't understand. It's probably better simply to go with the flow, she surmised.

"Oh, I don't know. I can see how some kids need 'special attention.' But sometimes, parents get too angry."

"C'mon Carol," Nancy interrupted. "You can't have it both ways. There are a lot of . . ."

"Well, I guess I agree with it. I hope that it's not done that often, though."

As the volunteer arrived at the table to pour more coffee, the conversation quickly turned to other news. Privately, Carol thought about why she had deferred to the group's will. She didn't want to be alone in her viewpoint, nor did she want to explain the personal and sordid details of her past. As Nick began to talk about last night's city council meeting, Carol wondered whether she would ever speak up on the subject again.

Our opinions of events, people, and topics change periodically in our lives. Consider, for example, your opinions about dating when you were a 15-year-old and your opinions about dating now. Or consider the opinions you held of your parents during your adolescence and those you hold today. Your opinions on various topics—including premarital sex and raising children—may have evolved over the years. Our opinions are not static and frequently change over the years.

One important influence on our opinions is the media. Media have helped to shape who we are today. Often, this influence is subtle; at other times it is more direct. The media's influence on public opinion is what Elisabeth Noelle-Neumann studied, dating back to the 1930s and 1940s. It was in the early 1970s, however, that she conceptualized the Spiral of Silence Theory.

Although Noelle-Neumann's theory is pre-Internet age, her interpretation of the media's influence still holds true. Today, given the popularity in usage of blogs, e-mail, Listservs, and YouTube, we are bombarded with mediated messages. The messages emanating from websites, television news, and e-commentary have contributed to our cultural discourse. Indeed, these media have even affected the direction of public discourse on socially significant issues (Butsch, 2007). Finally, the theory is important to address "because it directly relates to speech freedom, which is the cornerstone of our democracy" (Liu, 2006). Therefore, the value of examining Spiral of Silence Theory remains high.

Noelle-Neumann focuses on what happens when people provide their opinions on a variety of issues that the media have defined for the public. The Spiral of Silence Theory suggests that people who believe that they hold a minority viewpoint on a public issue will remain in the background where their communication will be restrained; those who believe that they hold a majority viewpoint will be more encouraged to speak. Noelle-Neumann (1983) contends that the media will focus more on the majority views, underestimating the minority views. Those in the minority will be less assertive in communicating their opinions, thereby leading to a downward spiral of communication. Interestingly, those in the majority will overestimate their influence and may become emboldened in their communication. Subsequently, the media will report

> **Theory at a Glance** • *Spiral of Silence Theory*
>
> Because of their enormous power, media have a lasting and profound effect on public opinion. Mass media work simultaneously with majority opinion to silence minority beliefs on cultural and social issues in particular. A fear of isolation prompts those with minority views to examine the beliefs of others. Individuals who fear being socially isolated are prone to conform to what they perceive to be the majority view. Every so often, however, the silent majority raises its voice in activism.

on their opinions and activities. This theory, then, adheres to the belief that we alluded to in Chapter 2. Groups are highly influential in our lives.

The minority views of Carol Johansen and the behavior of her breakfast friends underscore the gist of the Spiral of Silence Theory. Listening to her colleagues' opinions on spanking, Carol feels that she is alone in thinking that spanking is wrong. The theory suggests that Carol is influenced by media reports of over 60 percent of the state supporting spanking for discipline and also by her own recollection of a television news show that lauded the benefits of spanking by adult children who had been spanked themselves. Carol perceives her opinion to be a minority view, and consequently she speaks less. Conversely, those in our sample who agree with spanking as discipline (Nick, Nancy, and Earl) are no doubt inspired by the state survey responses; this prompts even more assertive communication on their part.

The difference between this majority and minority view at the senior center is further clarified by Noelle-Neumann (1991). She believes that those in the majority have the confidence to speak out. They may display their convictions by wearing buttons, brandishing bumper stickers, and emblazoning their opinions on the clothes they wear. Holders of minority views are usually cautious and silent, which reinforces the public's perceptions of their weakness. Nick, Nancy, and Earl are clearly confident in their opinions, whereas Carol fosters a sense of weakness by her lack of assertiveness in expressing her opinion.

The Spiral of Silence Theory uniquely intersects public opinion and media. To understand this interface better, we first unravel the notion of public opinion, a key component of the theory. We then examine three assumptions of the theory.

The Court of Public Opinion

As a researcher, Noelle-Neumann was interested in clarifying terms that may have multiple meanings. At the core of the Spiral of Silence Theory is a term that is commonly accepted but one that she felt was misconstrued: public opinion. As a founder and director of the Allensbach Institute, a polling agency in Germany, Noelle-Neumann contended that interpretations of *public opinion* have been misguided. In fact, although she identified more than fifty definitions of the term since the theory's inception, none satisfied her.

Although many years have passed since the theory's original expression, the concept of public opinion "is particularly encumbered by the thicket of confusion, misunderstandings, and communication problems" (Noelle-Neumann & Petersen, 2004, pp. 339–340). Attempting to provide some understanding of this key term in the theory, Noelle-Neumann (1984, 1993) has provided some clarity. She separates *public opinion* into two discrete terms: *public* and *opinion.*

She notes that there are three meanings of **public.** First, there is a legal association with the term. Public suggests that it is open to everyone, as in "public lands" or "public place." Second, public pertains to the concerns or issues of people, as in "the public responsibility of journalists." Finally, public represents the social-psychological side of people. That is, people not only think inwardly but also think about their relationships to others. The phrase "public eye" is relevant here. Noelle-Neumann concludes that individuals know whether they are exposed to or sheltered from public view, and they adjust themselves accordingly. She claims that the social-psychological side of public has been neglected in previous interpretations of public opinion, and yet "this is the meaning felt by people in their sensitive social skin" (1993, p. 62).

public
legal, social, and social-psychological concerns of people

An **opinion** is an expression of an attitude. Opinions may vary in both intensity and stability. Invoking the early French and English interpretation of opinions, Noelle-Neumann notes that opinion is a level of agreement of a particular population. In the spiral of silence process, opinion is synonymous with something regarded as acceptable.

opinion
expression of attitude

Putting all of this together, Noelle-Neumann defines **public opinion** as the "attitudes or behaviors one must express in public if one is not to isolate oneself; in areas of controversy or change, public opinions are those attitudes one *can* express without running the danger of isolating oneself" (p. 178). So, for Carol Johansen, her opinion on spanking would not be regarded as acceptable by her breakfast club. Because she fears being isolated from her particular early-morning community, she silences her opinions.

public opinion
attitudes and behaviors expressed in public to avoid isolation

Noelle-Neumann and Petersen (2004) argue that public opinion is a dynamic process and limited by time and place. To that end, they note that "a spiral of silence only holds sway over a society for a limited period of time" (p. 350). So, there are both short- and long-term components to public opinion. For instance, in 2008, there was a difference between the public's opinion of having the first African American as a U.S. presidential candidate (short-term) and the public's opinion pertaining to race relations. In fact, Noelle-Neumann and Petersen note that in the United States, public opinion pertaining to race may pose a threat to "social cohesion" (p. 350).

Essentially, public opinion refers to the collective sentiments of a population on a particular subject. Most often, the media determine what subjects will be of interest to people, and the media often make a subject controversial. For example, the drug Viagra, used to treat impotence, was considered a medical marvel until the media discovered that many health plans covered this drug but did not cover female contraceptives. Many media outlets subsequently

T*I*P

Theory Into Practice

Carmine

I read about the Spiral of Silence Theory. At first, I thought it was too old a theory for someone like me (20 years old) to relate to. But I thought about how, when I'm around my fraternity brothers, I don't really speak up as I should. A few weeks ago, about five of us were talking about euthanasia. I felt that only God has the power to end a life; doctors should not be able to do that. Well, the other guys all said that it's "their right" to tell a doctor to do it. And they were knocking down those of us who think that no one—but God—should terminate a life. I didn't say a word, though, because they all were for it. This is, as I think about it, a lot like the Spiral of Silence. It certainly does apply to me today.

reported that this was an overtly sexist practice. Noelle-Neumann (1991) notes that public opinion may be influenced by who approves or disapproves of our views. In 2005 the U.S. Congress voted to repeal Medicare and Medicaid coverage of Viagra. Your opinion on whether you support this congressional action will likely be shaped by spokespeople on both sides of the issue as well as by friends and family members. A spiral of silence is the response to the shifting opinions of others.

Assumptions of Spiral of Silence Theory

With public opinion as our backdrop to the theory, we now explore three assumptions of the Spiral of Silence Theory. Noelle-Neumann (1991, 1993) has previously addressed these assertions:

- Society threatens deviant individuals with isolation; fear of isolation is pervasive.
- This fear of isolation causes individuals to try to assess the climate of opinion at all times.
- Public behavior is affected by public opinion assessment.

The first assumption asserts that society holds power over those who do not conform through threat of isolation. Noelle-Neumann believes that the very fabric of our society depends on people commonly recognizing and endorsing a set of values. And it is public opinion that determines whether these values have equal conviction across the populations. When people agree on a common set of values, then fear of isolation decreases. When there is a difference in values, fear of isolation sets in.

Like many theorists, Noelle-Neumann is concerned with the testability of this assumption. After all, she notes, are members of a society really threatened with isolation? How could this be? She believes that simple polling could not tap this area (for instance, How much do you fear isolation?). Questions such as these ask respondents to think too abstractly, because it's likely that few respondents have ever thought about isolation.

Noelle-Neumann employs the research values of Solomon Asch (1951), a social psychologist in the 1950s. Asch conducted the following laboratory experiment more than fifty times with eight to ten research subjects:

Which of the following lines on the right is equal to the line on the left?

_____

1. _____

2. _____

3. _____

You are probably quick to say that line 3 is equal to the line on the left. The group of research subjects, however, disagreed. After going around the room, the experimenter's assistants (who were in on the experiment) all named line 1 as the one that was equal to the line on the left. The unsuspecting subjects began to name line 1 as the correct response. In fact, Asch discovered that several times around, the unsuspecting subjects named the incorrect response. Asch believed that individuals frequently feel great pressure to agree with others, even though the others are incorrect. Borrowing from the theory, there is a very real fear of isolation.

Elizabeth Blakeslee (2005) of the *New York Times* notes that Asch's research conclusions on social conformity still exist today. She reports on the implications of following a group in many areas of society, including jury decisions and elections. She notes that "the unpleasantness of standing alone can make a majority opinion seem more appealing than sticking to one's own beliefs" (p. D3).

Responding to primary criticisms of the Asch studies—that people did not have a real fear of isolation but rather a lack of confidence in their own judgment—Noelle-Neumann engaged in a more realistic threat-of-isolation test. She believed that requiring subjects to assess a moral or aesthetic conviction was more realistic than any laboratory experiments conducted by Asch. Indeed, these moral issues should be contemporary (in the public spotlight) and issues on which the public is divided. Think about gay marriage, abortion rights, human cloning, marijuana for medical use, and other topics on which divergent points of view exist.

For Noelle-Neumann, freedom to smoke was (and continues to be) an issue "in the spotlight." During interviews with smokers, she showed them a picture with a person angrily saying, "It seems to me that smokers are terribly inconsiderate. They force others to inhale their health-endangering smoke." Respondents were asked to phrase responses to the statement. The results indicated that in the presence of nonsmokers, many smokers were less willing to support smokers' rights overtly.

The second assumption of the theory identifies people as constant assessors of the climate of public opinion. Noelle-Neumann contends that individuals receive information about public opinion from two sources: personal observation and the media. First, let's discuss how people are able to personally observe public opinion and then examine the role of the media.

quasi-statistical sense
personal estimation of the strength of opposing sides on a public issue

Noelle-Neumann (1991) states that people engage in a quasi-statistical ability to appraise public opinion. A **quasi-statistical sense** means that people are able to estimate the strength of opposing sides in a public debate. They are able to do this by listening to the views of others and incorporating that knowledge into their own viewpoints. For instance, Carol Johansen's quasi-statistical sense makes her believe that she is the only person at her breakfast table who opposes spanking. She can see that she is vastly outnumbered on the topic and therefore is able to assess the local public opinion on the subject. Noelle-Neumann calls this a quasi-statistical frequency "organ" in that she believes that people like Carol are able to numerically estimate where others fall on the topic. The theorist states that this organ is on "high alert" during periods of instability. So our quasi-statistical sense works overtime when we see that our opinions on a subject are different from those of the majority around us. This sense is, as a rule, an unconscious process.

pluralistic ignorance
mistaken observation of how most people feel

Personal observations of public opinion can often be distorted and inaccurate. Noelle-Neumann (1993) calls the mistaken observations about how most people feel **pluralistic ignorance**. She notes that people "mix their own direct perceptions and the perceptions filtered through the eyes of the media into an indivisible whole that seems to derive from their own thoughts and experiences" (p. 169). Consider Carol's assessment of the opinions on spanking. With the vast majority of people around her supporting this type of discipline, she may believe that she is clearly in the minority. One or both sides in the debate, however, can overestimate their ability to estimate opinion. Especially with such lopsided support on a topic (as with the group at the senior center), Noelle-Neumann believes that people can become disillusioned.

People not only employ their personal observations of public opinion but also rely on the media. Yet Noelle-Neumann insists that the media's effects are frequently indirect. Because people are inherently social in nature, they talk about their observations to others. People seek out the media to confirm or disconfirm their observations and then interpret their own observations through the media. This can be illustrated through Carol's future behaviors. First, if she returns home from the senior center and reveals her beliefs on spanking to others, she may encounter several neighbors who share her opinion. Next, if she watches the evening news and learns that the majority of the country oppose spanking, this will resonate deeply with her. She will also be affected by any media reports that disproportionately publicize opposition to spanking. Finally, later discussions that Carol might have on the subject may invoke the media. She may tell others that even the media reports underscore her point of view. We will return to the powerful role of the media in the Spiral of Silence Theory a bit later in the chapter.

The final assumption of the theory is that the public's behavior is influenced by evaluations of public opinion. Noelle-Neumann (1991) proposes that public behavior takes the form of either speaking out on a subject or keeping silent. If individuals sense support for a topic, then they are likely to communicate about it; if they feel that others do not support a topic, then they maintain silence. She continues, "The strength of one camp's signals, or the weakness of the other's, is the driving force setting the spiral in motion" (p. 271). In sum, people seem to act according to how other people feel.

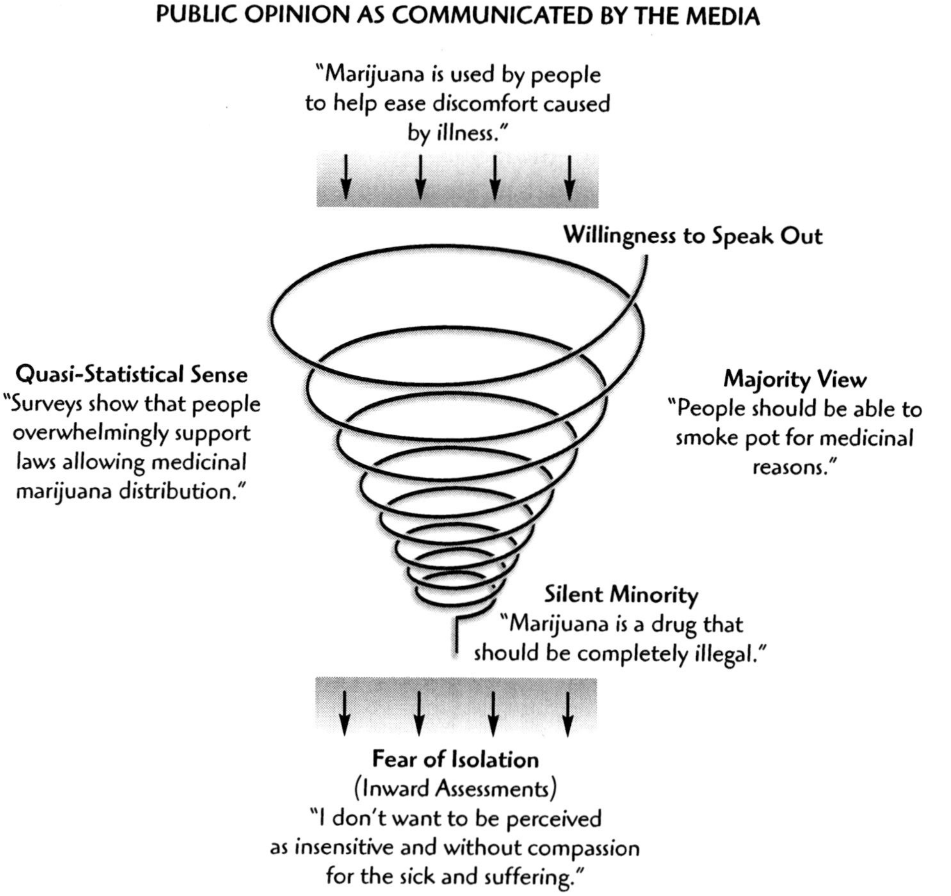

Figure 24.1
The Spiral of
Silence: Medicinal
Marijuana

PUBLIC OPINION AS COMMUNICATED BY THE MEDIA

"Marijuana is used by people
to help ease discomfort caused
by illness."

Willingness to Speak Out

Quasi-Statistical Sense
"Surveys show that people
overwhelmingly support
laws allowing medicinal
marijuana distribution."

Majority View
"People should be able to
smoke pot for medicinal
reasons."

Silent Minority
"Marijuana is a drug that
should be completely illegal."

Fear of Isolation
(Inward Assessments)
"I don't want to be perceived
as insensitive and without compassion
for the sick and suffering."

Noelle-Neumann believes that human beings have an aversion to discussing topics that do not have the support of the majority. To test this assumption, consider interviewing people on your campus about a controversial issue such as physician-assisted suicide. If straw polls in your campus newspaper show that almost 70 percent of the campus opposes this, then according to the theory, students, faculty, and staff are probably going to be less inclined to speak out in favor of the practice. A willingness to speak out may have more to do with one's convictions and an assessment of overall trends in society. That is, if there is a liberal climate on your campus, there may be more willingness to speak out; if a conservative climate exists, people may feel less inclined to offer their opposition.

These three assumptions are important to consider as we further delineate Noelle-Neumann's theory. In Figure 24.1, we illustrate several concepts and themes emerging from the theory's assumptions.

Personal opinions, a fear of being alone in those opinions, and public sentiment lay the groundwork for discussing the remainder of the theory. Each of these areas is influenced by a powerful part of U.S. society: the media. Let's now overview the powerful influence of the media in the Spiral of Silence Theory.

The Media's Influence

As we have discussed, the Spiral of Silence Theory rests on public opinion. Noelle-Neumann (1993) cautions, however, that "much of the population adjusts its attitudes to the tenor of the media" (p. 272). Nancy Eckstein and Paul Turman (2002) agree. They claim that "the media may provide the force behind the spiral of silence because it is considered a one-sided conversation, an indirect public form of communication where people feel helpless to respond" (p. 173). A willingness to speak out depends greatly on the media. Without support from others for divergent views, people will remain consonant with the views offered in the media. In fact, Noelle-Neumann (1993) believes that the media even provide words and phrases so people can confidently speak about a subject. If no repeated words or expressions are used, people fall silent. The extent to which Carol Johansen in our opening scenario will offer her views about spanking, then, will rest on what position the various media have taken on the subject. Yet, as George Gerbner (Cultivation Analysis, Chapter 22) says, television is the most influential of all media forms, although the Internet continues to be highly important.

In explaining why the media have such influence, Noelle-Neumann believes that the public is not offered a broad and balanced interpretation of news events. Consequently, the public is given a limited view of reality. This restrictive approach to covering news narrows an individual's perception.

ubiquity
the belief that media are everywhere

Consider the theorist's three characteristics of the news media: ubiquity, cumulativeness, and consonance. **Ubiquity** refers to the fact that the media are pervasive sources of information. Because media are everywhere, they are relied on when people seek out information. For instance, Nick, a member of Carol Johansen's morning group, is quick to point out the recent surveys done in the state about perceptions of spanking. He has the source immediately at hand. And as the media strive for agreement from the majority of the public, they will be everywhere.

cumulativeness
the belief that media repeat themselves

The **cumulativeness** of the media refers to the process of the media repeating themselves across programs and across time. Frequently, you will read a story in the morning newspaper, listen to the same story on the radio as you drive to work, and then watch the story on the evening news. Noelle-Neumann calls this a "reciprocal influence in building up frames of reference" (1993, p. 71). It can become problematic when the original source is left unquestioned, and yet four media (newspaper, radio, television, and the Internet) rely on that source. The theory suggests that conformity of voice influences what information gets released to the public to help them develop an opinion.

consonance
the belief that all media are similar in attitudes, beliefs, and values

Finally, **consonance** pertains to the similarities of beliefs, attitudes, and values held by the media. Noelle-Neumann states that consonance is produced from a tendency for newspeople to confirm their own thoughts and opinions, making it look as if those opinions were emanating from the public. Each of these three qualities—ubiquity, cumulativeness, consonance—allows for majority opinions to be heard. Those wishing to avoid isolation remain silent.

It is not surprising that the media are influential in public opinion. Many surveys have demonstrated that people consider the media to have too much

Research Notes

Eckstein, N. J., & Turman, P. D. (2002). "Children are to be seen and not heard:" Silencing students' religious voices in the university classroom. *Journal of Communication and Religion, 25,* 166–192.

This article is about one of the first research studies to examine the role of religion in the classroom from a communication vantage point. Eckstein and Turman explore how instructors silence students while discussing "controversial" issues, such as religion. The researchers note that silencing "often provides the task of marginalizing, excluding, centering, and privileging students in classroom discussion" (p. 175). They looked at three silencing behaviors: naming (uncovering a person's belief system), not-naming (avoiding problemitizing the fact that there are different belief systems), and smoothing over (passing on quickly to another student or topic). The results of the study show that "teachers' specific silencing behaviors of naming, not-naming, and smoothing over play a significant role in the silencing of students' religious beliefs during classroom discussion" (p. 185). Furthermore, they found that naming had the most significant effect on silencing, followed by smoothing over and not-naming. The authors conclude with a discussion of the consequences of silencing student views.

Moy, P., Domke, D., & Stamm, K. (2001). The spiral of silence and public opinion on affirmative action. *Journalism and Mass Communication Quarterly, 78,* 7–25.

The topic of affirmative action is rife with public opinion in the United States. People tend to favor or not favor affirmative action policies, and government, education, religion, and the media have all weighed in on this very controversial topic. Moy and her colleagues tested the principle "fear of isolation" in the Spiral of Silence Theory, which the authors consider the "driving force" (p. 16) behind the theory. They studied public discussions of affirmative action and analyzed data from more than 200 randomly selected adults. Looking at Initiative 200, a 1998 Washington state ballot proposal designed to remove race, ethnicity, and gender from consideration in hiring and public education, Moy and associates sampled ferry passengers in the greater Seattle area. The participants completed a questionnaire "in public" (p. 13) to ascertain the public's reaction to this topic. Results of the study indicated that people had a real fear of being isolated. However, unlike the Spiral of Silence Theory, Moy and her colleagues discovered that one's family and friends were instrumental in one's willingness to speak out. These reference groups remained influential. The media (e.g., newspapers) were somewhat influential; however, they were not as significant as Noelle-Neumann had originally proposed. The study concludes with a call for future research looking at the *process* of media effects on public opinion.

power in U.S. society. Consider also that, as we discussed in Chapter 22, information is frequently filtered through news reporters and their agencies. As a result, what is presented—or in the case of this theory, what is perceived—may not be an accurate picture of reality. For instance, most people can attest to the diversity found in the United States, and yet most media do not report with this diversity in mind. Imagine, for instance, the anxiety and frustration of many disabled individuals as they read or listen to media reports about the success of the Americans with Disabilities Act passed in the early 1990s, when the high percentage of disabled people who remain unemployed or who continue to experience discrimination in the workplace is often not reported. Or perhaps you have read or heard about the success of affirmative action policies, neglecting the fact that much of today's discrimination is often covert and subtle (Jandt, 2004). Maybe you have read about the many people who have been forced off of welfare, but you probably haven't seen many stories describing the dire circumstances of many families as a result of this decreased funding. If the media report these "success" stories often enough, Noelle-Neumann says, they are setting the news agenda—identifying what should be noticed, deciding what questions should be asked, and determining whether various social policies and programs are effective. In other words, people experience the climate of public opinion through the mass media.

As you can see, then, when people look to media for a glimpse into the perceptions and beliefs of the population, they are likely to receive anything but an impartial representation. **Dual climates of opinion** often exist—that is, a climate that the population perceives directly and the climate the media report. For instance, Carol Johansen may compare her personal perceptions of spanking with those surveyed perceptions published in the newspaper. What is remarkable is that despite the differences in opinion, many people decide to remain silent. To understand what motivates people to speak out, Noelle-Neumann developed the train test.

dual climates of opinion
difference between the population's perception of a public issue and the way the media report on the issue

The Train Test

Examining whether or not people will speak out requires a methodology that is clear, testable, representative, and replicable. To prove this, Noelle-Neumann conceptualized the train test (today the test can be applied on a plane or bus as well). The **train test** is an assessment of the extent to which people will speak out with their own opinion. According to the Spiral of Silence Theory, people on two different sides of an issue will vary in their willingness to express views in public. To study this, the researchers gave respondents sketches showing two people in conversation. The researcher asked a respondent, "Which of the two would you agree with, Person A or Person B?" This question would then be followed up with a more pivotal question; for example, one that might test opinions pertaining to food safety. Essentially, the train (or plane or bus) test asks people a question such as the following:

train test
assessment of the extent to which people will speak out

> Suppose that you have a five-hour train ride ahead of you, and a person sits next to you and starts to discuss the problems of food safety. Would you talk or not talk about the topic to the person?

This question was repeated several times with various subjects. It focused on a number of topics, ranging from nuclear power plants to abortion to racial segregation. The test revealed a number of factors that help determine whether a person will voice an opinion. They include the following:

- Supporters of a dominant opinion are more willing to voice an opinion than those in the minority opinion.

- Because of a fear of isolation, people tend to refrain from publicly stating their position if they perceive that this perception will attract laughter, mockery, or similar threats of isolation.

- There are various ways of speaking out—for example, hanging posters, displaying bumper stickers, and distributing flyers.
- People are more likely to voice an opinion if it agrees with their own convictions as well as fits within current trends and the spirit of the age.
- People will voice an opinion if it aligns with societal views.
- People tend to share their opinions with those who agree with them more than with those who disagree.
- People draw the strength of their convictions from a variety of sources, including family, friends, and acquaintances.
- People may engage in **last-minute swing,** or jumping on the bandwagon of the popular opinion during the final moments of conversation.

last-minute swing
jumping on the bandwagon of popular opinion after opinions have been expressed

The train test has proved to be an interesting approach to studying public opinion. The method simulates public behavior when two schools of thought exist on a subject. For those who are willing to speak out, there are opportunities to sway others. And there are times when the minority opinion speaks out loudly. We now examine this group.

The Hard Core

Every now and then, the silent minority rises up. This group, called the **hard core,** "remains at the end of a spiral of silence process in defiance of the threats of isolation" (Noelle-Neumann, 1993, p. 170). Noelle-Neumann recognizes that like most things in life, there is an exception to every rule or theory. The hard core represents a group of individuals who know that there is a price to pay for their assertiveness. These deviants try to buck the dominant way of thinking and are prepared to directly confront anyone who gets in their way (Figure 24.2).

hard core
group(s) at the end of the spiral willing to speak out at any cost

Noelle-Neumann invokes the work of social psychologist Gary Shulman in attempting to understand the hard core better. Shulman argues that if the majority opinion becomes large enough, the majority voice becomes less powerful because no alternative opinions exist. A few years back, for instance, it was not uncommon for people to believe that those with AIDS should be quarantined (majority opinion). It didn't take long, however, for people's opinions to reject this narrow-minded view, primarily as a result of the hard core's efforts to educate

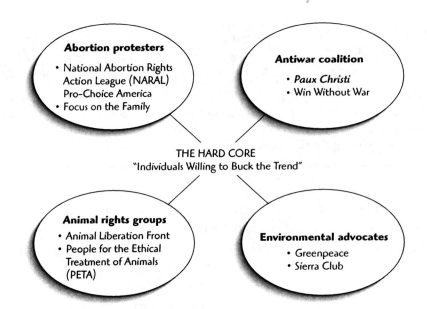

Figure 24.2
Examples of the "Hard Core" in the United States

the public. In fact, ironically, the media were pressed into educating the public about AIDS. It was not long before this silent hard core discovered that others had adopted their view. In this situation, the hard core was instrumental in changing public opinion.

For further evidence of the hard core, let's discuss an example pertaining to religion and religious opinion. Although we realize that not all people believe in God, God pervades our intellectual, political, and popular culture. For instance, people often say "God bless you" when others sneeze. In the political environment, each session of the U.S. Congress begins with some sort of prayer (there's even a U.S. House of Representatives chaplain), and many politicians conclude their speeches with "God bless America." "In God We Trust" appears on paper money, and the Pledge of Allegiance contains clear references to God ("one nation under God").

Despite pervasive references to God, many people in the United States do not believe in God. Some of these individuals contend that the country's Constitution requires a separation between church and state, and therefore any religious references in tax-supported venues should be eliminated. However, this opinion may not be shared by the majority because over half of the country affiliates with an organized religion (Lindner, 2008). Whether the media report on visits by the pope, present video clips of politicians leaving religious services each week, or solicit quotes for news stories from the clergy, they continue to imply that religion is an integral part of people's lives.

The minority—civil libertarians who advocate extracting religion from public-supported activities—have been vocal regarding their opinions; these hard-core dissenters have not blended into the background. Some of the effects of this hard core can be seen in that the Pledge of Allegiance is no longer required in every school district. In fact, in 2002 a federal appeals court in San Francisco ruled that the Pledge was unconstitutional in that it referenced God and violated the separation of church and state clause. Although the ruling was unsuccessfully appealed to the U.S. Supreme Court, it prompted considerable discussion on the references to God in state-sponsored efforts. The hard core might also claim victory as they see villages and cities remove religious icons (nativity sets, crucifixes, and so forth) from city parks during holidays. And with media outlets covering such legal victories, the hard core may be reconfiguring majority opinion.

Noelle-Neumann (1993) indicates that the hard core consists of people like Don Quixote, a literary figure who, because of his outdated clothing and weaponry, found himself ridiculed, defeated, and isolated. This tragic hero, according to Noelle-Neumann, had a desire to engender the respect of the world; his endless and futile combats were testimony to his undying commitment to chivalry. She concludes, "The 'hard core' [like Quixote] remains committed to the past, retaining the old values while suffering the isolation of the present" (p. 218). She adds that the hard core is the minority at the end of the spiral of silence who defy any threats of isolation.

Integration, Critique, and Closing

The Spiral of Silence Theory is one of the few theories in communication that focuses on public opinion. Indeed, the theory has been identified as an important foundation for examining the human condition (Csikszentmihalyi, 1991). The consequence of studying public opinion as Elisabeth Noelle-Neumann proposes is identified by Mihaly Csikszentmihalyi: "In an electoral democracy, but indeed even in the most tyrannical forms of government . . . the right to lead and to decide must eventually rest on the agreement of a significant segment of the population" (p. 288). The theory has been called "dynamic" (Merten, 1985), meaning that it underscores the process nature of communication that we discussed in Chapter 1. We examine two criteria for theory effectiveness: logical consistency and heurism.

Integration

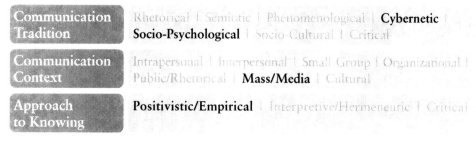

| Communication Tradition | Rhetorical | Semiotic | Phenomenological | **Cybernetic** | **Socio-Psychological** | Socio-Cultural | Critical |

| Communication Context | Intrapersonal | Interpersonal | Small Group | Organizational | Public/Rhetorical | **Mass/Media** | Cultural |

| Approach to Knowing | **Positivistic/Empirical** | Interpretive/Hermeneutic | Critical |

Critique

| Evaluation Criteria | Scope | **Logical Consistency** | Parsimony | Utility | Testability | **Heurism** | Test of Time |

Logical Consistency

Noelle-Neumann's theory has not avoided substantial criticism. And much of that criticism pertains to the lack of logical consistency in several of the terms and concepts. Charles Salmon and F. Gerald Kline (1985) state that the Spiral of Silence fails to acknowledge a person's ego involvement in an issue. At times, people may be willing to speak because their ego is involved in the topic (for example, if a promotion at work depends on assertiveness). Carroll Glynn, Andrew Hayes, and James Shanahan (1997) raise the issue of various selectivity processes, such as cognitive dissonance, which we explored in Chapter 7. Individuals will avoid a topic that conflicts with their own views. Glynn and colleagues also note that there is little empirical support for the claim that people speak out only because they perceive support for their views. J. David Kennamer (1990) supports this criticism: "[I]t is hard to imagine either the pro-life or the pro-choice sides of the abortion issue giving up the fight because they perceive themselves to be in the minority" (p. 396).

Carroll Glynn and Jack McLeod (1985) note two additional shortcomings pertaining to the logical consistency of the theory. First, they believe that the fear of isolation may not motivate people to express their opinions. They claim that Noelle-Neumann did not empirically test her assumption that fear of isolation prompts people to speak out. Second, they argue that Noelle-Neumann does not acknowledge the influence that people's communities and reference groups have on their opinions. They believe that she focuses too much on the media. Along with that concern, the fact that the development of the Spiral of Silence relies on the media in 1985 West Germany troubles Glynn and McLeod. They doubt whether the characteristics of the media then and there (ubiquitous, cumulative, and consonant) apply to the media in the United States today. During their examination of a U.S. presidential election, Glynn and McLeod discovered little support for media bias. They do not question the relatively intimate bond among media in Germany, but they do wonder whether the theory has limited cultural application in the United States.

Noelle-Neumann has responded to several of her critics, notably in defending her emphasis on the media. She remains convinced that the media is instrumental in public opinion. She writes that "by using words and arguments taken from the media to discuss a topic, people cause the point of view to be heard in public and give it visibility, thus creating a situation in which the danger of isolation is reduced" (Noelle-Neumann, 1985, p. 80). She continues by noting that not once did the spiral of silence process contradict the media's position on a topic (Noelle-Neumann, 1993). In terms of application across cultures, Noelle-Neumann agrees that any theory of public opinion must have cross-cultural applicability. However, she posits, it is important to note that most U.S. researchers desire a rational explanation for human behavior, but not all behavior can be explained sensibly. Still, she does accept that the train test may be limited in cross-cultural adaptation. As a result, Noelle-Neumann updated the version to read:

> Assume you are on a five-hour bus trip, and the bus makes a rest stop and everyone gets out for a long break. In a group of passengers, someone

Theory Into Practice

Soshanna

T*I*P

The fact that the media have power over the public is really nothing new to me. I think an example of this is the war in Iraq. There is no way that the public bought into that war, but the president kept telling people that we will get rid of terrorism if we invade Iraq, and the media kept reporting it over and over again. Now, of course, we know that the invasion had nothing to do with terrorism. But the fact that the media reported the "justification" on TV, radio, and the Internet just kept those of us who hated the invasion more silent, while those so-called "patriots" had their voices heard in media broadcasts.

starts talking about whether we should support [insert topic] or not. Would you like to talk to this person, to get to know his or her point of view better, or would you prefer not to? (p. 217)

Of course, you may doubt whether simply changing a train test to a bus test broadens the cross-cultural application of the theory.

Heurism

The theory has attracted writers and scholars who have discussed its merits in a variety of ways. First, some writers (Simpson, 1996) have attempted to discredit the theory because of its lack of application beyond one culture; other scholars have supported the cross-cultural application of the theory (Moy, Domke, & Stamm, 2001). This sort of scholarly dialogue enhances the heuristic appeal of the theory.

Researchers have employed the theory and many of its central concepts in their studies, including the following topics: declaring English as the official language of the United States (Lin & Salwen, 1997), religion in the classroom (Eckstein & Turman, 2002), the Persian Gulf War in the 1990s (Signorielli, Eveland, & McLeod, 1995), communication apprehension (Neuwirth, Frederick, & Mayo, 2007), college student sexual values (Chia & Lee, 2008), chat rooms (McDevitt, Kiousis, & Wahl-Jorgensen, 2003), and computer-mediated communication (Ernste, Fan, Sheets, & Elmasry, 2007). Such an array of topics and activity suggests that the theory and its prevailing concepts are worth studying.

The Spiral of Silence will continue to generate discussion among media scholars. The theory has sustained considerable criticism, and with a central emphasis on political discussion, researchers will continue to assess the theory's vitality. We live in a political world, dominated by a bold and intrusive Western media. Whether people openly express majority or minority viewpoints on an issue may not be directly proportional to the media's involvement on the issue, but it is clear that the public will come to rely on the media in the global society. The theory, therefore, may have lasting effects that have not been imagined.

Discussion Starters

1. Carol Johansen feels embarrassed about offering her opinions to a group that does not share her beliefs. Consider a similar time in your life. Did you speak out, or did you decide to remain quiet? What motivated your decision?

2. Discuss the times that you have been part of the hard-core minority. How did you behave? How did your confidence and self-esteem influence your behavior?

3. Does it make a difference to you to learn that Noelle-Neumann was once a newspaper journalist for Nazi publications? Why or why not?

4. Do you believe that the U.S. media are ubiquitous, consonant, or cumulative? Justify your answer.

5. Noelle-Neumann believes that the media help to influence minority views. Based on your observations of the media over the past several years, do you agree or disagree with this claim? What examples can you provide to defend your position?

6. Comment on the influence of the Internet on public opinion.

7. What do you suppose influences the "last-minute swings" of people?

Online Learning Center   www. mhhe.com/west4e

Visit the Online Learning Center at www.mhhe.com/west4e for chapter-specific resources, such as story-into-theory and multiple-choice quizzes, as well as theory summaries and theory connection questions.

CHAPTER 25

Media Ecology Theory

*Based on the research of **Marshall McLuhan***

Tiera Abrams

Tiera Abrams was bored. She was studying for her midterm in statistics and needed a break. She felt as though she would freak out if she continued to look at and memorize any more calculations. As she got up to get a drink, she thought about going online to a chat room she had found while surfing the Internet. Tiera figured a 5-minute break from studying wouldn't hurt too much. She liked the chat rooms because they featured like-minded people all together in one place. As she sat and chatted on e-mail, she became particularly interested in a man from Canada. As a New Yorker, Tiera was accustomed to meeting interesting people every day. Today, though, she soon found herself in private e-mail discussions with Marcus. Marcus seemed very different from any other person she had "chatted" with over the Internet—so much so that the two exchanged e-mail addresses.

Over the course of a month, Tiera and Marcus continued to e-mail each other. They were amazed how much they had in common. They both loved country music and had dozens of country music CDs. They also were amazed to find out that they were both "tech junkies" in that they both were interested in the latest palm organizers and personal video recorders, and they couldn't imagine what life would be like without digital cable (Tiera's local cable company offered 800 channels!). They also talked about each other's family and each other's views of relationships. Neither of them was especially excited about being married, and

neither one wanted children. Tiera thought that Marcus was simply too good to be true. And Marcus seemed to be quite enamored with her. All of this, and they had never even met in person!

Eventually, they decided to talk over the phone. Tiera was quite nervous; she wasn't sure whether she and Marcus would make as good a "connection" talking to each other as they had through e-mail. The conversation went great! They talked nonstop and covered a range of topics. Of course, they couldn't talk that long because of the long distance. Yet the half-hour phone call would be the beginning of something more significant.

In fact, after the phone call, Tiera called her best friend to tell her about it. The two talked for hours. Tiera was seriously thinking of trying to hook up with her newfound friend, but she still felt a bit afraid of the entire thing. She had heard horror stories about these sorts of Internet connections and wasn't sure if she should meet Marcus in Albany, a city in upstate New York. Tiera had relatives in Albany whom she could stay with, and she thought it would be a good central location for the two to meet. She decided that during spring break she would meet Marcus and would make sure that her friends and mother knew where she was all the time.

As she drove, Tiera talked to her friends and family on her cell phone. She assured them that she would be careful and had thought about the trip a lot before she made her decision. Despite their urging her to stay at home, Tiera wanted to meet the man whom she thought would be part of her future.

The two met at a parking lot in a strip mall outside of Albany. When Tiera saw Marcus's car, she dialed her cell phone to her mother and got out of the car to meet him (even though she was confident that everything would go okay, she didn't want to take any chances). Marcus was a complete gentlemen. They took separate cars to a restaurant, had dinner, went to the bar to have a drink, and talked all the while they were together. As they stood outside the restaurant, Tiera and Marcus spoke of getting together the next day for breakfast. She said that she could be reached at her uncle's house and gave Marcus the phone number. The two embraced and went to their respective cars.

As she pulled out of the parking lot of the restaurant, Tiera was a bit surprised to hear her cell phone ring. It was Marcus. He called to thank her again and to tell her to have a great night's sleep. When she hung up the phone, Tiera's head was spinning. She still couldn't believe that all of this happened because she went online during a night of studying!

Technology is often described as the most important influence on society. Few can challenge this claim. The Western world is filled with examples of how technology influences life. For instance, no doubt many of you begin your day by turning off your alarm clock, waiting for the coffeemaker to finish, turning on morning television, and going to work or school, immediately booting up the computer once you start the workday. Maybe you rely on instant messaging or blog on a subject near and dear to you. Perhaps you use a hand-held electronic organizer for your appointments or respond to voice mail by using your cell phone. When you return home, you probably turn on the television or radio to listen to the day's events. And it's fair to say, you begin and end each weekday in pretty much the same manner, probably unaware of your reliance on communication technology.

Like a lot of people today, Tiera Abrams finds herself in the middle of what could be called tech-dating. Although she is a self-described "tech junkie," very few could have predicted—even twenty years ago—that our society would find itself where Tiera Abrams is. There was a time when seeing a person up close was a primary prerequisite to communication with that person (your authors remember it well). Yet the technological times we live in have been expanded to the extent that "up close" simply means up close to one's computer monitor!

One theorist who could understand and interpret Tiera's relational circumstance is Marshall McLuhan. In his book *Understanding Media* (1964; Gordon, 2002), McLuhan wrote about the influence of technologies such as clocks, televisions, radios, movies, telephones, and even roads and games. Although today we would not classify some of these as technologies, at the time, McLuhan was interested in the social impact of these primary mediated forms of communication. In other words, what is the relationship between technology and members of a culture? It's fair to say that McLuhan himself was part of the culture's media. He appeared regularly on television talk shows, spoke to policy-makers, had a cameo role in the Woody Allen film *Annie Hall,* and even was interviewed by *Playboy* (Jenkins, 2008).

> **Media Ecology Theory • Theory at a Glance**
>
> Society has evolved as its technology has evolved. From the alphabet to the Internet, we have been affected by, and affect, electronic media. In other words, the medium *is* the message. The laws of media—enhancement, obsolescence, retrieval, and reversal—demonstrate that technology affects communication through new technology. Media Ecology Theory centers on the principles that society cannot escape the influence of technology and that technology will remain central to virtually all walks of life.

McLuhan was a Canadian scholar of literary criticism who used poetry, fiction, politics, musical theatre, and history to suggest that mediated technology shapes people's feelings, thoughts, and actions. McLuhan suggests that we have a symbiotic relationship with mediated technology; we create technology, and technology in turn re-creates who we are.

Electronic media have revolutionized society, according to McLuhan. In essence, McLuhan feels that societies are highly dependent on mediated technology and that a society's social order is based on its ability to deal with that technology. Recall that this theory was conceptualized nearly fifty years ago and, even today, McLuhan's assertion about technology rings true. Indeed, "since the public's growing consciousness of the Internet and the World Wide Web, starting in the mid-1990s, McLuhan's reputation has experienced an astounding upsurge" (Morrison, 2006, p. 170). Media, in general, act directly to mold and organize a culture. This is McLuhan's Media Ecology Theory (MET). Although some writers have referred to the theory as Technological Determinism, the growing consensus among scholars is that the term is an overstatement of McLuhan's theory (Cohen, 2000; Grosswiler, 1997; Levinson, 2001) and that it renders an audience passive and detached. In fact, audiences in McLuhan's writings are capable of being active: "Today, electronics and automation make mandatory that everybody adjust to the vast global environment as if it were his [*sic*] little home town" (McLuhan & Fiore, 1968, p. 11).

Because it centralizes the many types of media and views media as an environment unto itself, scholars aptly term McLuhan's work Media Ecology. For our purposes, we define **media ecology** as the study of how media and communication processes influence human perception, feeling, understanding, and value (Parameswaran, 2008). Given that McLuhan's writing spans a number of different academic disciplines, given that it focuses on a variety of technologies (e.g., radio, television, and so forth), and given that it pertains to the intersection of technology and human relationships and how media affect human perception and understanding (Postman, 1971), the ecological view of media proposed by McLuhan is appropriate and sensible. Paul Levinson (2000) describes the relationship of Media Ecology to communication this way: "McLuhan's work was startlingly distinct from the others [scholars] in that he

media ecology
the study of how media and communication processes affect human perception, feeling, emotion, and value

put communications at center stage. Indeed, in McLuhan's schema, there was nothing else on the stage."

McLuhan (1964) based much of his thinking on his mentor, Canadian political economist Harold Adams Innis (1951). Innis felt that major empires in history (Rome, Greece, and Egypt) were built by those in control of the written word. Innis argued that Canadian elites used a number of communication technologies to build their "empires." Those in power were given more power because of the development of technology. Innis referred to the shaping power of technology on a society as the **bias of communication**. For Innis, people use media to gain political and economic power and, therefore, change the social order of a society. Innis claimed that communication media have a built-in bias to control the flow of ideas in a society.

McLuhan extended the work of Innis. Philip Marchand (1989) observes that "not long after Innis's death, McLuhan found an opportunity to explore the new intellectual landscape opened up by his [Innis's] work" (p. 115). McLuhan, like Innis, felt that it's nearly impossible to find a society that is unaffected by electronic media. In fact, Michael Bugeja (2005) tends to agree; he notes that "the media use learners in a symbiotic marketing relationship. Content becomes biased in the process" (p. 133). Our perceptions of the media and how we interpret those perceptions are the core issues associated with MET. We now discuss these themes in the three main assumptions of the theory.

bias of communication
Harold Innis's contention that technology has a shaping power on society

Assumptions of Media Ecology Theory

We have noted that the influence of media technology on society is the main idea behind Media Ecology Theory. Let's examine this notion a bit further in the three assumptions framing the theory:

- Media infuse every act and action in society.
- Media fix our perceptions and organize our experiences.
- Media tie the world together.

Our first assumption underscores the notion that we cannot escape media in our lives: Media permeate our very existence. We cannot avoid nor evade media, particularly if we subscribe to McLuhan's broad interpretation of what constitutes media. Many Media Ecology theorists interpret media in far-reaching terms. For instance, in addition to looking at more traditional forms of media (e.g., radios, movies, and television), McLuhan also looks at the influence that numbers, games, and even money can have on society. We explore these three in more detail in order for you to understand the breadth of McLuhan's definition of media.

McLuhan (1964) views numbers as mediated. He explains: "In the theater, at a ball, at a ball game, in church, every individual enjoys all those others present. The pleasure of being among the masses is the sense of the joy in the multiplication of numbers, which has long been suspect among the literate members of

Western society" (p. 107). McLuhan felt that in numbers a "mass mind" (p. 107) was constructed by the elites in society to establish a "profile of the crowd" (p. 106). Therefore, it may be possible to create a homogenized population, capable of being influenced.

In addition to numbers, McLuhan looks at games in society as mediated. He observes that "games are popular art, collective, social reactions to the main drive or action of any culture" (p. 235). Games are ways to cope with everyday stresses and, McLuhan notes, they are models of our psychological lives. He further argues that "all games are media of interpersonal communication" (p. 237), which are extensions of our social selves. Games become mass media because they allow for people to simultaneously participate in an activity that is fun and that reflects who they are.

An additional mediated form is money. McLuhan concludes that "like any other medium, it is a staple, a natural resource" (p. 133). The theorist also calls money a "corporate image" that relies on society for its status and sustenance. Money has some sort of magical power that allows people access. Money allows people to travel the globe, serving as transmitters of knowledge, information, and culture. McLuhan notes that money is really a language that communicates to a diverse group, including farmers, engineers, plumbers, and physicians.

McLuhan, then, contends that media—interpreted in the broadest sense—are ever-present in our lives. These media transform our society, whether through the games we play, the radios we listen to, or the televisions we watch. At the same time, media depend on society for "interplay and evolution" (p. 49).

A second assumption of Media Ecology Theory relates to our previous discussion: We are directly influenced by media. Although we alluded to this influence earlier, let's be more specific about how McLuhan views the influence of media in our lives.

Media Ecology theorists believe that media fix perceptions and organize our lives. McLuhan suggests here that media are quite powerful in our views of the world. Consider, for instance, what occurs when we watch television. If television news reports that the United States is experiencing a "moral meltdown," we may be watching stories on child abductions, illegal drug use, or teenage pregnancies. In our private conversations, we may begin to talk about the lack of morals in society. In fact, we may begin to live our lives according to the types of stories we watch. We may be more suspicious of even friendly strangers, fearing they may try to kidnap our child. We may be unwilling to support laws legalizing medicinal marijuana, regardless of their merits, because we are concerned about possible increases in drug activity. We may also aggressively advocate an "abstinence-only" sex education program in schools, fearing that any other model would cause more unwanted pregnancies.

What occurs with each of these examples is what McLuhan asserts happens all the time: We become (sometimes unwittingly) manipulated by television. Our attitudes and experiences are directly influenced by what we watch on television, and our belief systems apparently can be negatively affected by television. Some writers (e.g., Bugeja, 2005) contend that McLuhan perceived television as instrumental to the erosion of family values. Marie Winn (2002) underscores the effect of television by calling it a "plug-in drug."

A third assumption of Media Ecology Theory has elicited quite a bit of popular conversation: Media connect the world. McLuhan used the phrase **global village** to describe how media tie the world into one great political, economic, social, and cultural system. Recall that although the phrase is almost a cliche these days, it was McLuhan who argued that the media can organize societies socially. Electronic media, in particular, have the ability to bridge cultures that would not have communicated prior to this connection.

global village
the notion that humans can no longer live in isolation, but rather will always be connected by continuous and instantaneous electronic media

The effect of this global village, according to McLuhan (1964), is the ability to receive information instantaneously (an issue we return to later in the chapter). As a result, we should be concerned with global events, rather than remaining focused on our own communities. He observes that "the globe is no more than a village" (p. 5) and that we should feel responsible for others. Others "are now involved in our lives, as we in theirs, thanks to the electric media" (p. 5).

Let's revisit our opening example of Tiera Abrams to illustrate this assumption further. As a consumer of the Internet, Tiera frequently visited "chat rooms," which allowed her to communicate with a number of different people at once. During this time, she encountered Marcus, whom she decided to meet. As a Canadian, Marcus would not normally visit the same social places as Tiera. It was electronic media that allowed this international relationship to get off the ground. If the two were to continue to see each other, they would naturally find out more about the other's family, community, and culture.

The global village of Marshall McLuhan follows the General Systems perspective we outlined in Chapter 3. You will recall that Systems theorists believe that one part of a system will affect the entire system. Media Ecology theorists believe that the action of one society will necessarily affect the entire global village. Therefore, floods in Europe, famine in Africa, and war in the Middle East affect the United States, Australia, and China. According to McLuhan, we can no longer live in isolation because of "electronic interdependence" (McLuhan & Fiore, 1996).

epoch
era or historical age

You have now been introduced to the primary assumptions of MET. McLuhan's theory relies heavily on a historical understanding of media. He asserts that the media of a particular time period were instrumental in organizing societies. He identifies four distinct time periods, or **epochs**, in history (Table 25.1). We address them next.

Making Media History and Making "Sense"

McLuhan (1962, 1964) and Quentin Fiore (McLuhan & Fiore, 1967, 1996) claim that the media of an era define the essence of a society. They present four eras, or epochs, in media history, each of which corresponds to the dominant mode of communication of the time. McLuhan contends that media act as extensions of the human senses in each era, and communication (technology) is the primary cause of social change (Hakanen, 2007).

Table 25.1 McLuhan's Media History

HISTORICAL EPOCH	PROMINENT TECHNOLOGY/ DOMINANT SENSE	McLUHAN'S COMMENTS
Tribal Era	Face-to-Face Contact/Hearing	"An oral or tribal society has the means of stability far beyond anything possible to a visual or civilized and fragmented world" (McLuhan & Fiore, 1968, p. 23).
Literate Era	Phonetic Alphabet/Seeing	"Western man [woman] has done little to study or to understand the effects of the phonetic alphabet in creating many of his [her] basic patterns of culture" (McLuhan, 1964, p. 82).
Print Era	Printing Press/Seeing	"Perhaps the most significant of the gifts of typography to man [woman] is that of detachment and noninvolvement—the power to act without reacting" (McLuhan, 1964, p. 173).
Electronic Era	Computer/Seeing, Hearing, Touching	"The computer is by all odds the most extraordinary of all the technological clothing ever devised . . . since it is the extension of our central nervous system" (McLuhan & Fiore, 1968, p. 35).

The Tribal Era

According to McLuhan, during the **tribal era,** hearing, smell, and taste were the dominant senses. During this time, McLuhan argues, cultures were "ear-centered" in that people heard with no real ability to censor messages. This era was characterized by the oral tradition of storytelling whereby people revealed their traditions, rituals, and values through the spoken word. In this era, the ear became the sensory "tribal chief" and for people, hearing was believing.

tribal era
age when oral tradition was embraced and hearing was the paramount sense

The Literate Era

This epoch, emphasized by the visual sense, was marked by the introduction of the alphabet. The eye became the dominant sensory organ. McLuhan and Fiore (1996) stated that the alphabet caused people to look at their environment in visual and spatial terms. McLuhan (1964) also maintained that the alphabet made knowledge more accessible and "shattered the bonds of tribal man" (p. 173). Whereas the tribal era was characterized by people speaking, the **literate era** was a time when written communication flourished. People's

literate era
age when written communication flourished and the eye became the dominant sense organ

messages became centered on linear and rational thinking. Out was storytelling; in were mathematics and other forms of analytic logic. This "scribal world" had the unintended consequence of forcing communities to become more individualistic rather than collectivistic (McLuhan & Fiore, 1967). People were able to get their information without help from their communities. This was the beginning of people communicating without the need to be face-to-face.

The Print Era

print era
age when gaining information through the printed word was customary, and seeing continued as the dominant sense

The invention of the printing press heralded the **print era** in civilization and the beginning of the industrial revolution. Although it was possible to do a great deal of printing by woodcut prior to this era, the printing press made it possible to make copies of essays, books, and announcements. This provided for even more permanency of record than in the literate age. The printing press also allowed people other than the elite to gain access to information. Furthermore, people didn't have to rely on their memories for information as they had to do in the past.

McLuhan (1964) observed that the book was "the first teaching machine" (p. 174). Consider his words today. Very few courses in college exist without a textbook. Even with technological teaching approaches such as distance learning or interactive television, the large majority of courses still require textbooks. Books remain indispensable in the teaching—learning process.

Exemplifying the print era more specifically, McLuhan writes:

> Margaret Mead has reported that when she brought several copies of the same book to a Pacific island there was great excitement. The natives had seen books, but only one copy of each, which they had assumed to be unique. Their astonishment at the identical character of several books was a natural response to what is after all the most magical and potent aspect of print and mass production. It involves a principle of extension by homogenization that is the key to understanding Western power. (p. 174)

What McLuhan notes here is that mass production produces citizens who are similar to each other. The same content is delivered over and over again by the same means. This visual-dependent era, however, produced a fragmented population because people could remain in isolation reading their mass-produced media.

The Electronic Era

Few can argue with the fact that the age we live in now is electronic. Interestingly, McLuhan (1964) and his colleague (McLuhan & Fiore, 1967) note that this epoch, characterized by the telegraph, telephone, typewriter, radio, and television, has brought us back to tribalization and the art of oral communication. Instead of books being the central repository of information, electronic media decentralized information to the extent that individuals are now one of several primary sources of information. This era has returned us to a primitivelike

Research Notes

Calavita, M. (2003). Within the context of many contexts: Family, news media engagement, and the ecology of individual political development among "Generation Xers." *Communication Review,* 6, 23–43.

The politics of fifteen young people (22–33 years old) were analyzed to determine who and what influenced their "political socialization" (p. 24). Prompted by "the apparently sorry state of this generation's political and civic attitudes and orientations" (p. 25), Calavita investigated the attitudes of a sample of young people who had completed two years of college. The researcher felt that "the news media is an environment in which individuals develop politically [and] the news media are of subtle-but-fundamentally powerful ecological importance" (p. 24) in shaping individuals. This study underscores the importance of family members—specifically parents—in contributing toward Generation Xers' political identity. According to several participants in this research, the media and family intersect to form a special "connective tissue" (p. 29) between the child and the world of politics. Calavita affirms that Generation Xers vicariously experienced their parents' news media "engagement." Two participants, for example, remembered the day President Nixon resigned because their parents were watching it on television, and at one point they watched their mother crying as the news unfolded.

The results of this research suggest that the political leanings of the participants' parents influenced Generation Xers. Furthermore, the research results underscore "the media ecology theorization of media as environments with structuring biases" (p. 24).

Strate, L. (2004). A media ecology review. *Communication Research Trends, 23*, 3–6.

Strate presents an essay that is a tribute to two leading scholars of Media Ecology, Walter Ong and Neil Postman. The two are posthumously honored by Strate, who articulates their contributions to Media Ecology Theory. First, Strate examines the influences Ong had on current questions pertaining to the media and the ecological issues surrounding media. Ong remains a crucial influence on how Media Ecology has evolved both as a cultural perspective and as a theoretical model. Strate then presents a tribute to Neil Postman, a more contemporary figure in Media Ecology (in fact, Postman conceptualized the media ecology "movement"). Postman, clearly influenced by Marshall McLuhan, looked at Media Ecology as a "field of inquiry" (p. 4) whereas in McLuhan's writings, Media Ecology is viewed in more practical terms. The essay is important as it contributes to our understanding of two central figures in Media Ecology and their relationship to Marshall McLuhan, the media pioneer associated with the theory.

reliance on "talking" to one another. Today, though, we define "talking" differently than the way it occurred in the tribal era. We talk through television, radio, records/tapes/CDs, photographs, answering machines, cell phones, blogs, and e-mail. The **electronic era** allows different communities in different parts of the world to remain connected, a concept we discussed earlier as the global village.

McLuhan (1964) provocatively relates a description of various technologies in the electronic age:

The telephone: speech without walls.

The phonograph: music hall without walls.

The photograph: museum without walls.

electronic era
age in which electronic media pervades our senses, allowing for people across the world to be connected

The electric light: space without walls.

The movie, radio, and TV: classroom without walls (p. 283).

The electronic era presents unique opportunities to reevaluate how media influence the people they serve. This age allows for ear and eye and voice to work together.

This historical presentation of media by McLuhan suggests that the primary media of an age prompts a certain sensory reaction in people. McLuhan and Fiore (1968) theorize that a **ratio of the senses** is required by people, which is a conversation of sorts between and among the senses. That is, a balance of the senses is required, regardless of the time in history. For instance, with the Internet, we reconcile a variety of senses, including visual stimulation of website pictures and the auditory arousal of downloaded music.

ratio of the senses
phrase referring to the way people adapt to their environment (through a balance of the senses)

The Medium Is the Message

the medium is the message
phrase referring to the power and influence of the medium—not the content—on a society

Media Ecology Theory is perhaps best known for the catchphrase **the medium is the message** (McLuhan 1964), a "humble and fascinating" phrase (Hodge, 2003, p. 342). Although followers of McLuhan continue to debate the precise meaning of this equation, it appears to represent McLuhan's scholarly values: The content of a mediated message is secondary to the medium (or communication channel). The medium has the ability to change how we think about others, ourselves, and the world around us. So, for instance, in our opening example of Tiera Abrams, what she and Marcus communicated is less important than that they communicated via a computer, the Internet, and e-mail.

McLuhan did not dismiss the importance of content altogether. Rather, as Paul Levinson (2001) points out, McLuhan argued that content gets our attention more than the medium does. McLuhan thinks that although a message affects our conscious state, it is the medium that largely affects our unconscious state. So, for example, we often unconsciously embrace television as a medium while receiving a message broadcast around the world. Consider the fact that the 2001 terrorist attacks in New York City, the train bombs in Madrid in 2004, Hurricane Katrina's devastating effects in 2005, and the 2008 earthquake in China were reported not only immediately after the events but, in some cases, during the events (interestingly, all these events occurred in the morning rush hours at each city around 9 A.M.). Many of us went to TV immediately and instinctively, captivated by the horror and the images as they occurred. We were pretty much unconscious of the medium, but rather consumed with the message. Nonetheless, we turned to television again and again for updates as the days and months progressed, rather unaware of its importance in our lives. This represents McLuhan's hypothesis that the medium shapes the message and it is, ironically enough, our unawareness of the medium that makes a message all the more important.

McLuhan and Fiore (1967) claim that in addition to the medium being the message, the medium is the "massage." By changing one letter, they creatively presented readers with another view of media. It's not clear whether the authors were making a pun on the "mass-age" or whether they were reinforcing McLuhan's earlier writings on the power of the media. McLuhan and Fiore argue that not only are we influenced by the media, but we can become seduced by it. As a population, we are entranced with new technologies. For instance, it is now customary for national media such as the *New York Times* and *USA Today* to feature special sections on technology and culture. New gadgets, gizmos, and technological inventions (and their prices) are featured for those desiring the latest. Indeed, the medium massages the masses, is part of the "mess-age" (McLuhan & Parker, 1969), and can be understood in a "mass-age" (McLuhan & Nevitt, 1972). James Morrison (2006) sums it up best by stating that "'the medium is the message' because the contents of a medium vary and may even be contradictory, but the medium's effects remain the same, no matter what the content" (p. 178).

We have presented several key assumptions and issues associated with Media Ecology Theory. We have also discussed media in very broad terms. McLuhan said that some unifying and systematic way of differentiating media was necessary. The result was an interesting analysis of hot and cool media.

Gauging the Temperature: Hot and Cool Media

To understand the "large structural changes in human outlook" (McLuhan, 1964, p. vi) of the 1960s, McLuhan set out to classify media. He explains that media can be classified as either hot or cool, language he borrowed from jazz slang. This classification system remains confounding to many scholars, and yet it is a pivotal aspect of the theory. We distinguish between the two media next and provide examples of each in Figure 25.1.

Hot media are described as media that demand very little from a listener, reader, or viewer. Hot media are high-definition communications that have

hot media
high-definition communication that demands little involvement from a viewer, listener, or reader

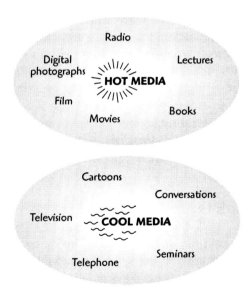

Figure 25.1
Examples of McLuhan's Hot and Cool Media

relatively complete sensory data; very little is left to the audience's imagination. Hot media, therefore, are low in audience participation. Meaning is essentially provided. An example of a hot medium is a movie, because it requires very little of us. We sit down, watch the film, react, maybe eat some popcorn, and then watch the credits. Hot media give the audience what they need—in this case, entertainment.

We should add that McLuhan believes that radio is a hot medium. He acknowledges that radio can serve as background sound, as noise-level control, or for listening pleasure. No involvement is needed with radio. However, McLuhan wrote before the proliferation of radio talk shows. Would he consider radio to be low involvement today?

cool media
low-definition communication that demands active involvement from a viewer, listener, or reader

Unlike hot media, **cool media** require a high degree of participation; they are low definition. Little is provided by the medium, so much has to be filled in by the listener, reader, or viewer. Cool media require audiences to create meaning through high sensory and imaginative involvement. Consider, for instance, cartoons. Generally, we get a few frames of illustrations and perhaps some brief phrases. Cartoons are low definition and provide very little visual information. We need to determine the meaning of the words and the pictures, and even supply missing words or ideas that are not provided in the cartoon.

Let's make one more point about cool media. Interestingly, McLuhan (1964) contended that television can be considered a cool medium. He argued that TV is a medium that requires viewers to be actively involved. In fact, he notes that television "engages you. You have to be *with* it" (p. 312). Yet, with the digital age upon us, television has taken on new meaning that perhaps even McLuhan could never have imagined. Would he still consider television a cool medium today? In a personal interview with media scholar Guido Stempel, Michael Bugeja (2005) reports that Stempel considers television to be "passive . . . [e]xcept for the remote control. In that sense . . . television is interactive" (p. 125). Bugeja and others wonder how McLuhan would place HDTV (high-definition television), which has the precise and clear audio and visual quality.

To illustrate the hot and cool media, McLuhan analyzed the 1960 presidential debates between John F. Kennedy and Richard Nixon. McLuhan discovered that for those who watched the debate on television, Kennedy had won because he exuded an objective, cool persona, perfect for the cool medium. For those who listened to the debates on the radio (a hot medium), Nixon was the winner. He was considered hot (which, in fact, his sweating showed he was!). So, the medium influences others' perceptions. Arthur Asa Berger (2007) notes that McLuhan's thinking pertaining to hot and cool media is prompting more research interest as communication theorists try to understand the passion that people have for their cell phones.

The Circle Is Complete: The Tetrad

We continue our discussion of Media Ecology Theory by examining the most recent expansion of McLuhan's thinking about the media. With his son, Eric (McLuhan & McLuhan, 1988), and to respond to those who believed that

> ### Theory Application in Groups (TAG)
>
> How might McLuhan respond to the role of the Internet today? Would he applaud its existence, lament its existence, or be cautious? Does it promote "the global village" as he believed, or does it serve another function? Use examples in your response.

there was no scientific grounding in his work, McLuhan developed a way to look further into the effects of technology on society. His expansion of the theory included a thorough discussion of the **laws of media.**

Although McLuhan's earlier work identified in this chapter did not fully take into account the advent of the computer, his posthumous work with his son took into consideration the influence of the Internet. Their work was an effort to bring the theory full circle: Technology affects communication through new technology, the impact of the new technology affects society, and the changes in society cause further changes in technology. McLuhan and McLuhan offer the **tetrad** as an organizing concept that allows scholars to understand the past, present, and current effects of media.

To give us a new way of looking at the role of technology in our culture, McLuhan and McLuhan offer four laws of media, phrased as questions (Table 25.2): (1) What do media *enhance*? (2) What do media make *obsolete*? (3) What do media *retrieve*? (4) What do media *reverse*? Let's examine each and identify examples of their role in culture. We pay particular attention to the role of the Internet in our discussion.

laws of media
further expansion of Media Ecology Theory with focus on the impact of technology on society

tetrad
organizing concept to understand the laws of media

Enhancement

The first law of media is **enhancement**; that is, media enhance or amplify society. The telephone enhanced the spoken word found in face-to-face conversations. Radio, of course, amplified the voice across distance. Television amplified the word and the visual across continents.

enhancement
law that states media amplify or strengthen society

Table 25.2 Laws of Media

LAWS OF MEDIA	DESCRIPTION
Enhancement	What does the medium enhance or amplify?
Obsolescence	What does the medium push aside or make obsolete?
Retrieval	What does the medium retrieve from the past?
Reversal	When pushed to its limits, what does the medium reverse or flip into?

The Internet has enhanced society in different ways. First, it has the potential to enhance a number of senses, including sight and sound. Second, the existence of the Internet has enhanced the accessibility of information. For instance, we can now obtain birth records, credit card balances, and missing person information over the Internet. Third, the Internet can enhance class division. The "haves and the have-nots" exist along this information superhighway. Finally, decentralization of authority is enhanced by the Internet. No longer do our political leaders solely possess information; that information becomes available online.

Obsolescence

McLuhan and McLuhan (1988) note that the second law of media is that media eventually render something obsolete or out of date. Television made radio obsolete, although many of us continue to turn to radio each day while we drive. Levinson (2001) notes that radio rendered motion pictures obsolete, which in turn resulted in fewer movies to watch. VCRs and DVD players may have also attempted to make movies obsolete, but we know that their efforts have been only somewhat successful.

obsolescence
law that states media eventually render something out of date

The Internet, too, has brought about **obsolescence**. For example, as we learned earlier, the global village now exists, thanks largely to the Internet. The geographical splits are pretty hard to find; even the remote villages of Africa are becoming accessible by the Internet. Second, the Internet is slowly targeting micromedia (specific audiences) rather than macromedia (large masses), thereby making traditional media outlets such as CBS, NBC, and ABC change their news reporting. Finally, face-to-face dialogues are becoming outdated with the Internet. Former "tribal" conversations are now electronically derived.

Retrieval

retrieval
law that states media restore something that was once lost

The third law is **retrieval**, meaning that media recover or restore something that was once lost. What older, previously obsolesced media is brought back? Television, for instance, restored the importance of the visual that radio did not achieve, but that was once in face-to-face conversations. Radio retrieved the town crier, the prominent voice of newsworthy events well over 200 years ago in the United States. Print retrieved the tribe's universality of knowledge. And the Internet recovers a community that was once lost to other media. For instance, chat rooms visited by people like Tiera Abrams from our opening vignette have electronically rekindled conversations that flourished before radio and television.

Reversal

reversal
law that states media will—when pushed to their limit—produce or become something else

When "pushed to the limit of its potential" (McLuhan & McLuhan, 1988, p. 99), what do media produce or become? What do media reverse into? When too many constraints exist on a medium, it will "overheat" and become ineffective. **Reversal** contains characteristics of the system from which it arose. For

> ### Theory Into Practice
> #### Olga
>
> When I read about the "global village," considering that McLuhan wrote about this in the 1960s, I thought it was amazing! Here's this pretty zany guy who almost fifty years ago was writing about how we are connected with the rest of the world. And he was right! As someone who has lived in four countries, I have turned on the TV, gone to a website, or blogged about what is happening around the world. We are all connected more than ever, and McLuhan knew this before anyone else did.

T * I * P

instance, the public's desire to have access to entertainment in a relatively cheap medium led to the creation of radio dramas and comedy programs. The need to "see" what was heard led to the creation of these programs on television. Yet we can videotape television programs and what was once seen by millions of people at the same time is reversed into private videotaped "performances." Television, then, reversed into the early days of the print era when people could consume media privately.

The Internet—as a medium pushed to its potential—reverses society into a new and unique place. The Internet has the potential to bring tribal people together when they discuss websites or chat room conversations with one another. Looking at the number of people who "surf the net" each day, we can confidently state that the Internet can isolate people just as television can. With the ability to download music, television shows, and short films, the Internet has reversed itself into a medium with significant visual and auditory appeal. Finally, the Internet is a medium that "flips" on its user. That is, although it can serve to erode power, it can also perpetuate power differences among people. As a result, the Internet provides opportunities for both. Furthermore, the Internet has ushered in a generation of youth who "think like Pentium rather than like Plato" (Bugeja, 2005, p. 132).

Carrying the McLuhan Banner: Postman and Meyrowitz

Two influential contemporary scholars have worked to integrate McLuhan's thinking into their own scholarship. Neil Postman (1992), in *Technopoly: The Surrender of Culture to Technology,* and Joshua Meyrowitz (1985), in *No Sense of Place,* remain influential in understanding McLuhan. We close our discussion with an overview of this scholarly expansion.

Neil Postman, who died in 2003, is credited with formally introducing the term *media ecology* in 1968 (Gencarelli, 2006). Postman's biography is an interesting one and is available elsewhere (Thaler, 2006; Gencarelli, 2006). Nonetheless, it is important to give you a glimpse into Postman's credentials.

As Thomas Gencarelli (2006) observes, "Postman is first and foremost an educator" (p. 239). Indeed, most of his books pertained to public education in the United States. In some cases, he encouraged changes to the educational system by stating that it needed to be revitalized. Nowhere can that revitalization occur other than with an infusion of technology, according to Postman. The media environment, he believed, helped shape children's lives. Television, in particular, was ripe in allowing young people to be exposed to all sorts of information that was originally intended for adults. This conflation of the child and adult worlds was an ongoing concern for Postman.

Postman was clearly a man who practiced what he preached. Jim Benning (2003) relates a relevant anecdote. Shopping for a new car, Postman is quoted as saying: "Why do I need electric windows? My arm and hand work. If I were paralyzed I could use an electric window." His colleague and friend noted that "Neil would always take what he would call an ecological perspective, a balanced view."

Postman wrote over 200 articles for the public and over 20 popular and scholarly books. Postman's research is underscored by a central theme: "All technologies are human impositions into the natural order of things and, as a result, change that order" (Gencarelli, 2006, p. 244). Among the most influential of his published works is *Technopoly: The Surrender of Culture to Technology*. In the book, Postman (1992) hypothesized that technology negatively changes the fabric of society. Specifically, he believed that culture is subservient to the invisible (e.g., I.Q. scores) and visible (e.g., computers).

technopoly
a term coined by Postman that means we live in a society dominated by technology

Postman coined the term **technopoly**, which means that we live in a culture in which technology dominates our thinking and behaviors. In a technopoly, Postman argued, technological tools serve to take over the culture in which they thrive. We live in a society where being technologically driven may result in being driven mad! We trust that our technology will bring us safety and salvation, and seem to lose any sense of humility, discipline, and rationality regarding our reliance on and trust in current media. As a result, Postman laments that "tradition, social mores, myth, politics, ritual, and religion have to fight for their lives" (p. 28). Postman, like McLuhan, asked whether we want to live in a culture with such unwavering dependence on technology.

In addition to Postman, Joshua Meyrowitz's (1985) research interconnects with McLuhan's work. Meyrowitz's *No Sense of Place* ushered in a unique way of thinking related to space. First, he argues that space is more than physical (Dresner, 2006). That is, social situations such as contesting a parking ticket at city hall include more than the physical surroundings of the building and courtroom. Meyrowitz contends that the influence that communication has on the situation also needs to be considered.

As a communication scholar, Meyrowitz is interested in uncovering the effects of communication technology, namely, television, on a social situation. Consider, for instance, a private discussion between a husband and wife on marital infidelity. The discussion is likely to be free-wheeling, underscoring the intimacy that the couple shares. Now, put that discussion in front of a live

Oprah television audience. A new pattern of communication will begin, with different information flow and new rules of conduct. It is this new communication medium that Meyrowitz is interested in and one that has cultural consequences. Television is a medium that reconfigures boundaries that were once in place (Dresner, 2006).

Meyrowitz agrees with McLuhan that electronic media have social consequences. Meyrowitz expands the notion that power relations and social class can be traced to electronic media. He draws on sociology research to conclude that media have brought about a blurring of formerly distinct roles or places. He states that "many Americans may no longer seem to 'know their place' because the traditionally interlocking components of 'place' have been split apart by electronic media. Wherever one is now—at home, at work, or in the car—one may be in touch and tuned in" (p. 308).

Meyrowitz points to television. For instance, examine talk shows and you can get a sense of how the blurring of place occurs. What was once private (for instance, discussing your mother's alcoholism) is now public on *Jerry Springer*. Masculine and feminine roles now blur. Even our political leaders are now at the level of everyone else. In fact, in small states such as Maine, the governor can be contacted directly by phone, e-mail, or fax!

Both Postman and Meyrowitz remain articulate and effective stewards of Marshall McLuhan. They carry the banner which boldly proclaims that electronic media have unraveled Western society's foundation and many of its core values. To be sure, the two scholars prompt us to consider McLuhan's work in more contemporary ways. As Gary Wolf (1996) noted in *Wired* magazine: "McLuhan is relevant" (p. 124).

Integration, Critique, and Closing

You probably have already figured out that Marshall McLuhan has caused quite a reaction in both academic and public circles. His ideas are provocative, and at times, have been unilaterally dismissed by many. In fact, if you reviewed his original work, you may be challenged by frequently eccentric writing style. Some have labeled his thinking "McLuhanacy" (Gordon, 1982), while others feel his writing is equivalent to "genre bending" (Carey, 1998).

McLuhan's work and reputation, however, have been invoked with considerable regard. *Wired* magazine named him their "Patron Saint," and *Life* magazine called him the "Oracle of the Electronic Age." There exists a concentration in McLuhan Studies at the University of Toronto, a McLuhan newsletter, a *McLuhan Studies* journal, symposia on McLuhan's research, a McLuhan festival, a McLuhan reading club, and even a secondary high school in Canada named the Marshall McLuhan Catholic School. It's hard to escape his influence both in research and in societies around the world. The theory, despite its popularity, has been evaluated by scholars and writers. We will examine these critiques on the criteria of testability and heurism.

Integration

Communication Tradition	Rhetorical	Semiotic	Phenomenological	Cybernetic	Socio-Psychological	**Socio-Cultural**	**Critical**
Communication Context	Intrapersonal	Interpersonal	Small Group	Organizational	Public/Rhetorical	**Mass/Media**	Cultural
Approach to Knowing	Positivistic/Empirical	Interpretive/Hermeneutic	**Critical**

Critique

| Evaluation Criteria | Scope | Logical Consistency | Parsimony | Utility | **Testability** | **Heurism** | Test of Time |

Testability

Media Ecology Theory has been criticized because many of its concepts are difficult to understand, thereby making testability of the theory challenging and, indeed, nearly impossible. The question becomes apparent: How does one test something one has trouble understanding?

Criticism pertaining to the testability of the theory is represented in comments that have been offered by media scholars over the years. For instance, critics have blasted MET as "overly optimistic" about the role of technology in society (Baran & Davis, 2009). They believe that McLuhan put too much emphasis on how much technology influences society, making the very foundation of the theory rather shaky. George Gordon (1982) is more direct: "Not one bit of sustained and replicated scientific evidence, inductive or deductive, has to date justified any one of McLuhan's most famous slogans, metaphors, or dicta" (p. 42). Dwight Macdonald (1967) also attacked McLuhan's writing, noting that "he has looted all culture from cave painting to *Mad* magazine for fragments to shore up his system against ruin" (p. 203).

A great deal of criticism has been directed at McLuhan's use of words and his clarity. To some, his ideas make little sense. Some writers believe that McLuhan failed to define his words carefully and used too much exaggeration. In the *Chronicle of Higher Education,* Paul Levinson (1999) concludes that his work "was not your professor's writing—no long paragraphs of logically developed argument" (p. B10). He writes in a zigzag fashion, weaving in one point after another with no apparent topic sentence or sustained idea. Although some writers indict this process, McLuhan (1967) offers no apology: "I don't explain—I explore" (p. i).

Heurism

Media Ecology Theory and McLuhan's thinking have been met with considerable enthusiasm. Because McLuhan was a key figure in popular culture, it's important to keep in mind that his writing has prompted both academic and lay reaction. One hallmark of the heuristic value of Media Ecology Theory is the fact that there is now a Media Ecology Association (www.media-ecology.org). This organization is dedicated to promoting the theory in both practical and theoretical ways, thereby ensuring the theory's visibility. The association publishes a journal (*EME: Explorations in Media Ecology*) dedicated to the theory, a testimony to the fact that mass communication scholars continue to integrate the theory into their research.

Researchers have discussed McLuhan and his contributions in a variety of ways. Scholars have provided a comprehensive understanding of the theory and have discussed the theory's influential pioneers (Lum, 2006). Additional writers have applied several of McLuhan's premises in research (Strate & Wachtel, 2005). Furthermore, many of the theory's concepts have been incorporated into research on such diverse topics as human–computer interaction (Edsall, 2007) and YouTube as "cool" media (Trier, 2007). Media Ecology Theory, then, has high heuristic value.

Marshall McLuhan and Media Ecology Theory will continue to resonate for years to come. Perhaps one day we will revisit McLuhan's original thinking on historical epochs in media history! New media will continue to evolve in our society and so will the application of McLuhan's thinking. Was McLuhan an absurd reactionary? Or was McLuhan a cultural prophet? On his gravestone are the words "The Truth Will Set You Free." Did McLuhan think he discovered Truth? Or, even in his death, does he continue to play with our imaginations? Perhaps one of McLuhan's biographers, Philip Marchand (1989), best illustrates McLuhan's contribution to the study of media: "McLuhan's comments had at least one virtue: They seemed to suggest that the world was more interesting than any of us had previously thought it to be" (p. xiii).

Discussion Starters

1. Discuss whether Tiera Abrams's experience with an online relationship is representative of the future of relationships or if similar experiences will eventually fade away.

2. How might Media Ecology theorists like Marshall McLuhan react to the current news on television today? What would be his major criticisms and his major objections? What would he be particularly interested in?

3. Do you agree or disagree with McLuhan regarding television being a cool medium? Use examples to defend your view.

4. Suppose you were asked to have dinner with scholars Neil Postman and Joshua Meyrowitz. What types of questions would you ask them? How would the conversation proceed?

5. Interpret and comment on the following statement: "Technology is the end of our beginning." Use examples to defend your view.

6. Discuss your response to theorists who choose to be part of the popular culture, including participating on talk shows and appearing in films?

7. Apply any principle of MET to (a) YouTube, (b) Google, and (c) Facebook.

Online Learning Center    www. mhhe.com/west4e

Visit the Online Learning Center at www.mhhe.com/west4e for chapter-specific resources, such as story-into-theory and multiple-choice quizzes, as well as theory summaries and theory connection questions.

Major Continental Theories Influencing Media Studies

C H A P T E R   **2**

Karl Marx

Chapter Outline

Introduction

Marx began his most famous work, *The Manifesto of the Communist Party* (Marx and Engels 1848/1948), with the following line: "There is a spectre haunting Europe, the spectre of communism." It might be said that the same ghost is haunting our understanding of Marx. It is difficult to separate the ideas of Marx from the political movements that they inspired. Nevertheless, as Tom Rockmore (2002:96) tells us, we must try "to free Marx from Marxism."

For many, Marx has become more of an icon than a thinker deserving of serious study. The symbolism of his name tends to muddle understanding of his ideas. Marx is the only theorist we will study who has had political movements and social systems named after him. He is probably the only theorist your friends and family have strong opinions about. He is often criticized, as well as praised, by people who have never actually read his work. Even among his followers, Marx's ideas frequently are reduced to slogans such as "the opium of the people" and "the dictatorship of proletariat," but the role of these slogans in Marx's encompassing theory often is ignored.

There are many reasons for this lack of understanding of Marx's social theory, the main one being that Marx never really completed his social theory. He planned, early in his career, to publish separate works on economics, law, morals, politics, and so forth, and then "in a special work, to present them once again as a connected whole, to show the relationship between the parts" (Marx, 1932/1964:280). He never did this final work and never even completed his separate work on economics. Instead, much of his time was taken up by study, journalism, political activity, and a series of minor intellectual and political arguments with friends and adversaries.

In addition, although Marx could write clear and inspiring prose, especially in his political tracts, he often preferred a vocabulary that relied on complex philosophical traditions, and he made these terms even more difficult to understand by implicitly redefining them for his own use. Vilfredo Pareto made the classic critique of Marx by comparing his words to a fable about bats. When someone said they were birds, the bats would cry, "No, we are mice." When someone said they were mice, they protested that they were birds. Whatever interpretation one makes of Marx, others can offer alternative interpretations. For example, some stress Marx's early work on human potential and tend to discount his political economy (see, for example, Ollman, 1976; Wallimann, 1981; Wartenberg, 1982). Others stress Marx's later work on the economic structures of society and see that work as distinct from his early, largely philosophical work on human nature (see Althusser, 1969; Gandy, 1979; McMurty, 1978).[1] A recent interpreter of Marx made the following comment, which applies equally to this chapter: "Virtually every paragraph in this chapter could be accompanied by three concise paragraphs describing why other readers of Marx, erudite and influential, think that this paragraph is wrong, in emphasis or substance" (R. Miller, 1991:105). And, of course, the differing interpretations have political consequences, making any disagreement extremely contentious.[2]

Despite these problems, Marx's theories have produced one of sociology's most productive and significant research programs. When Marx died in 1883, the eleven mourners at his funeral seemed to belie what Engels said in his eulogy: "His name and work will endure through the ages." Nevertheless, Engels seems to have been right. His ideas have been so influential that even one of his critics admitted that, in a sense, "we are all Marxists now" (P. Singer, 1980:1). As Hannah Arendt (2002:274) wrote, if Marx seems to be forgotten, it is not "because Marx's thought and the methods he introduced have been abandoned, but rather because they have become so axiomatic that their origin is no longer remembered."

It is for these reasons that a return to Marx has proven so productive to those working in sociology. Thinking about Marx helps to clarify what sociology and, indeed, our society have taken for granted. Rediscoveries and reinterpretation of Marx have often renewed sociology and opened up a fresh perspective on such issues as alienation, globalization, and the environment (Foster, 2000).

Despite differing interpretations, there is general agreement that Marx's main interest was in the historical basis of inequality, especially the unique form that it takes under capitalism. However, Marx's approach is different from many of the theories that we will examine. For Marx, a theory about how society works would be partial, because

---

[1] The approach here is based on the premise that there is no discontinuity or contradiction between Marx's early work on human potential and his later work on the structures of capitalist society—that his early ideas continue, at least implicitly, in his later work even though these ideas were certainly modified by his study of the economic structures of capitalism.
[2] In Joseph Stalin's Soviet Union, there was no problem about the "correct" interpretation of Marx. Stalin himself provided the interpretation and brutally eliminated all those, such as Leon Trotsky, who disagreed.

what he mainly sought was a theory about how to change society. Marx's theory, then, is an analysis of inequality under capitalism and how to change it.

As capitalism has come to dominate the globe and the most significant communist alternatives have disappeared, some might argue that Marx's theories have lost their relevance. However, once we realize that Marx provides an analysis of capitalism, we can see that his theories are more relevant now than ever (McLennan, 2001:43). Marx provides a diagnosis of capitalism that is able to reveal its tendencies to crises, point out its perennial inequalities, and, if nothing else, demand that capitalism live up to its own promises. The example of Marx makes an important point about theory. Even when their particular predictions are disproved—even though the proletariat revolution that Marx believed to be imminent did not come about—theories still hold a value as an alternative to our current society. Theories may not tell us what will happen, but they can argue for what should happen and help us develop a plan for carrying out the change that the theory envisions or for resisting the change that the theory predicts.

The Dialectic

Vladimir Lenin (1972:180) said that no one can fully understand Marx's work without a prior understanding of the German philosopher G.W.F. Hegel. We can only hope that this is not true, because Hegel was one of the most purposefully difficult philosophers ever to have written. Nevertheless, we must understand some of Hegel in order to appreciate the central Marxian conception of the dialectic.

The idea of a dialectical philosophy had been around for centuries (Gadamer, 1989). Its basic idea is the centrality of contradiction. While most philosophies, and indeed common sense, treat contradictions as mistakes, a dialectical philosophy believes that contradictions exist in reality and that the most appropriate way to understand reality is to study the development of those contradictions. Hegel used the idea of contradiction to understand historical change. According to Hegel, historical change has been driven by the contradictory understandings that are the essence of reality, by our attempts to resolve the contradictions, and by the new contradictions that develop.

Marx also accepted the centrality of contradictions to historical change. We see this in such well-known formulations as the "contradictions of capitalism" and "class contradictions." However, unlike Hegel, Marx did not believe that these contradictions could be worked out in our understanding, that is, in our minds. Instead, for Marx these are real, existing contradictions (Wilde, 1991:277). For Marx, such contradictions are resolved not by the philosopher sitting in an armchair but by a life-and-death struggle that changes the social world. This was a crucial transformation because it allowed Marx to move the dialectic out of the realm of philosophy and into the realm of a study of social relations grounded in the material world. It is this focus that makes Marx's work so relevant to sociology, even though the dialectical approach is very different from the mode of thinking used by most sociologists. The dialectic leads to an interest in the conflicts and contradictions among various levels of social reality, rather than to the more traditional sociological interest in the ways these various levels mesh neatly into a cohesive whole.

For example, one of the contradictions within capitalism is the relationship between the workers and the capitalists who own the factories and other means of production with which the work is done. The capitalist must exploit the workers in order to make a profit from the workers' labor. The workers, in contradiction to the capitalists, want to keep at least some of the profit for themselves. Marx believed that this contradiction was at the heart of capitalism, and that it would grow worse as capitalists drove more and more people to become workers by forcing small firms out of business and as competition between the capitalists forced them to further exploit the workers to make a profit. As capitalism expands, the number of workers exploited, as well as the degree of exploitation, increases. This contradiction can be resolved not through philosophy but only through social change. The tendency for the level of exploitation to escalate leads to more and more resistance by the workers. Resistance begets more exploitation and oppression, and the likely result is a confrontation between the two classes (Boswell and Dixon, 1993).

Dialectical Method

Marx's focus on real, existing contradictions led to a particular method for studying social phenomena that has also come to be called "dialectical" (T. Ball, 1991; Friedrichs, 1972; Ollman, 1976; L. Schneider, 1971; Starosta, 2008).

Fact and Value

In dialectical analysis, social values are not separable from social facts. Many sociologists believe that their values can and must be separated from their study of facts about the social world. The dialectical thinker believes that it is not only impossible to keep values out of the study of the social world but also undesirable, because to do so would produce a dispassionate, inhuman sociology that has little to offer to people in search of answers to the problems they confront. Facts and values are inevitably intertwined, with the result that the study of social phenomena is value-laden. Thus to Marx it was impossible and, even if possible, undesirable to be dispassionate in his analysis of capitalist society. But Marx's emotional involvement in what he was studying did not mean that his observations were inaccurate. It could even be argued that Marx's passionate views on these issues gave him unparalleled insight into the nature of capitalist society. A less passionate student might have delved less deeply into the dynamics of the system. In fact, research into the work of scientists indicates that the idea of a dispassionate scientist is largely a myth and that the very best scientists are the ones who are most passionate about, and committed to, their ideas (Mitroff, 1974).

Reciprocal Relations

The dialectical method of analysis does not see a simple, one-way, cause-and-effect relationship among the various parts of the social world. For the dialectical thinker, social influences never simply flow in one direction as they often do for cause-and-effect thinkers. To the dialectician, one factor may have an effect on another, but it is just as likely that the latter will have a simultaneous effect on the former. For example, the increasing exploitation of the workers by the capitalist may cause the workers to become increasingly dissatisfied and more militant, but the increasing militancy of the proletariat may well cause the capitalists to react by becoming even more exploitative in order to crush the resistance of the workers. This kind of thinking does not mean that the dialectician never considers causal relationships in the social world. It does mean that when dialectical thinkers talk about causality, they are always attuned to reciprocal relationships among social factors as well as to the dialectical totality of social life in which they are embedded.

Past, Present, Future

Dialecticians are interested not only in the relationships of social phenomena in the contemporary world but also in the relationship of those contemporary realities to both past (Bauman, 1976:81) and future social phenomena. This has two distinct implications for a dialectical sociology. First, it means that dialectical sociologists are concerned with studying the historical roots of the contemporary world as Marx (1857–1858/1964) did in his study of the sources of modern capitalism. In fact, dialectical thinkers are very critical of modern sociology for its failure to do much historical research. A good example of Marx's thinking in this regard is found in the following famous quotation from *The Eighteenth Brumaire of Louis Bonaparte*:

> Men make their own history, but they do not make it just as they please; they do not make it under circumstances chosen by themselves, but under circumstances directly encountered from the past. The tradition of all the dead generations weighs like a nightmare on the brain of the living.
>
> (Marx, 1852/1970:15)

Second, many dialectical thinkers are attuned to current social trends in order to understand the possible future directions of society. This interest in future possibilities is one of the main reasons dialectical sociology is inherently political. It is interested in encouraging practical activities that would bring new possibilities into existence. However, dialecticians believe that the nature of this future world can be discerned only through a careful study of the contemporary world. It is their view that the sources of the future exist in the present.

No Inevitabilities

The dialectical view of the relationship between the present and the future need not imply that the future is determined by the present. Terence Ball (1991) describes Marx as a "political possibilist" rather than a "historical inevitabilist." Because social phenomena are constantly acting and reacting, the social world defies a simple, deterministic model. The future may be based on some contemporary model, but not inevitably.[3] Marx's historical studies showed him that people make choices but that these choices are limited. For instance, Marx believed that society was engaged in a class struggle and that people could choose to participate either in "the revolutionary reconstitution

---

[3] Marx did, however, occasionally discuss the inevitability of socialism.

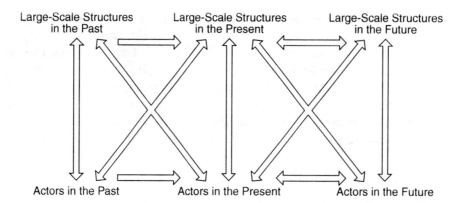

FIGURE 2.1   *Schematic Representation of a Sociologically Relevant Dialectic*

of society at large, or in the common ruin of the contending classes" (Marx and Engels 1848/1948). Marx hoped and believed that the future was to be found in communism, but he did not believe that the workers could simply wait passively for it to arrive. Communism would come only through their choices and struggles.

This disinclination to think deterministically is what makes the best-known model of the dialectic—thesis, antithesis, synthesis—inadequate for sociological use. This simple model implies that a social phenomenon will inevitably spawn an opposing form and that the clash between the two will inevitably lead to a new, synthetic social form. But in the real world, there are no inevitabilities. Furthermore, social phenomena are not easily divided into the simple thesis, antithesis, and synthesis categories adopted by some Marxists. The dialectician is interested in the study of real relationships rather than grand abstractions. It is this disinclination to deal in grand abstractions that led Marx away from Hegel and would lead him today to reject such a great oversimplification of the dialectic as thesis, antithesis, synthesis.

Actors and Structures

Dialectical thinkers are also interested in the dynamic relationship between actors and social structures. Marx was certainly attuned to the ongoing interplay among the major levels of social analysis. The heart of Marx's thought lies in the relationship between people and the large-scale structures they create (Lefebvre, 1968:8). On the one hand, these large-scale structures help people fulfill themselves; on the other, they represent a grave threat to humanity. But the dialectical method is even more complex than this, because, as we have already seen, the dialectician considers past, present, and future circumstances—both actors and structures. Figure 2.1 is a simplified schematic representation of this enormously complex and sophisticated perspective.

Human Potential

A good portion of this chapter will be devoted to a discussion of Marx's macrosociology, in particular his analysis of the macrostructures of capitalism. But before we can analyze these topics, we need to begin with Marx's thoughts on the more microsociological aspects of social reality. Marx built his critical analysis of the contradictions of capitalist society on his premises about human potential, its relation to labor, and its potential for alienation under capitalism. He believed that there was a real contradiction between our human potential and the way that we must work in capitalist society.

Marx (1850/1964:64) wrote in an early work that human beings are an "ensemble of social relations." He indicates by this that our human potential is intertwined with our specific social relations and our institutional context. Therefore, human nature is not a static thing but varies historically and socially. To understand human potential, we need to understand social history, because human nature is shaped by the same dialectical contradictions that Marx believed shapes the history of society.

For Marx, a conception of human potential that does not take social and historical factors into account is wrong, but to take them into account is not the same as being without a conception of human nature. It simply complicates this conception. For Marx, there is a human potential in general, but what is more important is the way it is "modified in each historical epoch" (Marx, 1842/1977:609). When speaking of our general human potential, Marx often used the term *species being*. By this he meant the potentials and powers that are uniquely human and that distinguish humans from other species.

Some Marxists, such as Louis Althusser (1969:229), have contended that the mature Marx did not believe in human nature. There are certainly reasons to downplay human nature for someone interested in changing society. Ideas about human nature— such as our "natural" greed, our "natural" tendency to violence, our "natural" gender differences—have often been used to argue against any social change. Such conceptions of human nature are innately conservative. If our problems are due to human nature, we had better learn to just adapt instead of trying to change things.

Nevertheless, there is much evidence that Marx did have a notion of human nature (Geras, 1983). Indeed, it makes little sense to say there is no human nature. Even if we are like a blank chalkboard, the chalkboard must be made out of something and must have a nature such that chalk marks can show up on it. Some conception of human nature is part of any sociological theory. Our concept of human nature dictates how society can be sustained and how it can be changed, but most important for Marx's theory, it suggests how society *should* be changed. The real question is not whether we have a human nature, but what kind of nature it is— unchanging or open to historical processes (the use of the idea human potential here indicates that we think it is open):

> Unless we confront the idea, however dangerous, of our human nature and species being and get some understanding of them, we cannot know what it is we might be alienated from or what emancipation might mean. Nor can we determine which of our "slumbering powers" must be awakened to achieve emancipatory goals. A working definition of human nature, however tentative and insecure, is a necessary step in the search for real as opposed to fantastic alternatives. A conversation about our "species being" is desperately called for.
>
> (D. Harvey, 2000:207)

50   **Part I**   Classical Sociological Theory

KARL MARX

A Biographical Sketch

Karl Marx was born in Trier, Prussia, on May 5, 1818 (Beilharz, 2005e). His father, a lawyer, provided the family with a fairly typical middle-class existence. Both parents were from rabbinical families, but for business reasons the father had converted to Lutheranism when Karl was very young. In 1841 Marx received his doctorate in philosophy from the University of Berlin, a school heavily influenced by Hegel and the Young Hegelians, supportive, yet critical, of their master. Marx's doctorate was a dry philosophical treatise, but it did anticipate many of his later ideas. After graduation he became a writer for a liberal-radical newspaper and within ten months had become its editor in chief. However, because of its political positions, the paper was closed shortly thereafter by the government. The early essays published in this period began to reflect a number of the positions that would guide Marx throughout his life. They were liberally sprinkled with democratic principles, humanism, and youthful idealism. He rejected the abstractness of Hegelian philosophy, the naive dreaming of utopian communists, and those activists who were urging what he considered to be premature political action. In rejecting these activists, Marx laid the groundwork for his own life's work:

> Practical attempts, even by the masses, can be answered with a cannon as soon as they become dangerous, but ideas that have overcome our intellect and conquered our conviction, ideas to which reason has riveted our conscience, are chains from which one cannot break loose without breaking one's heart; they are demons that one can only overcome by submitting to them.
>
> (Marx, 1842/1977:20)

Marx married in 1843 and soon thereafter was forced to leave Germany for the more liberal atmosphere of Paris. There he continued to grapple with the ideas of Hegel and his supporters, but he also encountered two new sets of ideas—French socialism and English political economy. It was the unique way in which he combined Hegelianism, socialism, and political economy that shaped his intellectual orientation. Also of great importance at this point was his meeting the man who was to become his lifelong friend, benefactor, and collaborator—Friedrich Engels (Carver, 1983). The son of a textile manufacturer, Engels had become a socialist critical of the conditions facing the working class. Much of Marx's compassion for the misery of the working class came from his exposure to Engels and his ideas. In 1844 Engels and Marx had a lengthy conversation in a famous café in Paris and laid the groundwork for a lifelong association. Of that conversation Engels said, "Our complete agreement in all theoretical fields became obvious . . . and our joint work dates from that time" (McLellan, 1973:131). In the following year, Engels published a notable work, *The Condition of the Working Class in England*. During this period Marx wrote a number of abstruse works (many unpublished in his lifetime), including *The Holy Family* (1845/1956) and

The German Ideology (1845–1846/1970) (both coauthored with Engels), but he also produced *The Economic and Philosophic Manuscripts of 1844* (1932/1964), which better foreshadowed his increasing preoccupation with the economic domain.

While Marx and Engels shared a theoretical orientation, there were many differences between the two men. Marx tended to be theoretical, a disorderly intellectual, and very oriented to his family. Engels was a practical thinker, a neat and tidy businessman, and a person who did not believe in the institution of the family. In spite of their differences, Marx and Engels forged a close union in which they collaborated on books and articles and worked together in radical organizations, and Engels even helped support Marx throughout the rest of his life so that Marx could devote himself to his intellectual and political endeavors.

In spite of the close association of the names of Marx and Engels, Engels made it clear that he was the junior partner:

> Marx could very well have done without me. What Marx accomplished I would not have achieved. Marx stood higher, saw farther, and took a wider and quicker view than the rest of us. Marx was a genius.
>
> (Engels, cited in McLellan, 1973:131–132)

In fact, many believe that Engels failed to understand many of the subtleties of Marx's work (C. Smith, 1997). After Marx's death, Engels became the leading spokesperson for Marxian theory and in various ways distorted and oversimplified it, although he remained faithful to the political perspective he had forged with Marx.

Because some of his writings had upset the Prussian government, the French government (at the request of the Prussians) expelled Marx in 1845, and he moved to Brussels. His radicalism was growing, and he had become an active member of the international revolutionary movement. He also associated with the Communist League and was asked to write a document (with Engels) expounding its aims and beliefs. The result was the *Communist Manifesto* of 1848 (1848/1948), a work that was characterized by ringing political slogans (for example, "Working men of all countries, unite!").

In 1849 Marx moved to London, and, in light of the failure of the political revolutions of 1848, he began to withdraw from active revolutionary activity and to move into more serious and detailed research on the workings of the capitalist system. In 1852, he began his famous studies in the British Museum of the working conditions in capitalism. These studies ultimately resulted in the three volumes of *Capital,* the first of which was published in 1867; the other two were published posthumously. He lived in poverty during these years, barely managing to survive on a small income from his writings and the support of Engels. In 1864 Marx became reinvolved in political activity by joining the International, an international movement of workers. He soon gained preeminence within the movement and devoted a number of years to it. He began to gain fame both as a leader of the International and as the author of *Capital*. But the disintegration of the International by 1876, the failure of various revolutionary movements, and personal illness took their toll on Marx. His wife died in 1881, a daughter in 1882, and Marx himself on March 14, 1883.

Labor

For Marx, species being and human potential are intimately related to labor:

> Labour is, in the first place, a process in which both man and Nature participate, and in which man of his own accord starts, regulates, and controls the material reactions between himself and Nature . . . .By thus acting on the external world and changing it, he at the same time changes his own nature. He develops his slumbering powers and compels them to act in obedience to his sway . . . .We presuppose labour in a form that stamps it as exclusively human. A spider conducts operations that resemble those of a weaver and a bee puts to shame many an architect in the construction of her cells. But what distinguishes the worst architect from the best of bees is this, that the architect raises his structure in imagination before he erects it in reality. At the end of every labour process we get a result that existed in the imagination of the labourer at its commencement. He not only effects a change of form in the material on which he works, but he also realizes a purpose. (Marx, 1867/1967:177–178)

We see in that quotation many important parts of Marx's view of the relation between labor and human nature. First, what distinguishes us from other animals— our species being—is that our labor creates something in reality that previously existed only in our imagination. Our production reflects our purpose. Marx calls this process in which we create external objects out of our internal thoughts *objectification*. Second, this labor is material (Sayers, 2007). It works with the more material aspects of nature (e.g., raising fruits and vegetables, cutting down trees for wood) in order to satisfy our material needs. Finally, Marx believed that this labor does not just transform the material aspects of nature but also transforms us, including our needs, our consciousness, and our human nature. Labor is thus at the same time (1) the objectification of our purpose, (2) the establishment of an essential relation between human need and the material objects of our need, and (3) the transformation of our human nature.

Marx's use of the term *labor* is not restricted to economic activities; it encompasses all productive actions that transform the material aspects of nature in accordance with our purpose. Whatever is created through this free purposive activity is both an expression of our human nature and a transformation of it.

As we will see below, the process of labor has been changed under capitalism, making it difficult for us to understand Marx's conception, but we get close to Marx's concept when we think of the creative activity of an artist. Artwork is a representation of the thought of the artist. In Marx's terms, artwork is an objectivation of the artist. However, it is also true that the process of creating the art changes the artist. Through the process of producing the art, the artist's ideas about the art change, or the artist may become aware of a new vision that needs objectivation. In addition, the completed artwork can take on a new meaning for the artist and transform the artist's conceptions of that particular work or of art in general.

Labor, even artistic labor, is in response to a need, and the transformation that labor entails also transforms our needs. The satisfaction of our needs can lead to the creation of new needs (Marx and Engels, 1845–1846/1970:43). For example, the production of cars to satisfy our need for long-distance transportation led to a new need for highways. Even more significantly, although few people thought they needed cars when cars were first invented, now most people feel that they need them. A similar change has occurred with the computer. Whereas a generation ago few thought they needed a personal computer, now many people need one, as well as all of the software and peripherals that go with it.

We labor in response to our needs, but the labor itself transforms our needs, which can lead to new forms of productive activity. According to Marx, this transformation of our needs through labor is the engine of human history.

> Not only do the objective conditions change in the act of production . . . but the producers change, too, in that they bring out new qualities in themselves, develop themselves in production, transform themselves, develop new powers and ideas, new modes of intercourse, new needs and new language.
> (Marx, 1857–1858/1974:494).

Labor, for Marx, is the development of our truly human powers and potentials. By transforming material reality to fit our purpose, we also transform ourselves. Furthermore, labor is a social activity. Work involves others, directly in joint productions, or because others provide us with the necessary tools or raw materials for our work, or because they enjoy the fruits of our labor. Labor does not transform only the individual human; it also transforms society. Indeed, for Marx, the emergence of a human as an individual depends on a society. Marx wrote, "Man is in the most literal sense of the word a *zoon politikon,* not only a social animal, but an animal which can develop into an individual only in society" (1857–1858/1964:84). In addition, Marx tells us that this transformation includes even our consciousness: "Consciousness is, therefore, from the very beginning a social product, and remains so as long as men exist at all" (Marx and Engels, 1845–1846/1970:51). Consequently, the transformation of the individual through labor and the transformation of society are not separable.

Alienation

Although Marx believed that there is an inherent relation between labor and human nature, he thought that this relation is perverted by capitalism. He calls this perverted relation *alienation* (Beilharz, 2005a; Cooper, 1991; Meisenhelder, 1991). The present discussion of Marx's concept of human nature and of alienation is derived mainly from Marx's early work. In his later work on the nature of capitalist society, he shied away from such a heavily philosophical term as *alienation,* yet alienation remained one of his main concerns (Barbalet, 1983:95).

Marx analyzed the peculiar form that our relation to our own labor has taken under capitalism. We no longer see our labor as an expression of our purpose. There is no objectivation. Instead, we labor in accordance with the purpose of the capitalist who hires and pays us. Rather than being an end in itself—an expression of human capabilities— labor in capitalism is reduced to being a means to an end: earning money (Marx, 1932/1964:173). Because our labor is not our own, it no longer transforms us. Instead we are alienated from our labor and therefore alienated from our true human nature.

Although it is the individual who feels alienated in capitalist society, Marx's basic analytic concern was with the structures of capitalism that cause this alienation (Israel, 1971). Marx uses the concept of alienation to reveal the devastating effect of capitalist production on human beings and on society. Of crucial significance here is the two-class system in which capitalists employ workers (and thereby own workers' labor time) and capitalists own the means of production (tools and raw materials) as well as the ultimate products. To survive, workers are forced to sell their labor time to capitalists. These structures, especially the division of labor, are the sociological basis of alienation.

> First, the fact that labor is external to the worker, i.e., it does not belong to his essential being; that in his work, therefore, he does not affirm himself but denies himself, does not feel content but unhappy, does not develop freely his physical and mental energy but mortifies his body and ruins his mind. The worker therefore only feels himself outside his work, and in his work feels outside himself. He is at home when he is not working, and when he is working he is not at home. His labor therefore is not voluntary, but coerced; it is forced labor. It is therefore not the satisfaction of a need; it is merely a means to satisfy needs external to it.
>
> (Marx, 1850/1964:72)

As a result, people feel freely active only in their animal functions—eating, drinking, procreating. In the essentially human process of labor, they no longer feel themselves to be anything but animals. What is animal becomes human, and what is human becomes animal. Certainly eating, drinking, procreating, and so on are human functions, but when separated from the sphere of all other human activity and turned into sole and ultimate ends, they become animal functions.

Alienation can be seen as having four basic components.

1. Workers in capitalist society are alienated from their *productive activity*. They do not produce objects according to their own ideas or to directly satisfy their own needs. Instead, workers work for capitalists, who pay them a subsistence wage in return for the right to use them in any way they see fit. Because productive activity belongs to the capitalists, and because they decide what is to be done with it, we can say that workers are alienated from that activity. Furthermore, many workers who perform highly specialized tasks have little sense of their role in the total production process. For example, automobile assembly-line workers who tighten a few bolts on an engine may have little feel for how their labor contributes to the production of the entire car. They do not objectivate their ideas, and they are not transformed by the labor in any meaningful way. Instead of being a process that is satisfying in and of itself, productive activity in capitalism is reduced, Marx argued, to an often boring and stultifying means to the fulfillment of the only end that really matters in capitalism: earning enough money to survive.

2. Workers in capitalist society are alienated not only from productive activities but also from the object of those activities—the *product*. The product of their labor belongs not to the workers but to the capitalists, who may use it in any way they wish because it is the capitalists' private property. Marx (1932/1964:117) tells us, "Private property is thus the product, the result, the necessary consequence of alienated labour." The capitalist will use his or her ownership in order to sell the product for a profit.

If workers wish to own the product of their own labor, they must buy it like anyone else. No matter how desperate the workers' needs, they cannot use the products of their own labor to satisfy their needs. Even workers in a bakery can starve if they don't have the money to buy the bread that they make. Because of this peculiar relation, things that we buy—that are made by others—seem to us to be more an expression of ourselves than do the things we make at our jobs. People's personalities are judged more by the cars they drive, the clothes they wear, the gadgets they use—none of which they have made—than by what they actually produce in their daily work, which appears to be an arbitrary and accidental means for making money in order to buy things.

3. Workers in capitalist society are alienated from their *fellow workers*. Marx's assumption was that people basically need and want to work cooperatively in order to appropriate from nature what they require to survive. But in capitalism this cooperation is disrupted, and people, often strangers, are forced to work side by side for the capitalist. Even if the workers on the assembly line are close friends, the nature of the technology makes for a great deal of isolation. Here is the way one worker describes his social situation on the assembly line:

> You can work next to a guy for months without even knowing his name. One thing, you're too busy to talk. Can't hear . . . .You have to holler in his ear. They got these little guys coming around in white shirts and if they see you runnin' your mouth, they say, "This guy needs more work." Man, he's got no time to talk.
>
> (Terkel, 1974:165)

Of course, much the same is true in the newest version of the assembly line: the office cubicle. But in this social situation, workers experience something worse than simple isolation. Workers often are forced into outright competition, and sometimes conflict, with one another. To extract maximum productivity and to prevent the development of cooperative relationships, the capitalist pits one worker against another to see who can produce more, work more quickly, or please the boss more. The workers who succeed are given a few extra rewards; those who fail are discarded. In either case, considerable hostility is generated among the workers toward their peers. This is useful to the capitalists because it tends to deflect hostility that otherwise would be aimed at them. The isolation and the interpersonal hostility tend to alienate workers in capitalism from their fellow workers.

4. Workers in capitalist society are alienated from their own *human potential*. Instead of being a source of transformation and fulfillment of our human nature, the workplace is where we feel least human, least ourselves. Individuals perform less and less like human beings as they are reduced in their work to functioning like machines. Even smiles and greetings are programmed and scripted. Consciousness is numbed and, ultimately, destroyed as relations with other humans and with nature are progressively controlled. The result is a mass of people unable to express their essential human qualities, a mass of alienated workers.

Alienation is an example of the sort of contradiction that Marx's dialectical approach focused on. There is a real contradiction between human nature, which is defined and transformed by labor, and the actual social conditions of labor under capitalism. What Marx wanted to stress is that this contradiction cannot be resolved merely in thought. We are not any less alienated because we identify with our employer or with the things that our wages can purchase. Indeed, these things are a symptom of our alienation, which can be resolved only through real social change.

The Structures of Capitalist Society

In Europe in Marx's time, industrialization was increasing. People were being forced to leave agricultural and artisan trades and to work in factories where conditions were often harsh. By the 1840s, when Marx was entering his most productive period, Europe was experiencing a widespread sense of social crisis (Seigel, 1978:106). In 1848 a series of revolts swept across Europe (soon after the publication of Marx and Engel's *Communist Manifesto*). The effects of industrialization and the political implications of industrialization were especially apparent in the mostly rural states collectively referred to as Germany.

At the beginning of the nineteenth century, cheap manufactured goods from England and France began to force out of business the less efficient manufacturers in Germany. In response, the political leaders of the German states imposed capitalism on their still mainly feudal societies. The resulting poverty, dislocation, and alienation were particularly evident because of the rapidity of the change.

Marx's analysis of alienation was a response to the economic, social, and political changes that Marx saw going on around him. He did not view alienation as a philosophical problem. He wanted to understand what changes would be needed to create a society in which human potential could be adequately expressed. Marx's important insight was that the capitalist economic system is the primary cause of alienation. Marx's work on human nature and alienation led him to a critique of capitalist society and to a political program oriented to overcoming the structures of capitalism so that people could express their essential humanity (Mészáros, 1970).

Capitalism is an economic system in which great numbers of workers who own little produce commodities for the profit of small numbers of capitalists who own all of the following: the commodities, the means of producing the commodities, and the labor time of the workers, which they purchase through wages (H. Wolf, 2005b). One of Marx's central insights is that capitalism is much more than an economic system. It is also a system of power. The secret of capitalism is that political powers have been transformed into economic relations (Wood, 1995). Capitalists seldom need to use brute force. Capitalists are able to coerce workers through their power to dismiss workers and close plants. Capitalism, therefore, is not simply an economic system; it is also a political system, a mode of exercising power, and a process for exploiting workers.

In a capitalist system, the economy seems to be a natural force. People are laid off, wages are reduced, and factories are closed because of "the economy." We do not see these events as the outcomes of social or political decisions. Links between human suffering and the economic structures are deemed irrelevant or trivial.

For example, you might read in the newspaper that the Federal Reserve Board of the United States has raised interest rates. A reason often given for this action is that the economy is "overheated," which is to say that there is the possibility of inflation. Raising interest rates does indeed "cool off?" the economy. How does it do so? It puts some people out of work. As a result, workers become afraid to demand higher wages, which might get passed on as higher prices, which might lead to additional interest-rate increases and to still more workers losing their jobs. Thus, inflation is averted. By raising interest rates, the Federal Reserve Board adopts a policy that helps capitalists and hurts workers. This decision, however, usually is presented as a purely economic one. Marx would say that it is a political decision that favors capitalists at the expense of workers.

Marx's aim is to make the social and political structures of the economy clearer by revealing "the economic law of motion of modern society" (quoted in Ollman, 1976:168). Furthermore, Marx intends to reveal the internal contradictions that he hopes will inevitably transform capitalism.

Commodities

The basis of all of Marx's work on social structures, and the place in which that work is most clearly tied to his views on human potential, is his analysis of commodities, or products of labor intended primarily for exchange. As Georg Lukács (1922/1968:83) put it, "The problem of commodities is . . . the central, structural problem of capitalist society." By starting with the commodity, Marx is able to reveal the nature of capitalism.

Marx's view of the commodity was rooted in his materialist orientation, with its focus on the productive activities of actors. As we saw earlier, it was Marx's view that in their interactions with nature and with other actors, people produce the objects that they need in order to survive. These objects are produced for personal use or for use by others in the immediate environment. Such uses are what Marx called the commodity's *use value*. However, in capitalism this process takes on a new and dangerous form. Instead of producing for themselves or for their immediate associates, the actors produce for someone else (the capitalist). The products have *exchange value*; that is, instead of being used immediately, they are exchanged in the market for money or for other objects.

Use value is connected to the intimate relation between human needs and the actual objects that can satisfy those needs. It is difficult to compare the use values of different things. Bread has the use value of satisfying hunger; shoes have the use value of protecting our feet. It is difficult to say that one has more use value than the other. They are *qualitatively* different. Furthermore, use value is tied to the physical properties of a commodity. Shoes cannot satisfy our hunger and bread cannot protect our feet because they are physically different kinds of objects. In the process of exchange, however, different commodities are compared to one another. One pair of shoes can be exchanged for six loaves of bread. Or if the medium of exchange is money, as is common, a pair of shoes can be worth six times as much money as a loaf of bread. Exchange values are *quantitatively* different. One can say that a pair of shoes has more exchange value than a loaf of bread. Furthermore, exchange value is separate from the physical property of the commodity. Only things that can be eaten can have the use value of satisfying hunger, but any type of thing can have the exchange value of a dollar.

Fetishism of Commodities

Commodities are the products of human labor, but they can become separated from the needs and purposes of their creators. Because exchange value floats free from the actual commodity and seems to exist in a realm separate from any human use, we are led to believe that these objects and the market for them have independent existences. In fully developed capitalism, this belief becomes reality as the objects and their markets actually become real, independent phenomena. The commodity takes on an independent, almost mystical external reality (Marx, 1867/1967:35). Marx called this process the *fetishism of commodities* (Dant, 1996; Sherlock, 1997). Marx did not mean that commodities take on sexual meanings, for he wrote before Freud gave the term *fetish* this twist. Marx was alluding to the ways in which the practitioners of some religions, such as the Zunis, carve figures and then worship them. By fetish, Marx meant a thing that we ourselves make and then worship as if it were a god.

In capitalism, the products that we make, their values, and the economy that consists of our exchanges all seem to take on lives of their own, separate from any human needs or decisions. Even our own labor—the thing that, according to Marx, makes us truly human—becomes a commodity that is bought and sold. Our labor acquires an exchange value that is separate from us. It is turned into an abstract thing and used by the capitalist to make the objects that come to dominate us. Hence, commodities are the source of the alienation discussed above. Even the labor of self-employed commodity producers is alienated, because they must produce for the market instead of to achieve their own purposes and satisfy their own needs.

Thus, the economy takes on a function that Marx believed only actors could perform: the production of value. For Marx, the true value of a thing comes from the fact that labor produces it and someone needs it. A commodity's true value represents human social relations. In contrast, in capitalism, Marx tells us, "A definite social relation between men . . . assumes, in their eyes, the fantastic form of a relation between things" (1867/1967:72). Granting reality to commodities and to the market, the individual in capitalism progressively loses control over them. A commodity, therefore, is "a mysterious thing, simply because in it the social character of men's labor appears to them as an objective character stamped upon the product of that labor: because the relations of the producers to the sum total of their own labor is presented to them as a social relation, existing not between themselves, but between the products of their labor" (Marx, 1867/1967:72).

Think, for example, of the cup of coffee that you might have bought before sitting down to read this text. In that simple transaction, you entered into a relationship with hundreds of others: the waitperson, the owner of the coffee shop, the people working at the roaster, the importer, the truck driver, dockworkers, all the people on the ship that brought the beans, the coffee plantation owner, the pickers, and so on. In addition, you supported a particular trading relation between countries, a particular form of government in the grower's country that has been historically shaped by the coffee trade, a particular relation between the plantation owner and the worker, and many other social relations. You did all this by exchanging money for a cup of coffee. In the relation between those objects—money and coffee—lies hidden all those social relations.

Marx's discussion of commodities and their fetishism takes us from the level of the individual actor to the level of large-scale social structures. The fetishism of commodities imparts to the economy an independent, objective reality that is external to, and coercive of, the actor. Looked at in this way, the fetishism of commodities is translated into the concept of *reification* (Lukács, 1922/1968; Sherlock, 1997). Reification can be thought of as "thingification," or the process of coming to believe that humanly created social forms are natural, universal, and absolute things. As a result of reification, social forms do acquire those characteristics. The concept of reification implies that people believe that social structures are beyond their control and unchangeable. Reification occurs when this belief becomes a self-fulfilling prophecy. Then structures actually do acquire the character people endowed them with. People become mesmerized by the seeming objectivity and authority of the economy. People lose their jobs, make career choices, or move across the country because of the economy. According to Marx, however, the economy is not an objective, natural thing. It is a form of domination, and decisions about interest rates and layoffs are political decisions that tend to benefit one group over another.

People reify the whole range of social relationships and social structures. Just as people reify commodities and other economic phenomena (for example, the division of labor [Rattansi, 1982; Wallimann, 1981]), they also reify religious (Barbalet, 1983:147), political, and organizational structures. Marx made a similar point in reference to the state: "And out of this very contradiction between the individual and . . . the community the latter takes an independent form as the State, divorced from the real interests of individual and community" (cited in Bender, 1970:176). Capitalism is made up of particular types of social relations that tend to take forms that appear to be and eventually are independent of the actual people involved. As Moishe Postone (1993:4) tells us, "The result is a new, increasingly abstract form of social domination—one that subjects people to impersonal structural imperatives and constraints that cannot be adequately grasped in terms of concrete domination (e.g., personal or group domination)."

Capital, Capitalists, and the Proletariat

Marx found the heart of capitalist society within the commodity. A society dominated by objects whose main value is exchange produces certain categories of people. The two main types that concerned Marx were the proletariat and the capitalist. Let us start with the proletariat.

Workers who sell their labor and do not own their own means of production are members of the proletariat. They do not own their own tools or their factories. Marx (1867/1967:714–715) believed that proletarians would eventually lose their own skills as they increasingly serviced machines that had their skills built into them. Because members of the proletariat produce only for exchange, they are also consumers. Because they don't have the means to produce for their own needs, they must use their wages to buy what they need. Consequently, proletarians are completely dependent on their wages in order to live. This makes the proletariat dependent on those who pay the wages.

Those who pay the wages are the capitalists. Capitalists are those who own the means of production. Before we can fully understand capitalists, we must first understand capital itself (H. Wolf, 2005a). Capital is money that produces more money, capital is money that is invested rather than being used to satisfy human needs or desires. This distinction becomes clearer when we look at what Marx considered to be "the starting-point of capital" (1867/1967:146): the *circulation of commodities.* Marx discussed two types of circulation of commodities. One type of circulation is characteristic of capital: Money → Commodities → (a larger sum of) Money (M_1-C-M_2). The other type is not: Commodities → Money → Commodities (C_1-M-C_2).

In a noncapitalist circulation of commodities, the circuit C_1-M-C_2 predominates. An example of C_1-M-C_2 would be a fisherman who sells his catch (C_1) and then uses the money (M) to buy bread (C_2). The primary goal of exchange in noncapitalist circulation is a commodity that one can use and enjoy.

In a capitalist circulation of commodities (M_1-C-M_2), the primary goal is to produce more money. Commodities are purchased in order to generate profit, not necessarily for use. In the capitalist circuit, referred to by Marx as "buying in order to sell" (1867/1967:147), the individual actor buys a commodity with money and in turn exchanges the commodity for presumably more money. For example, a store owner would buy (M_1) the fish (C) in order to sell them for more money (M_2). To further increase profits, the store owner might buy the boat and fishing equipment and pay the fisherman a wage. The goal of this circuit is not the consumption of the use value, as it is in the simple circulation of commodities. The goal is more money. The particular properties of the commodity used to make money are irrelevant. The commodity can be fish or it can be labor. Also, the real needs and desires of human beings are irrelevant; all that matters is what will produce more money.

Capital is money that produces more money, but Marx tells us it is more than that: it is also a particular social relation. Money becomes capital only because of a social relation between, on the one hand, the proletariat, which does the work and must purchase the product, and, on the other hand, those who have invested the money. The capacity of capital to generate profit appears "as a power endowed by Nature— a productive power that is immanent in Capital" (1867/1967:333); but, according to Marx, it is a relation of power. Capital cannot increase except by exploiting those who actually do the work. The workers are exploited by a system, and the irony is that the system is produced through the workers' own labor. The capitalist system is the social structure that emerges from that exploitive relationship.

Capitalists are those who live off the profit of capital. They are the beneficiaries of the proletariat's exploitation. Within the idea of capital is contained a social relation between those who own the means of production and those whose wage labor is exploited.

Exploitation

For Marx, exploitation and domination reflect more than an accidentally unequal distribution of wealth and power. *Exploitation* is a necessary part of the capitalist economy. All societies have exploitation, but what is peculiar in capitalism is that the exploitation is accomplished by the impersonal and "objective" economic system. It seems to be less a matter of power and more a matter of economists' charts and figures. Furthermore, the coercion is rarely naked force and is instead the worker's own needs, which can now be satisfied only through wage labor. Dripping irony, Marx describes the freedom of this wage labor:

> For the conversion of his money into capital . . . the owner of money must meet in the market with the free labourer, free in the double sense, that as a free man he can dispose of his labour-power as his own commodity, and that on the other hand he has no other commodity for sale, is short of everything necessary for the realization of his labour-power.

(Marx, 1867/1967:169)

Workers appear to be "free laborers," entering into free contracts with capitalists. But Marx believed that the workers must accept the terms the capitalists offer them, because the workers can no longer produce for their own needs. This is especially true because capitalism usually creates what Marx referred to as a *reserve army* of the unemployed. If a worker does not want to do a job at the wage the capitalist offers, someone else in the reserve army of the unemployed will. This, for example, is what Barbara Ehrenreich discovered is the purpose of many of the want ads for low-paying jobs:

> Only later will I realize that the want ads are not a reliable measure of the actual jobs available at any particular time. They are . . . the employers' insurance policy against the relentless turnover of the low-wage workforce. Most of the big hotels run ads almost continually if only to build a supply of applicants to replace the current workers as they drift away or are fired.

(Ehrenreich, 2001:15)

The capitalists pay the workers less than the value that the workers produce and keep the rest for themselves. This *practice* leads us to Marx's central concept of *surplus value,* which is defined as the difference between the value of the product when it is sold and the value of the elements consumed in the formation of that product (including the worker's labor). The capitalists can use this profit for private consumption, but doing so would not lead to the expansion of capitalism. Rather, capitalists expand their enterprises by converting profit into a base for the creation of still more surplus value.

It should be stressed that surplus value is not simply an economic concept. Surplus value, like capital, is a particular social relation and a form of domination, because labor is the real source of surplus value. "The rate of surplus-value is therefore an exact expression for the degree of exploitation of labor-power by capital, or of the laborer by the capitalist" (Marx, 1867/1967:218). This observation points to one of Marx's more colorful metaphors: "Capital is dead labor, that, vampire-like, only lives by sucking living labor, and lives the more, the more labor it sucks" (1867/1967:233).

Marx (1857–1858/1974:414) makes one other important point about capital: "Capital exists and can only exist as many capitals." What he means is that capitalism is always driven by incessant competition. Capitalists may seem to be in control, but even they are driven by the constant competition between capitals. The capitalist is driven to make more profit in order to accumulate and invest more capital. The capitalist who does not do this will be outcompeted by others who do. "As such, he shares with the miser an absolute drive towards self-enrichment. But what appears in the miser as the mania of an individual is in the capitalist the effect of a social mechanism in which he is merely a cog" (Marx, 1867/1967:739).

The desire for more profit and more surplus value for expansion pushes capitalism toward what Marx called the *general law of capitalist accumulation.* Capitalists seek to exploit workers as much as possible: "The constant tendency of capital is to force the cost of labor back towards . . . zero" (Marx, 1867/1967:600). Marx basically argued that the structure and the ethos of capitalism push capitalists in the direction of the accumulation of more and more capital. Given Marx's view that labor is the source of value, capitalists are led to intensify the exploitation of the proletariat, thereby driving class conflict.

Class Conflict

Marx often used the term *class* in his writings, but he never systematically defined what he meant (So and Suwarsono, 1990:35). He usually is taken to have meant a group of people in similar situations with respect to their control of the means of production. This, however, is not a complete description of the way Marx used the term. *Class,* for Marx, was always defined in terms of its potential for conflict. Individuals form a class insofar as they are in a common conflict with others over the surplus value. In capitalism there is an inherent conflict of interest between those who hire wage laborers and those whose labor is turned into surplus value. It is this inherent conflict that produces classes (Ollman, 1976).

Because class is defined by the potential for conflict, it is a theoretical and historically variant concept. A theory about where potential conflict exists in a society is required before identifying a class.[4] Richard Miller (1991:99) tells us that "there is no rule that could, in principle, be used to sort out people in a society into classes without studying the actual interactions among economic processes on the one hand and between political and cultural processes on the other."

For Marx, a class truly exists only when people become aware of their conflicting relation to other classes. Without this awareness, they only constitute what Marx called a class *in itself.* When they become aware of the conflict, they become a true class, a class *for itself.*

In capitalism, Marx's analysis discovered two primary classes: bourgeoisie and proletariat.[5] Bourgeoisie is Marx's name for capitalists in the modern economy. The bourgeoisie owns the means of production and employs wage labor. The conflict between the bourgeoisie and the proletariat is another example of a real material contradiction. This contradiction grows out of the previously mentioned contradiction between labor and capitalism. None of these contradictions can be resolved except by changing the capitalist structure. In fact, until that change occurs, the contradiction will only become worse. Society will be increasingly polarized into these two great opposing classes.

[4] Marx did acknowledge that class conflict often is affected by other forms of stratification, such as ethnic, racial, gender, and religious; however, he did not accept that these could be primary.
[5] Although his theoretical work looked mainly at these two classes, his historical studies examined a number of different class formations. Most significant are the petty bourgeois—small shopkeepers employing at most a few workers—and the lumpenproletariat—the proletariat who readily sell out to the capitalists. For Marx, these other classes can be understood only in terms of the primary relationship between bourgeoisie and proletariat.

Competition with megastores and franchise chains will shut down many small, independent businesses; mechanization will replace skilled artisans; and even some capitalists will be squeezed out through attempts to establish monopolies, for example, by means of mergers. All these displaced people will be forced down into the ranks of the proletariat. Marx called this inevitable increase in the proletariat *proletarianization.*

In addition, because capitalists have already reduced the workers to laboring machines performing a series of simple operations, mechanization becomes increasingly easy. As mechanization proceeds, more and more people are put out of work and fall from the proletariat into the industrial reserve army. In the end, Marx foresaw a situation in which society would be characterized by a tiny number of exploitative capitalists and a huge mass of proletarians and members of the industrial reserve army. By reducing so many people to this condition, capitalism creates the masses that will lead to its own overthrow. The increased centralization of factory work, as well as the shared suffering, increases the possibility of an organized resistance to capitalism. Furthermore, the international linking of factories and markets encourages workers to be aware of more than their own local interests. This awareness is likely to lead to revolution.

The capitalists, of course, seek to forestall this revolution. For example, they sponsor colonial adventures with the objective of shifting at least some of the burden of exploitation from the home front to the colonies. However, in Marx's view (1867/1967:10), these efforts are doomed to failure because the capitalist is as much controlled by the laws of the capitalist economy as are the workers. Capitalists are under competitive pressure from one another, forcing each to try to reduce labor costs and intensify exploitation—even though this intensified exploitation will increase the likelihood of revolution and therefore contribute to the capitalists' demise. Even good-hearted capitalists will be forced to further exploit their workers in order to compete: "The law of capitalist accumulation, metamorphosed by economists into pretended law of nature, in reality merely states that the very nature of accumulation excludes every diminution in the degree of exploitation" (Marx, 1867/1967:582).

Though not a Marxist, Robert Reich, a former U.S. secretary of labor, echoes Marx's analysis that it is not the evil of individual capitalists but the capitalist system itself that explains the increasing layoffs in America and the movement of manufacturing to take advantage of cheaper overseas labor:

> It's tempting to conclude from all this that enterprises are becoming colder-hearted, and executives more ruthless—and to blame it on an ethic of unbridled greed that seems to have taken hold in recent years and appears to be increasing. But this conclusion would be inaccurate. The underlying cause isn't a change in the American character. It is to be found in the increasing ease by which buyers and investors can get better deals, and the competitive pressure this imposes on all enterprises.
>
> (Reich, 2000:71)

Whether they want to or not, capitalists must move their factories where labor is cheaper; they must exploit workers. A capitalist who does not will not be able to compete with capitalists who do.

Marx usually did not blame individual members of the bourgeoisie for their actions; he saw these actions as largely determined by the logic of the capitalist system. This is consistent with his view that actors in capitalism generally are devoid of creative independence.[6] However, the developmental process inherent in capitalism provides the conditions necessary for the ultimate reemergence of such creative action and, with it, the overthrow of the capitalist system. The logic of the capitalist system is forcing the capitalists to produce more exploited proletarians, and these are the very people who will bring an end to capitalism through their revolt. "What the bourgeoisie, therefore, produces, is, above all, its own gravediggers" (Marx and Engels, 1848/1948).

It is not only the ultimate proletariat revolution that Marx sees as caused by the underlying contradictions of capitalism, but also many of the various personal and social crises that beset modern society. On the personal side, we have already discussed some of the facets of the alienation that Marx believed was at the root of the feeling of meaninglessness in so many people's lives. At the economic level, Marx predicted a series of booms and depressions as capitalists overproduced or laid off workers in their attempts to increase their profits. At the political level, Marx predicted the increasing inability of a civil society to discuss and solve social problems. Instead we would see the growth of a state whose only purposes are the protection of the capitalists' private property and an occasional brutal intervention when economic coercion by the capitalists fails.

Capitalism as a Good Thing

Despite his focus on the inevitable crises of capitalism and his portrayal of it as a system of domination and exploitation, Marx saw capitalism as primarily a good thing. Certainly, Marx did not want to return to the traditional values of precapitalism. Past generations were just as exploited; the only difference is that the old exploitation was not veiled behind an economic system. The birth of capitalism opened up new possibilities for the freedom of the workers. Notwithstanding its exploitation, the capitalist system provides the possibility for freedom from the traditions that bound all previous societies. Even if the worker is not yet truly free, the promise is there. Similarly, as the most powerful economic system ever developed, capitalism holds the promise of freedom from hunger and from other forms of material deprivation. It was from the viewpoint of these promises that Marx criticized capitalism.

In addition, Marx believed that capitalism is the root cause of the defining characteristics of the modern age. Modernity's constant change and propensity to challenge all accepted traditions are driven by the inherent competition of capitalism, which pushes capitalists to continuously revolutionize the means of production and transform society:

> Constant revolutionizing of production, uninterrupted disturbance of all social conditions, everlasting uncertainty and agitation distinguish the bourgeois epoch from all earlier ones. All fixed, fast-frozen relations, with their train of ancient and venerable prejudices and opinions, are swept away, all new-formed ones become antiquated before they can ossify. All that is solid melts into air, all that is holy is profaned, and man is at last compelled to face with sober senses, his real conditions of life, and his relations with his kind.
>
> (Marx and Engels, 1848/1948:11)

---

[6] Marx might be seen as an exception to his own theory. He does acknowledge that it is possible for some individuals among the bourgeoisie to lay aside their class characteristics and adopt a communist consciousness (Marx and Engels, 1845–1846/1970:69).

Capitalism has been a truly revolutionary force. It has created a global society; it has introduced unrelenting technological change; it has overthrown the traditional world. But now, Marx believed, it must be overthrown. Capitalism's role is finished, and it is time for the new stage of communism to begin.

Materialist Conception of History

Marx was able to criticize capitalism from the perspective of its future because of his belief that history would follow a predictable course. This belief was based on his materialist conception of history (often simply shortened to the term *historical materialism* [Vandenberghe, 2005]). The general claim of Marx's historical materialism is that the way in which people provide for their material needs determines or, in general, conditions the relations that people have with each other, their social institutions, and even their prevalent ideas.[7]

Because of the importance of the way in which people provide for their material needs, this, along with the resultant economic relations, is often referred to as the *base*. Noneconomic relations, other social institutions, and prevalent ideas are referred to as the *superstructure*. It should be noted that Marx's view of history does not envision a straightforward trend in which the superstructure simply comes into line with the base. Human history is set into motion by the attempt to satisfy needs, but as noted above, these needs themselves are historically changing. Consequently, advances in the satisfaction of needs tend to produce more needs so that human needs are both the motivating foundation and the result of the economic base.

The following quotation is one of Marx's best summaries of his materialist conception of history:

> In the social production which men carry on they enter into definite relations that are indispensable and independent of their will. These relations of production correspond to a definite stage of development of their material forces of production. The totality of these relations of production constitutes the economic structure of society, which is the real foundation on top of which arises a legal and political superstructure to which correspond definite forms of social consciousness. At a certain stage of their development, the material forces of production in society come in conflict with the existing relations of production or—what is but a legal expression of the same thing—with the property relations within which they had been at work before. From forms of development of the forces of production these relations turn into their fetters. Then occurs a period of social revolution. With the change of the economic foundation the entire immense superstructure is more or less rapidly transformed.
>
> (Marx, 1859/1970:20–21)

---

[7] Antonio (2000:119–120) distinguishes between a hard and a soft material determinism. "Although hard determinist passages exist in Marx's texts, he suggested much more often a complex, historically contingent materialism, which ought not to be reduced to 'technological determinism' (i.e., social change arises from technical change) or to 'reflection theory' (i.e., ideas are mere emanations of material reality)."

The place to start in that quotation is with the "material forces of production." These are the actual tools, machinery, factories, and so forth used to satisfy human needs. The "relations of production" are the kinds of associations that people have with each other in satisfying their needs.

Marx's theory holds that a society will tend to adopt the system of social relations that best facilitates the employment and development of its productive powers. Therefore, the relations of production correspond to the state of the material forces of production. For example, certain stages of low technology correspond to social relations characterized by a few large landowners and a large number of serfs who work the land in return for a share of the produce. The higher technology of capitalism corresponds to a few capitalists who are able to invest in the expensive machinery and factories and a large number of wage workers. As Marx succinctly, if somewhat simplistically, puts it, "the hand-mill gives you society with the feudal lord; the steam-mill society with the capitalist" (Marx, 1847/1963:95). Marx adds that these relations between people also can be expressed as property relations: the capitalist owns the means of production, and the wage laborer does not.

Capitalist economies foster unique relations between people and create certain expectations, obligations, and duties. For example, wage laborers must show a certain deference to capitalists if they want to keep their jobs. For Marx, what was important about these relations of production was their propensity to class conflict, but it is also possible to see the effect of the relations of production in family and personal relations. The socialization necessary to produce the "good" male worker also produces a certain type of husband. Similarly, early capitalism's requirement that the man leave the home to work all day led to a definition of the mother as the primary caretaker of the children. Hence, changes in the forces of production led to deep changes in the family structure. These changes too can be seen as relations of production.

Marx is never quite clear about where the relations of production leave off and the superstructure starts. However, he clearly felt that some relations and forms of "social consciousness" play only a supporting role in the material means of production. Marx predicted that although these elements of the superstructure are not directly involved, they tend to take a form that will support the relations of production.

Marx's view of history was a dynamic one, and he therefore believed that the forces of production will change to better provide for material needs. For example, this is what happened with the advent of capitalism, when technological changes made factories possible. However, before capitalism could actually occur, there had to be changes in society, changes in the relations of production. Factories, capitalists, and wage laborers were not compatible with feudal relations. The feudal lords, who derived their wealth solely from the ownership of land and who felt a moral obligation to provide for their serfs, had to be replaced by capitalists who derived their wealth from capital and who felt no moral obligation to wage laborers. Similarly, the serf's feeling of personal loyalty to the lord had to be replaced by proletarians' willingness to sell their labor to whoever will pay. The old relations of production were in conflict with the new forces of production.

A revolution is often required to change the relations of production. The main source of revolution is the material contradiction between the forces of production and the relations of production. However, revolution also results from another contradiction: between exploiters and the exploited. According to Marx, this contradiction, which has always existed, leads to revolutionary change when the exploited line up in support of a change in the relations of production that favors changes occurring in the forces of production. Marx did not believe that all workers' revolts could be effective, only those in support of a change in the forces of production. An effective revolution, according to Marx, will cause the supporting relations, institutions, and prevalent ideas to change so that they validate the new relations of production.

Cultural Aspects of Capitalist Society

In addition to his focus on the material structures of capitalism, Marx also theorized about its cultural aspects.

Ideology

Not only do the existing relations of production tend to prevent changes necessary for the development of the forces of production, but similarly, the supporting relations, institutions, and, in particular, prevalent ideas also tend to prevent these changes. Marx called prevalent ideas that perform this function *ideologies*. As with many terms, Marx is not always precise in his use of the word *ideology*. He seems to use it to indicate two related sorts of ideas.

First, *ideology* refers to ideas that naturally emerge out of everyday life in capitalism but, because of the nature of capitalism, reflect reality in an inverted manner (Larrain, 1979). To explain this meaning of the term, Marx used the metaphor of a camera obscura, which employs an optical quirk to show a real image reflected upside down. This is the type of ideology represented by the fetishism of commodities or by money. Even though we know that money is nothing but a piece of paper that has value only because of underlying social relations, in our daily lives we treat money as though it had inherent value. Instead of our seeing that we give money its value, it often seems that money gives us our value.

This first type of ideology is vulnerable to disruption because it is based on underlying material contradictions. Human value is not really dependent on money, and we often meet people who are living proof of that contradiction. In fact, it is at this level that we usually become aware of the material contradictions that Marx believed will drive capitalism to the next phase. We become aware, for example, that the economy is not an objective, independent system, but a political sphere. We become aware that our labor is not just another commodity and that its sale for wages produces alienation. Or if we don't become aware of the underlying truth, we at least become aware of the disruption because of a blatantly political move in the economic system or our own feeling of alienation. It is in addressing these disruptions that Marx's second use of *ideology* is relevant.

When disruptions occur and the underlying material contradictions are revealed, or are in danger of being revealed, the second type of ideology will emerge. Here Marx uses the term *ideology* to refer to systems of ruling ideas that attempt once again to hide the contradictions that are at the heart of the capitalist system. In most cases, they do this in one of three ways: (1) They lead to the creation of subsystems of ideas—a religion, a philosophy, a literature, a legal system—that makes the contradictions appear to be coherent. (2) They explain away those experiences that reveal the contradictions, usually as personal problems or individual idiosyncrasies. Or (3) they present the capitalist contradiction as really being a contradiction in human nature and therefore one that cannot be fixed by social change.

In general, members of the ruling class create this second type of ideology. For example, Marx refers to bourgeois economists who present the commodity form as natural and universal. Or he criticizes bourgeois philosophers, such as Hegel, for pretending that material contradictions can be resolved by changing how we think. However, even the proletariat can create this type of ideology. People who have given up the hope of actually changing society need such ideologies. But no matter who creates them, these ideologies always benefit the ruling class by hiding the contradictions that would lead to social change.

Freedom, Equality, and Ideology

For an example of ideology, we will look at Marx's ideas about the bourgeois conception of equality and freedom. According to Marx, our particular ideas of equality and freedom emerge out of capitalism. Although we take our belief in freedom and equality to be an obvious thing, any historical study will demonstrate that it is not. Most societies would have considered the idea that all people are essentially equal as absurd. For most cultures throughout history, slavery seemed quite natural. Now, under capitalism, we believe quite the opposite: inequality is absurd, and slavery is unnatural.

Marx thought that this change in our ideas could be traced to the everyday practices of capitalism. The act of exchange, which is the basis of capitalism, presupposes the equality of the people in the exchange, just as it presupposes the equality of the commodities in the exchange. For the commodities, the particular qualitative differences of their use values are hidden by their exchange value. In other words, apples and oranges are made equal by reducing them to their monetary value. The same thing happens to the differences between the people involved in the exchange. Most exchanges in advanced capitalism involve people who never meet and don't know each other. We don't care who grew the apples and oranges we buy. This anonymity and indifference constitutes a kind of equality.

Furthermore, freedom is assumed in this exchange, since any of the partners to the exchange are presumed to be free to exchange or not as they see fit. The very idea of capitalist exchange means that commodities are not taken by force but are freely traded. This is also true of the exchange of labor time for wages. It is assumed that the worker or the employer is free to enter into the exchange and free to terminate it. Marx (1857–1858/1974:245) concludes that "equality and freedom are not only respected in exchange which is based on exchange values, but the exchange of exchange values is the real productive basis of all equality and freedom." Nevertheless, Marx believed that capitalist practices result in an inverted view of freedom. It seems that we are free; but in fact, it is capital that is free and we who are enslaved.

According to Marx, freedom is the ability to have control over your own labor and its products. Although individuals may seem free under capitalism, they are not. Under previous social forms, people were directly dominated by others and so were aware of their unfreedom. Under capitalism, people are dominated by capitalist relations that seem objective and natural and therefore are not perceived as a form of domination. Marx (1857–1858/1974:652) decries "the insipidity of the view that free competition is the ultimate development of human freedom. . . . This kind of individual freedom is therefore at the same time the most complete suspension of all individual freedom, and the most complete subjugation of individuality under social conditions which assume the form of objective powers."

Because the capitalist owns the means of production, the exchange of wages for labor time cannot be free. The proletariat must work in order to live, but the capitalist has the choice to hire others from the reserve army of labor, or to mechanize, or to let the factory sit idle until the workers become desperate enough to "freely" accept the capitalist's wages. The worker is neither free nor equal to the capitalist.

Hence, we see that the first level of the ideology of freedom and equality emerges from the practices of exchange in capitalism, but that our ideas are inverted and do not represent real freedom and equality. It is capital that is freely and equally exchanged; it is capital that is accepted without prejudice; it is capital that is able to do as it wishes, not us. This first type of ideology is easily disrupted, and our awareness of this disruption drives capitalism to the next phase. Despite the ideology of equality and freedom, few workers feel equal to their employers; few feel free in their jobs. This is why the second type of ideology is necessary. These disruptions somehow must be explained away or made to look inevitable.

This is especially true with the ideology of equality and freedom, because these ideas are among the most threatening to capitalism. They are another example of how capitalism creates its own gravediggers. Older forms of unfreedom and inequality were clearly tied to people, and there was hope, therefore, of becoming free and equal by changing the hearts of the people who oppressed us. When we become aware of the source of unfreedom and inequality under capitalism, we begin to realize that capitalism itself must be changed. Ideologies therefore must be created to protect the capitalist system, and one way in which they do this is by portraying inequality as equality and unfreedom as freedom.

Marx believed that the capitalist system is inherently unequal. The capitalists automatically benefit more from the capitalist system, while the workers are automatically disadvantaged. Under capitalism, those who own the means of production, those with capital, make money from their money. Under capitalism, capital begets more capital—that is, investments give a return—and as we saw above, Marx believed that this was derived from the exploitation of the workers. Not only are the workers automatically exploited, they also bear the burden of unemployment due to technological changes, geographical shifts, and other economic dislocations, all of which benefit the capitalist. The rule of capitalism is reflected in the common saying that the rich get richer while the poor get poorer. Constantly increasing inequality is built into the capitalist system.

Any attempt toward a more equal society must take into account this automatic propensity of the capitalist system to increased inequality. Nevertheless, attempts to make the capitalist system more equal often are portrayed as forms of inequality. From the Marxist viewpoint these attempts would be the second form of ideology. For example, ideologues promote a "flat tax" which taxes the rich and the poor at the same rate. They argue that because the rate is the same for rich and poor, it is equal.

They ignore the fact that a graduated tax rate may be just compensation for the built-in inequality of capitalism. They create an ideology by portraying the obvious inequalities of the capitalist system as inevitable or as being due to the laziness of the poor. In this way, inequality is portrayed as equality, and the freedom of the rich to keep the fruits of exploitation trumps the freedom of the workers.

We see in this example not only the two types of ideology but also another instance of how Marx thought that capitalism is a good thing. The ideas of freedom and equality emerge from capitalism itself, and it is these ideas that drive us toward the dissolution of capitalism, toward communism.

Religion

Marx also sees religion as an ideology. He famously refers to religion as the opiate of the people, but it is worthwhile to look at the entire quotation:

> Religious distress is at the same time the expression of real distress and also the protest against real distress. Religion is the sigh of the oppressed creature, the heart of a heartless world, just as it is the spirit of spiritless conditions. It is the opium of the people.

(Marx, 1843/1970)

Marx believed that religion, like all ideology, reflects a truth but that this truth is inverted. Because people cannot see that their distress and oppression are produced by the capitalist system, their distress and oppression are given a religious form. Marx clearly says that he is not against religion per se, but against a system that requires the illusions of religion.

This religious form is vulnerable to disruption and therefore is always liable to become the basis of a revolutionary movement. We do indeed see that religious movements have often been in the forefront of opposition to capitalism (for example, liberation theology). Nevertheless, Marx felt that religion is especially amenable to becoming the second form of ideology by portraying the injustice of capitalism as a test for the faithful and pushing any revolutionary change off into the afterlife. In this way, the cry of the oppressed is used to further oppression.

Marx's Economics: A Case Study

This chapter is devoted to an analysis of Marx's sociology, but of course it is his economics for which he is far better known. Although we have touched on a number of aspects of Marx's economics, we have not dealt with it in a coherent fashion. In this section, we look at Marx's economics, not as economics per se but rather as an exemplification of his sociological theory (Mazlish, 1984).[8] There is much more to Marxian economics, but this is the most relevant way to deal with it in a book devoted to sociological theory.

---

[8] *One* way of looking at Marx's economic theory (for example, the labor theory of value) is as a specific application of his more general sociological theory. This stands in contrast to G. A. Cohen's (1978) work, in which his overriding concern is the underlying *economic* theory in Marx's work. Although Cohen sees the "economic" and the "social" as being interchangeable in Marx's work, he clearly implies that Marx's economic theory is the more general.

A starting point for Marxian economics is in the concepts, previously touched on, of use value and exchange value. People have always created use values; that is, they have always produced things that directly satisfy their wants. A *use value* is defined qualitatively; that is, something either is or is not useful. An *exchange value*, however, is defined quantitatively, not qualitatively. It is defined by the amount of labor needed to appropriate useful qualities. Whereas use values are produced to satisfy one's own needs, exchange values are produced to be exchanged for values of another use. Whereas the production of use values is a natural human expression, the existence of exchange values sets in motion a process by which humanity is distorted. The entire edifice of capitalism, including commodities, the market, money, and so forth, is erected on the basis of exchange values.

To Marx, the basic source of any value was the amount of socially necessary labor-time needed to produce an article under the normal conditions of production and with the average degree of skill and intensity of the time. This is the well-known *labor theory of value*. Although it is clear that labor lies at the base of use value, this fact grows progressively less clear as we move to exchange values, commodities, the market, and capitalism. To put it another way, "The determination of the magnitude of value by labor-time is therefore a secret, hidden under the apparent fluctuations in relative values of commodities" (Marx, 1867/1967:75). Labor, as the source of all value, is a secret in capitalism that allows the capitalists to exploit the workers.

According to Peter Worsley, Marx "put at the heart of his sociology—as no other sociology does—the theme of exploitation" (1982:115). The capitalists pay the workers *less* than the value the workers produce and keep the rest for themselves. The workers are not aware of this exploitation, and often, neither are the capitalists. The capitalists believe that this extra value is derived from their own cleverness, their capital investment, their manipulation of the market, and so on. Marx stated that "so long as trade is good, the capitalist is too much absorbed in money grubbing to take notice of this gratuitous gift of labor" (1867/1967:207). In sum, Marx said:

> The capitalist does not know that the normal price of labor also includes a definite quantity of unpaid labor, and that this very unpaid labor is the normal source of his gain. The category, surplus labor-time, does not exist at all for him, since it is included in the normal working-day, which he thinks he has paid for in the day's wages.
>
> (Marx, 1867/1967:550)

This leads us to Marx's central concept of *surplus value*. This is defined as the difference between the value of the product when it is sold and the value of the elements consumed in the formation of that product. Although means of production (raw materials and tools, the value of which comes from the labor involved in extracting or producing them) are consumed in the production process, it is labor that is the real source of surplus value. "The rate of surplus-value is therefore an exact expression for the degree of exploitation of labor-power by capital, or of the laborer by the capitalist" (Marx, 1867/1967:218). This points to one of Marx's more colorful metaphors: "Capital is dead labor, that, vampire-like, only lives by sucking living labor, and lives the more, the more labor it sucks" (1867/1967:233).

The surplus derived from this process is used by the capitalists to pay for such things as rent to landowners and interest to banks. But the most important derivation from it is profit. The capitalists can use this profit for private consumption, but that would not lead to the expansion of capitalism. Rather they expand their enterprise by converting it into a base for the creation of still more surplus value.

The desire for more profit and more surplus value for expansion pushes capitalism toward what Marx called the *general law of capitalist accumulation*. The capitalists seek to exploit workers as much as possible: "The constant tendency of capital is to force the cost of labor back towards . . . zero" (Marx, 1867/1967:600). Marx basically argued that the structure and the ethos of capitalism push the capitalists in the direction of the accumulation of more and more capital. In order to do this, given Marx's view that labor is the source of value, the capitalists are led to intensify the exploitation of the proletariat. Ultimately, however, increased exploitation yields fewer and fewer gains; an upper limit of exploitation is reached. In addition, as this limit is approached, the government is forced by pressure from the working class to place restrictions on the actions of capitalists (for example, laws limiting the length of the workday). As a result of these restrictions, the capitalists must look for other devices, and a major one is the substitution of machines for people. This substitution is made relatively easy, because the capitalists already have reduced the workers to laboring machines performing a series of simple operations. This shift to capital-intensive production is, paradoxically, a cause of the declining rate of profit since it is labor (not machines) which is the ultimate source of profit.

As mechanization proceeds, more and more people are put out of work and fall from the proletariat to the "industrial reserve army." At the same time, heightening competition and the burgeoning costs of technology lead to a progressive decline in the number of capitalists. In the end, Marx foresaw a situation in which society would be characterized by a tiny number of exploitative capitalists and a huge mass of proletarians and members of the industrial reserve army. In these extreme circumstances, capitalism would be most vulnerable to revolution. As Marx put it, the expropriation of the masses by the capitalists would be replaced by "the expropriation of a few usurpers by the mass of people" (1867/1967:764). The capitalists, of course, seek to forestall their demise. For example, they sponsor colonial adventures with the objective of shifting at least some of the burden of exploitation from the home front to the colonies. However, in Marx's view these efforts are ultimately doomed to failure, and the capitalists will face rebellion at home and abroad.

The key point about the general law of capitalist accumulation is the degree to which actors, both capitalist and proletarian, are impelled by the structure and ethos of capitalism to do what they do. Marx usually did not blame individual capitalists for their actions; he saw these actions as largely determined by the logic of the capitalist system. This is consistent with his view that actors in capitalism generally are devoid of creative independence. However, the developmental process inherent in capitalism provides the conditions necessary for the ultimate reemergence of such creative action and, with it, the overthrow of the capitalist system.

Communism

Marx often wrote as though changes in the mode of production were inevitable, as in the quotation about the hand-mill giving you feudalism and the steam-mill giving you capitalism. Unless one wishes to find reasons for rejecting Marx's theories, it is probably best to interpret Marx's historical materialism as motivated by a desire to identify some predictable trends and to use these trends to discover the points where political action could be most effective. This is certainly the way that Marx used his theories in his concrete political and economic studies, such as *Class Struggles in France* (1850) and *The Eighteenth Brumaire of Louis Bonaparte* (1869). The truth of historical materialism, then, does not depend on the inevitability of its historical predictions, but on whether a focus on the way that we satisfy our material needs is the best way to reveal the opportunities for effective political intervention.

If the goal of Marx's materialist view of history was to predict those points where political action could be most effective, then it is his view of what changes will lead to the next stage that is most important. Marx thought that capitalism had developed its productive powers so that it was ready to enter a new mode of production, which he called *communism*. Most of his analysis dwelt on conflicts in the present that will lead to this new economic form.

Despite the importance to Marx of the future communist society, he spent surprisingly little time depicting what this world would be like. He refused to write "recipes for the kitchens of the future" (Marx, cited in T. Ball, 1991:139). The era in which Marx wrote was filled with talk of revolutions and new forms of society—of communism, socialism, anarchy, and many more now forgotten. Charismatic political leaders appeared on the historical stage and stirred audiences with their speeches. Marx, however, was intellectually opposed to painting utopian visions of the future. To Marx, the most important task was the critical analysis of contemporary capitalist society. He believed that such criticism would help bring down capitalism and create the conditions for the rise of a new socialist world. There would be time to construct communist society once capitalism was overcome. In general, however, Marx believed that communism would involve taking decisions about what is to be produced away from the reified economy that runs in the interests of the few capitalists and putting in its place some sort of social decision making that would allow the needs of the many to be taken into account.

Criticisms

Five problems in Marx's theory need to be discussed. The first is the problem of communism as it came to exist. The failure of communist societies and their turn to a more capitalistically oriented economy raise questions about the role of Marxian theory within sociology (Antonio, 2000; Aronson, 1995; Hudelson, 1993; Manuel, 1992). Marx's ideas seem to have been tried and to have failed. At one time, almost one-third of the world's population lived under states inspired by the ideas of Marx. Many of those formerly Marxist states have become capitalist, and even those (except perhaps for Cuba) that still claim to be Marxist manifest nothing but a highly bureaucratized form of capitalism.

Against this criticism, it could be argued that those states never truly followed Marxist precepts, and that it is unfair for critics to blame Marx for every misuse of his theory. However, those making the criticism claim that Marx himself insisted that Marxist theory should not be split from its actually existing practice. As Alvin Gouldner (1970:3) writes, "Having set out to change the world, rather than produce one more interpretation of it, Marxist theory must ultimately be weighed on the scales of history." If Marxism never works out in practice, then, for Marx, the theory would be useless at best and ideological at worst. Furthermore, it seems clear that Marx's lack of a theory regarding the problems of state bureaucracy has contributed to the failures of actually existing communism. Had he developed a complete theory of state bureaucracy, it is conceivable that Marx might have preferred the evils of capitalism.

The second problem is often referred to as the *missing emancipatory subject.* Critics say that although Marx's theory places the proletariat at the heart of the social change leading to communism, the proletariat has rarely assumed this leading position and often is among the groups that are most opposed to communism. This problem is compounded by the fact that intellectuals—for example, academic sociologists—have leapt into the gap left by the proletariat and substituted intellectual activity for class struggle. In addition, the intellectuals' disappointment at the proletariat's conservativism is transformed into a theory that emphasizes the role of ideology much more strongly than Marx did and that tends to see the "heroes" of the future revolution as manipulated dupes.

The third problem is the *missing dimension of gender.* One of the main points of Marx's theory is that labor becomes a commodity under capitalism, yet it is a historical fact that the commodifying of labor has happened less to women than to men. To a large degree, men's paid labor still depends on the *unpaid* labor of women, especially the all-important rearing of the next generation of workers. Sayer (1991) points out that the missing dimension of gender not only leaves a hole in Marx's analysis but also affects his primary argument that capitalism is defined by its growing dependence on wage labor, because the growth of wage labor has been dependent on the unpaid labor of women. Patriarchy may be an essential foundation for the emergence of capitalism, but Marx simply ignores it.

The fourth problem is that Marx saw the economy as driven almost solely by production, and he ignored the role of consumption. The focus on production led him to predict that concerns for efficiency and cost cutting would lead to proletarianization, increasing alienation, and deepening class conflict. It could be argued, however, that the central role of consumption in the modern economy encourages some creativity and entrepreneurship and that these provide at least some wage labor jobs that are not alienating. People who create new video games or direct movies or perform popular music are less alienated from their work, even though they are firmly entrenched in a capitalist system. Although there are only a few such jobs, their existence gives hope to the alienated masses, who can anticipate that they, or at least their children, might someday work in interesting and creative jobs.

Finally, some might point to Marx's uncritical acceptance of Western conceptions of progress as a problem. Marx believed that the engine of history is humanity's always improving exploitation of nature for its material needs. In addition, Marx thought that the essence of human nature is our ability to shape nature to our purposes. It may be that these assumptions are a root cause of many of our current and future ecological crises.

Summary

Marx presents a complex and still relevant analysis of the historical basis of inequality in capitalism and how to change it. Marx's theories are open to many interpretations, but this chapter tries to present an interpretation that makes his theories consistent with his actual historical studies.

The chapter begins with a discussion of the dialectical approach that Marx derived from Hegel and that shapes all of Marx's work. The important point here is that Marx believed that society is structured around contradictions that can be resolved only through actual social change. One of the primary contradictions that Marx looked at was between human potential (nature) and the conditions for labor in capitalism. For Marx, human nature is intimately tied to labor, which both expresses and transforms human potential. Under capitalism, our labor is sold as a commodity, and the commodifying of our labor leads to alienation from our productive activity, from the objects that we make, from our fellow workers, and even from ourselves.

Next the chapter presents Marx's analysis of capitalist society. We begin with the central concept of commodities and then look at the contradiction between their use value and their exchange value. In capitalism, the exchange value of commodities tends to predominate over their actual usefulness in satisfying human needs; therefore, commodities begin to appear to be separate from human labor and from human need and eventually appear to have power over humans. Marx called this the fetishism of commodities. This fetishism is a form of reification, and it affects more than just commodities; in particular, it affects the economic system, which begins to seem like an objective, nonpolitical force that determines our lives. Because of this reification we don't see that the very idea of capital contains a contradictory social relation between those who profit from their investments and those whose actual labor provides the surplus value that constitutes profit. In other words, the ability of capital to generate profit rests on the exploitation of the proletariat. This underlying contradiction leads to class conflict between the proletariat and bourgeoisie, which eventually will result in revolution because proletarianization will swell the ranks of the proletariat. This section concludes by stressing that despite his criticisms of capitalism, Marx believed that capitalism has been good and that his criticisms of it are from the perspective of its potential future.

Marx felt that he was able to take the view from capitalism's potential future because of his materialist conception of history. By focusing on the forces of production, Marx was able to predict historical trends that allowed him to identify where political action could be effective. Political action and even revolution are necessary because relations of production and ideology hold back the necessary development of the forces of production. In Marx's view these changes eventually will lead to a communist society.

We also offer a discussion of some of the most important nonmaterial (cultural) aspects of Marx's theory—especially ideology and religion—as well as some of his famous ideas on economics, especially the labor theory of value.

The chapter ends with some criticisms of Marx's theories. Despite their significance, these criticisms have contributed to the strength of the Marxist approach, even where the strengthening of some Marxist approaches has meant abandoning some of Marx's most strongly held positions.

4 Structuralism and semiotics

Introduction

This chapter focuses on structuralist theories of media and the method of **semiotics** that emerged from theoretical themes which underpin **structuralism**. The work of a linguist, Ferdinand de Saussure, will begin our discussion. Central to Saussure's theory of language is the distinction between synchronic and diachronic forms of analysis. Synchronic analysis explores language as a system at a given moment in time. It is a 'snapshot' form of analysis. Diachronic analysis, on the other hand, explores a language system as it evolves over a period of time. Etymology is a type of diachronic analysis. By contrast:

> Structuralism as a whole is necessarily synchronic; it is concerned to study particular systems or structures under artificial and ahistorical conditions, neglecting the systems or structures out of which they have emerged in the hope of explaining their present functioning.
>
> (Sturrock 1979: 9)

Unlike theories of modernity, structuralism is oblivious to history in its search for what language means and represents here and now. Semiotics is the method that serves this purpose. Semiotics analyses language as a whole system that structures its individual parts into distinct units of meaning. These units of meaning are referred to as signs. Since the system is constantly changing – new signs emerge, old signs become obsolete – what semiotics does is freeze the moment in order to analyse the system at work. Structuralism is the theoretical framework that seeks to understand how systems work to structure their individual parts at any given moment in time.

Language is the system *par excellence*, but inextricably linked to language are social, cultural, political and economic systems. Societies, like languages, structure their individual parts (i.e. citizens) precisely through processes of differentiation. Our social lives are structured by powerful agents of the social system such as governments. Media institutions are also powerful agents of the social system, but at the same time these agents are structured by the system too. As we will discuss in relation to structuralist theories of myth, ideology and hegemony, it is possible to theorize media texts (especially news) and the institutions that produce them as meaning-makers. The ways in which we perceive our social and cultural lives are shaped to a great extent by what we see on television or read in newspapers or hear on the radio. Media – among other meaning systems – structure our lives. Of course, we do not simply accept what we see on television or read in the newspapers or hear on the radio. As Hall (1980) notes, we 'decode' media texts in different ways – sometimes we agree, sometimes we disagree. Nonetheless, the power to decide what stories, ideas, tastes and values are offered to us via media communications is structured unequally in favour of some interests (the ruling ones) rather than others (the interests of the silent majority). Hebdige's subcultural theory reminds us that ideological and hegemonic power can be met with resistance, but for Foucault resistance is banal because we have internalized the power structures that oppress us.

Saussure and Barthes: language and myth

Before we can begin to understand structuralist theories of media, it is first necessary to probe in greater depth the theory of **language** outlined by Saussure's *Course in General Linguistics* (first published in 1916). Saussure dismissed the notion that language simply reflects reality and instead suggested that language operates within its own system. This system *constructs* meanings within a language – meanings do not evolve in any natural or unique way. He called this approach semiology, which means the study of signs, but we will use the more common term for this approach, known as semiotics. A sign (word) such as 'rat', for instance, has two properties: a sound and an idea. But there is no connection between the sound and the idea: 'the choice of a given slice of sound to name a given idea is completely arbitrary' (Saussure 1966: 113). Even a sign like 'sizzle' – which some would cite as an example of onomatopoeia – has no meaning in relation to its sound, according to Saussure's theory of language. Working as a system, the signs (i.e. words) that form a language are able to signify ideas precisely because they are different from other signs: 'Language is a system of interdependent terms in which the value of each term results solely from the simultaneous presence of the others' (Saussure 1966: 114). So language is structured through difference, and different ideas depend on different sounds, or 'the phonic differences that make it possible to distinguish this word from all others, for differences carry signification' (Saussure 1966: 118).

For example, we can only understand the word 'rat' as a unit of meaning in the English language because its sound – as well as the idea or thing it signifies – differs from that of other words, such as 'mouse' or 'cat'. If 'rat' was the word used to signify all of these 'real' things (i.e. mouse and cat as well as rat), its meaning would be imprecise and the whole system of language would have effectively failed to signify. However, in Latin there is only one term – 'mus' – to refer to both a rat and a mouse. Latin speakers, historically, have

56   STRUCTURALISM AND SEMIOTICS

not distinguished between the two creatures because they are 'indifferent' to Latin cultures. Likewise, Eskimos have several different words to describe 'snow' whereas English speakers only use one. As Umberto Eco rightly demonstrates in support of Saussure, 'any cultural phenomenon is *also* a sign phenomenon' (Eco 1973: 61). Cultural meanings are therefore specific to language systems that operate within the rules of semiotics.

Saussure shows, therefore, that any single sign (or word) in a language system is inextricably linked with the system as a whole. A word's 'content is really fixed only by the concurrence of everything that exists around it' (Saussure 1966: 115). In order to illustrate this, he makes a distinction between the *langue* (the whole system or structure) and the *parole* (specific utterances within this system) of a given language. An utterance (*parole*) can only signify meaning effectively in its relation to the whole system of a language (*langue*). The analogy to a game of chess is a good one:

> Each individual move in chess is selected from the whole system of possible chess moves. So we could call the system of possible chess moves the *langue* of chess. Any individual move in a game of chess would be *parole*, the selection of a move from the whole set of possible moves in the *langue* of chess.
>
> (Bignell 2002: 8)

This distinction between *langue* and *parole* can be applied not only to the formal properties of a language (linguistics) but also to uses of language in social contexts. As Figure 4.1 shows, language usage is structured by a system that works along two axes: the *syntagmatic* (meanings which exist at a specific moment in time) and the *paradigmatic* (meanings which could be used to substitute existing ones). The examples in Figure 4.1 prove Saussure's point that changes in the paradigmatic features of a language system alter the whole structure of meaning as carried by the syntagmatic features, and vice versa.

Following Saussure, Roland Barthes's theory of **myth** is indebted to his predecessor's claim that a word's idea (its signified element) and its sound (its signifier element) are unconnected but together make up the total meaning of that word (its sign), which can only be understood in relation to all other signs – as in the relationship between *langue* and *parole*. However, Barthes extends Saussure's theory of language systems by applying it to the systems by which societies and cultures develop 'myths'. Societies and cultures, like languages, are considered to be structured by a 'whole' system that determines their individual parts. Of course, language as a system is also fundamental to how societies or cultures persist. But Barthes suggests that purely linguistic meanings are radically changed by social and cultural practices.

Barthes's most important work in this respect is *Mythologies* (first

PARADIGMATIC DIMENSION

(vertical substitutions of meaning)

	Politicians		suffered	defeat
The	**Media**	have	**expressed**	**anger**
	Courts		enjoyed	success

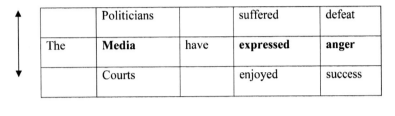

SYNTAGMATIC DIMENSION (horizontal substitutions of meaning)

Figure 4.1 Syntagmatic and paradigmatic dimensions of semiotics

published in 1957). Here he develops Saussure's notion that meanings do not simply refer to real things. Furthermore, meanings can develop beyond their linguistic properties and take on the status of myths. Saussure suggested that the meaning of any term in a language system consists of a signifier plus a signified to give a sign (Figure 4.2).

SIGNIFIER (sound/phonetic quality) + SIGNIFIED (idea) = SIGN (total meaning)

Figure 4.2 Saussure's semiotic theory of language

Barthes, on the other hand, introduces an extra dimension to this equation (Figure 4.3).

Language { SIGNIFIER + SIGNIFIED = SIGN
↓
Myth { **SIGNIFIER + SIGNIFIED = SIGN**

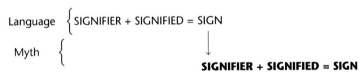

Figure 4.3 Barthes's semiotic theory of language and myth

Source: Barthes (1993: 115)

Language – the first order of signification in Barthes's model – is therefore capable of generating a second order of signification called myth. This is the basis for Barthes's approach to semiotics. In Figure 4.3 we can see how a sign (i.e. an idea plus a sound) such as 'rat', which operates in a first order of signification, becomes a signifier within a second-order 'myth' system of signification. In the case of rat, therefore, its sign in the 'language' order of

58   STRUCTURALISM AND SEMIOTICS

signification defines it as, say, 'a small rodent with a pointed snout'. However, its sign in the 'myth' order of signification would be extended to what rat means in particular social and cultural contexts. In English-speaking, Western countries such as Britain, rat as a myth signifies dirt, disease, the darkness of underground sewers and cellars. Most of the mythical meanings that we attach to 'rat' are negative, because most of us dislike or even fear the 'real' creature which the word signifies. The distinction between language and myth is sometimes equated to the distinction between denotation and connotation. Denotation is similar to a dictionary definition of a sign; connotation, by contrast, refers to the wider social and cultural meanings (myths) attached to a sign. Rat denotes rodent; it connotes much, much more (dirt, disease, and so on).

How does Barthes's semiotic – or structuralist – theory of myth apply to media? If we consider media to be an important – perhaps *the* most important – element within a social and cultural system of signs that are capable of generating myths, then clearly television, the internet and other mass communications can help to nurture some myths and not others. Barthes's best-known example of myth-making derives from a medium. He analyses the front cover of an issue of *Paris-Match*, a French magazine, which depicts a black boy in military outfit looking upwards and saluting what is assumed to be the French flag. Barthes reads this image (i.e. sign) as language and myth. On the level of language, the image denotes a black boy giving a French salute. Far more can be read into what this image *connotes* though. As a myth, Barthes suggests that the image signifies 'that France is a great Empire, that all her sons, without any colour discrimination, faithfully serve under her flag' (Barthes 1993: 116). The image of the proud black soldier connotes a myth that France is a multicultural land of opportunity far from an oppressive colonizer of foreign peoples. Clearly, the meanings signified by this image as language and myth are only *made* possible in how they compare with the vast range of other meanings that an image like this might depict if it was configured differently. If the boy in the image is white and not black, the image's meaning is radically changed.

Barthes applies his theory of myth to several 'mythologies' associated with his native French culture, such as wine and Citroen cars. We can apply his theory to contemporary media mythologies, although we would need to stretch our imagination and thought processes in the same way that Barthes did. For instance, BBC News 24 occasionally broadcasts a pre-recorded trailer just before headlines appear 'on the hour'. In the order of a language system, the moving images shown denote foreign correspondents 'on location' in various parts of the world, reporting on different kinds of news stories (environmental, political, financial, and so on). A timer counts down the seconds from 30 to 0 in anticipation of the headlines that will immediately follow once the trailer has finished. But we can read this sequence of images on the more sophisticated order of a myth system. From this reading we can appreciate how the BBC News 24 channel – and its journalists – takes on connotations of a professional organization dedicated to fast, concise, global news coverage. BBC foreign correspondents are eyewitnesses to international affairs in a not dissimilar way that Britain has its metaphorical eyes on the world. We seek out evil, we search out poverty and disease – 'we' the BBC, like the country we represent, are a force for good, and a picture of fine health compared to the tyranny and misfortune of others. The timer, moreover, connotes punctuality and recency (i.e. BBC news values). News does not occur on the hour – in reality, it can occur at any time – but news is always made fresh by headlines 'on the hour' to reinforce the myth that news is always 'new'. A timer that began counting down the seconds from 30 *minutes* to zero, rather than 30 seconds, would generate very different meanings (and myths) about BBC News 24. Instead of pandering to breaking news or the headline stories, we might read this news channel as dedicated to programming that deals with in-depth debate and dialogue.

The need to 'stretch one's imagination' when identifying media mythologies points to a weakness with semiotics as a method and the structuralist theory it informs. Far from a science, semiotics is a highly subjective method of reading social and cultural myths that depends entirely on 'the analytical brilliance of the semiotician' (Couldry 2000a: 75). Moreover, as well as being unable to account for historical changes in language and myth, given its focus on synchronicity, semiotics is only able to analyse one particular text in isolation. What Nick Couldry calls the 'total textual environment' (Couldry 2000a: 73) – the multitude of media texts and technologies that we interact with on a daily basis – cannot be penetrated by semiotic analysis. Moreover, semiotics as a method of textual analysis is easily abused to make claims about how media texts signify meanings in everyday use. Angela McRobbie acknowledges that while semiotics can 'read' ideologies in media texts, it cannot account for the views of readers/audiences and therefore cannot 'understand the complex and contested social processes which accompany the construction of new images [and texts]' (McRobbie 1994: 165). Similarly in relation to semiotic analysis of music texts, Tia DeNora rightly interprets 'an epistemologically naïve move' in 'a tacit shift in many semiotic "readings" of music . . . from description of musical material and its social allocation to the theorization of that material's "wider" significance and cultural impact' (DeNora 2000: 28). Semiotics, given that it can only ever be one person's interpretation of what they read, hear or see, is certainly not a substitute for empirical audience research.

Hall: Encoding/Decoding, ideology and hegemony

While he does not theorize **ideology** in any great depth, Barthes is none-theless clear that myths contain ideological meanings. Myth and ideology in their structuralist senses are synonymous. For Barthes, the ideology of French colonialism is expounded in the proud salute of the black soldier. It is only by deconstructing a myth, or reading a myth's hidden meanings, that its ideology – the values and beliefs it upholds – can be exposed. The concept of 'ideology' has been theorized to a greater extent by structuralist Marxists who followed Barthes, such as Louis Althusser and Stuart Hall. Althusser (1971) argued that individuals in capitalist societies are governed by ideological state apparatuses (ISAs), including schools, legal systems, religious institutions, media communications, and so on. These ISAs espouse the ideologies of powerful political institutions, such as governments and armies, in implicit – not explicit – ways, and sometimes without knowing it. As such, individuals 'internalize' ruling capitalist ideologies, unaware that their lives are repressed by the very institutions that represent and serve them (and perhaps even employ them). As Hall notes, Althusser's approach was more sophisticated than the classical Marxist notion of top-down 'false consciousness' which suggests that ideology is imposed 'from above' by elite powers upon the unknowing masses (see discussion of Adorno in Chapter 7, for a version of classical Marxism). ISAs point to a 'more linguistic or "discursive" conception of ideology' (Hall 1996a: 30) that is reproduced by various institutional practices and structures. Ellis Cashmore (1994) applies Althusser's theory of ISAs to television by suggesting that viewers are given a partial view of the world that fits with state interests, even when television is not explicitly state-controlled.

Although Althusser's ideas can be applied to media, the ideas of Hall rework structuralist theories of ideology into a more systematic theory of media in their social and cultural functions. Hall also criticizes Althusser for assuming that ideology, although internalized, always functions to reproduce state capitalist values: 'how does one account for subversive ideas or for ideological struggle?' (Hall 1996a: 30). As such, Hall defines ideology in a discursive sense as 'ideas, meanings, conceptions, theories, beliefs, etc. and the form of consciousness which are appropriate to them' (Hall 1977: 320). Hall, along with other theorists associated with the Birmingham Centre for Contemporary Cultural Studies (CCCS) such as Dick Hebdige and David Morley, investigated the relationship between media and ideology through semiotic analysis of systems of signification in texts such as television news bulletins.

Hall's aim is to rediscover ideology as a concept that can reveal the 'politics of signification' engaged in by media institutions. His starting point is to attack behaviourist theories of media. Models of 'effects' such as Lasswell's formula theorize the communication process in terms of its reliability (see Chapter 2). If messages are not received as intended, this is deemed to be a failure of communication in a technical or behavioural sense. According to 'effects' perspectives, messages are not received correctly if the channels of communication from sender to recipient are distorted by electrical or human error. The meanings of messages themselves, however, are assumed to be distortion-free and universally transferable. But Hall argues that behaviourist models are flawed because they fail to situate media communications within existing social, economic and political structures. The meanings of messages, then, are able to be distorted and interpreted differently than intended according to the positions of producers (senders) and audiences (recipients) within these existing structures:

> Meaning is a social production, a practice. The world has to be *made to mean*. Language and symbolization is the means by which meaning is produced. This approach dethroned the referential notion of language, which had sustained previous content analysis, where the meaning of a particular term or sentence could be validated simply by looking at what, in the real world, it referenced.
>
> (Hall 1982: 67)

Content analysis – a favoured method of cultivation theory (see Chapter 2) – is rendered meaningless by this structuralist perspective on meaning as social production. Like Saussure and Barthes, Hall states that meaning is a discursive process that operates within a language system (what he terms 'a set of codes') loaded with ideological signification.

Media institutions and the texts they generate are important ideological dimensions through which we make sense of the world. Hall deploys semiotics to understand the sense-making process by which media transmit messages to their audiences. Language is *encoded* (made to mean something) by those with 'the means of meaning production' (i.e. producers) and is then *decoded* (made to mean something) by audiences (Hall 1982: 68). Hall extends this semiotic theory of meaning construction to a model of media production and reception which is commonly known as the Encoding/Decoding model (see Figure 4.4). Unlike the behaviourist approach to communication, Hall's Encoding/Decoding approach does not assume a direct correspondence between the meaning intended by a sender and how that meaning is interpreted by a recipient: 'The codes of encoding and decoding may not be perfectly symmetrical' (Hall 1980: 131). Hall is interested in how media represent – and misrepresent – what they mean rather than simply reflect those meanings on to their audiences. While encoding and decoding are separate processes, they are not arbitrary however. Encoding – at the phase of

62   STRUCTURALISM AND SEMIOTICS

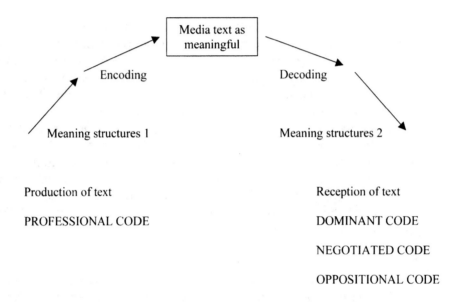

Figure 4.4   The Encoding/Decoding model

Source: Adapted from Hall (1980: 130)

production – operates within a set of *professional codes* such as technical competence and high-budget production values. These professional codes generate preferred meanings that 'have the institutional/political/ideological order imprinted in them and have themselves become institutionalized' (Hall 1980: 134). Television is the medium that Hall is most interested in. In Britain, for example, the BBC operates a professional code in line with their public service ethos. One characteristic of this code relates to political impartiality – the BBC is not allowed to take sides in party politics, otherwise it would be breaking its code and being unprofessional. The preferred meanings encoded by BBC news channels, therefore, include political impartiality. The assumption is that audiences will not decode partial political points of view if – as seems likely – they adopt the BBC's preferred meanings in their news broadcasts.

While Hall argues that preferred meanings have considerable weight in determining how messages are decoded, they are not *determinate*. This returns us to a basic – but crucial – theory of structuralism that informs the Encoding/Decoding model: 'In a "determinate" moment the structure employs a code and yields a "message"; at another determinate moment the "message", via its decodings, issues into the structure of social practices' (Hall 1980: 130). It is precisely because encoding and decoding are distinct, determinate moments that explains why the meaning structures of media messages do not reflect reality in an objective sense. Rather, in the case of television, messages 'can only be signified within the aural-visual forms of the televisual discourse' (Hall 1980: 129). A news event such as a state funeral, for instance, cannot represent the experience of actually being in attendance at the funeral – it can only signify what the experience is 'really' like through the meaning structures (rules and conventions) of the televisual message. Media – like language systems – are therefore structured through a set of rules, codes and values that make them highly prone to ideological constructions of meaning, or what Barthes refers to as myths. Television is a primary myth-maker – constructer of ideology – according to Hall. Processes of editing, selection, camera operation and arrangement are all important aspects of encoding, in the sense of determining preferred meanings (Hall 1975). BBC news bulletins – like those of all news institutions – are loaded with the ideology of professionalism. What news stories are selected, how each of them are edited, and how they are arranged in a particular order (of importance) are just some of the ways in which the ideology of media professionalism is constructed. Ideologies of newsworthiness do not correspond to an objective set of criteria. On the contrary, newsworthiness is highly subjective and differs from institution to institution, and from country to country. Nonetheless, wherever newsworthiness is practised (on the BBC, CNN, Al Jazeera, and so on), it exerts its preferred meanings upon its audience.

Encoded ideologies such as media professionalism and newsworthiness, however, do not determine meaning structures at the reception phase. Hall (1980) identifies three categories of decoding through which audiences make meaning of media messages. First and in keeping with the professional code, an audience member may adopt a *dominant code* which accepts the preferred meanings intended by the encoders (i.e. media producers). A second possibility is that an audience member adopts a *negotiated code* which accepts some preferred meanings of a media production but opposes others. On a general level, the encoded meanings may be understood and endorsed; but on a more specific, local level these meanings and the rules within which they operate may be discarded, as audience members consider their own positions to be exceptions to the general rule. For example, a parent may adopt a negotiated code when decoding a television show about how to care for babies. He may agree that, in general, the best advice is to lay a baby on its back when placing her in a cot, but disagree in the case of his own son who only ever goes to sleep on his front. Third and finally, an audience member may completely disagree with the preferred meanings of media producers (both on a general and local level), in which case they adopt an *oppositional code* and 'decode the message in a *globally* contrary way' (Hall 1980: 137–8). For example, a news story might be encoded with an ideological message about how 'yobbish' youths are becoming more troublesome and anti-social than previous generations of young people. An oppositional code is adopted at the moment of decoding, however, by someone with historical knowledge of how young

64 STRUCTURALISM AND SEMIOTICS

people have committed crimes and been stigmatized by societies (including mass media institutions) since time immemorial.

Hall's Encoding/Decoding model is an attempt to rediscover and rescue ideology from its conception as an omnipotent, oppressive force wielded by the ruling classes upon the masses in the classical Marxist tradition of political economy theory (as we will discuss in Chapter 7). However, in a later work (Hall 1996a), he refers to the 'problem of ideology' as a concept. Can it still withstand application in contemporary, democratic societies where media institutions appear free from the power of states and commercial forces? He acknowledges that Marxist theories of ideology tend to overemphasize 'negative and distorted features' of bourgeois capitalist ideas and values (Hall 1996a: 28). Nevertheless, he remains sympathetic to Marx's original formulation of ideology and particularly to the related concept of **hegemony** formulated by Antonio Gramsci. Unlike many Marxist conceptions of ideology (such as that of Adorno), Marx did not suggest that ideology amounts to mass deception but rather to a situation where individuals within capitalist social systems can only gain a limited impression of the consequences of such systems, given ideological constraints imposed by ruling power elites. The best revision of Marx's ideas, argues Hall, is by Gramsci who contends that 'in particular historical situations, ideas "organize human masses, and create the terrain on which men [*sic*] move, acquire consciousness of their position, struggle, etc."' (Hall 1996a: 41, quoting Gramsci 1971). Social, economic and political ideas create struggle, and 'ideological struggle is a part of the general social struggle for mastery and leadership – in short, for hegemony' (Hall 1996a: 43).

Gramsci's theory of hegemony marks a fundamental shift from orthodox structuralism to a more discursive form of post-structuralism with which Hall, among others (see also discussion of Foucault in this chapter), has identified. Hegemony, unlike orthodox approaches to myth and ideology, is about a dialogue between those parts of a society with and without the power to signify their values and intentions:

> [H]egemony is understood as accomplished, not without the due measure of legal and legitimate compulsion, but principally by means of winning consent of those classes and groups who were subordinated within it … This approach could also be used to demonstrate how media institutions could be articulated to the production and reproduction of the dominant ideologies, while at the same time being 'free' of direct compulsion, and 'independent' of any direct attempt by the powerful to nobble them.
>
> (Hall 1982: 85–6)

In other words, hegemony is a 'give and take' form of power. Hegemony works to permit dissenting voices and oppositional politics, but to suppress the force of dissent and opposition by actively seeking out support from all parts of a society. Media are argued by Hall to encode their products in the interests of dominant hegemonic forces, such as governments: 'The professional code operates *within* the "hegemony" of the dominant code' (Hall 1980: 136). Even if media institutions do not intend to collude with the forces of hegemony that operate in their countries or regions, they are likely to do so unwittingly because hegemony – unlike more orthodox versions of ideology – is a function of existing social structures and practices; not an intention of individuals. Unlike behaviourists such as Katz and Lazarsfeld, who argued that media have no direct effects other than to reflect the consensus opinion among people, Gramsci and Hall would argue that media – in their propensity to serve a hegemonic function for the good of those in power – effectively manufacture consent (see discussion of Herman and Chomsky in Chapter 7 for a political economy approach to hegemony).

Glasgow Media Group: the ideology of news

Structural Marxist theories about the ideological function of media have been tested out using the types of empirical methods associated with media effects research. Perhaps the most substantial and innovative examples of this research were undertaken by the Glasgow Media Group (GMG) in Britain from the mid-1970s to the mid-1990s. Its findings suggest that Hall's Encoding/Decoding model affords the audience too much scope for alternative decodings of television productions:

> although there are variations in audience 'readings' of media reports, there are pervasive common themes in the meanings conveyed to the public ... even though people may 'resist' the dominant message of a programme, it may still have the power to convey facts and to influence their ideas, assumptions, and attitudes.
>
> (Eldridge et al. 1997: 160)

John Eldridge et al. have tended to theorize media – television news organizations in particular – as influential shapers of public opinion. Rather than take the 'effects' approach associated with behaviourism, though, the GMG has re-articulated the debate in terms of the power of media to serve the interests of dominant ideologies. Media are ideological in the sense that they present 'a way of seeing and understanding the world which favours some interests over others' (GMG 1982: 3).

Early studies by the GMG (1976; 1980; 1982) centred on television news reports. Extensive textual and image analysis – inspired by Barthes's ideas about denotative and connotative levels of signification – revealed that 'news

66   STRUCTURALISM AND SEMIOTICS

is not a neutral product ... it is a sequence of socially manufactured messages, which carry many of the culturally dominant assumptions of our society' (GMG 1976: 1). The GMG aimed to 'unpack the coding of television news' and 'reveal the structures of the cultural framework which underpins the production of apparently neutral news' (GMG 1976: 1). News presents itself as 'truth' and 'fact' under the guise of impartiality, as Hall argues, but GMG researchers set out to deconstruct what they called its ideology of truth and neutrality. Analysis of news programming was coupled with participant observation of newsroom practices at the two main news broadcasters in Britain, the BBC and ITN (Independent Television News). The ideological functions of television news are laid bare in the case of reports on industrial strikes by trade unions. Analysis revealed that these reports tended to represent bosses as rational, civilized individuals who were often invited to the studio for interviews, while trade union officials and ordinary workers were represented as emotive members of the baying crowd. In its worst forms, such media **representation** can construct a biased perspective in favour of dominant ideological interests (i.e. those of bosses) and 'the laying of blame for society's industrial and economic problems at the door of the workforce' (GMG 1976: 267). While the workforce is never directly criticized by 'neutral' news presenters and journalists, its side of the argument is presented in a less favourable light by being ignored, sensationalized or juxtaposed with negative images of violent confrontation on picket lines – confrontation that it is often provoked by police and other state authorities.

Akin to Hall, the GMG's argument is that the structural qualities of television news productions determine the ways in which they are interpreted as much as the content of specific news stories. News media therefore possess 'the power to tell people the *order* in which to think about events and issues' (GMG 1982: 1). As well as industrial disputes, the GMG's later studies examined media representations of AIDS (Kitzinger 1993; Miller and Williams 1993), child abuse (Eldridge et al. 1997) and the women's peace movement (Eldridge 1995) among other topics. In each case, news reports were deconstructed to reveal an ideological bias in the way media represented certain groups (police, politicians, doctors, and so on) in comparison to others (social workers, gay people, feminists, and so on). While the GMG's research has achieved the status of a long and established tradition in media studies, its theoretical framework has been criticized in at least two respects. First, it could be argued that the ideological force of media is most pervasive and least noticeable in their capacity to be impartial, as suggested by Hall's professional code. This would problematize the GMG's claim about the ideological function of biased news reporting because

> [the] ideological effectivity of the news is greatest in those areas where the operation of the particular signifying conventions which

constitute the news and seem to secure impartiality ... conceal the operation of another, ideologically loaded set of signifying conventions.

(Bennett 1982: 304)

In other words, the ideological bias of news reporting is powerful precisely because it is concealed under a veil of impartiality that not even the most perceptive textual analysis could detect. A second criticism of the GMG has been its lack of sustained audience research to test whether the ideological functions of media representations actually affect viewers' opinions at the point of reception and thereafter. This leaves the GMG open to an elitist fallacy given the underlying assumption – by not analysing audience responses – that media researchers and theorists can *see* what the rest of us cannot.

Williamson: the ideology of ads

Structuralist theories of ideology have also been applied to the meanings of advertisements. As well as selling goods, ads create structures of meaning, and 'in providing us with a structure in which we, and those goods, are inter-changeable, they are selling us ourselves' (Williamson 1978: 13). Informed by structural Marxism, Judith Williamson analyses how ads structure the ways we identify with ourselves in relation to the goods they sell to us. She agrees with Althusser's idea that ideology is 'internalized' in individuals through subtle or subliminal techniques on the part of ISAs. The advertising industry, Williamson suggests, is a highly pervasive ISA in advanced capitalist societies. One such function served by the ideology of ads is to mask the reality of stark class differences in such societies – ads assume that we all have equal access to wealth and luxury. Not everyone can afford a Versace dress but ads – and advertisers – take insufficient account of different consumer needs and expenditure. Williamson does not attempt to measure the effects of adver-tising on people's spending habits. This kind of research – typical of the behaviourist approach – would be worthwhile to some extent but would tell us little about how advertising structures our values, tastes, ideas and expectations. Instead, Williamson's semiotic analysis of visual signs in ads reveals their hidden ideological meanings and intentions, and their ideolo-gical power to structure our lives.

How do ads signify their ideology? Williamson's answer to this question forms her main theoretical argument, which is that ads construct ideological meaning 'not on the level of the overt signified but via the signifiers' (Wil-liamson 1978: 24). She states that 'the signifier of the overt meaning in an advertisement has a function of its own, a place in the process of creating

68   STRUCTURALISM AND SEMIOTICS

another, less obvious meaning' (Williamson 1978: 19). In other words, beneath the surface images (i.e. signifiers) contained in any ad can be deciphered hidden meanings using the method of semiotics. So ads make their meaning through a play on the meaning of signifiers rather than what is being signified (i.e. the obvious product meaning). Perfume ads are a good example because they cannot give any 'real' meaning or information about the products they are selling. How can smell be signified without a sample of perfume being attached? In the absence of sufficient 'signifieds', then, perfume products are sold as 'unique, distinctive' consumables through less overt 'signifiers' – images that are attached to those products. Perfume becomes associated with a particular style or 'look' rather than – as it ought to be associated – with a particular smell. These signifiers that work their meaning beneath the surface messages of ads are drawn from what Williamson calls a 'referent system', akin to systems of signification that operate on the basis of differentiation (see discussion of Saussure). Referent systems make connections with images that are auxiliary to those of the product being advertised. There are, in fact, only superficial differences between one perfume product and another (even if one is ten times more expensive than another!), but referent systems are sophisticated enough to carve out and manufacture differentiation even so. As such, referent systems constitute the ideological dimension of ads.

Nonetheless, the ideology of ads can only work its ulterior motives – to mask class differences, to present a world of glamour and happiness, and so on – at the moment in which they are received by consumers. Williamson explains that the reason why the ideological meaning buried in an ad is so elusive and invisible to us is because 'we constantly re-create it. It works *through* us, not at us' (Williamson 1978: 41). As consumers, we are lured into accepting the ideology of ads because they afford us an active role in deciphering their hidden meanings. However, this 'activity' afforded to us is a phoney activity that sucks us into an ideological vacuum wherein we are prevented from seeing a real world – outside referent systems – of inequalities and hardship. One way that we re-create and, moreover, appear to embrace the ideology of ads is by falsely decoding them as personal invitations to improve ourselves. Ads appear, through their signifiers, to address us as individuals, but although we might sense that ads are addressed to lots of people – not just you or I – we are still inclined to accept the invitation: 'You have to exchange yourself with the person "spoken to", the spectator the ad creates for itself ... The "you" in ads is always transmitted plural, but we receive it as singular' (Williamson 1978: 50). Ads provide consumers with an activity, but in partaking in this activity – substituting yourself for 'you' – we are internalizing its preferred ideology, which is that you 'yourself' can be like the ideal 'you' represented in the ad. So while 'we can "consciously work" in "producing" a meaning ... we do not produce a genuine "meaning" but consume a predetermined "solution"' (Williamson 1978: 75). Ads pretend to empower us but only in ways that they would wish us to be empowered.

They wish us to think 'I am empowered enough to convince myself that I am like the woman in that ad with men flocking around her as she sits in that expensive sports car, which I can also afford and am seriously thinking of buying ... if I can arrange another high-cost loan with my bank!' The 'ideal' types in ads, moreover, are stereotypes that conform to dominant ideological representations of what 'success' and 'happiness' look like (see Qualter 1997). The 'people' represented by ads are typically white, affluent, relatively young and physically attractive but these shiny, happy people are hardly a typical cross-section of society.

Morley: the *Nationwide* audience

The work of David Morley, by contrast to Williamson's study of ads and the GMG's research on television news, has sought to apply structuralist theories of ideological meanings in media texts – particularly Hall's Encoding/Decoding model – to empirical research on media audiences. Echoing Hall and Williamson, Morley suggests in *The Nationwide Audience* (first published in 1980) that 'audiences, like the producers of messages, must also undertake a specific kind of "work" in order to read meaningfully what is transmitted' (Morley and Brunsdon 1999: 125). Moreover, media can only reproduce the dominant ideology of powerful institutions by articulating this ideology to audiences at their level of common sense. He states: 'I would want to insist on the active nature of readings and of cultural production. Too often the audience subject is reduced to the status of an automated puppet pulled by the strings of the text' (Morley and Brunsdon 1999: 273). This audience-centred approach to structuralist theory was tested out by the author in a research project that interviewed groups of people about their responses to viewing two episodes of *Nationwide*, a long-running BBC current affairs television programme that was popular in Britain between 1969 and 1984. These groups were selected according to occupational status and their opinions of what they viewed were applied to the three categories of decoding outlined in Hall's Encoding/Decoding model.

Morley's findings are interesting, even though – as he later recognizes (Morley 1992) – the somewhat contrived method of grouping people's pre-supposed ideological positions on the basis of their occupations alone must question the validity of these findings. What Morley found, however, to some extent met but in other ways contradicted expectations. Those groups who tended to decode the stories and debates presented by *Nationwide* using a dominant code (i.e. the preferred meaning suggested by the programme's representation of these stories and debates) included bank managers – who it

70   STRUCTURALISM AND SEMIOTICS

might be expected would accept the ideological consensus worked by the professional code at the encoding stage given their middle-class status – but also working-class apprentices (semi-skilled manual workers) whose subordinate position in existing social and economic structures might suggest that they were more than likely to disagree with dominant or preferred meanings. Moreover, those groups who tended to decode *Nationwide* using a negotiated code (accepting some preferred meanings but opposing others) included trade union officials and university art students, who it might be assumed would be more hostile (i.e. oppositional) to the capitalist-driven, dominant ideologies reinforced by the programme. While some groups decoded *Nationwide* along expected class lines, other groups confounded expectations. Moreover, a group of black further education students did not understand the programme's content, which would suggest the need for a further category of decoding – a rejection code.

Morley's subsequent critique of the Encoding/Decoding model is perhaps more significant than what he found initially by testing it out. He argues that 'in the case of each of the major categories of decoding (dominant, negotiated or oppositional) we can discern different varieties and inflections of what, for purposes of gross comparison only, is termed the same "code"' (Morley 1992: 118). There are three problems with the model that arise from its theoretical foundations in structuralism and semiotics. First, as referred to in the quote above, decoding suggests a single, universal form of audience interpretation of media texts which is surely too simplistic and fails to account for more subtle nuances in how we read the different meanings that a television programme or pop song might *convey to us*. The complexities of audience interpretations are tackled in a later study (see Morley 1986). Second, there is the issue of intentionality or what literary critics would term 'the intentional fallacy'. Morley notes that the Encoding/Decoding framework is too liable to confuse the ideological meanings of texts with the ideological motivations of producers or authors. Texts themselves are often difficult to interpret in terms of their political, economic or ideological bias without implicating producers with the self-same biases. And third, Morley criticizes the notion of preferred meanings that generate 'preferred readings'. Certain media texts, such as party political broadcasts and possibly news bulletins, can be deemed to present a preferred reading that corresponds more or less with that of the dominant ideology of ruling interests – politicians and big business owners, for example. However, it is much harder to identify the preferred reading of a fictional text such as a romantic film or pop song. Morley asks: 'is the preferred reading a property of the text, the analyst or the audience?' (1992: 122).

In order to bridge this institution–text–audience split in the ideological transfer of meaning, Morley suggests an alternative approach: genre theory (Morley 1992: 126–30; see also Morley 1980). Genre theory derives from the work of Stephen Neale who claims that 'genres are not to be seen as forms of textual codifications, but as systems of orientations, expectations and conventions that circulate between industry, text and subject' (Neale 1980: 19). So media genres characterized by certain expectations and conventions – horror films, house music, reality TV, and so on – are defined as such by a combination of the institutions that produce them, the texts that constitute them, and the audiences that receive them. Genres ensure that audience expectations and prejudgements about a given media text are generally satisfied by industry production techniques. Genres, unlike the individual texts which make up their parts, are categorized by sets of rules determining how they signify meaning that must be governed by both producers and audiences in order for those genre categories to withstand signification. However, genres are not ideologically neutral in the way they generate this semiotic harmony between producers and audiences. On the contrary, certain genres demand different forms of 'cultural competence' (Morley 1992) that tend to result in one genre becoming associated with a different class of audience in comparison to another. In crude terms, working-class women are more likely to become culturally adept at watching soap operas, while middle-class men locate cultural competence in financial news programming. Morley's discussion of cultural competence in relation to genre theory is not dissimilar to the concept of cultural capital (see discussion of Bourdieu in Chapter 9).

Hebdige: *Subculture*

The most systematic attempt to analyse oppositional forms of decoding in media and cultural texts is Dick Hebdige's subcultural theory. Hebdige deployed semiotics to analyse how texts and products are used in subversive ways by youth subcultures such as punks and mods in order to articulate their resistance to dominant ideologies in society such as education and housing policies. Subcultures operate through a system of oppositional codes that offend the majority, threaten the status quo and contradict the 'myth of consensus' suggested by dominant codes (Hebdige 1979: 18). Like Hall, Hebdige applies hegemony theory to his structuralist approach, but his concern is more with how a dominant hegemony can be challenged and threatened rather than with how it maintains its hold over society. What does he mean by a 'subculture'? Essentially, a subculture is an underground set of practices – usually working-class in character – that try to resist surveillance by the dominant culture (e.g. police) as well as incorporation into mainstream cultures. A subculture ceases to exist when it becomes incorporated, manufactured and packaged by commercial interests. Punks' use of dog collars, bought from pet shops, cease to retain their subcultural value when they can be purchased for twice the price in High Street shops, for example.

72 STRUCTURALISM AND SEMIOTICS

According to Hebdige, subcultures resist surveillance and incorporation by creating their own internal logic of identity and cohesion. Two structuralist concepts underpin this claim: theories of homology and *bricolage*. Referring to Willis's (1978) theoretical conception, homology is defined as 'the symbolic fit between the values and lifestyles of a group, its subjective experience and the musical forms it uses to express or reinforce its focal concerns' (Hebdige 1979: 113). Music is only one media and cultural form, though, in which subcultures reinforce their concerns, fit together their values and experiences. Table 4.1 suggests some others, including the system of language (what Hebdige calls 'argot') adopted by a subculture to reinforce its unity.

Table 4.1 Homologies of youth subcultures

	Teds	*Mods*	*Punks*	*Ravers*
Music	Rock 'n' Roll	Ska/reggae	Heavy rock	Acid house
Clothes	Suits	Smart casual	Homemade	Baggy casual
Objects	Cigars	Scooters	Dog collars	Whistles
Drugs	Tobacco	LSD	Dope	Ecstasy
Argot/slang	'Spiv'	'About town'	'Piss off'	'Buzzin'

Each subculture, therefore, becomes associated with a cultural inventory of signs and symbols that 'fit' with its identities and concerns. This model harps back to Saussure's syntagmatic and paradigmatic dimensions (see Figure 4.1). Through homologies, therefore, subcultures develop exclusive, sophisticated systems of signification that protect them from censure or exploitation by outsiders. However, we can see that any single change in the syntagmatic features of a subculture would affect the whole paradigmatic fit of meanings and therefore break down its homological unity. As soon as the scooter becomes a mass-produced fashion object not solely used by the mod subculture, the whole homological unity of mods is fractured.

Related to homology is the concept of *bricolage* (first used by Claude Lévi-Strauss, a well-known structural anthropologist) and its sister term, appropriation. *Bricolage* and appropriation refer to the way in which symbolic objects are invested with subcultural meanings that are borrowed from different contexts and oppose their original functions. Dog collars had their original meaning – that is, as a pet-restraining device – opposed and appropriated by punks to fit with their own style and values. Similarly, 'the teddy boy's theft and transformation of the Edwardian style revived in the early 1950s by Savile Row for wealthy young men about town can be construed as an act of *bricolage*' (Hebdige 1979: 104). Black subcultures such as Rastafarians and rude boys had a particularly powerful influence on the *bricolage* practices of white working-class youth subcultures in Britain during the post-war per-iod. Rasta haircuts, fashions, reggae and cannabis use were all appropriated by white subcultures such as mods in order to express their resistance to domi-nant white, middle-class ideologies. This is akin to playing with Barthes's interpretations of cultural myths to suit the interests of one's own subculture while opposing the interests of the dominant culture. Mass media texts and the institutions that produce them are clearly outside the reference systems in which subcultures make their oppositional meanings. The most effective way to escape the ideological function of media, according to Hebdige's sub-cultural theory, is to ignore them and seek out cultural forms untarnished by media exposure.

Despite the ongoing currency of 'subculture', concepts of homology and *bricolage* informed by theories of structuralism have undergone significant critiques and revisions since Hebdige's account (see, for example, Clarke 1990; Muggleton 2000). This is partly because new media, information and manufacturing technologies have simultaneously widened and restricted the scope of opportunities for subcultures to evolve. Faster and more sophisti-cated production techniques enable the latest 'subcultural' music, fashion, argot, and so on to be delivered direct from 'the street' into multinational retail outlets in such short time that a subculture is strangled of its authen-ticity before it can get to its feet. Commercial incorporation is more ruthless now than in the days of mods and punks. Genre theory (see discussion of Morley) has been cited as an alternative to subcultural theory given its twin concerns with cultural production and (subcultural) consumption (Hes-mondhalgh 2005). This would seem to offer a way forward in understanding how the internet provides new opportunities for subcultural networks such as Goths to form and disseminate their values and experiences among them-selves (Hodkinson 2002). Indeed, the internet has served as a subcultural medium of consumption, albeit under the constant shadow of 'offline' pro-duction interests. For example, some resistant consumer practices – such as illegal music file-sharing – have become serious threats to dominant eco-nomic interests, such as major record companies. Whether or not unlawful music uploading and downloading is a subcultural practice in its strictest sense is open to debate, but it has certainly enabled consumers to wrestle authority from producers by forcing the music industry to explore alternative styles of music and forms of distribution (see Chapter 9 for further discussion of consumer authority in a non-subcultural sense).

Foucault: discourse and disciplinary society

The work of Michel Foucault is wide-ranging and not specifically concerned with media, so for the purposes of this book we will only focus on his theory

74   STRUCTURALISM AND SEMIOTICS

of **discourse** in relation to surveillance and what he called 'panopticism'. In *The Archaeology of Knowledge* (first published in 1972), Foucault (1989) argues that discourse functions to make certain ideas and values *present* while others are made *absent*. Discourse is an exclusionary mechanism that allocates power and knowledge to those whose ideas are included and made present at a given moment in time, but at the same time exerts power and knowledge over the excluded/absent. Foucault defines discourse – much like Saussure's definition of language – as a system of signification governed by rules that structure the ways in which we classify and divide its different meanings. He differs from orthodox structuralism, though, by investigating how discourse evolves and changes through history (diachronic rather than synchronic analysis) in the shape of discursive practices (see White 1979). The historical dividing of meanings and practices into different classifications (e.g. good versus evil) ensures 'the infinite continuity of discourse and its secret presence to itself in the interplay of a constantly recurring absence' (Foucault 1989: 25). People can gain power over time, for example, by articulating a discourse of goodness and comparing their own ideas with an absent discourse of evil that exists elsewhere. As such, discourse disperses power and knowledge by dividing and differentiating itself into what Foucault (1989) calls discursive formations.

An example of what he means by discursive formations is found in *Discipline and Punish* (first published in 1975):

> Generally speaking, all the authorities exercising individual control function according to a double mode; that of binary division and branding (mad/sane; dangerous/harmless; normal/abnormal); and that of coercive assignment, of differential distribution (who he [*sic*] is; where he must be; how he is to be characterized; how he is to be recognized; how a constant surveillance is to be exercised over him in an individual way, etc.).
>
> (Foucault 1995: 199)

The power to decide, say, what is criminal or lawful is exercised by those authorities who speak the discourse of law and construct discursive formations out of it. This is what Foucault means by 'binary division and branding'. The other half of the double mode that exercises control over individuals – the technique of discipline through coercion – is surveillance, the best example of which for Foucault is Jeremy Bentham's design for the 'panopticon'. Designed to be the ultimate prison, the panopticon consisted of a central watchtower in which prison officers could observe the inmates in their cells situated along several 'corridor-like' wings extended out from the watchtower. The cells housing the prisoners appear to those who watch over them 'like so many cages, so many small theatres, in which each actor is alone, perfectly individualized and constantly visible. The panoptic mechanism arranges spatial unities that make it possible to see constantly and to recognize immediately' (Foucault 1995: 200). Moreover, the panopticon's all-seeing power extends to situations in which the watchtower is unmanned. Inmates act and behave in a disciplined manner, as if they are being observed all the time, given their uncertainty as to whether they are or are not because they cannot see into the watchtower. As such, panopticism is both an externalized and an internalized power mechanism: 'Disciplinary power ... is exercised through its invisibility; at the same time it imposes on those whom it subjects a principle of compulsory visibility' (Foucault 1995: 187). Like Foucault's theory of discourse, panopticism disperses power in such a way that it becomes instilled into individuals' consciousness until they accept the discursive formations exercised upon them (good versus evil, lawful versus criminal, and so on).

What has all this to do with media theory? Perhaps most importantly, Foucault argues that the panoptic mechanism of surveillance and its 'infinitesimal distribution of the power relations' extends beyond prison walls to what he calls the 'disciplinary society' (Foucault 1995: 216). As such, panopticism can be considered a function of media as well as prisons and other powerful social institutions. Television in particular has the power to make visible certain kinds of ideas and forms of behaviour to the exclusion of others. The powerful discourse of media – like the discourse of crime and punishment – classifies certain forms of knowledge as 'true' and others as 'false'. For example, health advice from medical 'experts' on television is classified as the truth in interplay with other, 'false' sources of medical knowledge – such as alternative medicines. At first, this seems awfully similar to the ideological function of media as theorized by Hall, Williamson and the GMG, among others. However, unlike ideology or hegemony which are forms of power external to individuals, Foucault conceives discourse as dispersed internally *into* individuals. There is no manufacture of consent, and there are no oppositional or resistant codes that individuals can adopt against a dominant culture, because power has been distributed everywhere into our hearts and minds. Media institutions – like hospitals, schools and other state apparatuses – disperse and distribute power through discourses that we cannot help but internalize and accept as 'the truth'. *Big Brother* (2000–) and the reality television genre could be theorized as a panoptic media discourse that includes and excludes certain types of participants. However, an Orwellian 'Big Brother' watching over us – the BBC is nicknamed 'Big Brother' by those who see its public service values as excessively paternal – does not fit with Foucault's theory of discourse as infinitesimally distributed. Rather, we are all 'little brothers' – or 'little sisters' – partaking in surveillance of ourselves and each other, regardless of what Big Brother might be doing.

76   STRUCTURALISM AND SEMIOTICS

Summary

This chapter has considered:

- Saussure's theory of language – 'differences carry signification' – that underpins structuralism and semiotics.
- Barthes's theory of myth that develops Saussure's ideas and shows how signs operate within wider social and cultural – not just linguistic – structures.
- Theories of ideology and hegemony in relation to the production and reception of media texts – with particular reference to the Encoding/Decoding model (Hall) and its subsequent application to media audience research (Morley).
- The ideology of news (GMG) and ads (Williamson) – and how the meaning structures of these media texts represent ruling political and commercial interests.
- Hebdige's subcultural theory, including concepts of homology and *bricolage* as forms of resistance to dominant cultural structures.
- Foucault's theory of discourse in relation to the disciplinary mechanisms of panopticism, and how this theory applies to media surveillance.

Further reading

Bignell, J. (2002) *Media Semiotics: An Introduction*, 2nd edn. Manchester: Manchester University Press.

Semiotics is clearly explained and then thoughtfully applied to examples from ads, magazines, newspapers, reality TV, cinema and interactive media. Accessible to all media students.

Hall, S. (ed.) (1997) *Representation: Cultural Representations and Signifying Practices*. London: Sage and The Open University.

Even if somewhat dated, this edited collection of articles remains seminal to structuralist theories of representation, developed through semiotic, sociological, Foucauldian and gender perspectives. Suitable for all media students.

Morley, D. and Chen, K-H. (eds) (1996) *Stuart Hall: Critical Dialogues in Cultural Studies*. London: Routledge.

This edited collection of articles charts and evaluates the wide variety of Hall's work, from questions of ideology and hegemony to postmodernism and postcolonial theory (note that this book is also useful in relation to post-colonial perspectives discussed in Chapter 7). Recommended for advanced undergraduates and postgraduates.

Tudor, A. (1999) *Decoding Culture: Theory and Method in Cultural Studies.* London: Sage.

A thoroughly critical analysis of structuralism, post-structuralism and the CCCS tradition of media and cultural theory. Suitable for all media students.

CHAPTER 21

Cultural Studies

*Based on the research of **Stuart Hall***

Lisa and John Petrillo

Lisa and John Petrillo have lived in the same trailer park for four years, and, with two young children, they realize that the wages they earn as migrant workers will probably never permit them to own their own home. They appreciate that Mr. DeMoss, the owner of the egg farm where they work, has provided housing for them, but they wish that they could have more privacy so that their neighbors would not be able to hear every word they say in the evening. The Petrillos do not have any desire to leave their tiny city because they realize that jobs are not that plentiful in New England. So they get by in the trailer park, and they dream about a big backyard where their two kids and their dog, Scooter, can play.

The Petrillos' dream often unfolds on the television shows they watch at night. Even though cable TV is expensive and not a necessity, they both love to watch shows that help them escape their daily routines. Watching TV, Lisa and John are bombarded with messages about the low home prices. They both know that the housing market is taking a dive, yet they keep seeing the same commercial over and over again promoting home ownership as the "American Dream." They watch the infomercials that promote "Ten Ways to Get Your American Dream." They look at each other, wondering why they continue to live the way they do—two children, two bedrooms, and a common bathing area in the migrant camp. They both know that they don't have the money to purchase a home, but they also know that they aren't happy with the way things are.

Recently, Mr. DeMoss's farm was investigated by the government for unsanitary living and working conditions. DeMoss was told to clean up the place and was threatened with stiff fines unless he improved the situation. As a result, he had authorized spending a lot of money for individual lavatory facilities and was talking to the local grocery chain to ask for their help in granting discounts to employees at the egg farm. As a gesture of goodwill, and to avoid a media attack, DeMoss was also prepared to increase each worker's paycheck by 15 percent by the end of the month. He also promised to help relocate families with children to more suitable accommodations.

The Petrillos were ecstatic. They dreaded the "communal" bathing area and welcomed more privacy for their children and themselves. They were very excited about the opportunity to save money on food, and, of course, they were thrilled that their paychecks would increase almost immediately. This, they thought, was the beginning of saving for their American Dream. They knew that they made just enough money to pay all of their bills, and now with the raise, the extra money would go into a rainy day fund that could eventually be used to purchase a home.

Lisa wrote to her brother in South America to tell him the good news. She wrote about how relatively easy it is to get a home in the United States. She quoted the commercials she saw so frequently on television: "Good sense, good money, and a good deal," she related. She had watched the evening news reports about the low interest rates and had even gone to the library to read up on mortgages. She thought that if they saved their extra money, within a year, she and her family could be living in a new home. For now, though, Lisa was excited about the chance to move to what DeMoss called "suitable" housing. "It has to be better than this," she thought. Lisa was starting to think that her luck was changing.

■

We cannot overstate how much the U.S. culture relies on the media. Each day, for instance, millions of homes tune in to dozens of different "news" programs on television. In fact, Stanley Baran and Dennis Davis (2009) conclude that "the media have become a primary means by which many of us experience or learn about many aspects of the world around us" (p. 215). However, the manner in which the media report events can vary significantly. Some journalists take pride in their fact finding. Others rely on personal testimony. Still others seek out experts to comment on events and topics as they unfold, whether they pertain to celebrity trials, natural disasters, refugees' plight, war, terrorist attacks, or school shootings. A consistent process for following a school shooting, for instance, resulted from the coverage of the 1999 Columbine school shooting in which twelve students and a teacher were killed. It is now predictable: First, the tragedy is usually reported in "real time," that is, as it happens. Next, reporters interview witnesses to get firsthand accounts of the shootings. Finally, journalists gather experts on both sides of the gun control issue to assess whether gun control laws are sufficiently tough. This last activity involving experts seems to beg other questions about the media's role in such events: Are they trying to convey a larger message about society in general? Is the reporting of images and stories done thoughtfully and conscientiously? Do the media have hidden agendas?

Reporting events with a hidden agenda has several implications. When the media fail to report all aspects of a story, someone or some group is inevitably affected. Nowhere is this more apparent than in the early coverage of AIDS, which was first diagnosed in the gay community. Edward Alwood (1997) notes that because most news editors did not consider gay deaths to be newsworthy, major news outlets (including the *New York Times*) failed to provide coverage of the disease. In fact, the disease was killing far more people than the thirty-four who died from Legionnaires' disease in 1976 and the eighty-four women who died of toxic shock syndrome in 1980. Yet it wasn't until the death of actor Rock Hudson in 1985 that major news stories were devoted to the subject of AIDS. By that time, however, more than 6,000 people had died from the disease. Again, the media's message is implied but significant: The deaths of gay men are not newsworthy.

Theorist Stuart Hall questioned the role of the media and their frequently false and misleading images. Unlike other communication theorists, however, Hall focused on the role of the media and their ability to shape public opinions of marginalized populations, including people of color, the poor, and others who do not reflect a White, male, heterosexual (and wealthy) point of view.

For Hall, the personal is the political. A former high school teacher who taught English, math, and geography, Hall's background influenced his conceptualization of cultural studies. He speaks of doing graduate work and, as a Jamaican, of "trying to understand what my relationship was to Jamaican culture, and what Jamaican culture was about because, basically, I'd left it behind and then it came to meet me" (cited in MacCabe, 2008, p. 13). This kind of philosophical thinking resonates throughout Cultural Studies.

This orientation underscores his work in Cultural Studies. Cultural Studies is a theoretical perspective that focuses on how culture is influenced by powerful, dominant groups. Cultural studies is clearly rooted in politics, but "too often, the politics pervades the body of work, where we are supposed to be figuring out what is going on, in all of its complexity" (cited in Cho, 2008, p. 103). Unlike several other theoretical traditions in this book, Cultural Studies does not refer to a single doctrine of human behavior. In fact, Stuart Hall (1992) persuasively argues that "Cultural Studies has multiple discourses; it has a number of different histories. It is a whole set of formations; it has its own different conjunctures and moments in the past. . . . I want to insist on that!" (p. 278). Although Hall and other theorists in Cultural Studies have applied many of the theory's concepts to the media, Cultural Studies extends beyond the media and has often been referred to as "audience studies" (Angus, Jhally, Lewis, & Schwichtenberg, 1989). Cultural Studies concerns the attitudes, approaches, and criticisms of a culture. Culture and media are the principle features of the theory, and it has provided an intellectual framework that has prompted scholars to discuss, disagree, challenge, and reflect. In fact, John Hartley (2003) observes that researchers have come to "little agreement about what counts as cultural studies, either as a critical practice or an institutional apparatus . . . the field is riven by fundamental disagreements about what cultural studies is for, in whose interests it is done, what theories, methods and objects of study are proper to it, and where to set its limits" (p. 2).

Cultural Studies has its background and its beginnings in Britain, although the United States has also taken a lead in understanding Cultural Studies (e.g., Grossberg, 1997). As a cultural theorist and the former director of the Center for Contemporary Cultural Studies (CCCS) at the University of Birmingham in England, Stuart Hall (1981, 1989) contends that the media are powerful tools of the elite. Media serve to communicate dominant ways of thinking, regardless of the efficacy of such thinking. Cultural Studies emphasizes that the media keep the powerful people in control while the less powerful absorb what is presented to them. Our Lisa and John Petrillo, for instance, exemplify a marginalized group (the poor) who have been taken in by the American Dream of owning a home. Of course, cultural theorists would argue that the media—in this case, the infomercial sponsors—are taking advantage of a couple who will probably never have enough money to own a home. Yet the message from the popular media is that it is possible. All that is needed, according to the message, is good sense and good money.

Cultural Studies is a tradition rooted in the writings of German philosopher Karl Marx. Because Marxist principles form the foundation of the theory,

> ### Cultural Studies • Theory at a Glance
>
> The media represent ideologies of the dominant class in a society. Because media are controlled by corporations (the elite), the information presented to the public is consequently influenced and targeted with profit in mind. The media's influence and the role of power must be taken into consideration when interpreting a culture.

let's look further into this theoretical backdrop. We then examine two assumptions of Cultural Studies.

The Marxist Legacy: Power to the People

Philosopher Karl Marx (1818–1883) is generally credited with identifying how the powerful (the elite) exploit the powerless (the working class; 1963). He believed that being powerless can lead to **alienation,** or the psychological condition whereby people begin to feel that they have little control over their future. For Marx, though, alienation is most destructive under capitalism. Specifically, when people lose control over their own means of production (as happens in capitalism) and must sell their time to some employer, they become alienated. Capitalism results in a profit-driven society, and workers in a capitalistic society are measured by their labor potential.

alienation
perception that one has little control over his or her future

Marx believed that the class system—a monolithic system that pervades all society—must be unearthed by the collective working class, or *proletariat.* He felt that laborers were often subjected to poor working and living conditions because the elite were unwilling to yield their control. As with Lisa and John Petrillo, laborers across society are constantly relegated to secondary status. The elite, or ruling, class's interests become socially ingrained, and therefore people become enslaved in society. One of Marx's principal concerns was ensuring that some revolutionary action of the proletariat be undertaken to break the chains of slavery and ultimately to subvert alienation under a capitalistic society. The capitalistic society, according to Marxist tradition, shapes society and the individuals within it (Weedon, 2004).

Marxist thinkers who believed the working class was oppressed because of corporate-owned media have been called the **Frankfurt School theorists.** These thinkers and writers believed that the media's messages were constructed and delivered with one goal in mind: capitalism. That is, although the media might claim that they are delivering information for the "common good," the bottom line (money) frames each message. Those affiliated with the Frankfurt School felt that the media could be considered an "authoritarian personality," which meant that they were opposed to the male-centered/male-owned media. In fact,

Frankfurt School theorists
a group of scholars who believed that the media were more concerned with making money than with presenting news

T*I*P *Theory Into Practice*

Elena

I love the phrase "the power of the people" but it seems like Cultural Studies says that the power is *not* in the people. I wouldn't call myself a Marxist, and yet I can understand why he wanted to return the power to the people. In America, it seems the media have so much power. During the 2008 presidential election primary, I noticed that the media dissed Hillary Clinton a lot. Even when she won a state, the media (mostly men) would say "Well, she has a long way to go." It seemed like the male-owned media had a voice in the process . . . too big of a voice, I think. There were times that I felt alienated as a woman because of the sexism that some of the men in the media were perpetuating.

Herbert Marcuse, a Frankfurt thinker, was the leader of a group of social revolutionaries whose goal was to break down this patriarchal system.

The application of Marxist principles to Cultural Studies is more subtle than direct. This has prompted some scholars to consider the theory to be more **neo-Marxist,** which means the theory diverges from classical Marxism to some extent. First, unlike Marx, those in Cultural Studies have integrated a variety of perspectives into their thinking, including those from the arts, the humanities, and the social sciences. Second, theorists in Cultural Studies expand the subordinate group to include additional powerless and marginalized people, not just laborers. These groups include gay men and lesbians, ethnic minorities, women, and even children. Third, everyday life for Marx was centered on work and the family. Writers in Cultural Studies have also studied recreational activities, hobbies, and sporting events in seeking to understand how individuals function in society. In sum, Marx's original thinking may have been appropriate for post–World War II populations, but his ideas now require clarification, elaboration, and application to a diverse society. Cultural Studies moves beyond a strict, limited interpretation of society toward a broader conception of culture.

Now that you have a brief understanding of how theorists in Cultural Studies were influenced by the writings of Marx, we examine two primary assumptions of Cultural Studies.

neo-Marxist
limited embracement of Marxism

Assumptions of Cultural Studies

Cultural Studies is essentially concerned with how elite groups such as the media exercise their power over subordinate groups. The theory is rooted in a few fundamental claims about culture and power:

- Culture pervades and invades all facets of human behavior.
- People are part of a hierarchical structure of power.

The first assumption pertains to the notion of culture, a concept we addressed in Chapter 2. To review, we identified culture as a community of meaning. In Cultural Studies, we need a different interpretation of the word, one that underscores the nature of the theory. The various norms, ideas, values, and forms of understanding in a society that help people interpret their reality are part of a culture's ideology. According to Hall (1981), **ideology** refers to "those images, concepts and premises which provide the frameworks through which we represent, interpret, understand, and 'make sense' of some aspect of social existence" (p. 31). Hall believes that ideologies include the languages, the concepts, and the categories that different social groups collect in order to make sense of their environments.

ideology
framework used to make sense of our existence

To a great extent, cultural practices and institutions permeate our ideologies. We cannot escape the cultural reality that, as a global community, actions are not performed in a vacuum. Graham Murdock (1989) emphasizes the pervasiveness of culture by noting that "all groups are constantly engaged in creating and remaking meaning systems and embodying these meanings in expressive forms, social practices, and institutions" (p. 436). Interestingly and predictably, however, Murdock notes, being part of a diverse cultural community often results in struggles over meaning, interpretation, identity, and control. These struggles, or **culture wars,** suggest that there are frequently deep divisions in the perception of the significance of a cultural issue or event. Individuals often compete to help shape a nation's identity. For example, both pro-life and pro-choice groups want to define the "product" of conception. One wants to define it as a "fetus" and the other as a "baby." Both groups strive to make their meanings dominant. This struggle takes place not only in the courts but also in the media and in the classroom.

culture wars
cultural struggles over meaning, identity, and influence

In addition to the various ideologies, Dreama Moon (2008) notes that culture includes a number of diverse activities of a population. In the United States, there are many behaviors, some done daily and others less frequently. For instance, it is common for people to date within their ethnicity, for families to visit one another during holidays, and for people to attend religious services at least once a week. There are also more mundane behaviors, such as getting your driver's license renewed, running on the treadmill, pulling weeds from your garden, or listening to public radio while driving home from work. For those interested in Cultural Studies, it is crucial to examine these activities to understand how the ideology of a population is maintained. Paul du Gay, Stuart Hall, Linda Janes, Hugh Mackay, and Keith Negus (1997) explain that these practices intersect to help us understand the production and dissemination of meaning in a culture. At the same time, the meaning of a culture is reflected by such practices. Culture, then, cannot be separated from meaning in society. In fact, uncovering prevailing cultural meanings is one important aim of researchers in Cultural Studies.

Meaning in our culture is profoundly sculpted by the media. The media could simply be considered the technological carrier of culture, but as this chapter will point out, the media are so much more. Consider the words of Michael Real (1996) regarding the media's role in U.S. culture: "Media invade our living space, shape the taste of those around us, inform and persuade us on products and policies, intrude into our private dreams and public fears, and in turn, invite us to inhabit them" (pp. xiii–xiv). No doubt, for example, that the media contain messages—intentional or unintentional—that get the Petrillos to accept the goals, dreams, and standards of success portrayed in the media.

**"Power corrupts, but not like it did
when I was younger."**

A second assumption of cultural theory pertains to people as an important part of a powerful social hierarchy. Power operates at all levels in society. However, power in this sense is not role based, as we considered it in our discussion of Structuration Theory in Chapter 15. Rather, Hall is interested in the power held by social groups or the power between groups. Meaning and power are intricately related, for as Hall (1989) contends, "Meaning cannot be conceptualized outside the field of play of power relations" (p. 48). In keeping with the Marxist tradition, power is something that subordinate groups desire but cannot achieve. Often there is a struggle for power, and the victor is usually the person at the top of the social hierarchy. An example of what we are discussing here can be observed in the U.S. culture's preoccupation with beauty. Theorists in Cultural Studies contend that because beauty is often defined as thin and good-looking, anyone not matching these qualities would be considered unattractive. Hall may believe that the attractive people—at the top of the social hierarchy— are able to wield more power than those at the bottom (the unattractive).

Perhaps the ultimate source of power in our society, however, is the media. Hall (1989) maintains that the media are simply too powerful. He is not shy in his indictment of the media's character by calling it dishonest and "fundamentally dirty" (p. 48). In a diverse culture, Hall argues, no institution should have the power to decide what the public hears. Gary Woodward (1997) draws a similar conclusion when he states that there is a tradition whereby journalists serve as guardians of the nation's cultural activities: If the media deem something to have importance, then something has importance; an otherwise unimportant event suddenly carries importance.

Let's revisit our story of Lisa and John Petrillo. Theorists in Cultural Studies would argue that as members of a minority population, the Petrillos have been inherently relegated to a subordinate position in society. Their work environment—as migrant workers on a large egg farm—is the product of a capitalistic society, one in which laborers work under difficult conditions. Although they will inevitably have difficulty owning their own home because of their low wages, writers in Cultural Studies would point to the media's barrage of images and stories touting the American Dream. Although the message may convey hope for the Petrillos, their dream of owning their own home might better be called a fantasy because the elite power structure (the media) does not honestly convey the reality of their circumstances. Perhaps unknown to the Petrillos, the media are a tool of the dominant class. The future of Lisa and John Petrillo, then, will overtly and covertly be influenced by the ruling class.

Hegemony: The Influence on the Masses

The concept of hegemony is an important feature of Cultural Studies, and much of the theory rests on an understanding of this term. Scott Lash (2007) contends that "from the beginnings of cultural studies in the 1970s, 'hegemony' has been perhaps *the* pivotal concept" (p. 55). **Hegemony** can be generally defined as the influence, power, or dominance of one social group over another. The idea is a complex one that can be traced back to the work of Antonio Gramsci, one of the founders of the Italian Communist Party who was later imprisoned by the Italian fascists. Writers in Cultural Studies have called Gramsci a "second progenitor Marxist" (Inglis, 1993, p. 74) because he openly questioned why the masses never revolted against the privileged class:

hegemony
the domination of one group over another, usually weaker, group

> The study of hegemony was for him [Gramsci], and is for us, the study of the question why so many people assent to and vote for political arrangements which palpably work against their own happiness and sense of justice. What on earth is it, in schools or on the telly, which makes rational people accept unemployment, killing queues [wards] in hospitals, ludicrous waste on needless weaponry, and all the other awful details of life under modern capitalism? (Inglis, 1993, p. 76)

Gramsci's notion of hegemony was based on Marx's idea of **false consciousness**, a state in which individuals are unaware of the domination in their lives. Gramsci contended that audiences can be exploited by the same social system they support (financially). From popular culture to religion, Gramsci felt the dominant groups in society manage to direct people into complacency. Consent is a principal component of hegemony. Consent is given by populations if they are given enough "stuff" (e.g., freedoms, material goods, and so forth). Ultimately, people will prefer to live in a society with these "rights" and consent to the dominant culture's ideologies.

false consciousness
Gramsci's belief that people are unaware of the domination in their lives

The application of Gramsci's thinking on hegemony is quite applicable to today's society. Under a hegemonic culture, some profit (literally) while others lose out. What happens in hegemonic societies is that people become susceptible to a subtle imbalance in power. That is, people are likely to support tacitly the dominant ideology of a culture. The complexity of the concept is further discussed by Hall (1989). He notes that hegemony can be multifaceted in that the

Research Notes

Ott, B. L. (2003). "I'm Bart Simpson, who the hell are you?" A study in postmodern identity (re)construction. *Journal of Popular Culture, 37,* 56–78.

Ott outlines his analysis of the longest-running comedy in television history, *The Simpsons.* He believes that "television furnishes consumers with the symbolic resources—the actual cultural bricks—with which to (re)construct identity" (p. 58). Ott argues that the television show has transformed the way viewers look at the family in society. After heavy doses of traditional images of the family for decades, Ott believes, *The Simpsons* models a new way to configure family identity. He zeroes in on Bart, the adolescent son, who, among others, emulates and looks up to Krusty the Clown. Sadly, Krusty is always getting into trouble with law enforcement, and, as Ott asserts, the clown provides a mediated example of a "countercultural image" (p. 63). Ott presents a number of examples from the series and assert that the show has

frequently influenced viewers and their perceptions and configurations of identity.

Weedon, C. (2004). *Identity and culture: Narratives of difference and belonging.* New York: Open University.

This book is an in-depth examination of the intersection of race, class, and gender and its relationship to Cultural Studies. The author presents both personal insights and research findings from Stuart Hall and his followers. Weedon looks primarily at the British "version" of Cultural Studies, although, to make his point, he articulates its relationship to U.S. Cultural Studies theorists. Weedon extrapolates from a number of examples, including the Bible, the Confederate flag, the Aboriginal people, and "Islamaphobia" in the Western world. The book provides readers with concrete examples of many of the themes inherent in Cultural Studies. Weedon gives a scholarly account of the ways in which identity is constituted for a number of different cultural communities.

dominant, or ruling, class is frequently divided in its ideologies. That means that during the subtle course of being influenced, the public may find itself pushed and pulled in several directions. Unraveling such complexity is one goal of researchers in Cultural Studies.

Hegemony can be further understood by looking at today's corporate culture, where—using Marx's thinking—ruling ideas are ideas of the ruling class. In most corporate cultures, where decision making is predominantly made by White, heterosexual males, we expect certain ideologies to be present that support this class of people. Hall questions whether this dominant way of thinking and relating is legitimate or whether it simply perpetuates the subordination of the masses. How is consciousness raised and how is new consciousness presented? Perhaps it is the language used in an organization, for as Hall (1997) states, "Language in its widest sense is the vehicle of practical reasoning, calculation and consciousness, because of the ways by which certain meanings and references have been historically secured" (p. 40). People must share the same way of interpreting language, however, to achieve meaning in a context, and Hall notes that meanings change from one culture or era to another. So what exists in one organizational setting may not exist in another.

What all this means is that there are multiple ideologies in a society as complex as the United States. This translates into what Hall calls a **theatre of struggle**, which means that various ideologies in society compete and are in temporary states of conflict. Thus, as attitudes and values on different topics shift in society, so do the various ideologies associated with these topics. For example, think about what it meant to be a woman before 1920 and what it means to be a woman today. Before 1920, women were unable to vote and were generally regarded as subordinate and subservient to men. Then in August 1920, the amendment giving women the right to vote was ratified. Today, of course, women not only vote but hold high political office. Although U.S. society still does not provide entirely equal opportunity for women, and women continue to be targets of discrimination, the culture and ideology pertaining to women's rights have changed with the times.

Hegemony is but one component of the intellectual currents associated with Cultural Studies. Although people (audiences) are frequently influenced by dominant societal forces, at times people will demonstrate their own hegemonic tendencies. We explore this notion further.

theatre of struggle
competition of various cultural ideologies

Counter-Hegemony: The Masses Start to Influence the Dominant Forces

We have noted that hegemony is one of the core concepts associated with Cultural Studies. Yet audiences are not always duped into accepting and believing everything presented by the dominant forces. At times, audiences will use the same resources and strategies of dominant social groups. To some extent, individuals will use the same practices of hegemonic domination to challenge that domination. This is what Gramsci called **counter-hegemony.**

Counter-hegemony becomes a critical part of Cultural Studies thinking because it suggests that audiences are not necessarily willing and compliant. In other words, we—as audience members—are not dumb and submissive! Danny Lesh in *Counter Heg* (a newsletter dedicated to the counter-hegemonic movement; www.lesstreet/com/dan/counterheg) observes that part of the goal of counter-hegemony "is to understand history from other lenses, particularly from women's, workers', and racial minorities' perspectives." That is, in counter-hegemony, researchers try to raise the volume on muted voices. Think of counter-hegemony as a point where individuals recognize their consent and try to do something about it.

Counter-hegemonic messages, interestingly enough, occur in television programming. In particular, two shows—*The Cosby Show* and *The Simpsons*—exemplify counter-hegemony. Both shows are effective examples of how television content challenges the priorities established by the dominant forces. With respect to *The Cosby Show,* the Number 1 show on TV in the 1980s and 1990s, Bishetta Merrit (1991) notes that, in an effort to defy social stereotypes, this television family featured two working parents, one a gynecologist and the other an attorney. Furthermore, instead of having five

counter-hegemony
when, at times, people use hegemonic behaviors to challenge the domination in their lives

children who argued all the time, Herman Gray (1989) claimed that in almost every episode, the children were taught the values of honesty, respect, and responsibility. Finally, the show was an educational tool as well, referencing many historically Black colleges, playing music by Black artists (e.g., jazz and rap), and depicting symbols of African American heritage. To this end, the show was an effort to dispel the messages that the media elite were presenting on nightly news: the absent father, the uneducated family members, and the poverty-ridden living environment. Counter-hegemony, then, takes shape with the presentation of the Cosbys as "Black America."

The Simpsons, the longest running comedy on television, also contains satiric counter-hegemonic messages aimed at showing that individuals who are dominated use the same symbolic resources to challenge that domination. The relevance of *The Simpsons* to the lives of people has been persuasively argued. Tim Delaney (2008) succinctly notes that the show reveals so much about us because so much of the show intersects with the social institutions (family, school, jobs, houses or worship, etc.) to which we belong. The show has included references to such diverse topics as talk shows, Kafka, the Beatles, Tennessee Williams, gay marriage, the invention of television, and hormone therapy! The core cast of characters—Marge (mother), Homer (father), Bart (son), Lisa (daughter), and Maggie (infant daughter)—all present different counter-hegemonic messages. For Marge, although cultural representations of a homemaker/housewife suggest a doting and supportive wife and mother, she is arguably the most independent of all the characters. She has tried a number of other professions, from police officer to protester against handgun violence. Homer, an employee at a local nuclear power plant, shows that despite what the government may tell us about the safety of these facilities, bumbling, inept people like Homer continue to stay employed. Lisa, contesting societal expectations that a "child should be seen and not heard," shows that she is intellectually curious, artistically savvy, and environmentally aware.

One of the more central characters of the show is Bart Simpson. Interestingly, although society tends to shut down boys of Bart's age (and girls to some extent), Bart manages to shut down the same society that tries to subdue him. His pranks range from harassing a local bar with sophomoric phone calls to disrespecting his grade school principal to calling his father by his first name. In the end, however, despite the 20 minutes of chaos, the family members show that they have high regard for one another in personal ways. As Carl Matheson (2001) notes, the show advocates "a moral position of caring at the level of the individual, one which favors the family over the institution" (p. 4).

A closer look at the television series illustrates other counter-hegemonic tones. Brian Ott (2003), for example, calls *The Simpsons* the "anti-show show" (p. 58). He states that "*The Simpsons* has always represented a sort of anti-show, spoofing, challenging, and collapsing the traditional codes, structures, and formulas of network television" (p. 59). Ott contends that the characters of Bart, Homer, and Lisa help viewers understand "lessons about selfhood" (p. 61) and that the show is watched by a number of different

> ### Theory Application in Groups (TAG)
>
> Find other examples of counter-hegemony in society. You may examine film, video, the Internet, or other types of communication. Further, identify the specific counter-hegemonic message in your discussions.

cultural communities, including Whites, African Americans, and Hispanics. Ott and other scholars contend that the show has managed to transcend traditional images of the family that demonstrated and embraced patriarchal control. Indeed, a close examination of the series shows that children are frequently viewed as subverting or overthrowing parental control and asserting dominance in their family. *The Simpsons* continues to challenge prevailing religious, political, and cultural notions that the family is weakening.

Audience Decoding

No hegemonic or counter-hegemonic message can exist without an audience's ability to receive the message and compare it with meanings already stored in their minds. This is called **decoding**, the final topic of Cultural Studies we wish to address. When we receive messages from others, we decode them according to our perceptions, thoughts, and past experiences. So, for instance, when Lisa Petrillo, from our opening story, interprets information on purchasing a home, she is relying on several mental behaviors. These include her desire to have a home, her conversations with people who have already purchased a home, her library visits, and the fact that she and her family have never owned a home. Lisa will store the information she receives pertaining to a new home and retrieve it when someone engages her in a conversation on the topic. All of this is done instantaneously; that is, she will make immediate decisions about how to interpret a message once she receives it.

 Decoding is central to Cultural Studies. But before we delve further into this, let's review the gist of Cultural Studies up to this point. You will recall that the public receives a great deal of information from the elite and that people unconsciously consent to what dominant ideologies suggest. Theorists reason that the public should be envisioned as part of a larger cultural context, one in which those struggling for a voice are oppressed (Budd & Steinman, 1992). As we discussed previously, hierarchical social relations (between the elite bosses and the subordinate workers, for example) exist in an uneven society. This results in subordinate cultures decoding the messages of the ruling class. Usually, according to Hall, the media connote the ruling class in Western society.

 Hall (1980a) elaborates on how decoding works in the media. He recognizes that an audience decodes a message from three vantage points, or positions:

decoding
receiving and comparing messages

dominant-hegemonic, negotiated, and oppositional. We explore each of these next.

Hall claims that individuals operate within a code that dominates and exercises more power than other codes. He terms this the **dominant-hegemonic position.** The professional code of television broadcasters, for instance, will always operate within the hegemony of the dominant code. Hall relates that professional codes reproduce hegemonic interpretations of reality. This is done with subtle persuasion. Consider John and Lisa Petrillo from our opener. The television images of owning a home prompt the Petrillos to believe that owning a home is within their reach. The selection of words, the presentation of pictures, and the choice of spokespeople in infomercials are all part of the staging in the professional code. Audiences, like the Petrillos, are prone to either misunderstanding a message or selectively perceiving only certain parts of a message. Why? Hall writes, "The viewer does not know the terms employed, cannot follow the complex logic of argument or exposition, is unfamiliar with the language, finds the concepts too alien or difficult or is foxed by the expository narrative" (1980a, p. 135). Television producers are worried that people like the Petrillos will not accept the intended and preferred media message of owning a home. They (the media) therefore place their professional code placed in the larger, dominant cultural code of meaning. This ensures that John and Lisa Petrillo will work toward buying a home.

The second position is a **negotiated position;** audience members are able to accept dominant ideologies but will operate with some exceptions to the cultural rule. Hall holds that audience members always reserve the right to apply local conditions to large-scale events. This happens frequently when the media report on laws that are enacted at the national level and interpreted at the state or community level. For example, Hall might argue that although audiences may accept the elite's interpretation of a welfare reform bill in Washington, D.C. ("All people should work if they are able to"), they may have to negotiate when it does not coincide with a local or personal principle ("Children need parents at home"). Hall notes that due to the difficulty of negotiations, people are prone to communication failures.

The final way in which audiences decode messages is by engaging in an oppositional position. An **oppositional position** occurs when audience members substitute an alternative code for the code supplied by the media. Critical consumers reject the media's intended and preferred meaning of the message and instead replace it with their own way of thinking about a subject. Consider, for instance, the manner in which the media communicate feminine images of beauty. To many, the media present feminine beauty as a way to serve the sexual desire of men (Schwichtenberg, 1987). Some consumers, however, reject this capitalistic message and substitute more realistic portrayals.

Hall accepts the fact that the media frame messages with the covert intent to persuade. Audience members have the capacity to avoid being swallowed up in the dominant ideology, yet, as with the Petrillo family, the messages the audience receives are often part of a more subtle campaign. Theorists in Cultural Studies do not suggest that people are gullible, but rather that they often unknowingly become a part of the agenda of others (Hall, 1980b).

dominant-hegemonic position
operating within a code that allows one person to have control over another

negotiated position
accepting dominant ideologies, but allowing for cultural exceptions

oppositional position
substituting alternative messages presented by the media

Integration, Critique, and Closing

Although Cultural Studies began at the CCCS in England, its influence on writers, researchers, and theorists in the United States has been profound. The theory has attracted the attention of critical theorists in particular because it is founded on the principles of criticism. Its Marxist influence has also drawn scholars from philosophy, economics, and social psychology, and its emphasis on underrepresented groups in society has enticed writers in sociology and women's studies to take notice (Long, 1989). For additional criticism, we discuss three criteria for evaluating a theory: logical consistency, utility, and heurism.

Integration

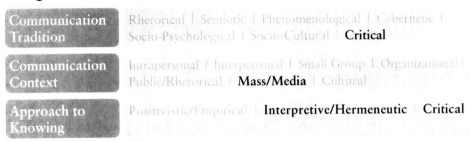

Communication Tradition	Rhetorical	Semiotic	Phenomenological	Cybernetic	Socio-Psychological	Socio-Cultural	**Critical**
Communication Context	Intrapersonal	Interpersonal	Small Group	Organizational	Public/Rhetorical	**Mass/Media**	Cultural
Approach to Knowing	Positivistic/Empirical	**Interpretive/Hermeneutic**	Critical

Critique

| Evaluation Criteria | Scope | **Logical Consistency** | Parsimony | **Utility** | Testability | **Heurism** | Test of Time |

Logical Consistency

Despite some glowing endorsements, the logical consistency of the theory has been challenged. This criticism relates to the audience. Even though some audiences resist the role of dupe, are they able to become interpretive and active resisters? In other words, to what extent can audiences be counter-hegemonic? Mike Budd, Robert Entman, and Clay Steinman (1990) suggest that some cultural and critical theorists overestimate the ability of oppressed and marginalized populations to escape their culture. For evidence of this thinking, reexamine our opening story of the Petrillos and assess the extent to which you believe they can "escape" their circumstances. Budd and colleagues believe that these communities frequently lack the skills, insights, and networks to be so political in their resistance. This dialogue is not likely to go away because "debates over the audience were once, and continue to be, a major field of contestation in cultural studies" (Kellner & Hammer, 2004, p. 79).

Utility

Cultural Studies "makes up a vehicle that can alter our self-image" (Carey, 1989, p. 94). Therefore, it's possible to translate some of the theory into daily

T∗I∗P

Theory Into Practice

Mirri

When someone said that Stuart Hall was concerned with oppression, I couldn't help but think of my own background in Haiti. The country is very poor, and we don't have a lot of resources like the United States. We rely on other countries a lot, which makes the dominance of the elites over ordinary people pretty common. The government acts like the people's voice is important, but everyone knows that simply is not the case. Media there are controlled by the government in a lot of ways and tells people both truthful and deceitful things. It's a perfect example of the dominance over the masses.

life, making it useful to some extent. Its utility can also be found in its dedication to studying the cultural struggles of the underprivileged. According to Hall (1997), these populations have remained subordinate for too long. By concentrating on these marginalized social groups, a number of subfields have emerged; namely, ethnic studies and gay, lesbian, bisexual, transgender studies (Surber, 1998). Hall's theory has been called "empirically elegant" (Carey, 1989, p. 31), and its usefulness beyond the written page has been widely articulated.

Heurism

Many of the principles and features of Cultural Studies have been investigated. Ideology has been examined (Lewis & Morgan, 2001; Soar, 2000), and the concept of hegemony has been applied to episodes of the long-running situation comedy *The Mary Tyler Moore Show* (Dow, 1990) and to the HBO series, *Sex in the City* (Brasfield, 2007). Research by Janice Radway (1984, 1986) focused on romance novels and the women who read them. She discovered that many women read these books silently to protest male domination in society. Lawrence Grossberg (1986) and Linda Steiner (1988) found oppositional coding with audiences in their research. Grossberg noted that punk music was an oppositional response to rock and roll music because rock and roll allowed for "new possibilities" (1986, p. 57). Steiner looked at a decade of the "No Comment" section of *Ms.* magazine, which is partly devoted to overt and covert male domination in society. Steiner claimed that the manner in which women read these sections is tantamount to oppositional decoding; they read the comments in a way that suits their own interests and not the superiority of males. Finally, counter-hegemony has been applied to Nike's Bode Miller Olympic Advertising campaign (Ryan, 2007) and to issues of globalization (de Sousa Santos, 2006).

Cultural Studies remains one of the few theoretical traditions that has attracted the attention of scholars from a variety of disciplines outside communication. Researchers interested in understanding the thinking, experiences, and activities of historically oppressed populations usually endorse Cultural Studies. Although some critics have faulted the theory for a number of reasons, Stuart Hall is credited with criticizing the elite and with drawing attention to oppressed voices in society. Hall's commitment to understanding the everyday acts and commonly accepted events is admirable.

Discussion Starters

1. Is the Petrillo family responsible for not trying to leave their current situation? If they are not able to achieve the American Dream of owning a home, should the media be blamed? Include examples when expressing your opinion.

2. Discuss how hegemony functions in world events. Now apply the concept to your campus. Identify any similarities and differences between the two applications. Use examples in your response.

3. What other cultural artifacts exist in our society that could be studied within a Cultural Studies framework?

4. British Cultural Studies is strongly focused on class differences. What do you think about applying the thinking of British Cultural Studies to Cultural Studies in North America? Do you believe that the concepts and principles are relevant to all countries? Why or why not?

5. Do you agree or disagree with the belief that oppressed populations have little voice in the United States? How does this view relate to how you feel about the theory?

6. How might Cultural Studies theorists view poverty in the United States?

7. Apply counter-hegemony to a contemporary television show.

Online Learning Center   www. mhhe.com/west4e

Visit the Online Learning Center at www.mhhe.com/west4e for chapter-specific resources, such as story-into-theory and multiple-choice quizzes, as well as theory summaries and theory connection questions.

8   Postmodernity and the information society

Introduction

Postmodernity and **postmodernism** are difficult theoretical themes to
define succinctly. The two terms are closely related, although – like the distinction between modernity and modernism – there are fundamental differences. Postmodernity refers to social, economic, political and technological
developments that have characterized the transition from modern to newly-
organized, postmodern ways of life. Two aspects of postmodernity are often
marked out: first, the emergence and proliferation of new media, information
and communications technologies that trigger social change and are particularly indicative of globalization; and, second, the rise of consumer culture
and simultaneous demise of certain forms of production (Lyon 1999: 10).
Some other important developments related to postmodernity are listed in
Figure 8.1. Essentially we see a transition from the elitist values of modernity –
espoused by a capitalist ruling elite and manifested in 'high culture' – to a
postmodern 'flattening of hierachies' (Bauman 1992: 34). At first, this seems
like social progress, but postmodern critics such as Zygmunt Bauman consider
postmodern relationships to be fragmentary, shallow, driven by consumerism, and lacking moral responsibility to others – especially disadvantaged
groups unable to reap the rewards of this so-called progress (see Bauman
1996). In contrast to postmodernity, the term 'postmodernism' refers to art,
literature and cultural criticism that have supplanted the modernist tradition.
Postmodernism is seen as a reaction to the elitism of high modernism (evident in, for example, the Leavisite tradition as discussed in Chapter 3) and a
rejection of realism – the artistic endeavour to represent an objective reality
(e.g. Dickens's realist novels about everyday poverty).

This chapter deals with *postmodernity* in relation to media theory, but by
definition there are significant overlaps with theories of postmodernism.
Dominic Strinati (1995) refers to five key features of postmodernism:

1   *Breakdown of the distinction between culture and society*: as he states,
    'the importance and power of the mass media and popular culture
    mean that they govern and shape all other forms of social relation-
    ships' (Strinati 1995: 224). Our perceptions of the social environment
    in which we live are largely informed by mediated cultural repre-
    sentations such as news images.
2   *An emphasis on style over substance*: we consume images and

> Women gain the right to vote (1920 in the United States, 1928 in Britain).
>
> Education and literacy levels increase throughout the social strata.
>
> Increased affluence – also experienced by the working-class population – means greater social mobility.
>
> Rise in demand for service industries to serve the masses (mass retail, mass consumerism, mass media).
>
> Technological innovation propels globalization – a combination of cultural homogenization and diversity.

Figure 8.1 Postmodernity and the empowered masses: some reasons for the decline of modernism and elitist 'high culture'

spectacles, as opposed to forms of communication such as the written word that encourage us to ponder and reflect.

3 *Breakdown of the distinction between high art and popular culture*: this is a modernist distinction that is now threatened by postmodern media culture that embraces both 'art' and 'the popular' (pop music, Hollywood, and so on).

4 *Confusions over time and space*: the globalizing tendencies of communications technologies, economics and politics are distorting traditional conceptions of time and space dimensions.

5 *Decline of metanarratives*: grand theories such as Marxism, Christianity and, of course, modernism have lost their currency for modern societies.

All these five features – in their original conceptions – will be applied to media and postmodernity in the course of this chapter. Somewhat challenging the fifth feature, however, will be our discussion of the **information society** thesis that could be construed, paradoxically, as a postmodern metanarrative.

Baudrillard: hyperreality and simulation

Jean Baudrillard is the best known and arguably the most elusive theorist of postmodernity. His elusiveness is partly due to the cryptic style in which he writes but is also due to the controversial – and apparently absurd – character of his theories. 'The Gulf War did not take place' and 'Disneyland is the *real* America' appear to be ridiculous claims but, as we shall see, Baudrillard presents a complex argument that offers a specific interpretation of these theoretical statements. He argues that postmodern societies – saturated by media and information technologies – have entered an age of **simulation**, and more particularly an age of third-order simulation. Third-order simulation differs from two earlier forms of simulation, as detailed in Table 8.1.

Table 8.1 Baudrillard's three orders of simulation

Order of simulation	Type	Description
First-order	Signification (signs which imitate real things)	Reality is constructed through representation (e.g. maps, paintings)
Second-order	Reproduction (signs refer to signs which imitate real things)	Representations of reality (first-order) are reproduced by mechanical technologies (e.g. photography, film)
Third-order	Simulation (signs no longer represent real things but serve to mask this absence of reality)	No connection exists between reality and representation – instead we have hyperreality (e.g. Disneyland)

First-order and second-order simulation maintain a relationship between reality and representations (signs) of reality – indeed, second-order simulation is the type celebrated by Benjamin (as discussed in Chapter 3). By contrast, third-order simulation amounts to a system of signs that bear no relation to reality or its representations, but function to conceal this absence of genuinely real things. Disneyland, according to Baudrillard, is a third-order simulation. Disneyland is pure fantasy, of course, but it simultaneously functions 'to make us believe that the rest is real, when in fact all of Los Angeles and the America surrounding it are no longer real, but of the order of the hyperreal and of simulation' (Baudrillard 1983: 25). This is what Baudrillard means when he states that Disneyland is the *real* America, because the *real* America is actually a hyperreal phenomenon divorced from the once genuinely real place called America that has now vanished from human experience. **Hyperreality**, therefore, is the outcome of simulated imagery – what Baudrillard calls **simulacra**: 'The simulacrum denies not reality, but the difference between the image and the real ... there is no difference between the image and other orders of experience' (Fiske 1991b: 57–8). Los Angeles *is* its media images and cultural myths more so than it is a real, material, geographical location. We have nothing real to believe in except hyperreal (more *real* than genuinely real) simulation and simulacra.

What has brought about this postmodern age of simulation and hyperreality? For Baudrillard, the transformation of signs no longer referring to real things as they are channelled through media and communications

150   POSTMODERNITY AND THE INFORMATION SOCIETY

technologies – especially television – has collapsed the separation between the real (the physical, terrestrial habitat) and the metaphysical (knowledge beyond this habitat). Like 'an astronaut in his capsule' each human being is 'at the controls of a micro-satellite, in orbit, living no longer as an actor or dramaturge but as a terminal of multiple networks. Television is still the most direct prefiguration of this ... regulating everything from a distance' (Baudrillard 1985: 128). Just as prisons conceal the fact that society as a whole is imprisoned in the sense of being unable to access genuine reality, so television and other electronic media conceal processes of simulation which effectively regulate and restrict our versions of the 'reality' (hyperreality actually) we sense around us. As Bauman states, 'For Baudrillard, society itself is now made to the measure of television ... One can no longer speak of the distortion of reality: there is nothing left to measure the image against' (Bauman 1992: 33). Similarly, the omnipresence of mediated advertising 'invades everything, as public space (the street, monument, market, scene) disappears ... Not a public scene or true public space but gigantic spaces of circulation, ventilation and ephemeral connections' (Baudrillard 1985: 129–30). This media power to saturate public and private spaces or *scenes* by harassing us with *obscene* simulations – what he refers to as 'a whole pornography of information and communication' – is what Baudrillard calls 'the ecstasy of communication. All secrets, spaces and scenes abolished in a single dimension of information' (Baudrillard 1985: 130–1). Television, telephone and radio are just three media technologies that partake in this ecstasy of communication – they invade our lives and confuse our sense of knowing what we want. This, in turn, creates a new form of schizophrenia caused by 'too great a proximity to everything' (Baudrillard 1985: 132).

Baudrillard's theory of media-saturated simulation owes much to McLuhan's statement that 'the medium is the message' (as discussed in Chapter 3). His suggestion that information devours its own content and that 'Only the medium can make an event – whatever the contents' (Baudrillard 1994: 82) is clearly McLuhan-esque, and Baudrillard draws on McLuhan's ideas in several of his works. However, Baudrillard's hyperreality theory goes a step further than McLuhan's medium theory:

> there is not only an implosion of the message in the medium, there is, in the same movement, the implosion of the medium itself in the real, the implosion *of the medium and of the real* in a sort of hyperreal nebula, in which even the definition and distinct action of the medium can no longer be determined
>
> (Baudrillard 1994: 82).

The medium is the real message in McLuhan's theory of modernity but, having undergone postmodern transformation, the medium and the message collapse into a third-order simulation of *the real* (i.e. the hyperreal). For Baudrillard, medium (technology) and message (content) are no longer real because they saturate any genuine sense of reality that distinguishes between them. There are some other fundamental differences between the two theorists that are often understated. One commentator argues that McLuhan's emphasis on the power of technological form over content is counteracted by Baudrillard's theory of simulation which emphasizes 'the sign-form, not technology per se' (Merrin 2005: 50). The semiotic transformation of signs and symbols (that no longer refer to real things) is not determined by technology but by human perception of – and participation in – the ecstasy of communication. Technology is therefore secondary to the implosion of the message (and the medium) into simulation. Another difference cited by William Merrin is McLuhan's 'global village' perspective that electronic media foster retribalization compared to Baudrillard's vision of 'an indistinct mass created by, refusing and imploding with the circuit of communication' (Merrin 2005: 53). Baudrillard's claim that media power abolishes social relations and transforms individuals into networked terminals is far less optimistic than McLuhan's version, the latter of which is closer to theories of progressive information society (as discussed later in this chapter).

We cannot leave our discussion of Baudrillard, however, without considering how his theory of simulation casts doubt on the 'reality' of the first Gulf War (Baudrillard 1995) as well as the 9/11 terrorist atrocities (Baudrillard 2002). The Gulf War did not take place, according to Baudrillard, because it was won by the mighty US Air Force before it had begun. The lasting memories of this war for most people were screened images – transmitted via military operations to CNN and other Western media – showing how US pilots pinpointed and then bombed Iraqi targets (bridges, hospitals, military camps) from thousands of miles above land. As such, 'This war is conducted according to the media model: war as a technological relationship . . . founded on the abolition of symbolic exchange and the simulation of real communication' (Merrin 2005: 84). This is not a war in the sense of prolonged combat and conflict (the first two world wars, by contrast, *really* did take place); instead, we experience a virtual war, much like a video game simulates real warfare, and therefore this real-time, media-saturated spectacle is nothing other than what Baudrillard calls a 'non-event'. Subsequent wars in Afghanistan and Iraq amount to 'a rehash of the past, with the same deluge of military forces, bogus information, senseless bombardment, emotive and deceitful language, technological deployment and brainwashing. Like the Gulf War: a non-event, an event that does not take place' (Baudrillard 2002: 34).

What happened to the weapons of mass destruction that Iraq was supposed to possess? They did not exist. Baudrillard might use this evidence of 'bogus information' and the emotive language it engendered to argue that the subsequent conflict is a mere simulation to those who fight and witness it. Then again, one obvious criticism of this 'non-event' thesis is that no simulated, virtual war that 'did not take place' has ever resulted in so many casualties and fatalities, not to mention changes to world order. It is easy to sympathize with one critic who refers to Baudrillard's 'stupid and irresponsible position' and 'his rampant relativism which refuses to discriminate between degrees of authenticity' (Webster 2002: 256–7).

9/11, on the other hand, did take place and was 'the absolute event': 'The whole play of history and power is disrupted by this event' (Baudrillard 2002: 4). Terrorist violence – unlike the violence of the Gulf War – amounts to an exchange of symbolic violence in which 'the media are part of the event, they are part of the terror' (Baudrillard 2002: 31). Although the destruction of the World Trade Center was a real event, however, its symbolic collapse was more significant and came before its physical collapse. According to Baudrillard, 'The architectural object was destroyed, but it was the symbolic object which was targeted and which it was intended to demolish ... no one, not even the terrorists, had reckoned on the total destruction of the towers' (Baudrillard 2002: 48). The objective of the terrorists was to demonstrate 'the terrorism of spectacle' as opposed to the spectacle of terrorism (Baudrillard 2002: 30). Even though the twin towers did collapse and thousands of people died, Baudrillard insists that this Manhattan disaster movie was not a real event for those who witnessed it on television because 'the fascination of the attack is primarily a fascination with the image', and 'The image consumes the event, in the sense that it absorbs it and offers it for consumption' (Baudrillard 2002: 27–9). The event and the image present entirely different experiences. In the case of real-time media coverage, 'the image is there first, and the *frisson* of the real is added' to create 'a fiction surpassing fiction' (Baudrillard 2002: 29). While Baudrillard makes a convincing point about the power of imagery over unmediated experience in contemporary culture, he neglects to pursue his initial claim in *The Spirit of Terrorism* (2002) that the events of 9/11 – far from mere simulation – had a very *real* consequence for history and the events that were to follow.

Boorstin and Debord: the image and the spectacle

Two important influences on Baudrillard's theory of simulation are Daniel J. Boorstin's *The Image* (first published in 1961) and Guy Debord's *The Society of the Spectacle* (first published in 1967). Boorstin explores the concept of 'pseudo-events', especially rife in news media and not dissimilar to Baudrillard's media-simulated 'non-events'. Boorstin argues that the omnipresence of images, which are so easy to produce and distribute via multi-media channels in the late twentieth century, are indicative of a Graphic Revolution

(Boorstin 1992: 13) – a wholesale change in the way we view the reality of our world. Instead of increasing our awareness of the world, however, Boorstin suggests that news media do not usually report 'real', truthful events but instead deal in a currency of false, pseudo-events. A pseudo-event is 'not spontaneous, but comes about because someone has planned, planted, or incited it. Typically, it is not a train wreck or an earthquake, but an interview' (Boorstin 1992: 11). Boorstin lays the blame for this state of affairs at the feet of public relations and journalistic practices. The press conference, for example, is a contrived pseudo-event carefully planned by newsworthy individuals or institutions in order to satisfy journalists' insatiable appetite for fresh 'news'. It is a self-fulfilling pseudo-event that offers little genuine news value at all. The British Prime Minister's weekly press briefing, for example, is staged and usually reported in news bulletins even if the Prime Minster has nothing really *new* to say. An up-to-date image of the Prime Minster along with his latest spin doctoring message is enough to hit the headlines. Boorstin even suggests that pseudo-events have diminished what it means to be a famous public figure. Real heroes of the past who undertook great feats have been replaced by manufactured, image-conscious celebrities who have no genuine talent. The technological progress that would lead to intellectual and political enlightenment – as promised by Benjamin and McLuhan – is not shared by the impotence of this postmodern Graphic Revolution.

Guy Debord offers a similarly cynical perspective on what he terms 'the spectacle' which 'is both the outcome and the goal of the dominant mode of production' (Debord 1994: 13). He notes: 'the world we see is the world of the commodity' (Debord 1994: 29). By extension, Debord's theory of the spectacle is not limited to mass media images, but is more centrally to do with modern capitalist economies that produce a form of spectacle which isolates and alienates those who are forced to consume it. It is only when 'the spectacle is *capital* accumulated to the point where it becomes image' (Debord 1994: 24) that it fulfils this function of alienation, and the spectacle only becomes image when mediated through technologies such as television which 'serve as weapons for that [spectacular] system as it strives to reinforce the isolation of the "lonely crowd"' (Debord 1994: 22). The spectacle is therefore not primarily a collection of images but 'a social relationship between people that is mediated by images' (Debord 1994: 12). Nonetheless, this relationship is entirely based on appearances and images – a false reality – that conceals a real world of capitalist exploitation and class division. Echoing Baudrillard, Debord states that 'the spectacle's job is to cause a world that is no longer directly perceptible to be *seen* via different specialized mediations' (Debord 1994: 17). The word *seen* is italicized by Debord because sight is the human sense most vulnerable to deception and false belief. After all, *seeing is believing* – but we do not always *see through* artifice and manipulation.

Although originally intended as Marxist rather than postmodern theory,

154   POSTMODERNITY AND THE INFORMATION SOCIETY

Debord's work has since been closely associated with the postmodernist emphasis on style over substance; image over reality. This is particularly evident in one of the two forms of the spectacle he outlines (Debord 1994: 41–3). First, we have the concentrated form of spectacle, which is associated with bureaucratic ownership and restriction of choice in the capitalist realms of production and labour. More significant, though, is a second form that Debord calls the diffuse form of spectacle, which is associated with the abundance of commodities in the capitalist mode of consumption. He identifies 'the pseudo-need imposed by the reign of modern consumerism . . . Waves of enthusiasm for particular products, fuelled by the communications media, are propagated with lightning speed' (Debord 1994: 44). The triumph of the spectacular economy, therefore, springs from its 'ceaseless manufacture of pseudo-needs' (Debord 1994: 33) that strike a familiar chord with Boorstin's pseudo-events. One such 'specialized mediation' of these false needs is the media celebrity. While Boorstin ridicules the emptiness of the image-conscious media celebrity, Debord conceives them as spectacular representations of ordinary people who turn their spectacle into 'images of possible roles' for us to identify with so as 'to compensate for the crumbling of directly experienced diversifications of productive activity' (Debord 1994: 38). Celebrities provide us with false representations of life, which reinforces Debord's argument that the spectacle they produce – via media – is not perceptible to direct experience and is predominantly experienced as a series of appearances. However, this spectacle *becomes* the reality of our everyday lives to the extent that social life becomes an alienating scenario grounded entirely in appearances (first impressions). On the other hand, real class inequalities, poverty and social exclusion – created by the capitalist mode of production and its uneven distribution of wealth – are concealed by the spectacle in order to protect the dominant order of power from the proletariat uprising predicted by Marx.

Jameson: pastiche and intertextuality

Although principally a postmodernist, Fredric Jameson's theories of contemporary media and culture, like Debord's theory of spectacle, owe much to Marxism. Jameson argues that we have entered a stage of late capitalism associated with post-industrial, consumer societies and globalization in the shape of multinational economics. Postmodern culture 'replicates or reproduces – reinforces – the logic of consumer capitalism' (Jameson 1998: 20) by embracing all things 'popular' and rejecting the modernist values of non-commercial, 'high art'. While modernism sought to clearly distinguish high culture from mass or popular culture, the onset of postmodernism – from the post-war boom of the 1950s onwards – has meant that 'the line between high art and commercial forms seems increasingly difficult to draw' (Jameson 1998: 2). This cultural turn from modernism to postmodernism is centred on 'The disappearance of the individual subject, along with its formal consequence, the increasingly unavailability of the personal style' (Jameson 1991: 16). Modernist art and literature cherish the value of individuality and the 'first-person' voice in stark contrast to the hostility of an outside world marked by rampant modernity – industrialization, scientific and technological advance, rationalization, and so on (see theories of modernity in Chapter 3). James Joyce's 'stream of consciousness' technique – in which an author's thoughts and feelings are directly translated into a rambling written style – typifies the individual style of modernism. Postmodernist culture, from Jameson's point of view, dismisses the possibility that an individual style can still exist in a late capitalist era where all new styles are immediately incorporated to serve the intentions of global, consumer capitalism.

Jameson's notion of **pastiche** – and the way pastiche differs from the practice of 'parody' – is central to his postmodernist perspective on the disappearance of individuality and originality. Parody is a general technique of mimicry, not peculiar to postmodernism, which has the comic intention to 'produce an imitation which mocks the original' (Jameson 1998: 4). Impersonators deploy parody to mimic the actions and behaviour of others, especially famous people. Importantly, parody acknowledges what it imitates and does not ignore the sanctity of the original form. As such, 'there is a linguistic norm' (Jameson 1998: 4) behind parody. Parody mocks but does not threaten the existence of original meanings (language). By contrast, pastiche is a technique peculiar to postmodernism because it denies the existence of – refuses to acknowledge – the original form it *appears* to be imitating. Pastiche is less about comedy and more about plagiarism. Pastiche does not accept that 'some healthy linguistic normality still exists' (Jameson 1991: 17) because, unlike parody, it has no satirical purpose and does not distinguish its own mimic from an original form. As such, 'Pastiche is blank parody, parody that has lost its sense of humour' (Jameson 1998: 5). Pastiche is the outcome of wider trends in postmodernity that have arisen from the compartmentalization of the professions since the earlier developments of modernity. For Jameson, the fragmentation and privatization of language into different styles associated with these professional practices – medicine, law, literature, and so on – have meant these styles are now impossible to ridicule because there is no longer a universal 'linguistic norm' through which to parody such styles. Postmodernist, pastiche styles therefore arise from both the disappearance of originality (linguistic norms) and the disappearance of parody, which relies on an original form with which to mock.

Pastiche is closely linked with Jameson's theory of **intertextuality** that he defines 'as a deliberate, built-in feature of the aesthetic effect, and as the operator of a new connotation of "pastness" and pseudo-historical depth, in

156   POSTMODERNITY AND THE INFORMATION SOCIETY

which the history of aesthetic styles displaces "real" history' (Jameson 1991: 20). As well as the disappearance of individuality and originality, postmodern culture has lost its sense of the past because the past has become romanticized by artistic representations of history that are clouded by nostalgia. As the author states, 'we seem condemned to seek the historical past through our own pop images and stereotypes about the past, which itself remains forever out of reach' (Jameson 1998: 10). Mike Featherstone makes a similar point about the aestheticization of the present day as evidenced by 'the rapid flow of signs and images which saturate the fabric of everyday life in contemporary society' (Featherstone 1991: 66), of which MTV and its 'three-minute concentration span' philosophy is a prime example. For Jameson, intertextuality is a practice typically found in postmodern films and other media texts that borrow features from other texts. Like pastiche, intertextuality is not about an overt acknowledgement of the original text (or texts) from which it is borrowing certain features but rather about an insistence on the disappearing sense of anything original or historical that has gone before. Intertextuality operates in a perpetual present because postmodernity has effectively obliterated any genuine sense of the past. Jameson identifies the 'nostalgia film' as an example of pastiche and intertextuality in practice. *American Graffiti* (1973), for example, aims to 'recapture all the atmosphere and stylistic peculiarities of the 1950s United States' (Jameson 1998: 7–8) by imitating – in pastiche form – both the content and the formal filmic techniques associated with earlier representations of the rock and roll generation. *Chinatown* (1974) likewise is a pastiche of 1930s America and aesthetic styles of American filmmaking familiar to this period.

Pastiche as it operates in a nostalgic mode differs from imitation as practised in the more generic category of 'historical film', however, because it colonizes 'even those movies today which have contemporary settings, as though, for some reason, we were unable today to focus our own present' (Jameson 1998: 9). Films more or less about the present day – such as *Star Wars* (1977) and *The Day After Tomorrow* (2004) – are incapable of creating new, original representations of contemporary life, and are therefore forced to pastiche aesthetic (filmic) styles of a previous age, such as science-fiction literature and the 'disaster movie' genre, as evidenced by covert, intertextual references. Usually these references to previous films or generic conventions operate on an unconscious level and are not easily identifiable. In these cases, film directors may well refuse to acknowledge their indebtedness to a particular filmic style or scene – in keeping with the practice of pastiche – but instances of intertextuality are always able to be drawn because so-called 'new' styles have 'already been invented; only a limited number of combinations are possible; the unique ones have been thought of already' (Jameson 1998: 7). There are occasions, though, when intertextual references are self-consciously constructed for purposes of parody, in 'spoofs' like the *Naked Gun* films (1988; 1991). In these films or other media texts, intertextuality is not a specifically postmodern facet.

Jameson's postmodernist theories of pastiche and intertextuality can certainly be applied to various media and cultural examples, and not just films. Certain forms of popular music, for example, 'sample' or draw from previous sounds and tracks (pastiche), and these forms can be distinguished from overt 'covers' that – like parody – acknowledge an original version. We should be keen to critically evaluate these theories, though. Is originality really impossible today? This partly depends on what we mean by originality. Jameson appears to define the individual style as unique and entirely new, according to high modernism, but that famous modernist T. S. Eliot understood the 'individual talent' as emerging from a concern with both tradition and novelty; with an historical sense 'not only of the pastness of the past, but of its presence' (Eliot 1951: 14). Eliot's definition of originality, therefore, is not about uniqueness but about adding a distinctive contribution to an existing 'ideal order' of canonical art and literature. What Jameson defines as unoriginal intertextuality, then, amounts to a more conservative interpretation of tradition-minded individual talent in Eliotian terms. Another criticism we might level at Jameson is that by referring to the disappearance of our sense of history, he also appears conveniently to neglect a long history of pastiche-like intertextuality. Shakespeare's plays, for instance *Anthony and Cleopatra*, are full of intertextual references to earlier chronicles without overtly acknowledging the historical origins of their narratives. Jameson does make it clear that aesthetic practices of pastiche have existed longer than postmodernism but that 'we have something new when they become the central features of cultural production' (Jameson 1998: 18). Is pastiche so central to contemporary media and cultural texts? Films and music – associated with genre traditions – are perhaps often pastiche-like, but what about less predictable media texts such as live (television) coverage of news or sports events? Are not live, 'real-time' media texts, by definition, original? Jameson might argue that while the content of live media may be original, the formal ways in which media represent live action always draw on pre-existing aesthetic styles.

Lyotard: the decline of metanarratives

For Jean-François Lyotard, the forces of multinational capitalism have not so much brought about the death of modernist 'high art' as the delegitimation of assumed scientific knowledge. The sacred truth of science, like art, so coveted in the age of modernity, is threatened by the onset of postmodernity. Lyotard's postmodern theory of knowledge is grounded in the decline of two types of **metanarrative** (or **grand narrative**): the narrative of

158   POSTMODERNITY AND THE INFORMATION SOCIETY

emancipation and the narrative of speculation. Both of these narratives sought to legitimize – justify as true – their claims about the virtues of science and knowledge against the sins of ignorance, religion and superstition characteristic of pre-modern societies (see Figure 3.1 in Chapter 3). The narrative of emancipation or freedom is a political narrative, often utilized by the state in their provision of school education, which tells of science as a great, liberating force against the shackles of an older, feudal, medieval order (also known as the 'Dark Ages' given that the medieval period had not yet been enlightened by the truth of scientific knowledge). Likewise, the narrative of speculation sought to legitimize scientific knowledge, but in the form of a philosophical narrative associated with the rise of university education that was not so bound to state politics. Narratives of speculation differed from those of emancipation by not accepting statements of knowledge at face value and emphasizing a holistic approach to unified learning – combining the arts and sciences – rather than, in the unification of the narrative of emancipation, separating knowledge into distinct but related disciplines (e.g. physics, mathematics and economics). Regardless of their political and philosophical differences, both types of metanarrative are in decline. Lyotard's perspective is clearly contrary to Foucault's (1989) theory of discourse as exclusionary power and knowledge (see Chapter 4).

According to Lyotard, postmodern culture has led to a situation in which 'The grand narrative has lost its credibility, regardless of what mode of unification it uses, regardless of whether it is a speculative narrative or a narrative of emancipation' (Lyotard 1984: 37). Reasons for this loss of credibility in metanarratives are not fully accounted for by Lyotard, but he tentatively suggests that several outcomes of advanced liberal capitalism have affected such a decline in belief about grand ideas and ways of knowing the world. Like Jameson, he suggests that consumerism and 'the individual enjoyment of goods and services' are indicative of postmodernity in its denial of the 'communist alternative' (Lyotard 1984: 38) or any other grand theory about society other than a liberal capitalist one. As well as the capitalist prosperity enjoyed by advanced societies in the latter half of the twentieth century, Lyotard argues that it is understandable that 'the disorienting upsurge of technology would have an impact on the status of knowledge' (Lyotard 1984: 38). The proliferation of communications technologies including transportation, media and information systems have meant that 'knowledge has become the principal force of production over the last few decades' (Lyotard 1984: 5). Technological advances of this kind have also threatened the narrative of emancipation produced by nation-states because knowledge is able to flow freely across different nations regardless of attempts at state intervention. The computerization of society has meant that information and intellectual property rights, now 'even more mobile and subject to piracy' (Lyotard 1984: 6), have become the new battleground for knowledge and power, not between nation-states but between multinational corporations in pursuit of lucrative consumer markets.

As well as the decline of grand narratives such as communism, Marxism, Christianity and Einstein's theory of relativity as a result of this commodity production of knowledge by way of information-processing technologies, we might also point to the decline of media metanarratives such as public service broadcasting and 'freedom of the press' as the Fourth Estate. On the one hand, public service broadcasters such as the BBC have lost much of their belief in Reithian values of high culture, educative and informative programming. Competition from commercial media systems founded on consumer capitalist values has forced public service broadcasters to produce television and radio shows that appeal to popular tastes more so than the Arnoldian principle of 'the best of what has been thought' (see discussion of Schiller in Chapter 7). For example, the appeal of the 'reality TV' genre is equally embraced by public service and commercial broadcasters in Britain, given the widely held assumption that such programmes are popular among audiences. The 'high culture' metanarrative espoused by Lord Reith – appointed in 1927 as the BBC's first Director-General – has declined immeasurably in the present-day, ratings-obsessed BBC. The close association between popular aesthetics and postmodernity is no better manifested than in the case of twenty-first-century public service broadcasting, which in highly competitive television markets – such as the USA – is diminishing fast.

On the other hand, the grand narrative of emancipation associated with the Fourth Estate loses its credibility when we consider that access to knowledge production is mostly in the hands of a few multinational news conglomerates (see Chapter 7). Prior to postmodernity, access to mediated knowledge production was in the hands of either the state or a multitude of private enterprises, but concentration of (economic and knowledge) capital alongside a decline in metanarratives of emancipation have effectively delegitimized such knowledge and replaced it with the logic of mass media and mass consumption. A counter-argument in this case, though, is that public service broadcasters and the free press are still alive even if their narratives of emancipation are no longer so convincing. Another criticism we might level at Lyotard's account is that he appears to be implicitly condoning a *new* grand narrative of postmodernity despite his claim that grand narratives are no longer credible. If metanarratives really are in decline, nothing theoretically universal like 'the postmodern condition' would surely explain what is replacing them. Moreover, Lyotard's claims about the power of technology and computerized societies resonates with another paradoxical metanarrative of postmodernity, known as the information society thesis.

The information society

Theories of the information society are extensive and diverse in their arguments, and by no means exclusively postmodern in their approach. In the wider scheme of media theory, though, the idea of an information society is closer associated with postmodernity than modernity or any other theoretical theme. One of the most influential theorists in this regard is Daniel Bell, whose work entitled *The Coming of Post-industrial Society* (first published in 1973) inspired new ways of thinking about a post-industrial, postmodern, information age. Bell's perspective on technological innovations in the information sector is largely optimistic. He argues that 'technology has transformed social relationships and our ways of looking at the world' (Bell 1999: 188), increasing human control over nature and transforming economic productivity. Five positive outcomes in this technological transformation of the social world are that:

1   Living standards have risen throughout the world, wages have increased in real terms (taking into account inflation) and social class inequalities in Western societies have been reduced.
2   A 'new class' of engineers, technicians and other planning occupations has been created.
3   A new definition of rationality in the sense of efficiency and optimization – using resources with the least cost and effort – has introduced 'quantitative techniques of engineering and economics [that] now jostle the older modes of speculation, tradition, and reason' (Bell 1999: 189) by enabling more accurate forecasting of social and economic trends.
4   'New networks of social relationships have been formed' (Bell 1999: 189) which mark a shift from kinship to occupational ties.
5   Perceptions of time and space have been altered, as evidenced in modern art's portrayal of new standards of 'speed' and 'height' compared to an earlier age.

For Bell, these five areas of progress indicate a wider social change from an industrial to a post-industrial society, evident particularly in the United States. Table 8.2 indicates some of the radical differences between the two types of society.

Bell's conception of a post-industrial society is also one in which information and knowledge have replaced material forms of production in a post-Marxist, Baudrillardian sense. No longer is there a division between those who own the means of goods production and the proletarian masses – as some political economists would still suggest – but instead there is a

Table 8.2 Radical differences between the industrial and post-industrial societies

	Industrial society	*Post-industrial society*
Regions	Western Europe, Japan	United States
Technology	Energy	Information
Economic sector	Secondary (goods manufacturing and processing)	Tertiary (services), Quaternary (finance, insurance), Quinary (health, education, research)
Occupations	Semi-skilled worker Engineer	Professional and technical Scientist
Time perspective	Projections (ad hoc)	Forecasting (future orientation)

Source: Adapted from Bell's (1999: 117) 'General Schema of Social Change'.

bureaucratic division between 'those who have powers of decision and those who have not, in all kinds of organizations, political, economic and social' (Bell 1999: 119). Although post-industrial society is seen by Bell as expanding scientific and technical knowledge to all levels of the social strata, the central problem remains how to adapt public policies to these scientific and technological advances so that the full potential of free-market, post-industrial economics can be realized. In a 1999 Foreword to a new edition of his post-industrial society thesis, Bell discusses the internet as an example of technological empowerment: 'It provides enormous access to the cultural resources of humankind in a way never known of before. It multiplies the number of affinity groups – people with like-minded interests and common professions – across national boundaries' (Bell 1999: lvii). The internet could certainly be theorized in the optimistic terms of Bell's post-industrial, information age. Social relationships, economic productivity (i.e. e-commerce) and the means of forecasting consumer trends are – at least to some extent – transformed by new media infrastructures like the worldwide web.

Other theorists share Bell's optimism – for example, see Negroponte (1995) on the revolutionary promise of the digital age. Alvin Toffler's (1981) account of a third wave that follows the first wave (agricultural) and second wave (industrial) in the historical development of modern societies is not dissimilar to Bell's distinction between the pre-industrial, industrial and post-industrial. For Toffler, the third wave 'info-sphere' wrought by technological change is resulting in a de-massified media. Instead of mass media production that prevailed in the second wave, the third-wave emphasis on small-batch, localized production tailored to consumer trends has led to an expansion of choice and competition within media sectors. For example, mass-circulation newspapers that flourished in the second wave have declined in response to

162   POSTMODERNITY AND THE INFORMATION SOCIETY

third-wave news and magazine publications 'that serve not the metropolitan mass market but specific neighbourhoods and communities within it' (Toffler 1981: 170). Radio and television programming geared towards particular regions or common interests likewise mark this shift to a de-massified media in the third wave. The third wave also means – unlike Jameson's idea of postmodern pastiche – more diversity:

> Today, instead of masses of people all receiving the same messages, smaller de-massified groups receive and send large amounts of their own imagery to one another ... This, in part, explains why opinions of everything from pop music to politics are becoming less uniform. Consensus shatters.
>
> (Toffler 1981: 176)

The de-massification of media signals an enormous change in the range and quantity of information we exchange with each other. As we become more individualized and less uniform in our outlooks, we need more information to forecast how others will behave and respond to our behaviour (Toffler 1981: 178). This is why Toffler situates the third wave, above all, within the context of an information society (see also Toffler and Toffler 1995).

Reading Bell and Toffler, we might gain the impression that all is well with an information society. However, there are as many critics as there are exponents of the information society thesis. Philip Elliott (1995) outlines two criticisms: first, he questions the suggestion that information can be equally accessed by all by pointing out that it is in the interests of commercial corporations to keep secret certain kinds of information; and, second, he argues that what appears to be information is very often merely *infotainment* – a mixture of tabloidized information and entertainment – that has little educative substance. David Lyon's (1988) counter-perspective outlines three further problems with this so-called progressiveness in information societies. First, he argues that vested interests mean access to information technologies favours those who can afford to invest in them. For example, 'the collusion of military with microelectronic interests in the modern world' does not harness mutual communication among different social groups – quite the opposite, these vested interests are 'dedicated to hostile, destructive and lethal ends' (Lyon 1988: 18). Second and related to this first point, capitalist economic interests mean that 'private gain is constantly set against efforts to "socialize" production' (Lyon 1988: 18). Public information providers such as public libraries and public service broadcasters find it increasingly difficult to afford access to certain forms of information in competition with multinational corporations, and the privatization of previously public services such as the telephone network further pushes up prices. And third, the assumption that information society marks a 'natural' progression – following the agricultural and industrial revolutions – forecloses alternative ways of thinking about contemporary societies, including the starkly alternative Luddite argument that technologies restrict choice and should be (indeed, often are) resisted by individuals. Lyon's theory of information society is situated between optimistic and pessimistic (Luddite) accounts, although he is closer to pessimism than optimism in his later account of a Foucauldian surveillance society (see Lyon 2001).

Manuel Castells's theory of the network society (outlined in three large volumes first published in 1996 and 1997) is closely associated with the concept of the information society but is, in part, a sustained critique of the liberal, optimistic approach. Unlike Toffler, he considers the informational economy of the network society to be overlapping with and penetrating agricultural and industrial economies (informational agriculture, informational manufacturing) rather than replacing them. Castells also differs from Bell in arguing that while information flows within a global economy, 'This is not the same as a world economy' (Castells 1997: 7). While the global economy reaches out to the whole world, it only incorporates the wealthier nations who benefit one another through the technological systems of 'interconnected' global financial markets (Castells 2000: 102). International trade between powerful economies, however, is contrasted with un-networked societies in parts of Africa, South America and rural Asia that remain regionalized and untouched by global economics. The network society is also characterized by a transformation in employment that amounts to the individualization of work (Castells 1997: 9). In contrast to traditional full-time, salaried work closely tied to trade unions, more contemporary developments point to an increase in self-employment, temporary work and the practice of 'subcontracting' labour to specialist consultancies. Rather than create a new class of worker, information-led network societies create new types of employment that fragment or individualize 'labour's bargaining power' (Castells 1997: 10). Small and medium-sized enterprises engage in inter-firm networking – often with much larger businesses – and the inter-dependence between big and small firms largely maintains existing economic and social structures. Individualization of the workforce and the breakdown of the welfare state as a result of weakening trade unions also lead to what Castells identifies as widening social polarization and exclusion.

Castells is not a postmodern theorist *per se*, although what he calls 'the culture of real virtuality' serves to implicate electronic media in a theory of network society resembling the postmodern. As opposed to virtual reality, real virtuality implies that media texts are not substitutes for real experiences but have 'become the experience' (Castells 2000: 404) in a network society driven by mediated communications. Unlike the mass media age theorized by McLuhan in terms of a 'global village' where 'the medium is the message' (see Chapter 3), Castells argues that by the 1990s multi-media systems and their

164   POSTMODERNITY AND THE INFORMATION SOCIETY

power to target diverse audiences mean that 'the message is the medium' (Castells 2000: 368). This change is evident in multinational corporations that take certain messages (content), such as teenage music, and shape them into a niche medium (technological format), such as MTV. Furthermore, the mass media age is obsolete, given the rise of computer-mediated communications – not least the internet – that herald 'increased interaction by and among individuals that break up the uniformity of a mass audience' (Castells 1997: 11). Similar to Toffler's ideas about de-massified media, new media technologies enable the inclusion of different cultural expressions that, in turn, weaken mass media organizations that promote traditional cultural values (Castells 2000: 406). So despite social exclusion and maintenance of the economic status quo, the network society offers sophistication in catering for the diverse cultural traits and identities of those who experience it (see Castells 2004).

This culture of real virtuality carved out by interactive media also radically transforms time and space. Castells refers to 'timeless time' as an outcome of new media and information technologies that aim to annihilate time by compressing years into seconds and breaking 'natural' sequences (i.e. past, present and future). However, timeless time is only available to powerful groups that can, for example, fight and win 'instant wars' with enemies (Castells 2000: 484–91). Elsewhere, societies without new technologies rely on biological or clock time, and the wars they fight last for years. As well as timeless time, what Castells terms 'the space of flows' enable powerful groups – major financial markets, global media, and so on – to engage in distant interactions involving the movement of people and goods. The 'global city', such as New York or London, arises from this space of flows that link up production, management and information. By contrast, un-networked societies 'perceive their space as place-based' (Castells 2000: 453), fixed in a particular locale, and unaffected by the global space of flows in a network society. The notions of timeless time and the space of flows – as Castells acknowledges – are reminiscent of David Harvey's (1989) concept of time–space compression. Contrary to the work of Jameson which marks off postmodernity as a new era in reaction to modernity, Harvey sees continuities between the two. Indeed, 'the changing experience of sense and time had much to do with the birth of modernism' (Harvey 1989: 283). Nevertheless, 'the rapidity of time–space compression in recent years' caused by the pressures of capital accumulation – akin to Castells's interconnected global market economy – is distinctly postmodern and 'exacts its toll on our capacity to grapple with the realities unfolding around us' (Harvey 1989: 305–6). The technological endeavour to tighten time-spans and space-distances for economic gain has catastrophic implications when it hastens the need for quick, unconsidered decision-making in political, military and financial realms.

Ritzer: McDonaldization

It seems appropriate to end this chapter with what is, partly at least, a counter-perspective on postmodernity. George Ritzer suggests that there are more continuities than differences between modernity and a so-called postmodern age. According to Ritzer (1993), we live in a McDonaldized society reminiscent of advanced modernity. This is not to say that McDonald's is a typical feature of social life but that the corporate structure and practices associated with the fast-food chain are symptomatic of wider global production trends – a similar perspective, known as 'Coca-colonization', has a longer tradition (see Nederveen Pieterse 2004: 49). Based on Max Weber's theory of bureaucracy and rationalization, Ritzer's **McDonaldization** thesis states that the rules, regulations and structures characteristic of a McDonald's-style global corporation are put in place so as to maximize four profit-making concerns:

1. *Efficiency*: this is about being cost-effective and preventing waste. For example, 'The Egg McMuffin is basically an entire breakfast ... combined into one handy sandwich that can be eaten quickly, easily, and without utensils' (Ritzer 1993: 40).

2. *Calculability*: this is about uniformity of size, quantity and production time. So 'great care is taken to be sure that each raw McDonald's hamburger weighs 1.6 ounces, no more, no less ... The precooked hamburger measures precisely 3.875 inches across' (Ritzer 1993: 66).

3. *Predictability*: we expect the same tastes, packaging and people employed to serve us. Predictable ingredients and predictable forms of storage (i.e. freezing) aid this rationalizing process of McDonaldization.

4. *Control*: this is to be found in rigid management structures and huge wholesale purchasing of supplies. Not even the 'chefs' have much control over how the food is delivered to the customer: 'Much of the food prepared at McDonald's arrives at the restaurant preformed, precut, presliced, and preprepared, often by nonhuman technologies' (Ritzer 1993: 105).

These four features of McDonaldization are not only evident within fast-food industries. Ritzer refers to the media and information industries in terms of similar structures and practices of production as McDonald's. Efficiency, for instance, is identifiable in what the author terms 'News McNuggets' (Ritzer 1993: 57–8) – very short stories presented in tabloid newspapers such as *USA TODAY* and *The Sun* – in contrast to the more substantial and intellectually challenging reports found in inefficient broadsheets. Calculability is evident

166   POSTMODERNITY AND THE INFORMATION SOCIETY

in televised sports such as basketball and football with their uniform time periods which allow for easy programme scheduling and commercial breaks. By contrast, competitive pursuits less constrained by time and calculability – such as chess and mountaineering – are less media-friendly and therefore receive little media coverage. Predictability is an important technique by which the Hollywood film industry constantly searches for remakes, sequels and films based on 'tried and tested' formulas. Ritzer (1993: 89) uses the example of *Psycho* (1960), a box-office hit film which spurned predictable offshoots such as *Halloween* (1978) and *A Nightmare on Elm Street* (1984). Control is evident when politicians and other public figures utilize media training and spin-doctors in their media appearances: 'Most of [President Ronald] Regan's TV appearances were carefully managed to be sure that the right message was communicated' (Ritzer 1993: 117). Like Adorno's theory of standardization and Boorstin's concept of pseudo-events, Ritzer's McDonaldization thesis proposes that media and popular culture are starved of originality, creativity and diversity due to the rationalized structures of global capitalist corporations. The main challenge to the McDonaldization thesis is the concept of 'glocalization' or global localization, which is based on the premise that 'corporations only succeed if and to the extent that they adapt themselves to local cultures and markets' (Nederveen Pieterse 2004: 50; see also Sreberny 2000). The recent Bond film, *Casino Royale* (2006), may have all the hallmarks of a predictable Hollywood espionage thriller but it had to adapt to the lucrative Chinese market, for example, by renaming the main character 'Ling ling qi' – Chinese for 007 (Yahoo! News UK 2007). The importance of localizing global media productions further suggests the persistence of traditional, local ways of life in many aspects of contemporary culture – far from the breakdown of history and tradition associated with postmodernity.

In his original conception of a McDonaldized society, Ritzer argues that global capitalism today is an outcome of modernity rather than postmodernity – an argument clearly at odds with Jameson among other postmodernists. In a sequel to his first book on McDonaldization, however, Ritzer is less hostile to theories of postmodernity and instead refers to 'the utility of *both* modern and postmodern theory' (Ritzer 1998: 132) in our understanding of new means of production and consumption. Ritzer accords with Baudrillard's view of postmodern society as a consumer society saturated by simulations. Moreover, 'As a result of the necessity for ever-increasing consumption, the focus of capitalism has shifted from exploiting workers to exploiting consumers' (Ritzer 1998: 121). This, in part, explains why 'instead of "real" interactions with servers in fast-food restaurants ... we can think of these as simulated interactions' (Ritzer 1998: 121), determined by point-of-sale technologies including the electronic checkouts increasingly 'employed' by supermarket chains. These simulated interactions, which we might also apply to technologies such as video on-demand and internet banking, are now such a routine feature of postmodern life that any sense of real interaction between individuals is lost – indeed, consumed by simulations. Simulated interaction is more real than real, face-to-face interaction. Likewise, the fast food we are encouraged to eat in a consumer capitalist society – McDonald's hamburgers, pizzas, chicken nuggets – is akin to a simulation of 'real', homemade, freshly cooked food that we were once encouraged to consume, before the days of hyperreality. Notwithstanding plasticity, the McDonald's burger has become the 'real' American burger, concealing the *really* real origins of any authentic, original burger (Ritzer 1998: 122). Mediated advertising and promotional campaigns serve to reinforce this deception. Moreover, the simulated McUniversity – literally realized by CNN Ted Turner's idea of an electronic university (Ritzer 1998: 159) and supported more recently by Google's digitalization of millions of academic books and journals – is a postmodern manifestation of McDonaldization in practice.

Summary

This chapter has considered:

- Definitions of postmodernity and postmodernism, including the main features that characterize postmodernity.
- Baudrillard's theory of simulation, including concepts of hyperreality and media saturation as they apply to televised coverage of warfare and other global 'non-events'.
- Postmodern theories of image in relation to 'pseudo-events' (Boorstin) and spectacle in relation to the pseudo-needs of consumerism (Debord).
- Lyotard's theory of the decline of metanarratives – narratives of emancipation and of speculation – and how this theory applies to media metanarratives.
- Information society debates, including competing theories of the post-industrial society (Bell) and the network society (Castells), and ideas about media de-massification and time–space compression.
- The McDonaldization thesis, which both challenges and – in Ritzer's revised version – reaffirms the distinction between modernity and postmodernity.

Further reading

Genosko, G. (1999) *McLuhan and Baudrillard: The Masters of Implosion*. London: Routledge.

An interesting and amusing account that traces parallels between Baudrillard's postmodern theories of media and the renaissance enjoyed by McLuhan's medium theory since the boom in postmodernist perspectives. Recommended for advanced undergraduates and postgraduates.

McGuigan, J. (2006) *Modernity and Postmodern Culture*, 2nd edn. Maidenhead: Open University Press.

An innovative approach to theories of postmodernity that questions postmodern accounts and reaffirms the place of modernity in contemporary media culture. Chapters on 'declaring the postmodern' and the information age. Recommended for advanced undergraduates and postgraduates.

Slevin, J. (2000) *The Internet and Society*. Cambridge: Polity.

This book presents a social theory of the internet as an interactional community for the transmission of cultural values and information (note that this book is also useful in relation to interactionist perspectives discussed in Chapter 5). Chapters on globalization, regulation and 'the self'. Suitable for all media students.

Winston, B. (1998) *Media Technology and Society – A History: From the Telegraph to the Internet*. London: Routledge.

A cautious approach to the notion of an 'information society' revolution. Media technologies throughout history are seen to have suffered from problems of suppression (particularly economic constraints) and competence. Useful for all media students.

CPSIA information can be obtained
at www.ICGtesting.com
Printed in the USA
FFOW02n1209270814
7077FF